Happier?

HAPPIER?

The History of a Cultural Movement That Aspired to Transform America

Daniel Horowitz

OXFORD
UNIVERSITY PRESS

OXFORD
UNIVERSITY PRESS

Oxford University Press is a department of the University of Oxford. It furthers the University's objective of excellence in research, scholarship, and education by publishing worldwide. Oxford is a registered trade mark of Oxford University Press in the UK and certain other countries.

Published in the United States of America by Oxford University Press
198 Madison Avenue, New York, NY 10016, United States of America.

Library of Congress Cataloging-in-Publication Data
Names: Horowitz, Daniel, 1938– author.
Title: Happier? : the history of a cultural movement that
aspired to transform America / Daniel Horowitz.
Description: New York, NY : Oxford University Press, [2018] |
Includes index. Identifiers: LCCN 2017009917 | ISBN 9780190655648 (hardcover : alk. paper)
Subjects: LCSH: Happiness—United States. | Quality of life—United States. |
Well-being—United States. | United States—Social conditions.
Classification: LCC HN57 .H59 2018 | DDC 306.0973—dc23
LC record available at https://lccn.loc.gov/2017009917

9 8 7 6 5 4 3 2 1
Printed by Sheridan Books, Inc., United States of America

To Helen L. Horowitz

co-participant in Love and Work; in Hedonic and Eudaimonic pleasures

CONTENTS

ACKNOWLEDGMENTS

Positive psychologists point to the importance of the "Helper's High": the recipient of an altruistic gift may well feel its benefit, but the benefactor surely experiences an enhanced sense of subjective well-being. I can attest that this is true for me as I have this opportunity to thank those who assisted me in writing this book.

First, people in institutional settings. Those who labor at Harvard College Library, Occidental College Library, Smith College Library, and the public libraries of Pasadena, California, and Cambridge, Massachusetts, provided hospitable settings for my work and access to their holdings, both actual books and online materials. The Henry E. Huntington Library offered the location for an April 2015 informal seminar where Sarah Hanley, Helen L. Horowitz, Carol Rigolot, François Rigolot, Malcolm Rohrbaugh, Sharon Strom, Lee Theisen, and Fred Weaver compelled me forward with their useful suggestions.

Among those on the long list of people who in person, on the telephone, and in correspondence answered my questions, provided me with leads, and suggested avenues for exploration are Norman Abeles, Oscar Ax, Dana Becker, Tal Ben-Shahar, Sam Binkley, Kim Cameron, Avshalom Caspi, Mihaly Csikszentmihalyi, Ed Diener, Phoebe Ellsworth, Nancy Etcoff, Jonathan Freedman, Howard Gardner, Dan Gilbert, Art Goldsmith, Peter Gregory, Jessica Grogan, Anne Harrington, Barbara Held, John Helliwell, Ellen Herman, Marwan W. Kraidy, Sonja Lyubomirsky, Micki McGee, Bethany Moreton, Mike Norton, James Pawelski, Braco Pobric, Steve Quartz, Rachael Rosner, Melissa Schnapp, Arthur Schwartz, Barry Schwartz, Martin Seligman, Nima Daniel Shirazi, Michael Staub, Peter Stearns, Toby Stuart, George Vaillant, and Ruut Veenhoven.

Then there is a group of far-flung friends, family members, and colleagues who should experience the pleasure of the Helper's High because they offered all kinds of assistance—peppering me with leads, references, and, more generally, encouragement: Jerry Auerbach, Hal Barron, Alex

Bloom, Larry Blum, Leona Brandwene, Don Brenneis, Irene Q. Brown, Carol T. Christ, Carol Clark, Donna R. Divine, Rebecca D'Orsogna, Lucie Fielding, Larry Friedman, David Gordon, Maggi Gordon, Peter Gregory, Ellen Herman, Ben Horowitz, Sarah Horowitz, Gwen Jensen, Elizabeth Knoll, Kathy Kobayashi, Peter Kramer, Jackson Lears, Elizabeth Lunbeck, Darrin McMahon, Pat McPherson, Susan Matt, Heather Murray, Jeremy Nahum, Joe Newhouse, Meg Newhouse, Julie Norem, Monroe Price, Jennifer Ratner-Rosenhagen, Carol Rigolot, Ted Rogers, Catherine Sanderson, Dan Segal, Carl Smith, Emily Estafani Smith, Jane Smith, Al Warren, Don Weber, and Steve Whitfield.

Although the people at the Sandra Dijkstra Literary Agency made the fully understandable decision not to represent me, Sandy Dijkstra, Elise Capron, and Andrea Cavallaro nonetheless offered their wisdom and support.

I like to joke that University of California at Berkeley had a two-for-one sale: if one child, Ben, went there for his PhD in computer science, then the second child, Sarah, went free for hers in history. Truth to tell, they independently earned support and then education from that wonderful public university. Though there is no connection between their attendance and what came forward with this project, I must give a special shout-out to helpers there. Jason Marsh helped me understand the work of Cal's Greater Good Science Center and think through key issues. In a series of conversations, Dacher Keltner explored with me some of the questions that have animated positive psychology. He gave the manuscript a careful, perceptive reading—one that opened my eyes to new issues to focus on, saved me from making mistakes, and pushed me to clarify my argument. Dacher introduced me to a Berkeley graduate student in psychology, Luma Muhtadie. Her careful reading of the manuscript sharpened my prose, saved me from making mistakes, and educated me about key issues in the field. At key moments, her skills as editor, her engagement, and her commanding knowledge shaped my arguments—and her wisdom ended up in key sections of this book.

As a newcomer to much of the material and concepts I cover in this book, I had to rely on the aid of scholars with expertise beyond my ken. Jamie Cohen-Cole showed me the way in the history of science. Rachael Rosner used her familiarity with the life and work of Aaron Beck to urge me to clarify and strengthen my argument. Marc Steinberg of Smith College opened my eyes to current scholarship in sociology, including transformative work on cultural movements and self-help literature. In a series of wide-ranging conversations and emails, Steve Quartz explored with me the intersections of moral philosophy, philosophy of mind, and neuroscience.

Sarah Murray contributed greatly to how I might explore the connections between new media and the pursuit of happiness.

Finally, people who read the manuscript should experience a level of the Helper's High available only, perhaps, to major philanthropists engaged in more monetary exchanges. Three anonymous readers solicited by Oxford University Press offered unusually probing and suggestive comments on the portion of the manuscript they had access to. Helen L. Horowitz and Lynn Dumenil, among my most important writing buddies, read multiple drafts and urged me on at every step of the way with their care, intelligence, and proddings. Judy Smith helped me reconsider how to introduce the book. Bob Abzug and Chris Babits contributed their command of the history of psychology to key chapters. Fred Feldman came to a reading of the whole manuscript with the critical, probing eye of a philosopher, in the process clarifying the distinct ways scholars from two different disciplines engage with ideas and inching me, perhaps less than he would like, to tell readers my stance on what I report. With the help of two Washington and Lee summer research assistants, Katie Pettit and Laura Stagno, Art Goldsmith brought to bear his command of the economics of happiness and offered immensely helpful suggestions that helped me advance and strengthen my argument.

Sarah Igo justified my evaluation of her as one of the most astute and talented American cultural and intellectual historians by giving the manuscript a probing, insightful, commanding but critical reading that alerted me to important scholarship, saved me from making mistakes, clarified my arguments, helped me find my voice, and suggested how I might place my findings in more robust contexts.

Kimberly Probolus proved that a student could become a colleague when she gave the manuscript a reading that revealed her command of the history of psychology and of American history more generally, as well as her engagement and intelligence. She encouraged me to sharpen my analysis and connect my arguments to larger questions.

With her commanding knowledge of the history of American psychology, Nadine Weidman showed me ways to draw out and clarify what I was trying to say—and did so in ways so specifically and insightfully helpful that at key moments I have adopted or paraphrased her remarks.

From start to finish the people at Oxford University Press exceeded my expectations of what publishers could accomplish. Courtney McCarroll helped out on matters large and small, and did so with dispatch, humor, and intelligence. Shana Iden tracked down what I thought were impossible-to-find citations. Diane Lange copyedited the manuscript effectively. Amy Whitmer and Emily Perry expeditiously moved it through production. Above all,

Abby Gross did all that an author could hope for, and more. From the very beginning she understood and enthusiastically supported what I was trying to do. With a deep and extensive knowledge of positive psychology, she comprehended what writing the field's history involved. Moreover, she had an uncanny knack for balancing proddings to improve what I wrote and letting me say what I wanted to say. Throughout, she brought to a wide range of challenges a combination of intelligence and engagement.

ABBREVIATIONS USED

AP	*American Psychologist*
JHS	*Journal of Happiness Studies*
JPP	*Journal of Positive Psychology*
JPSP	*Journal of Personality and Social Psychology*
NYRB	*New York Review of Books*
NYT	*New York Times*
NYTBR	*New York Times Book Review*
NYTM	*New York Times Magazine*
PB	*Psychological Bulletin*
PS	*Psychological Science*
SIR	*Social Indicators Research*

Happier?

Introduction

In April 2015, a business owner in Seattle, having read that incomes over $70,000 do not make people appreciably happier, decides to reduce his own salary from $1 million to $70,000 and increase those of his employees to $70,000. Studies suggest that conservatives are happier than liberals, or is it the other way around? The *Washington Post* reports on the least and most happy nations. *Money* magazine publishes an article on the neuroscience of positive feelings. I pick up a flier at a local store—"Happiness, Stop Thinking"—and then an invitation to a Maum Meditation Center. I receive an email about crowdfunding to develop an online happiness course that will spread joy around the world. A *New Yorker* article on the Koch brothers talks of their rebranding; in an effort to appear less harsh and to appeal to a broader range of the American public, they decided to connect free markets and happiness.[1]

These anecdotes offer traces of the story I have to tell—how the study of happiness burst out of its bounds in the academic world to influence the lives of tens of millions of people. Happiness studies and positive psychology, two fields indistinguishable to most outsiders, helped shift the focus among researchers and a broader public from mental illness to emotional well-being. Starting in the late 1930s and continuing through the middle of the second decade of the twenty-first century, I draw on studies, both popular and scholarly, that built a basis for new ideas about enhancing personal well-being. A broad series of changes, including new media, Eastern spirituality, and neuroscience, come into play. All the while, many sources have amplified and altered the conversation, including evangelical ministers, TED talks, Oprah's enterprises, and funding from government agencies and private foundations, especially the transformative contributions of the John Templeton Foundation. Academic entrepreneurs created and sustained what is among the most influential of academic fields of the late twentieth and early twenty-first centuries.

Key paradoxes and tensions also drive this history. Strands as diverse as Eastern spiritual traditions, behavioral economics, neuroscience, evolutionary biology, and cognitive psychology shaped public discourse, yet they exist sometimes in combinations that allow reconciliation but sometimes remain in tension with one another. Interestingly, those born Jewish played a prominent role in a field often dominated by a sunny version of American Protestantism. Positive psychology's optimistic world view developed during a time that saw a worldwide refugee crisis, the spread of religiously and ethnically based violence, and the anger that arose from the adverse consequences of globalization and technological changes. Specialized knowledge within a discipline transferred into the public domain—with academics both enthusiastically crossing and policing the borders between the two, in the process revealing their love/hate relationship with popular psychology. As marketing ultimately triumphed, it transformed academic disciplines and spirituality into salable products. Literary agents and publishers played key roles in making it possible for professors to crash through the boundaries around the universities and take over public discussions. Broad audiences could be easily reached because experts gave the obvious—sleep more, have close friends, engage in work—a scientific basis.

Those involved in the worlds I explore continually debate the proper terms to describe what they are talking about—among them are happiness, positivity, pleasure, hedonic, eudaimonic, or subjective well-being. I often use these terms interchangeably—except when I am describing debates over terminology itself. Then there is the issue of the definition of happiness studies and positive psychology. The two fields came into existence separately in the post–World War II period but then merged so fully afterwards that it was and remains difficult for most observers to distinguish between them. Yet their beginnings are distinctive and their foci remain different, with happiness studies focused on improving society while its counterpart concentrated on improving the individual. Happiness studies emerged in the 1960s with scholarship on social indicators. Generally speaking, whereas happiness studies have focused on subjective well-being, life satisfaction, and a broadly defined hedonic happiness, positive psychology has concentrated on positive mental health, meaning, and eudaimonia, Aristotle's word for flourishing. Through publically available data, happiness studies placed greater emphasis on policy and collectivities. Concentrating on the individual, those involved in positive psychology created their own data in the lab.

Positive psychology appeared as a distinct field much later and at an apparently precise moment, namely Martin Seligman's address as president of the American Psychological Association in 1998.² Positive psychology under Seligman's leadership mobilized individuals and foundations in ways that, seemingly out of the blue, gave the field its name, visibility, self-conscious definition, and robust institutional heft. Whereas income inequality, environmentalism, social class, and gender were more important to happiness studies, character strengths were central to positive psychology. The *Journal of Happiness Studies* responded to the Great Recession as an important public event, while the reaction to terrorism, 9/11 especially, commanded attention in the *Journal of Positive Psychology*. Both fields came to emphasize their international and cross-cultural focus, but happiness studies took the leadership along these lines. Scholars in happiness studies involved themselves in politics and public policy from early on and have continued to do so, while the main arenas for positive psychologists were schools, corporations, therapeutic practice, and life coaching.³

The emergence of happiness studies and positive psychology is part of a long story of how writers have shifted back and forth between optimism and pessimism, a focus on mental health and mental illness. For centuries observers pondered the meaning of happiness, as Darrin M. McMahon has made abundantly clear in *Happiness: A History* (2006). In his *Nicomachean Ethics*, Aristotle identified eudaimonia, what he called "happiness as prosperity combined with virtue," as life's goal.⁴ If classical philosophers and Christian theologians believed that only certain people achieved life satisfaction in the afterlife, *philosophes* of the French Enlightenment made such a prospect potentially universal and relocated it on earth. In 1789 Jeremy Bentham called on governments to adopt the yardstick of utility to increase pleasure and decrease pain. In *Social Statics, or the Conditions Essential to Human Happiness* (1851), Herbert Spencer opposed Bentham by exploring how evolution depended on the free reign of the individual's search for survival or happiness. Charles Darwin laid the basis for evolutionary versions of psychology and biology in *The Descent of Man* (1871) by suggesting that both animals and humans had inheritable traits that shaped their moods and temperaments. He emphasized the conflict humans faced between their baser instincts, such as hatred, on the one hand, and their nobler ones, such as conscience and self-command, on the other. "The individuals which took the greatest pleasure in society would best escape various dangers," Darwin concluded in reference to all species, "whilst those that cared least for their comrades, and lived solitary, would perish in greater numbers."⁵ Then in the late nineteenth and early twentieth centuries, philosophically minded observers, most notably William James, increasingly turned their attention to the mental conditions that fostered happiness.⁶ If most of those who have contributed to positive psychology acknowledge the importance of Aristotle, Bentham, Darwin, and James, they often keep their distance from the American tradition of positive thinking, one that stretches back at least to Mary Baker Eddy, the founder of Christian Science, and reached a high point in the 1950s with the Protestant minister Norman Vincent Peale's wildly popular 1952 *The Power of Positive Thinking*.[7]

Nationality shapes and reflects happiness studies and positive psychology. They cross national boundaries, and their international cachet enhances their significance for American adherents. Nonetheless, the base of these fields lies in the United States. While international dimensions are essential, including the engagement by scholars from other nations, the importance of international comparisons of well-being, and the impact of Eastern traditions, the focus on the United States is appropriate for it is the locale of more practitioners, publications, and programs than any other nation. Moreover, with its emphasis on optimism and individualism, its concentration on personal transformations through rebirth, and its reliance on open market capitalism, the field reflected and reflects core, though not universally shared, American values. Advocates emphasized rebirth and the remaking of the self, believing as they did that they had a mission to transform the world.

A largely white, middle- and upper middle-class movement, positive psychology has devoted relatively little explicit attention to either class or race. Except for stating that poverty and unemployment make people miserable, while great wealth and income do not necessarily make people significantly happier, scholars pay little attention to class dynamics or privilege. African Americans are noticeably absent from the ranks of leading scholars, as is more than minimal discussion of race that might help us understand white privilege, racism, or the lives of African Americans. Homosexuality and more generally sexual ambiguity have received remarkably little notice from scholars. Gender has occupied an ambiguous position. As professors and popularizers, women have played prominent roles, but gender itself has remained a category that drew relatively little attention in terms of exploring who and why some persons were happier than others. With an emphasis on personalism, positive psychology, its language and advice, has been more feminine than feminist. What Dana Becker has written of the link between therapy and women's empowerment generally can be applied to positive psychology specifically. "The repackaging of the psychological as power reproduces what has long been the cultural norm for women: the colonization of both the interior world of the psyche and the small world of intimate relationships."[8]

The emergence of a focus on happiness comprises a recent chapter in the centuries-old story of how successive generations of Americans came to realize that there was more to life than increasing material consumption through greater levels of income. Yet much is distinctive to time and place, for the creation and development of happiness studies and positive psychology is enmeshed in the moments and movements of their time. Although many consider World War II as the Good War, for millions of citizens the traumas of the late 1930s and early 1940s provide the contexts for the origins of key concepts. Major events—including the social and cultural movements of the 1960s, the crisis of confidence of the 1970s, the Reagan revolution of the following decade, the attacks of 9/11, and the Great Recession of 2008—help explain the conceptual shifts that would eventually undergird these two fields.

A critical factor in shaping the development and reception of positive psychology stemmed from the way individualistic and market-based neoliberalism replaced the earlier Fordist vision, one in which cooperation of labor unions, the federal government, and major corporations was perceived to provide social stability. The last third of the twentieth century, approximately the same time the systematic study of happiness came to the fore, witnessed arrival of key aspects of a neoliberal economy, including an optimistic emphasis on unbounded choices and new beginnings. Social engineering by experts who fostered the commodification of feelings undergirds the connection between capitalism and emotions. Especially in the twenty-first century, it was ironic that positive psychology came to be promoted by marketing, even as many of its practitioners minimized the benefits of higher incomes or unbridled immersion in materialistic consumer culture, while others offered a gospel based on prosperity.[9] Incomes have been stagnant for vast stretches of American society, achieving economic security became more elusive for tens of millions, politics have been deadlocked, and inequalities of wealth and income have grown dramatically. In such circumstances, positive psychology promised tens of millions of ordinary people that they could rely on individual experiences to bypass, temporarily forget, or transcend social, political, and economic difficulties.[10] All the while, new technologies have made it possible for neuroscientists to understand the relationship between the brain and pleasure and, at the same time, the Internet has helped spread positive psychology's wisdom. Indeed, positive psychology developed simultaneously with the rise of TED talks and new kinds of social networks, amplifying the power of its discoveries.[11]

Despite or perhaps because of its popularity, virtually every finding of positive psychology under consideration remains contested, by both insiders and outsiders. Controversies go well beyond the question of replication or reproducibility.[12] Major conclusions have been challenged, modified, or even abandoned. Even what happiness means has been up for grabs.[13] Other key issues remain unsettled. Do higher incomes enhance well-being? What are the implications of international comparisons? What is the relevance of scholarly findings for public policy? What are or should be the relationships between morality and science?[14] Positive psychology is a relatively young field, one still evolving and in process of developing—with many challenges as yet unresolved. By moving quickly from scientific journals to popular books, key representatives in the field might be prematurely overreaching. Although at several points I discuss important controversies, my aim is not to review the abundant literature in order to offer my own specific judgments. Rather, as a historian it is to explore what writers assert and then to analyze their work in terms of the assumptions they make, the world views they create, and the contexts that shaped their perspectives. Although my narrative captures how a field developed in a manner that moved toward more unity and comprehensiveness, I hardly mean to deny controversy or to tell a story of an inevitable march toward scientific truth. Nor do I see positive psychology as moving teleologically, shaped by an intrinsic goal or commanding principle; rather it is driven by human actors in specific historical contexts.[15]

Also important historically is the relationship between character and personality. Historians have argued that in the early twentieth century, Americans shifted from "hard" traits of character, such as commitment to work, to "soft" personality traits, such as self-realization. Yet some positive psychologists have returned to an emphasis on character, often linking it with a strong moral sense and an emphasis on the practical results of virtue. Similarly, contrary to the postmodern emphasis on performativity, scholars in positive psychology have written about the significance of "eudaimonia: being true to one's inner self" and finding meaning in life.[16] Critics have been quick to point out some limitations of an emphasis on character. In response to Angela Duckworth's *Grit: The Power and Passion of Perseverance* (2016), one observer wrote "anyone who would tell a child that the only thing standing between him or her and world-class achievement is sufficient work ought to be jailed for child abuse." Another commentator insisted that positive psychologists should pay more attention to addressing and challenging "structural inequity" and suggested that "institutions of higher learning could start funding research that puts pressure not only on the individual but on the gritty system in which the individual travails." Moreover, the focus on character suggests that although positive psychologists insist on focusing on the present and future, in some important sense the field has embarked on a nostalgic invocation of an earlier era in an effort to reclaim virtue in a world gone wild.[17]

The problematic nature of positive psychology's relationships to a wider world became clear as the presidential election of 2016 approached. Set off by David Brooks's op-ed essay on Donald Trump as a lonely man, a heated discussion on the listserv Friends of Positive Psychology erupted in early October on the relationship of positive psychology to the election. Participants expressed the hope that they could rise above the fray of partisanship. Discussants could not decide whether the field's task was to bring healing positivity to their peers, their clients, or the society at large. How could positive psychology, they asked, help heal the nation's wounds? As discussions became more partisan and heated, email authors called on others to offer only inspiring responses. Eventually, agreement having emerged that a professional listserv should not permit political discussions, the listserv's moderator called for an end (only partially successful) to the intrusion of politics into this professional world. Yet from my perspective, several things were striking about all of this. Mirroring rather than transcending the campaign itself, most of the contributions focused not on policy but on personalities. Moreover, what was missing was any significant awareness that the campaign had revealed that a substantial percentage of American voters had a dire and distinctly negative view of life in America. The election of Donald Trump proved the power of negativity. In the days immediately after the election, no messages came on the listserv in response to the results.[18]

When positive psychologists have engaged a wider world, they have usually done so by emphasizing the importance of individual character in such institutions as schools, corporations, and the military. They have developed a comprehensive view of the world, but to a considerable extent they rarely consider whether phenomena beyond the individual's ken—war or peace, poverty or wealth, polluted or clean environments—influence people's happiness. This dovetails with contemporary emphasis on people's separation from a wider world that we see in Robert Putnam's *Bowling Alone: The Collapse and Revival of American Community* (2000), documenting how many Americans have lost a sense of obligation beyond the narrow compass of their lives.[19]

Nonetheless, positive psychology has helped create a cultural movement of tremendous reach and power. It is hard to think of an academic specialty that at the end of the twentieth century and the beginning of the twenty-first so fully entered the popular realm and so greatly affected the lives of tens of millions of people worldwide—one that, in effect, became a cultural movement.[20] As two prominent positive psychologists remarked in 2008, the field has "the extremely lofty goal of changing" their readers "and the society" they live in.[21] In using the word "cultural" as an adjective for a movement, I mean to distinguish what positive psychologists tried to do from the more overtly political and social efforts of others. After all, promoting mindfulness, resilience, or positivity is very different from changing the world by marching in the streets, organizing voters, or occupying a building. Political and social movements have been subject to more scrutiny than have cultural ones. Yet cultural movements share some characteristics with social and political ones: the importance of networks, media, organization, leadership, and transnational influences; connectedness over time and space to other movements; and the impulse to change the world.

Still, there are important differences. A cultural movement, such as one relying on neuroscience and mindfulness, does not involve collective action through social movements or political protests in the same way as its social and political counterparts. What positive psychology challenges is not so much existing organizations or social structures as existing beliefs and values. To its advocates, progress comes not from changing institutions but from transforming how people see the world. Proponents remain confident, perhaps naively, that this transformation might or should eventually lead to changes in society and politics. Yet it is also possible that things that give us pleasure—writing in a journal, expressing gratitude to a teacher, practicing mindfulness—can keep us from understanding the power of external events and forces in our lives and the lives of others.

Exploring the history of happiness studies and positive psychology continues my decades-long scholarly examination of the connections between morality, materialism, pleasure, and meaning. [22] In the fall of 2013, I learned firsthand about the scholarship of positive psychology when I audited "The Science of Happiness," a Harvard undergraduate seminar taught by Dr. Nancy Etcoff, in which she presented a state-of-the-art window into the field. I accepted Etcoff's generous invitation to give a talk at the end of the semester on how I, as an American cultural and intellectual historian, viewed what we had studied. I began my talk by locating our class geographically and historically. We were sitting in a room in the fifteen-story William James Hall, designed in 1963 by Minoru Yamasaki, the Japanese-American architect also responsible for the original World Trade Center. I noted that James might have objected to having his name associated with a modern, somewhat antiseptic building whose windows could not be opened. James, whom positive psychologists hail as one of their most important precursors, lived around the corner from where we sat. He struggled, as did those who later claimed his mantle, with the relationship between science and religion. Whenever we exited the building, across the street we saw the Swedenborgian Church, whose spiritual mysticism James's father embraced. If we left the building, turned right and headed north along Oxford Street, we would come near the labs of the geneticist James Watson, the behaviorist B. F. Skinner, and the sociobiologist E. O. Wilson. Simply put, in William James Hall we were located at the crossroads of religion, social sciences, and behavioral sciences that together shaped what we studied in the seminar.

I focused much of my talk on a contrast between the world of ideas I had inhabited as a teacher/scholar and the material I encountered in the seminar. What had come to dominate the approaches long familiar to me was an emphasis on race, class, gender, and sexuality, along with the cultural construction of just about everything. This relies on the notion that how we see the world involved historically shaped categories that, regardless of their truth value, were greatly influenced by the intellectual, social, political, and economic forces that influence the beliefs, rules, and daily practices that comprise culture. Course readings and discussions brought me into strange and unfamiliar territory—a world of cognitive science, behavioral psychology, neuroscience, evolutionary biology, and genetics, all fields whose advocates believed that to varying degrees that it was possible to know truth with scientific certainty. Moreover, immersion in the seminar prompted me to think about the relationships between the often highly specialized scholarly papers assigned and the larger social issues abroad in the historical profession and in the public worlds I inhabit.[23]

As I have studied this cultural movement since taking the seminar, I have often cast the historian's skeptical eye on what I read and learned, while not wanting to deny or call into question the benefits millions have derived from positive psychology. Indeed, I learned from my research on this book a number of practices that have made my own life more satisfying. Moreover, much of what I have read and heard in the course of research and writing reverberated with what I had concluded from decades of my own scholarship on what social observers and critics, from the 1830s to the present, had asserted—that experiences and relationships were more important than goods, that satiation with consumption set in at a fairly early point, that generosity and gratitude mattered, and that rituals made real differences in our lives. If I have never carried out some of the exercises experts in the field recommend, such as practicing mindful meditation or keeping a journal, I consider myself and those who know me well consider me a fulfilled, effective person, someone usually buoyed by cautious optimism.

In researching and writing *Happier?*, I have continually balanced appreciation of what the field has given many of those who follow its advice with skepticism of some of its more simplistic or exaggerated claims. Like others in and outside the field, I worry about the scientific claims scholars offer and about the consequences of popularization. I see more personal, social, and political tragedy in the world than many of positive psychology's proponents seem to envision. In addition, I join others who wonder whether the pursuit of subjective well-being is or should be *the* primary or even *a* primary goal of life. I recognize the variety of political positions advocates take, but associating myself as I do with many left-liberal critics of the field, I nonetheless dissent from many of the ideological implications of positive psychology. Moreover, problematic uses of the science of psychology in the past remind us of the necessity to proceed more cautiously than do those who in a relatively new field may rush too quickly from specific experiments to robust claims and applications.[24]

The development of happiness studies and positive psychology provides insights into more than the careers of two overlapping academic fields. If the political philosopher Danielle Allen is right in saying that a comma and not a period comes after the Declaration of Independence's call for the "pursuit of happiness," then that founding document is less about individual pleasure and more about communitarian values. As she writes, a period "interrupts an argument that leads from a recognition that individually we all pursue happiness to a subsequent recognition that our best instrument for doing so is what we make together: our government." Juxtaposing that realization with the often individualistic emphasis among positive psychologists complicates our understanding of the long-standing tension between communal and individual values. In the late twentieth century, as social connections both frayed and became more urgently needed, a shift gave rise to the individualistic end of the spectrum.[25]

Of course, while this book brings to a close my story, it is not the end of where the academic study of happiness and its popularization to a broad public will lead. *Happier?* offers a look at the past and how scholarly discoveries broke out of the confines that contained them to influence tens of millions of people around the world. Just as historical forces have helped shape the field in the past, so changing circumstances will reshape it in the future. Because it affects people both in the United States and throughout the world as they struggle to find meaning and attain a sense of well-being in often difficult times, the work of positive psychology and happiness studies is profoundly important.

NOTES

1. Jane Mayer, "New Koch," *New Yorker*, Jan. 25, 2016, 43, 45. For additional evidence of the prominence of happiness as a topic, see "Symposium: Understanding Happiness," which centers on the work of Amitai Etzioni, in the May/June 2016 issue of *Society*. Initially scholars suggested conservatives were happier than those on the left, but using big data a more recent study insists on the opposite: Sean P. Wojcik and Peter H. Ditto, "Motivated Happiness: Self-Enhancement Inflates Self-Reported Subjective Well Being," *Social Psychological and Personality Science* 5 (Sept. 2014): 825–34.

2. The full name is Martin E. P. Seligman; except for when in a publication the longer name is used, I refer to him as Martin Seligman.

3. Note also that a focus on immigration was more common in *JHS* and on the Holocaust in *JPP*. This discussion of the differences between the two fields relies heavily on email exchanges between the author and Ruut Veenhoven from May 2015 until March 2016

and on a comparison of articles in *Journal of Happiness Studies* and *Journal of Positive Psychology* from their beginnings through February 2016. The juxtaposition reveals that Ed Diener and Ruut Veenhoven are the key figures in the former; Martin Seligman and Barbara Fredrickson in the latter; with Mihaly Csikszentmihalyi as the most important crossover. Those in happiness studies gather around the *Journal of Happiness Studies* and International Society for Quality of Life Studies (ISQOLS), while positive psychologists focus on *Journal of Positive Psychology* and the International Positive Psychology Association (IPPA). ISQOLS has a more social activist focus than many positive psychology organizations. See also the interview of Richard J. Estes at http://sites.baylor.edu/ michael_b_frisch/oral-history-education-project/. This project, developed by Michael B. Frisch, includes interviews of, among others, Ed Diener, David G. Myers, and Ruut Veenhoven.

4. Aristotle, quoted in Darrin M. McMahon, *Happiness: A History* (New York: Atlantic Monthly Press, 2006), 46.

5. This discussion draws on but hardly captures the nuanced richness of McMahon, *Happiness* on Aristotle (41–50), the Enlightenment (13–14, 208–12, 245–52), Bentham (217–21), and Darwin (410–24, with the quote from *Descent of Man* on 417).

6. Howard Mumford Jones, *The Pursuit of Happiness* (Cambridge, MA: Harvard University Press, 1953), 146; William James, *The Varieties of Religious Experience: A Study in Human Nature* (New York: Longmans, Green, 1902); James Mackaye, *The Economy of Happiness* (Boston: Little, Brown, 1906); Henry Smith Williams, *The Science of Happiness* (New York: Harper, 1909); Jean Finot, *The Science of Happiness*, trans. Mary J. Safford (1909; New York: G.P. Putman's Sons, 1914). Among later precursors are Bertrand Russell, *The Conquest of Happiness* (London: George Allen and Unwin, 1930); Lewis M. Terman, *Psychological Factors in Marital Happiness* (New York: McGraw-Hill, 1938).

7. For this tradition, see Donald B. Meyer, *The Positive Thinkers: A Study of the American Quest for Health, Wealth and Personal Power from Mary Baker Eddy to Norman Vincent Peale* (Garden City, NY: Doubleday, 1965); see also Peter N. Stearns, "The History of Happiness," *Harvard Business Review* 90 (Jan.–Feb. 2012): 104–9. Although happiness studies is a field that commands considerable attention, especially among economists and psychologists, American historians have paid remarkably little attention to the field. Google Scholar yields only one cite, José M. Edwards, "Joyful Economists: Remarks on the History of Economics and Psychology from the Happiness Studies Perspective," *Journal of the History of Economic Thought* 32 (Dec. 2010): 611–13. America-History and Life, the database for scholarship in American History, reveals no work by historians on happiness studies. Indeed, Darrin M. McMahon notes a "conspicuous" absence of discussions of positive emotions—joy or happiness included—in the extensive field of the history of emotions: Darrin M. McMahon, "Finding Joy in the History of Emotions," in *Doing Emotions History*, ed. Susan J. Matt and Peter N. Stearns (Urbana: University of Illinois Press, 2014), 103. Many scholars have studied the history of happiness, but no one has turned to examine the history of happiness studies extensively. Jackson Lears, "Get Happy!! For Margaret Thatcher as for Today's Happiness Industry, There Is No Such Thing as Society," *Nation*, Nov. 6, 2013, is a suggestive analysis.

8. Dana Becker, *The Myth of Empowerment: Women and the Therapeutic Culture in America* (New York: New York University Press, 2005), 1. On feminism and psychology more generally, see Alexandra Rutherford and Michael Pettit, "Feminism As/In/As Psychology: The Public Sciences of Sex and Gender," *History of Psychology* 18 (Aug. 2015): 223–37. From what I can tell, only one article in ten years of *Journal of Positive Psychology* has focused significantly on homosexuality: Dusty D. Jenkins and Alexander T. Vazsonyi, "Psychosocial Adjustment During the Transition from Adolescence to Young

Adulthood: Developmental Evidence from Sexual Minority and Heterosexual Youth," *JPP* 8 (May 2013): 185–91.

9. Daniel T. Rodgers, *Age of Fracture* (Cambridge, MA: Harvard University Press, 2011) explores the relationships between economics and emotions. On the connection between capitalism and emotions, see Arlie Russell Hochschild, *The Managed Heart: Commercialization of Human Feeling* (Berkeley: University of California Press, 1983).

10. James Turner, *Reckoning with the Beast: Animals, Pain, and Humanity in the Victorian Mind* (Baltimore: Johns Hopkins University Press, 1980) discusses how people in another age turned to human treatment of animals because their own lives seemed full of uncertainty and pain.

11. On how inherent in self-help books is an antipathy to communal solutions, see Wendy Simonds, *Women and Self-Help Culture: Reading Between the Lines* (New Brunswick, NJ: Rutgers University Press, 1992), 227.

12. On problems with replicating findings, see Brian Nosek and Open Science Collaboration, "Estimating the Reproducibility of Psychological Science," *Science*, Aug. 28, 2015. One example of the unsettled terrain involves definitions of key words: see James Pawelski's careful discussion of different meanings of the word positive in key documents in the field, "Defining the 'Positive' in Positive Psychology," Dec. 10, 2015, https://jamespawelski. com/2015/12/10/defining-the-positive-in-positive-psychology/.

13. In *What Is This Thing Called Happiness?* (New York: Oxford University Press, 2010), the philosopher Fred Feldman offers a probing discussion of basic terms. For an examination of key concepts behind scientific claims, see Lorraine Datson and Peter Galison, *Objectivity* (New York: Zone Books, 2007); Theodore Porter, *Trust in Numbers: The Pursuit of Objectivity in Science and Public Life* (Princeton, NJ: Princeton University Press, 1995). For an ambitious effort to pin down data, see Bernard Van Praag and Ada Ferrer-i-Carbonell, *Happiness Quantified: A Satisfaction Calculus Approach* (New York: Oxford University Press, 2004).

14. For a heated discussion in the *New York Review of Books* of the relevance of positive psychology to moral questions, see Tamsin Shaw, "The Psychologists Take Power," Feb. 25, 2016, http://www.nybooks.com/articles/2016/02/25/the-psychologists-take-power/; Jonathan Haidt and Steven Pinker, "Moral Psychology: An Exchange" and reply by Tamsin Shaw, April 7, 2016, http://www.nybooks.com/articles/2016/04/07/moral-psychology-an-exchange/.

15. Most historians of psychology counter the distinction between internal and external focal points by insisting on integrating them: Graham Richards, "Of What Is the History of Psychology a History?" *British Journal for the History of Science* 20 (April 1987): 201–11; Roger Smith, "Does the History of Psychology Have a Subject?" *History of the Human Sciences* 1 (Oct. 1988): 147–77. On earlier struggles to establish legitimacy in light of popularized versions of what psychologists claimed, see Jill G. Morawski and Gail A. Hornstein, "Quandary of the Quacks: The Struggle for Expert Knowledge in American Psychology, 1890–1940," in *The Estate of Social Knowledge*, ed. JoAnne Brown and David K. van Keuren (Baltimore: Johns Hopkins University Press, 1991), 106–33.

16. Christopher Peterson et al., "Strengths of Character, Orientation to Happiness, and Life Satisfaction," *JPP* 2 (July 2007): 150. A key discussion of the shift from character to personality is Warren Susman, "'Personality' and the Making of Twentieth-Century Culture," in *Culture as History: The Transformation of American Society in the Twentieth Century* (New York: Pantheon, 1984), 271–85.

17. Mike Egan, letter to editor, *NYTBR*, May 22, 2016; Ben Wegner, letter to editor, *NYTBR*, May 22, 2016, 6.

18. Interestingly, after the election, advice on how to apply positive psychology to the political situation came most clearly from the left and right. On the one hand, the web site of Berkeley's Greater Good Science Center emphasized how mindfulness led to compassion and then to action; how fully social action intensified social connections; and how activism amplified caring and compassion: Stephen Murphy-Shigematsu, "How to Sustain Your Activism," March 13, 2017. On the other hand, Arthur C. Brooks, president of the American Enterprise Institute, wrote that political engagement made people happier by transforming them into problem solvers and giving them a sense of control: Arthur C. Brooks, "Depressed by Politics? Just Let Go," *NYT*, March 17, 2017. See also Carol Graham, *Happiness for All? Unequal Hopes and Lives in Pursuit of the American Dream* (Princeton, NJ: Princeton University Press, 2017).

19. Jonathan Haidt, *The Happiness Hypothesis: Finding Modern Truth in Ancient Wisdom* (New York: Basic, 2006), 45–58, explores the dynamics of reciprocity within circles that move out from the individual. Roy F. Baumeister and Mark R. Leary, "The Need to Belong: Desire for Interpersonal Attachments as a Fundamental Human Motivation," *PB* 117 (May 1995): 497–529, exemplifies this problem of the narrowing of scope.

20. The literature on social and political movements is immense, but among good places to start is David A. Snow, Sarah A. Soule, and Hanspeter Kriesi, eds., *The Blackwell Companion to Social Movements* (Malden, MA: Blackwell, 2004). On cultural movements, begin with Thomas R. Rochon, *Culture Moves: Ideas, Activism, and Changing Values* (Princeton, NJ: Princeton University Press, 1998) and Ron Eyerman and Andrew Jamison, *Social Movements: A Cognitive Approach* (University Park: Pennsylvania State University Press, 1991). Google's Ngram viewer, which counts the number of times a word appears in books from 1800 to the present, reveals a long, slow decline in the use of the word happiness from the early 1820s, a leveling off in the very early 1980s, and then the beginning of an ascent in the late 1990s to the level last seen in the late 1950s.

21. Ed Diener and Robert Biswas-Diener, *Happiness: Unlocking the Mysteries of Psychological Wealth* (Malden, MA: Blackwell, 2008), 233.

22. See the following books by Daniel Horowitz: *The Morality of Spending: Attitudes Toward the Consumer Society in America, 1875–1940* (Baltimore: Johns Hopkins University Press, 1985); *The Anxieties of Affluence: Critiques of American Consumer Culture, 1939–1979* (Amherst: University of Massachusetts Press, 2004); *Consuming Pleasures: Intellectuals and Popular Culture in the Postwar World* (Philadelphia: University of Pennsylvania Press, 2013).

23. Ann Cvetkovich, *Depression: A Public Feeling* (Durham, NC: Duke University Press, 2012) explores some of the consequences of the disconnect between the academic and larger social worlds. In the late 1970s and early 1980s, social scientists, aware of such issues, included in studies such as the National Survey of Black Americans (NSBA) and the Multi-City Survey of Urban Inequality (MCSUI) questions that sought to determine a sense of how intergroup relationships affected people's sense of fairness and well-being.

24. On historically inspired cautions against moving too fast in applying advances in brain science to social problems, see Jed S. Rakoff, "Neuroscience and the Law: Don't Rush It," *NYRB*, May 12, 2016, 30–33.

25. Danielle Allen, *Our Declaration: A Reading of the Declaration of Independence in Defense of Equality* (New York: W.W. Norton, 2014), 278.

CHAPTER 1
From Helplessness to Optimism

Martin Seligman and the Development
of Positive Psychology

In his 1998 presidential address to the American Psychological Association (APA), University of Pennsylvania professor Martin Seligman issued clarion calls. First, he urged practitioners to "better understand, predict, and even prevent" horrendous "ethnopolitical conflicts." With events in Kosovo most immediately in mind, he presciently predicted that "the warfare the world faces in the next century will be ethnic in its roots and hatreds" with "the destruction of whole communities and the ongoing problems of refugees and human rights abuse" amplifying these problems. Second, he called for psychology to return to "its original roots" by emphasizing "the understanding and building of the most positive qualities of an individual: optimism, courage, work ethic, future-mindedness, interpersonal skill, the capacity for pleasure and insight, and social responsibility." Though he acknowledged the importance of the work psychologists had done in the field of mental illness, he envisioned a more positive approach. He believed that especially after World War II the focus "on repairing damage within a disease model of human functioning" had been problematic. In doing so, psychologists neglected "the flourishing individual and the thriving community." For Seligman, flourishing was a richer and broader term than happiness, including as it did a wide range of positive emotions including the search for meaning, resilience, and vitality.

In his speech, coming not long after the disintegration of the Soviet Union, Seligman called for a reorientation of thinking about the relationship between the self and society. Celebrating that the United States stood "alone on the pinnacle of economic and political leadership," he challenged the nation to turn away from focusing on increasing its own materialistic consumption because that path ignored human needs at home and abroad. To continue would likely "lead to increasing selfishness, alienation between the more and the less fortunate, and eventually to chaos and despair." He therefore envisioned psychology playing a critical role in promoting an alternative course of action by developing a scientifically based "vision of the good life that is empirically sound and, at the same time, understandable and attractive. We can show the world what actions lead to well-being, to positive individuals, to flourishing communities, and to a just society." Aware that America's increasing affluence had, paradoxically, come along with dramatically higher rates of depression, especially among the young, he proposed turning away from an emphasis on "repairing damage." Social and behavioral scientists should instead study how to produce healthy children, a satisfying work life, and "the strongest civic commitment." A positive psychology would reveal how "growth, mastery, drive, and character building . . . can develop out of painful life events." Psychology, he insisted, was "surely more than a tenant farmer on the plantation of profit-motivated health schemes." Using a problematic analogy that revealed the scope of his ambitions, he asserted that "a new science of positive psychology can be the 'Manhattan Project' for the social sciences." The field held "the potential," he insisted, "to create, as a direct effect, an understanding and a scientifically informed practice of the pursuit of the best things in life and of family and civic virtue."

Seligman went beyond rhetorical assertions when he announced several initiatives. With the Canadian Psychological Association, the APA established a Task Force on Ethnopolitical Warfare, which had recently held a conference in Northern Ireland on that topic. With the help of money from the Mellon Foundation, the National Institute of Mental Health, and private donors, he could announce the allocation of $2 million to fund postdoctoral fellowships on ethnopolitical conflict at the University of Pennsylvania, the University of Cape Town in South Africa, and the University of Ulster in Northern Ireland. He told his audience that he had secured a grant for mid-career researchers from the John Templeton Foundation to the APA for an annual Templeton Positive Psychology Prize, "the largest monetary award ever given in psychology." He announced how he and some senior scholars had created a network of early and mid-career researchers they hoped would now become "the leaders of our reoriented science." Finally, he let it be known that a gathering of groups of senior researchers had begun work on "the taxonomy of the roots of a positive life," asking "what are the relationships among subjective well-being, positive individual traits, and positive community?" In addition, this group would seek "to transform the study of genius and extraordinary accomplishments," exploring how people with exceptional talents would "come into play in mastering human relationships, assuming moral responsibility, engaging in spirituality, and viewing life as a work of art."[1]

I start the story I am telling not in the 1940s but with this important moment in 1998—a moment significant because it is a widely accepted tale of positive psychology's origin; because it brings to the fore many of the themes that pulse through this history; because Seligman plays such a commanding role in the field's development; and because as an organized movement compared with how other academic fields originated, positive psychology, though not without significant precedents, began at a specific moment under the leadership of a specific person.

Yet Seligman's address was hardly the first call on professional psychologists to emphasize well-being instead of mental illness. In 1946 the World Health Organization announced its commitment to seeing "health" as "a state of complete physical, mental and social well-being and not merely the absence of disease or infirmity." Also notable are two presidential addresses of the 1950s: J. P. Guilford's one on "Creativity" in 1950 and Harry F. Harlow's on "The Nature of Love" in 1958. Yet though both of them spoke on positive aspects of human life, neither placed his talk in the context of a battle between an emphasis on health and illness or offered a program, let alone a capacious one, that reached beyond a specific research agenda to promote a bold turn among professional psychologists.

The APA, with its huge and unwieldly membership of 155,000, encompassed a wide range of constituencies: consultants; academics ranging from humanistic scholars to hard scientists; professors, including researchers at major universities and teachers at community colleges; and therapists, among them those with a variety of degrees whose practices relied on a number of approaches, including Freudian, Jungian, existential, humanistic, cognitive behavioral, and psychopharmacological. Because they believed that clinicians dominated the APA, in 1988 academic psychologists formed the Association for Psychological Science.

The professional politics that helped lead to Seligman's election sprang from the political dynamics of psychology's organizational life, something dramatically clear in Ronald E. Fox's presidential address four years earlier.[2] Like Seligman, Fox, a clinical psychologist who had earlier served as the founding dean of the School of Professional Psychology at Wright State University, bridged the world of clinicians and academics. Fox dramatically pictured the field of psychology in danger of tearing itself apart, with highly visible "internal squabbles" and "ad hominem attacks" that undermined support from the public and from funding agencies. "The lack of cooperation and collaboration" was exacerbating "schisms" long present in the field, especially the one between scientists and therapists. Although Fox went on to propose solutions, he remained unsure that there were grounds for productive exchange since he believed "research contributions to practice are about as useful as sails on an automobile." "Charlatans" and "quacks" among those who practiced therapy, seen most recently in the controversies surrounding suppressed memories, were "giving both our profession and our science a black eye." More generally, Fox cited an email whose author claimed that "so-called clinicians have taken control of the APA for no better purpose than to use it to push questionable treatments and to convince the public that they are a real profession with legitimate services to offer . . . perverting our science and misusing our reputations." Most of them, his correspondent asserted, "should be confined to . . . treating and diagnosing each other rather than innocent members of society." Nor did Fox find scholars blameless. Although most researchers understood the problems clinicians faced on a daily basis, he asserted, some of them "carelessly use the mace of science as a cudgel to publicly, and unfairly, pummel clinicians." In addition, much of their research, he reported someone remarking, was "useful only to help professors get promoted, period."[3] Seligman's candidacy held the promise of resolving some of these tensions. He had a proven track record of collaboration. Moreover, he had made major contributions that bridged the gap between researchers and practitioners. What he discovered in laboratories had proven successful in therapeutic situations. All of this helped Seligman win the presidency.[4]

BIOGRAPHY AND HISTORY

Seligman's attempt to shift the focus in psychology from illness, misery, and pessimism to well-being, happiness, and optimism paralleled the trajectory of his own scholarly interests and reverberated with major events of his life. Among the biographical data that may be germane to understanding his career are the following: (1) he grew up in a household where Judaism and awareness of the Holocaust mattered but turned away from his family's faith soon after his bar mitzvah; (2) his father's incapacitation soon after had a great impact on him; (3) the person who most influenced him at Princeton, from which he graduated in 1964 with a degree in philosophy, was the libertarian Robert Nozick; (4) at Cornell in April 1969 he was the youngest faculty member of the Committee of 41, which believed that the takeover of Willard Straight Hall by African American protestors and the administration's giving in to their demands threatened academic freedom; (5) he showed a long, sustained interest in science fiction; (6) he was divorced in 1978 and remarried in 1988.[5]

Seligman began his professional education at the University of Pennsylvania where he earned his PhD in psychology in 1967. Influenced by the work of several Penn professors, including cognitive psychologist Aaron T. Beck, Seligman focused on what he called learned helplessness. Carrying out experiments beginning in the late 1960s, first on dogs and then on humans, he brought his findings together in his 1975 *Helplessness: On Depression, Development, and Death*. When faced with adversity, he demonstrated, people developed a false sense that they lacked control to change their situations.

Although most of the book focused on the psychological problems an individual encountered, at one point Seligman broadened the scope of his inquiry. Speaking of the poverty that inner-city African Americans faced (a topic to which his later work paid little attention), he acknowledged that he understood that blacks resented "liberals and social workers who tried to alleviate" their conditions. "Effective protest," which involved "changing one's conditions by one's own actions," he insisted as he appeared to embrace community organizing, helped residents of inner cities overcome helplessness. Poverty involved more than the lack of adequate financial resources; it was "a problem of individual mastery, dignity, and self-esteem," solved by the "self-esteem–enhancing nature of social action," he remarked. His linking of self-esteem and social action reminds us that Seligman then believed that although therapy could help the individual overcome a sense of helplessness, for a group adversely affected by uncontrollable social conditions, social action was in order.[6]

Nonetheless, most of his book focused on the implications of helplessness for individuals, not social groups. Seligman showed how an inability to predict or control produced "three deficits": the undermining of "the motivation to respond," the retarding of "the ability to learn that responding works," and the development of "emotional disturbance, primarily depression and anxiety." Depressed people developed a problematic cognitive approach—a pessimistic explanatory style that involved rationalizations for highly personal adverse judgments of their situation that seemed incapable of ever being changed and globally extensive in their impact. In the end, Seligman remained optimistic that scientific understanding and cognitive therapy could remedy the situation. "I, for one, am not ready to abandon the search for plasticity" that drew its strength from "democratic, egalitarian ideals."[7]

Seligman has offered several origin stories, all of them dramatic, but only partial explanations of how he shifted his emphasis from pessimism to optimism. One appeared in his 1990 *Learned Optimism: How to Change Your Mind and Your Life*. Eight years earlier, he reported, he had settled into his seat on a long flight, scrunching up against the window, as he often did, in order to avoid being forced into conversation with a fellow passenger. In this case, John Leslie, the man sitting next to him, refused to play along. "Thus began the chance, uninvited conversation," Seligman related, which "started a dramatic shift in the focus of my work." As Leslie told Seligman about how he came to tell the difference between pessimists and optimists when he worked to motivate horses he raised and employees he supervised, Seligman realized that what he heard also explained how as a psychologist he learned to distinguish between those who succumbed to and resisted depression. Leslie helped prompt Seligman to act on what he had long wondered about: not just how to make unhappy people less miserable and but instead how to make "the lives of well people even better." Thinking back to a previous talk he had with the head of Metropolitan Life Insurance Company, Seligman realized that what Leslie told him was applicable to the selection of successful insurance salespeople. Before long, Seligman followed Leslie's advice, shifting the attention of his research and teaching "from pessimism to optimism, from failure to success."[8]

Then there was a second story, narrated in 1999 by a writer for a Penn publication and titled "Martin Seligman's Journey from Learned Helplessness to Learned Happiness." The article told how in the late 1980s, Seligman, a "self-admitted grouch," met with his literary agent about writing a popular book for a general audience. As they talked, Seligman suddenly realized that he might see the glass as half full rather than half empty. "*Learned Optimism*—that's your title," his agent remarked as they neared the end of their productive conversation. That talk transformed Seligman, the Penn reporter noted, "from one of the world's experts on pessimism and depression into its premier scientific authority on optimism."[9]

The third story, the one Seligman most frequently offered, appeared in the same Penn publication and elsewhere. One day, when he was working in his garden, Seligman yelled at his five-year-old daughter Nicki. "Despite all my work on optimism," he noted, "I've always been somewhat of a nimbus cloud around my house." His daughter "got a stern look on her face, and she walked right over to me. 'Daddy,' she said, 'I want to talk with you .... From the time I was three until I was five, I whined a lot. But I decided the day I turned five, to stop whining. And I haven't whined once since.'" Next, he remarked as part of the explanation of why he turned from grouch to an expert on happiness, she "looked me right in the eye, and said 'Daddy, if I could stop whining, you can stop being such a grouch.'" As Seligman recalled later, "This was an epiphany for me .... In that moment, I resolved to change." His five-year-old daughter "had found me my mission," as he deployed religious language to describe what he set out to do. Indeed, it is useful to think of Seligman as a *macher* (a Yiddish word for an influential person) on a mission—as a Jew to fully embrace being an American and as a positive psychologist to transform the world.[10]

In 2011, Seligman offered a fourth story. Soon after his election to the APA presidency, he received an elliptical phone call inviting him to come to New York. Several weeks later he traveled there and faced "an unmarked door on the eighth floor of a small, grimy office building in the bowels of lower Manhattan." Entering a "windowless room," he encountered two lawyers who announced that they represented " 'an anonymous foundation.' " They told him that they would fund his work but that "if you reveal our identity, any funding we give you will stop." After talking for five minutes about his project on ethnopolitical conflict, they asked him to send them a one-page proposal and a budget. Two weeks later, a check for $120,000 arrived. After he held the meeting in Northern Ireland, a second phone call came, asking him what he wanted to do next. Stunned and surprised, Seligman talked briefly about his hopes for positive psychology. During a second meeting in New York, the foundation's representatives asked for a three-page proposal and a budget. A few weeks later, a check for $1.5 million arrived. On his third visit to New York, he learned that the money came from Atlantic Philanthropies, funded by Charles Feeney, who was determined to give away the fortune of $5 billion he made by developing duty-free shops in airports.[11]

These tales, which stemmed from highly personal epiphanies—or that rely on an examination of his actual research and writing—tell only a partial story, at least for a historian. As we shall see, multiple contexts led to the flowering of positive psychology. To begin with, the half-empty/half-full analogy was hardly new to Seligman in the 1990s: it was integral to Aaron Beck's work on cognitive behavioral therapy, best expressed in his book *Depression,* published in 1967, the year Seligman earned his PhD. By understanding how poorly grounded in reality pessimistic assumptions about life were, Beck argued, a patient could become, if not happier, then at least more realistic, effective, and resolved.[12]

Moreover, although correlation is not causation, the multiple historical locations of Seligman's work are striking. It would be a stretch to suggest that what impelled him forward was that translated from German, Selig, the first part of his last name, means blissful. More germane is that he wrote on helplessness during the 1970s when pessimism suffused much of a nation that seemed helpless in face of the failure to win the war in Vietnam, to curb violent civil disorders, to stem the tide of rampant inflation, and to overcome the political malaise following Watergate. Then Seligman shifted the mood of his scholarship to optimism in the 1980s at the same time that President Ronald Reagan declared that it was "morning in America." With the United States "standing alone on the pinnacle of economic and political leadership," as Seligman put it in his 1998 address, a parallel and transformative moment for psychology was in order.[13]

Yet in the end, caution is in order when it comes to evaluating Seligman's role in the history of happiness studies and positive psychology. Before his talk, scholarly findings had already begun to find their way into popular arenas. One example will suffice: on September 16, 1996, the *New Yorker* published a cartoon by J. B. Handelsman that pictured a man standing in front of his mansion telling his friend he has learned that it was fruitless to work so hard when happiness depended more on genetic disposition than on high levels of wealth and income. Reaching back even further makes it clear that the American Ed Diener and the Dutch Ruut Veenhoven can, with more justification than Seligman, claim the mantle as the field's pathbreaking researchers and founders. Moreover, Seligman is a controversial, often polarizing figure. To his supporters, he is a larger-than-life, generous, scientific researcher whose scholarship, writing, and entrepreneurial organizing have been transformative. On the other hand, critics believe he has moved too quickly from scholarship to application and popularization; that his work is more derivative than original—often not measuring up to scientific standards; and that his political commitments have shaped his interventions.[14]

POSITIVE PSYCHOLOGY AND ITS ALTERNATIVES

Seligman and other proponents of positive psychology and happiness studies were reacting against a full complement of seemingly alternative traditions. They rejected the pessimism of Freudianism, which, they asserted, blamed the victim. Seligman wrote that "all mental suffering became a transmutation of some vile part of us" and doomed victims of depression "to years of one-way conversation about the murky, distant past" so they could solve problems that alternative therapeutic strategies could revolve more expeditiously. Seligman also rejected behaviorism, in this case for being too mechanistic. In addition, he found the biomedical approach problematic: "dependent on outside forces—pills dispensed by a benevolent physician" made "patients out of essentially normal people." Moreover, in ways that pointed forward to his increasing emphasis on a conservative politics that emphasized certain character strengths, he attacked "victimology." The focus on sexism and racism, he believed, was part and parcel of social science's emphasis on the negative that excluded "responsibility, decision-making, and free will."[15]

Seligman also opposed what he saw as the superficiality of the power of positive thinking offered by Norman Vincent Peale in the 1950s. "The skills of optimism," he remarked caustically and colorfully, "do not emerge from the pink Sunday-school world of happy events." Writing in 2002, Seligman insisted on characteristics that differentiated Peale's positive thinking from his own positive psychology. The former was "an armchair activity," the work of non-professionals; his approach was "tied to a program of empirical and replicable scientific activity." Peale accentuated the positive and eliminated the negative, but Seligman understood that there were times "when negative thinking is to be preferred." Noting that many major proponents of positive psychology had spent much of their careers on negative aspects of human existence, he reassured the profession that "Positive Psychology is a supplement to negative psychology, not a substitute."[16]

Above all, Seligman and his colleagues distanced themselves from the emphasis on self-esteem that grew out of the work of humanistic psychologists, even as they echoed concepts their predecessors had offered. While acknowledging the "enormous promise" of the "generous humanistic vision," positive psychologists critiqued writers such as Abraham Maslow and Carl Rogers for being insufficiently scientific. More problematic was the way humanistic psychology beginning in the 1960s had generated what Seligman and his colleagues considered excessive, even dangerous emphases on self-esteem. In the introductory essay to an issue on positive psychology in the *American Psychologist* that they edited in 2000, Seligman and Mihaly Csikszentmihalyi noted that "one legacy of the humanism of the 1960s" was on view in bookstores. "The 'psychology' section contains at least ten shelves on crystal healing, aromatherapy, and reaching the inner child for every shelf of books that tries to uphold some scholarly standard." In some instances, they insisted, humanistic psychology "encouraged a self-centeredness that played down concerns for collective well-being." For many positive psychologists, humanistic psychologists were narcissists who avoided engagement with the public arena in responsible ways. Seligman went so far as to connect self-esteem with violent danger. Citing a 1996 study by Roy Baumeister, he noted that self-esteem not only undermined commitments to hard work, achievement, and civic engagement but also produced more dangerous results. Genocidal killers, hitmen, gang leaders, and violent criminals, it turned out, had "unwarranted self-esteem" that caused violence.[17]

Seligman's critique of humanistic psychology, something that was strategic and driven by an insistence on the importance of science, prompted a storm of criticism that fully reflected the anxieties of influence—the impact of humanistic psychology both on the excesses of self-esteem movements and on positive psychology. Respondents to the 2000 essays in *American Psychologist* emphasized the pioneering contributions of Maslow and Rogers and went on to deny that these psychologists were narcissistic, given how much they emphasized social responsibility and supported progressive social movements. They also pointed to the substantial empirical research humanistic psychologists had carried out. Indeed, one scholar remarked that Seligman's and Csikszentmihalyi's reaction to their progenitors "was 99.6% pure rejection of their so-called ancestors (even purer than Ivory soap!)." In their response, Seligman and Csikszentmihalyi acknowledged that "positive psychology has been strongly influenced by our predecessors." However, they insisted they and their colleagues were "unblushingly, scientists first. The work we seek to support and encourage must be nothing less than replicable, cumulative, and objective. Insofar as humanistic psychology and Buddhist psychology share these premises, they will find us ready allies."[18]

Yet as the historian Jessica Grogan has remarked, "the similarities between humanistic psychology and positive psychology are numerous": they both rejected Freudianism and behaviorism, as well as a reliance on drugs; they both worked to shift the focus from pathology to well-being, from pessimism to optimism, from misery to happiness. They both developed their psychology through extensive grounding in philosophy. They shared a commitment to civic engagement and to reaching a broad public by popularizing scholarly findings. After all, in his *Motivation and Personality* (1954) Maslow used the term positive psychology and had remarked that "the science of psychology has been far more successful on the negative than on the positive side." Where the generations really differed was in the empirical and scientific grounding of their work— Maslow has relied significantly on soft evidence, especially biographies of the lives of famous people; Seligman and his colleagues on clinical observations, lab experiments, extensive firsthand investigations, and reviews of scholarly literature. Despite these similarities, according to Grogan, Seligman "distanced his theory from those of the founders of humanistic psychology and belittled the movement's impact." Many were the parallels between Maslow and the other progenitors of positive psychology and happiness studies, and all built the paths to the work of Seligman and his colleagues.[19]

In addition, the birth of positive psychology hardly came out of nowhere. For more than a decade scholars working within a loosely defined field of happiness studies had offered many aspects of a vision of psychology that presented an alternative to a negative emphasis on mental illness. Those interested in evolutionary biology, neuroscience, experimental psychology, meditation, religion, psychopharmacology, and character strengths had provided virtually all of the elements that soon came to be defined as essential components of positive psychology. More generally, a turn to wellness was abroad: in the mid-1990s, for example, Oprah Winfrey shifted the focus of her television program from personal problems to personal opportunities. More and more people practiced mindful meditation; advice books promising inner peace appeared in greater and greater numbers.[20]

ON A MISSION

This hardly minimizes the capaciousness and influence of Seligman's presidential address. Though as we shall see, the origins of happiness studies and positive psychology preceded his 1998 speech, his talk was nonetheless a major turning point, moreso in terms of building an infrastructure than for generating new and transformative ideas. He called on psychologists to work in the public sphere. He focused on ethnopolitical conflicts, mentioning situations in South Africa, Northern Ireland, and Eastern Europe. Yet, despite his stated ambition to have his colleagues and peers focus on major international conflicts, he avoided any reference to the Arab-Israeli conflict or to the bombing of two American embassies in Africa carried out just two weeks earlier by Jihadis, including members of al-Qaeda led by Osama bin Laden. Despite his mention of the "less fortunate," the "just society," and "civic virtue," Seligman made no mention of how psychologists could help solve domestic problems, such as the stagnation of middle-class and working-class incomes, the end of welfare as we know it, continuing expressions of racism, and an increasingly fractious political situation in the nation.

Despite these lacunae, Seligman offered an ambitious program, indeed one driven by a religious, mystical sense of a professional mission to which he had been summoned. "Positive psychology called to me," he remarked in 2011, "just as the burning bush called to Moses."[21] Four years later told of a dream he had in the early 1970s when "the godhead appears (yes: male, white-bearded with a booming bass voice). He says—unforgettably," Seligman recalled, " 'at least you are starting to ask the right questions.' " Aaron Beck had warned Seligman that if he persisted on the professional path on which he was at age thirty, he would be wasting his life. "A numinous dream," Seligman now remembered, had shaken the foundations of his career and life. "I changed my science to work on real people," he reported as he explained the implications of the dream and of Beck's advice, "not just in the laboratory, and using longitudinal methods in addition to experiments." Over time, Seligman came to seek nothing short of transforming psychology, and doing so with the ample backing of government, foundation, and private funds. Ambitious, entrepreneurial, and organized, he had already begun to move quickly with others to transform positive psychology from an idea to an organized movement. As he remarked in 2009, in a way that might lead us to think of Judaism's commitment to *Tikkun Olam* (to heal the world), the goal of positive psychology was "to increase the percentage of the world's population that is considered 'flourishing' from today's 7–33% to 51% by the year 2051." Positive psychology promised a wide-ranging expansion of the discipline's reach into the public arena that relied on its ambition to transform the world.[22]

ON THE BEACH

In January 1997, Seligman was walking with his family on a beach in Hawaii. One of his daughters heard a man call for help. "Sure enough," Seligman later recalled, "down in the surf was a snowy-haired man, being pounded against the lava walls, razor-sharp with barnacles, and then being tossed back out into the turbulence." Seligman "waded in and pulled the big man to safety, not realizing that he had just triggered a revolution," wrote the author of an article in the magazine *Live Happy*. Seligman's catch that day was momentous—he had rescued Mihaly Csikszentmihalyi, a psychologist whose decades-long work on flow, the intense and full immersion in an activity, dovetailed profoundly with Seligman's search for how to ground psychology in positivity. As they settled down, they realized they shared much in common, including a commitment to restore a positive vision to the field of psychology. Talking for hours and keeping in mind that Seligman, recently elected president of the American Psychological Association, had the ideal platform from which to launch a transformative movement, they decided they could cooperate on promoting a vision of positive psychology. On New Year's Day, 1998, the first day of Seligman's presidency, at their initial gathering held in Akumal, Mexico, Csikszentmihalyi, Seligman, and Raymond Fowler, the APA CEO, decided on a strategy. They would build three "pillars" for the scientific study of happiness. Ed Diener, long active in the field of happiness studies, would direct the study of positive emotions; Csikszentmihalyi, the examination of positive character, "the strengths and virtues whose exercise regularly produces positive emotion"; and Seligman, research into positive institutions.[23]

They also drew up a list of fifty young scholars, which over time they narrowed to eighteen. They then invited them, along with some senior psychologists, to the inaugural conference on positive psychology. In January of 1999 and 2000, Seligman brought together more than two dozen psychologists at the same resort in Akumal. In days marked by snorkeling, walking, and talking, they discussed key concepts of positive psychology—and how they might move forward. Among the eighteen younger psychologists gathered there, two soon emerged as especially influential—Barbara

Fredrickson and Sonja Lyubomirsky—both then in their early thirties, holders of PhDs from Stanford, and at the time assistant professors at the University of Michigan and the University of California at Riverside, respectively. Eventually, all five—three older men and two younger women—would earn places on a visually playful rendition of America's most influential presidents on Mount Rushmore as the founding fathers and mothers of positive psychology.[24]

The most immediate result of these meetings was the "Akumal Manifesto," initially drafted in 1999 and issued in a revised version in 2000. Here Seligman and his colleagues laid out an ambitious program—practical in its implementation and lofty in its aspirations, although they made no mention of ethnopolitical conflict. Yet they did sketch their plans to spread the wisdom of positive psychology through professional meetings, inter-university cooperation, listservs, foundation funding, and publications. They planned the creation of three networks of scholars, each with representatives from several social sciences: "Positive Science" that would focus on studying "positive subjective states"; "the good life/good person"; and "the good society." Moreover, they advocated the promotion of positive values, such as creativity, hope, meaning, commitment, and love, in schools, medical facilities, families, and workplaces. They heralded "improving organizations and societies by discovering conditions that enhance trust, communication, and altruism between persons" and "improving the moral character of society by better understanding and promoting the spiritual impulse within humans." Moving "beyond prior emphases upon disease and disorder," they proposed scientific investigations of what would enable "individuals and communities to thrive."[25]

NOTES

1. Martin E. P. Seligman, "The President's Address," 1998, AP 54 (Aug. 1999): 559–62. Elsewhere Seligman reiterated and expanded on what he meant by positive psychology: see, for example, Martin E. P. Seligman "Positive Psychology," in *The Science of Optimism and Hope: Research Essays in Honor of Martin E. P. Seligman*, ed. Jane E. Gillham (Philadelphia: Templeton Foundation Press, 2000), 415–29, and Martin E. P. Seligman and Mihaly Csikszentmihalyi, "Positive Psychology: An Introduction," AP 55 (Jan. 2000): 1–14.

2. "Constitution of the World Health Organization," 1946; J. P. Guilford, "Creativity," AP 5 (Sept. 1950): 444–54; Harry F. Harlow, "The Nature of Love," AP 13 (Dec. 1958): 673–85. Seligman understands his election as involving a challenge to how insiders had until then fixed the order of succession: Martin Seligman, conversation with author, Sept. 10, 2016. For Seligman's critique of clinicians who had dominated the field of psychology and given it a focus on mental illness, see Martin E. P. Seligman, *Authentic Happiness: Using the New Positive Psychology to Realize Your Potential for Lasting Fulfillment* (New York: Free Press, 2002), 19.

3. Ronald E. Fox, "Charlatanism, Scientism, and Psychology's Social Contract," *AP* 51 (Aug. 1996): 777–84, and correspondence quoted in same. For information on Fox's position and approach, I am relying on Ronald E. Fox, telephone conversation with author, Sept. 30, 2016.

4. Several years before his election, Seligman had published in *Consumer Reports* the results of his study that demonstrated the effectiveness of therapeutic approaches: Martin Seligman, conversation with author, May 19, 2016; Martin E. P. Seligman, "The Effectiveness of Psychotherapy: The *Consumer Reports* Study," *AP* 50 (Dec. 1995): 965–74.

5. Seligman, conversation; Art Carey, "Give Thanks," http://www.philly.com, April 1, 2004; Martin Seligman to author, May 29, 2016; Stacey Burling, "The Power of a Positive Thinker," http://www.philly.com, May 30, 2010. On his interest in prospective psychology, see the joint effort of the Templeton Foundation and University of Pennsylvania: http://www.prospectivepsych.org/content/research-awards.

6. Martin E. P. Seligman, *Helplessness: On Depression, Development, and Death* (San Francisco: W.H. Freeman, 1975), 164.

7. Seligman, *Helplessness*, 6, 36. In *Helplessness*, xiii, Seligman noted that when he returned to Penn in 1970, Beck was one of his two "main sponsors" as well as being a teacher and a source of "stimulation."

8. Martin E. P. Seligman, *Learned Optimism: How to Change Your Mind and Your Life* (New York: Simon & Schuster, 1900), 95–97.

9. Rob Hirtz, "Martin Seligman's Journey from Learned Helplessness to Learned Happiness," *Pennsylvania Gazette*, Jan./Feb. 1999.

10. Hirtz, "Seligman's Journey"; Seligman, *Authentic*, 28–29 (in this source, Seligman called this daughter Nikki). For an analysis of Seligman's shift, one that relies on a discussion of his research, see Steven F. Maier, Christopher Peterson, and Barry Schwartz, "From Helplessness to Hope: The Seminal Career of Martin Seligman," in Gillham, *Science of Optimism*, 11–37.

11. Martin E. P. Seligman, *Flourish: A Visionary New Understanding of Happiness and Well-Being* (New York: Simon & Schuster, 2011), 5–8.

12. Aaron T. Beck, *Depression: Clinical, Experimental, and Theoretical Aspects* (New York: Harper & Row, 1967).

13. Seligman is writing his memoir, and its publication will enable us to explore the interaction of biography, personality, and scholarship. On how other psychologists performed the theories they produced, see Jamie Cohen-Cole, "The Reflexivity of Cognitive Science: The Scientist as a Model of Human Nature," *History of the Human Sciences* 18 (Nov. 2005): 107–39, and articles by Jill Morawski, including "Self-Regard and Other-Regard: Reflexive Practices in American Psychology, 1890–1940," *Science in Context* 5 (Autumn 1992): 281–308; "Scientific Selves: Discerning Subjects and Experimenters in Experimental Psychology in the United States, 1900–1935," in *Psychology's Territories: Historical and Contemporary Perspectives from Different Disciplines,* ed. Mitchell Ash and Thomas Sturm (Mahwah, NJ: Erlbaum, 2007), 129–48.

14. For critical evaluations of Seligman, see the discussions in Chapters 6, 7, and 8, including works by Barbara Ehrenreich, Jeffrey B. Rubin, and Barbara Held, as well as the controversy surrounding the issue of psychologists' involvement in the CIA's torture or enhanced interrogation program captured in the 2016 essay by Tamsin Shaw in the *NYRB* and the response of Seligman and others to it.

15. Seligman, *Learned Optimism*, 11, 12; Seligman, "Positive Psychology," in Gillham, *Science of Optimism*, 416–17.

16. Seligman, *Learned Optimism*, 15; Seligman, *Authentic*, 288–89.

17. Seligman and Csikszentmihalyi, "Positive Psychology," 7; Martin E. P. Seligman, "Introduction to Second Edition," 1997, in Seligman, *Learned Optimism*, vii. Jeffrey J. Froh,

"The History of Positive Psychology: Truth Be Told," *NYS Psychologist*, 16 (May–June 2004), 18–20, both challenges the claim that positive psychology began with Seligman's talk in 1998 and correctly insists on the importance of Maslow as a precursor who used the term positive psychology in the 1950s. Similarly, the Winter 2001 issue of *Journal of Humanistic Psychology* called on positive psychologists to recognize humanistic psychology as an important element in origins of the field.

18. See, for example, the following in *American Psychologist* 56 (Jan. 2001): Arthur C. Bohart and Thomas Greening, "Humanistic Psychology and Positive Psychology," 81–82; Stewart B. Shapiro, "Illogical Positivism," 82 (source of the quote); Martin Seligman and Mihaly Csikszentmihalyi, "Reply to Comments," 89–90.

19. Jessica Grogan, *Encountering America: Humanistic Psychology, Sixties Culture & the Shaping of the Modern Self* (New York: HarperCollins, 2013), 313–14; A[braham] H. Maslow, *Motivation and Personality* (New York: Harper, 1954), 353–54.

20. For Oprah's shift, see Janice Peck, *The Age of Oprah: Cultural Icon for the Neoliberal Era* (Boulder, CO: Paradigm, 2008), 1–13.

21. Seligman, *Flourish*, 75.

22. Martin Seligman, "Introduction: How Are We Called into the Future?" in *Being Called: Scientific, Secular, and Sacred Perspectives*, ed. David Bryce Yaden, Theo D. McCall, and J. Harold Ellens (Santa Barbara, CA: Praeger, 2015), xxi; Martin E. P. Seligman, "Address to First World Congress of Positive Psychology," 2009, quoted in Sam Binkley, *Happiness as Enterprise: An Essay on Neoliberal Life* (Albany: State University of New York Press, 2014), 6.

23. John David Mann, "Happiness Revolution," *Live Happy*, Oct. 11, 2013, http://www.livehappy.com/science/positive-psychology/happiness-revolution; Seligman, *Authentic*, 265–66. I am grateful to Martin Seligman for helping me do my best to get the chronology right for this story, which he did in an email of May 8, 2017.

24. On the meetings and early history, see http://content.time.com/time/magazine/article/0,9171,1015832,00.html; http://www.ppc.sas.upenn.edu/akumalmanifesto.htm; illustration by William J. Chalhan, http://www.livehappy.com/science/positive-psychology/happiness-revolution. Also critical in the launching of the first Summit of Positive Psychology was support by the Gallup Foundation: see "Acknowledgments," in *Flourishing: Positive Psychology and the Life Well-Lived*, ed. Corey L. M. Keyes and Jonathan Haidt (Washington, DC: American Psychological Association, 2003), ix.

25. Ken Sheldon et al., "Akumal Manifesto," http://www.ppc.sas.upenn.edu/akumalmanifesto.htm. For one discussion of the Akumal meetings, see Seligman, *Authentic*, 277–78.

CHAPTER 2

Misery and Pleasure in the Origins of Happiness Studies, 1945–1970

Positive psychology and the science of happiness were born in misery—both personal and collective. "It may seem strange that a work on happiness should have been written at a time when men were suffering the greatest misfortunes," wrote a Polish author who composed his book on happiness during World War II in German-occupied Warsaw. During the uprising there the Germans set his house on fire and a German soldier threw his manuscript into the gutter; still, he was able to retrieve it. However, what appeared tragic taught him a valuable lesson: "We think more about happiness when we are unhappy than when we are happy," he remarked retrospectively. "And evil is easier to endure if in our thoughts we can escape to something better." Although it is possible to trace the origins of happiness studies and positive psychology to an earlier time, the years during and after World War II were among the most fertile periods for their development. Formative events include the Holocaust and the rise of Nazism, the multiple disruptions caused by World War II, the American economic boom of the postwar period, scientific discoveries, and changes in attitudes to mental health. In addition, advances in the social and behavioral sciences, along with those in pharmacology and neuroscience, pointed in new directions.[1]

By 1970, a time when the postwar economic boom and the accompanying optimistic mood had begun to falter, much had changed in the ways Americans—including social and behavioral scientists—understood the nature and dynamics of happiness, but the arrival of happiness studies and positive psychology as self-conscious fields still awaited future developments. Martin Seligman and Mihaly Csikszentmihalyi claimed that the national priority given to mental health research and treatment for veterans returning from World War II was responsible for the field's postwar emphasis on negativity. Ironically, however, the multiple traumas of the war years and their aftermath were themselves responsible for the origins of positive psychology.[2]

NORMAN VINCENT PEALE AND THE POWER
OF POSITIVE THINKING

Also influentially in play during the postwar period was the storied American New Thought tradition. Relying on a powerful amalgam of Protestantism, therapies, and mind cure, by the late nineteenth century it had coalesced into a movement complete with speaking tours, as well as scientific and religious organizations. In doing so it relied on connecting happiness, religion, and science. More than fifty years later, in 1952, New Thought's intellectual and spiritual heir, Norman Vincent Peale, authored *The Power of Positive Thinking*, which became the most widely read precursor of positive psychology, however much its practitioners kept their distance from it. His life and book, neither of which was born in pain or misery, provide a contrast to others under consideration here. In 1932 a thirty-four-year-old Peale had begun a fifty-two-year career as minister of Manhattan's Marble Collegiate Church. For the first two decades of his pastorate, he balanced the acknowledgment of tragedy with his conviction that faith-based optimism should triumph. *The Art of Real Happiness* (1950), co-authored with the appropriately named psychiatrist Smiley Blanton, began by observing that contemporary America "can claim more than its full share" of "misery of a most particular kind" given that, "surrounded by unmatched potentialities for the good life, we are overwhelmed by the deadly fear that all is lost!" By the time he wrote his 1952 book, Peale had perfected a formula. He learned to leave his anti-Communist, small government conservatism implicit or hidden and worked hard to minimize if not eliminate negative observations from what he wrote.[3]

This accentuating of the positive and minimizing the negative was evident in *The Power of Positive Thinking*. As one critic noted, Peale refused "to allow his followers to hear, speak or see any evil. For him real human suffering does not exist; there is no such thing as murderous rage, suicidal despair, cruelty, lust, greed, mass poverty, or illiteracy. All these things he would dismiss as trivial mental processes which will evaporate if thoughts are simply turned into more cheerful channels." In *The Power of Positive Thinking*, Peale appealed to suburban women and organization men, especially small businessmen who focused on achieving success but nonetheless felt something was missing in their lives. He counseled the men whom he met on trains, at public talks, and in the locker rooms of country clubs to operate effectively in a circumscribed world. He offered both stories and techniques to teach his readers how they could achieve "peace of mind, improved health, and a never ceasing flow of energy." By casting troubling thoughts from their minds, they could channel God-given spiritual powers and achieve happier, more influential lives.[4]

His was a relaxing and reassuring message in which the exercise of a therapeutic, Protestant version of mind control promised peace, happiness, and well-being. At the end of most chapters, he offered practical suggestions, for example, advising readers to say "I believe" three times upon arising in the morning, to "cultivate friendships with hopeful people," to "mark every passage in the Bible that speaks of faith, hope, happiness, glory, radiance," and to repeat over and over again that Christ was with them. What drove people toward salvation was thus a soothing form of sin and redemption achieved by replacing unhealthy, negative thoughts with "faith in the combined therapy of medical science in harmony with the healing power of God." The pursuit and achievement of happiness, a word Peale used frequently, was a constant refrain in *The Power of Positive Thinking*. Although he acknowledged that "not all unhappiness is self-created" because unspecified "social conditions" were "responsible for not a few of our woes," his remained a confidently optimistic vision. "The happiness habit," he advised, "is developed by simply practicing happy thinking." His vision was highly individualistic, though at moments he offered examples of the benefit of helping others, albeit on a one-to-one basis. Governmental, social, religious, and business organizations—and even kinship and family ones—seemed beyond the author's purview and that of his readers. Historian David Meyer dubbed it "Social Anesthesia," pointing to how Peale's version of mind cure involved "social passivity, apolitical quiescence and fear of reform."[5]

The Power of Positive Thinking appeared in the fall of 1952, just before Dwight Eisenhower defeated Adlai Stevenson for the presidency and when the power of McCarthyism and the Cold War were at their height. At a few moments, Peale offered glimpses into the outside world. These references were vague, as when he remarked that he was not ignoring or minimizing "the hardships and tragedies of the world." He implied that such adversity was individual in nature, rather than social or political. At a few other points, he was more specific. At a time when congressional action and corporate power had begun to weaken the influence of trade unions, Peale offered his own version of reassurance about labor–management relations. He drew on a conversation he had with an Ohio industrialist who assured him "that the best workmen in his plant are those who get into harmony with the rhythm of the machine on which they are working," which involved "an assembling of parts according to the law of God." If talk of Communists taking over the nation came up at a lunch, he would remark that this was untrue, something that hardly convinced his friends associated with the far-right John Birch Society. Peale's assurances were more generalized: "eliminate from conversations all negative ideas, for they tend to produce tension and annoyance inwardly." There might be times, which he did not specify, when it was necessary to face "harsh questions and deal with them objectively and vigorously," but "to have peace of mind, fill your personal and group conversations with positive, happy, optimistic, satisfying expressions."[6]

Peale's message was enormously influential. His book remained on the *New York Times* list of bestsellers for three and one half years and sold more than 20 million copies. Peale reached people through radio and television shows, phonograph records, sermons, and the publication *Guideposts*, as well as through a series of organizations that included the Horatio Alger Association and the Positive Thinking Foundation. Yet Peale was hardly beyond criticism, and its most trenchant expression came in 1955 from Stevenson's speech writer William Lee Miller. Peale, he noted, smoothed over very real problems by banishing any negative thoughts about oneself or the world. Ironically, Miller asserted, Peale was successful precisely because his reassuring truths were no longer so self-evident. His rejection of negative thinking glossed over very real problems people faced, including "failure, loneliness, death, war, taxes, and the limitations and fragmentariness of all human striving." Despite these problems, or more likely because of them, Peale holds a coveted place in the pantheon of positive thinkers. He revealed how a religious, highly individualistic, and psychologically simple message of hope and happiness could reach a huge audience, all the while avoiding tough questions about the world beyond the striving self. In the future, his work provided a perfect foil, offering as it did ideas familiar to a broad public but whose clichés appeared more weighty because their validity could be tested and even confirmed scientifically. Peale's messages resonated so deeply in mainstream America that again and again his more secular and serious successors drew on the notion of the power of positive thinking at the same time that they had to differentiate themselves from its most well-known proponent.[7]

VIKTOR FRANKL AND POSTTRAUMATIC GROWTH

"It may seem strange for a man to write a book about peace of mind in this age of fierce turmoil and harrowing doubts," wrote Rabbi Joshua L. Liebman in *Peace of Mind* (1946), an immensely popular book that appeared in the same year as the original edition of Viktor Frankl's *Man's Search for Meaning* and that was among the postwar precursors of Peale's *The Power of Positive*

Thinking. Liebman cited "mass violence and exterminatory bombing" as his proof of turmoil that produced doubt. Yet central to happiness studies and positive psychology later on was the notion that people benefited from such severely stressful experiences. More than anyone else, psychiatrist and concentration camp survivor Viktor Frankl provided the evidence for and the philosophy of what came to be known as posttraumatic growth.[8]

Born in Vienna in 1905 and educated as a psychiatrist who specialized in the prevention of suicide, beginning in September 1942 Frankl spent two and a half years in Nazi concentration camps at Theresienstadt, Auschwitz, and Dachau. Soon after his liberation by the Allies in April 1945, he began work on what became a book published in German in 1946 with a title that translated as "Saying Yes to Life in Spite of Everything: A Psychologist Experiences the Concentration Camps." First published in the United States in 1959 and eventually titled *Man's Search for Meaning*, it was translated into twenty-four languages and sold more than 10 million copies, earning a place on one list of the ten most influential books in the postwar world.[9] Frankl wrote about his concentration camp experiences using a combination of vivid descriptions, clinical observations, and philosophical considerations. Before and after five months of slave labor, he related, the Nazis assigned him to work in the camps as a doctor—initially as a general practitioner and then as a psychiatrist who helped fellow prisoners wrestle with disorientation, depression, and suicidal thoughts. Frankl conveyed the horrors he and others encountered. They suffered physical and mental torture at the hands of sadistic guards. Noise and discomfort deprived them of rest and sleep. If they survived, they did so on inadequate diets. They took showers with freezing cold water. They labored long hours under deplorable conditions. One recollection captured what Frankl and his fellow prisoners experienced: "Almost in tears from pain (I had terrible sores on my feet from wearing torn shoes)," he remembered, "I limped a few kilometers with our long column of men from the camp to our work site. Very cold, bitter winds struck us," and he kept "thinking of the endless little problems of our miserable life."[10]

Yet once back in Vienna Frankl responded to the horrible events he recounted with positive conclusions. Relying on canonical works by European writers and artists, he found reason for hope. He insisted "that love is the ultimate and the highest goal to which man can aspire." This was true even though he learned after the war that his wife, the principal object of his affection, had perished in the camps, along with almost all of his other family members. His embrace of love was central to his larger vision: even in the most horrendous of circumstances it provided a reason to keep on living. Focusing intensely on his inner life helped him (and others) find a refuge from the painful experiences he faced. What sustained him were memories from the past, professional skills in the present, and hope for the future. He came to see art, beauty, and humor as "the soul's weapons in the fight for self-preservation." He insisted that "a very trifling thing," such as noting upon arrival at a camp that it had no crematorium, "can cause the greatest of joys." Above all, what his experiences in concentration camps taught him was that, rather than being controlled by one's environment, "Man *can* preserve a vestige of spiritual freedom, of independence of mind, even in such terrible conditions of psychic and physical distress." To prove his point, he recalled fellow inmates giving up their last bit of food to comfort others as proof of the ability of humans—even though in such circumstances they were few in number—to have the freedom to choose. It was this "spiritual freedom" that made life purposeful. What saved people like him was the commitment to live and perhaps thrive "by looking to the future." In the end, what mattered was "taking the responsibility to find the right answer" to life's problems and "to fulfill the tasks which it constantly sets for each individual."[11]

From these experiences, and from his earlier psychiatric training, Frankl developed logotherapy, his version of a clinical approach based on existentialism. He distanced himself from Freudianism by focusing more on the future than on the past, on the drive to find meaning rather than relief from traumas, and on the spiritual rather than the sexual or instinctual. For him, conflict was not primarily neurotic but healthy. Rather than seeking "to bury his patient's existential despair under a heap of tranquilizing drugs," the therapist should help in the search for meaning in life, with tension as an "indispensable prerequisite of mental health." Striving and struggling were best understood as the distance between what one was and what one could become. His version of existentialism focused not on life's meaninglessness but on the search for "supra-meaning," a quest that in his mind seemed more spiritual than religious. His "self-determining" individual was forward-looking and "self-transcending." In the end, Frankl returned to where he began. His experience in concentration camps provided a "living laboratory" in which some behaved like swine and some like saints. Which kind of life an individual chose to pursue ultimately depended not on external conditions but on personal choices. Some humans invented the gas chambers while others entered them "upright, with the Lord's Prayer or the *Shema Yisrael* on their lips."[12]

With *Man's Search for Meaning*, Frankl offered abundant evidence and powerful arguments to show that people could benefit from the most horrible of situations. Writing the book so soon after his liberation was surely therapeutic for him, just as reading it over the ensuing decades was for so many people. Frankl offered strategies for survival under adverse conditions and an outlook that reassuringly provided comfort for anyone seeking self-determination or even transcendence under situations both ordinary and extraordinary. In many ways, including his celebration of the importance of tension in life and his emphasis on a contrast between traumatic events and optimistic determination, Frankl's approach differed from Peale's. The implication was clear: adversity was the seed bed of happiness, a word he did not use. It was as if his first name signified that he, and by implication those he helped as patients or readers, could be victorious over virtually anything.

Exactly what Frankl knew when he first sent his book off to the publisher is not clear, yet he knew enough to realize the horrors he and many others suffered. His father had died of illness in Theresienstadt; the Nazis had killed his mother in the gas chambers at Auschwitz; his wife perished at Bergen-Belsen; and his brother's life ended at Auschwitz. Unlike other Holocaust writers, he evidenced no survivor's guilt; indeed, some might find problematic his focus on his own resilience rather than on the pain of others. Nonetheless, as an influence on and precursor of happiness studies and positive psychology, Frankl's insistence on how people recovered from and even thrived after experiencing trauma remains important. To some it might seem bizarrely trivializing to apply what Frankl learned in concentration camps to the lives of people who suffered under more ordinary circumstances, especially humdrum setbacks in life or death of an aged loved one. However, both Frankl and psychologists who explore posttraumatic growth did precisely that—study recovery and resilience in response to events rarely as serious as imprisonment in a concentration camp.[13]

SEPARATION AND ATTACHMENT

If Frankl experienced loss under extreme conditions, John Bowlby did so through the lenses of a privileged man who faced a series of disruptions, ones not, however, as dramatic or horrendously extreme as life in a concentration camp. Born in 1907 into an elite English family, as a child Bowlby saw his mother for only an hour a day and his father even less often, then not at all when he left the family for four years to serve in World War I. Bowlby also experienced painful separation when his beloved nanny left her job when he was four and, later in 1918, when his parents sent him off to boarding school in part to prevent him from being injured during the air raids in London. Beginning at age eleven, he never again lived at home on a regular basis. Bowlby married in 1938, but during World War II he was often separated from his wife.

Such a series of losses and separations might immobilize some, but they spurred Bowlby to a lifetime of productive scholarly engagement. After graduating from Cambridge, he began working with delinquent children who suffered from problems that he saw as being caused by separation from the security of their families. During World War II, he continued his work with children whose relationships with their families war had disrupted: young Jewish refugees who came to Britain from Nazi Germany on the Kindertransport, as well as British children separated from their loved ones when their mothers took up work in factories or who were relocated because of the German bombing of major cities.[14]

Bowlby's scholarly work built on all these experiences in his own life and in the lives of others, as well as on the work of Harry Harlow, an American scientist who beginning in the 1930s studied the impact of social isolation and deprivation on rhesus monkeys. In 1949, the World Health Organization commissioned Bowlby to explore the lives of hundreds of thousands if not millions of children whom World War II had left homeless, including orphans and refugees separated from their families. In the resulting 1951 report, *Maternal Care and Mental Health*, he concluded that "the infant and young child should experience a warm, intimate, and continuous relationship with his mother (or permanent mother-substitute) in which both find satisfaction and enjoyment." In 1952, with James Robertson, he produced a movie, *A Two-Year-Old Goes to the Hospital*, which, contradicting the assertion of psychoanalysts about the centrality of fantasies and orality shaped by milk from the mother's breast, focused on the anxiety and pain experienced by very young people as a result of being physically separated from their loved ones. What shaped the child's early relationship to a primary care giver were not issues of dependence but of attachment.[15]

Over time, Bowlby built on these early experiences and studies to contribute to the development of attachment theory. His work helped shape how professionals and institutions treated children. He drew on evolutionary biology, ethology, developmental psychology, cybernetics, object-relations theory, and cognitive science. Instead of the Freudian emphasis on dreams and fantasies understood retrospectively, Bowlby began with the "loss of mother-figure in infancy or early childhood." He then worked "to trace the psychological and psychopathological processes that commonly result. It starts in fact with the traumatic experience and works prospectively." He came to understand how children struggled to resolve the tensions between separation and safety. Seen in pathological terms, attachment theory pointed to pain and a sense of loss; seen positively, it underscored the importance of what Bowlby captured in the title of his 1988 book, *A Secure Base: Parent-Child Attachment and Healthy Human Development*. Extended even further and elaborated by others, attachment theory underscored the importance of social connections more generally to human happiness.[16]

Two final notes, on gender and on politics. Central to Bowlby's attachment theory was that young children needed the love of a mother, without which they would develop psychological problems. Whatever Bowlby's issue of attachment to his own mother, there was one woman whose research and writing on the subject was crucial to his own scholarship—Mary Ainsworth. Working under Bowlby in London in the early 1950s and then carrying out her own studies of the mother–infant relationship, first in Africa and then at Johns Hopkins, Ainsworth transformed her relationship with her mentor to one of colleague. Moreover, in the 1950s, 1960s, and beyond, she developed nuanced, suggestive theories of the dynamics of attachment that grounded Bowlby's theories in empirical research, refined his findings, enhanced the gender dynamics of his work, and explored the relationships of infants not only to their mothers but also to caregivers and fathers. In addition, Bowlby's political commitments are also pertinent. In the vast amount of scholarly literature on Bowlby, observers give remarkably little attention to his broader commitments. In fact he did make clear the political implications of his views on attachment. Bowlby was a democratic socialist who believed that a close bond between mother and child would help unleash an individual's psychological potential for social responsibility and that state-funded social programs could assist in the development of altruistic children.[17]

AARON BECK: DEPRESSION AND RECOVERY THROUGH COGNITIVE BEHAVIORAL THERAPY

If what shaped Bowlby's work were the multiple tragedies of two world wars, the more specific but nonetheless momentous traumas World War II veterans experienced helped shape the work of Aaron Beck, the author of an influential book on depression and a father of cognitive behavioral therapy. Beck's role as Martin Seligman's teacher helps us understand one source of the transition from mental illness to mental health. Born in 1921 to Russian immigrant parents, Beck earned his medical degree in 1946 and worked in a military hospital as a psychiatrist soon after. As reported in two of his first published papers, in that hospital he treated men who had had traumatic experiences in World Wars I and II, as well as the Korean War. When reporting on how soldiers reacted to accidentally killing their buddies, Beck deployed insights that were central to his later work: once their defensive systems weakened, he remarked in 1953, "a flood of intense emotions, highly charged memories, and horrendous fantasies burst into consciousness." Over the course of his career, Beck developed ways of measuring and treating a host of mental illnesses that originated in such experiences, including anxiety disorders, drug abuse, alcoholism, suicide, and depression. Central to cognitive behavioral therapy that Beck and others developed by the late 1960s was the observation that patients reported experiencing highly negative ideas and emotions that seemed to pop up spontaneously. Once a therapist helped a patient develop an awareness of these as distorted thoughts, rooted in dysfunctional core beliefs, she or he could begin to approach life more realistically.[18]

In 1967, Beck, by this time a professor at the University of Pennsylvania, drew on years of research to produce his major work, *Depression: Causes and Treatment*. "The cognitive manifestations of depression," he wrote, included "the patient's distorted attitudes toward himself, his experience, and his future." These cognitive distortions meant that the "depressed patient was prone to magnify any failure or defects and to minimize or ignore any favorable characteristics." In therapy, as in life, these unrealistic appraisals appeared as "automatic" or involuntary. The task of the therapist was to help the patient understand these as illogical and idiosyncratic "misconstructions of reality" that unduly shaped the patient's life and led to "depressive feelings of sadness, guilt, loneliness, and pessimism." Using methods such as positing alternative explanations, developing realistic goals, learning to see reactions objectively, "neutralizing 'automatic thoughts,'" and understanding how to evaluate their accuracy, the patient would be better able to challenge and counteract them. If not happiness, a word Beck did not deploy, then at least a less depressive and more realistic approach to the world resulted.[19]

In 1967, when Beck published *Depression*, Seligman completed his PhD and began to work on the experiments that resulted in his 1975 *Helplessness: On Depression, Development, and Death*. Beck's contributions to cognitive psychology helped build a foundation for positive psychology— even though Seligman's work on optimism and positive psychology was more than a decade away.

ABRAHAM MASLOW AND SELF-ACTUALIZATION

By 1967 Abraham Maslow had developed an optimistic humanistic psychology that emerged from personal and social adversity. The threats of his superstitious and miserably unhappy mother that if he misbehaved as a child he would feel God's wrath turned him not only into an atheist but also into someone who embraced life rather than feared it and hoped that scientific rationality would bring a better world. When he ventured out of the Jewish neighborhood in Brooklyn where he grew up, his encounters with anti-Semitism stoked his curiosity about what made people angry and hateful. Reading Upton Sinclair's muckraking *The Jungle* helped turn him into a democratic socialist, optimistic about the prospect for a better world. During the 1930s in graduate school at the University of Wisconsin studying under Harry Harlow, Maslow explored hunger among primates. Reacting against behaviorism, Maslow distinguished between the physiological drive to overcome starvation and the appetite that drove monkeys to yearn for something more. Living in New York in the late 1930s, he came to know many of the émigré psychologists the Nazis had driven into exile—Alfred Adler, Erich Fromm, Kurt Goldstein, and Max Wertheimer among them. They intensified his interest in finding positive alternatives to mechanistic behaviorism and to pessimistic versions of Freudianism.[20]

By the early 1940s, Maslow's achievements as a psychology professor at Brooklyn College and as a scholar gave him a reason to feel satisfied, but as his biographer notes, "he wondered what such achievements really accomplished against the darker forces in the world," which were so evident to him when totalitarianism but especially fascism extended its sway in Europe. Tragic events in the broader world thus played an important role in impelling Maslow to develop humanistic psychology, a process for which his studies of self-realized people provided ample evidence. In 1941, looking across the ocean to Europe and without specifying whether he meant Nazi Germany and/or Soviet Russia, he wondered about the implications of "totalitarian states" for the psychologist's "attempts to bring order and simplicity into his conceptual systems." The situation on the other side of the Atlantic raised troubling issues: whether cultural relativism sufficed as a yardstick for judging behavior; whether an entire culture could be abnormal; and how far a psychologist could reasonably go in condemning political events.[21]

During World War II, Maslow differentiated between democratic and authoritarian personalities, something prompted by his close collaboration with émigré psychologists and his defense of American values against totalitarian ones. In a 1943 article titled "The Authoritarian Character Structure," he spelled out the world view of the authoritarian personality. Such a person could not love others because he or she saw the world as a jungle filled with antagonistic and angry people. If democratic people respected others while acknowledging their differences, authoritarian individuals classified others in hierarchical terms, relying on external characteristics to differentiate among them. Locked in fights, the authoritarian person sought power over others, an impulse connected with hatred of a group most conveniently at hand. If the democratic personality honored kindness toward others, his or her counterpart equated kindness with weakness. The former could achieve self-fulfillment while the latter engaged in a conflictual and unsuccessful pursuit of satisfaction. Although it is possible for us to read the essay as one in which Maslow made a case for the Allies against the Axis powers, his explicit references were somewhat more ambiguous. To be sure, he mentioned Hitler's *Mein Kampf* as the best source for understanding the authoritarian personality. Yet he began the essay by stating that "in this war it is difficult to differentiate our friends from our enemies" and went on to deny any necessary connection between fascism and nationality and any necessary link between anti-Semitism and authoritarianism.[22]

All these experiences, plus serious health problems that living in Pleasanton, California, from 1946 to 1949 helped him overcome, impelled Maslow to develop a holistic and positive theory of motivation, one that celebrated how individuals might aspire toward self-realization and how fully a psychologist could explore the ways society could complete the march toward democracy, social justice, and peace. He determined to focus on healthy and fulfilled people, to concentrate on a psychology of normality, not abnormality.

Maslow's vision found its most influential expression in his 1954 *Motivation and Personality*, in which he offered a full statement of his philosophy of self-realization, one based on the notion of the hierarchy of needs that he located in biological instincts. On the lower rungs were physiological processes necessary for the human body to maintain itself— drinking, eating, sleeping, excreting, and having sex. Once those basic needs were met, people concerned themselves with safety, the "peaceful, smoothly running, good society." Next in play were "the belongingness and love needs" when "the person will feel keenly, as never before, the absence of friends, or a sweetheart, or a wife, or children."[23] Linking higher needs with a commitment to democratic citizenship, Maslow asserted that the healthy person "will hunger for affectionate relations with people in general, namely, for a place in his group, and he will strive with great intensity to achieve this goal." What followed on the hierarchy was the quest "for a stable, firmly based, usually high evaluation of themselves, for self-respect, or self-esteem, and for the esteem of others." Maslow divided the desire for esteem into the pursuit of "confidence in the face of the world, and for independence and freedom" and for "reputation or prestige," which, he insisted, was best "based on *deserved* respect from others rather than on external fame or celebrity and unwarranted adulation." Finally, there was the need for self-actualization or the fulfillment of one's potential. A key characteristic of self-actualized people was the ability to reestablish their sense of themselves following a traumatic event. As Frankl might have remarked in *Man's Search for Meaning*, Maslow, perhaps influenced by the many émigrés among his colleagues and friends, insisted that the healthy person "can maintain a relative serenity and happiness in the midst of circumstances that would drive other people to suicide."[24]

Maslow based his theories of self-actualizing people not on laboratory experiments but on personal observations and on reading the biographies of historical figures who represented progressive aspects of social transformation, including Jane Addams, George Washington Carver, Eugene Debs, William James, Eleanor Roosevelt, Albert Schweitzer, and Walt Whitman. Self-actualizing people, who he believed could be found throughout society and not just among elites, were "lusty animals, hearty in their appetites, and enjoying themselves mightily without regret or shame or apology" who approached the world with spontaneity, simplicity, and naturalness. Nonconformists and "propelled by growth motivation," they possessed "the wonderful capacity to appreciate again and again, freshly and naïvely, the basic goods of life, with awe, pleasures, wonder, and even ecstasy." Invoking William James, Maslow emphasized the capacity for peak experiences, mystical moments that transformed his subjects' daily lives. Truly democratic and unaware of differences based on politics, race, and class, they moved beyond their selves as they strove to help others because they were "capable of more fusion, greater love, more perfect identification, more obliteration of the ego boundaries." Transcending their cultural origins and ruled by their own rather than by society's dictates, they had a childlike awe. Under the best of circumstances, they were capable of fusing sex and love, of loving and being loved, and of experiencing "no really sharp differentiation between the roles and personalities of the two sexes."

Maslow rarely used the word happiness, but the implication of his position was clear: if the study of unhealthy people "can yield only a cripple psychology," he insisted, "the study of self-actualizing people must be the basis for a more universal science of psychology." In the years remaining in his life after the publication of his pathbreaking 1954 book, Maslow experienced or wrote about virtually all aspects of the counterculture that emerged in the 1960s, among them Eastern religions, encounter groups, Esalen, organic farming, natural child birth, experiments in education, and drugs. Though in 1954 happiness studies as a field was far off, *Motivation and Personality*, concerned with psychological health and not mental illness, was a foundational document in both humanistic and positive psychology.[25]

With *Motivation and Personality*, Maslow was developing an analysis that transcended specific situations, but he generally left implicit any connection to them. Since much of the writing originated in the 1940s, the book offered hints of the political and historical locations and implications of his analysis. He mentioned race prejudice, as well as wartime disruption, injuries, displacement, and bombing. In what was for him an unusually direct statement, he wrote that "the war has taught us the lesson that the attack of the gangster and the defense of the righteously indignant are not the same psychologically." Moreover, he acknowledged that his work with Blackfoot natives had taught him that "human beings need not be even as aggressive or destructive as the average man in American society, let alone those of some parts of Europe."[26]

Above all, Maslow made clear the democratic implications of what he wrote. Self-actualizing people, he insisted, hostile to others only when called for, had "a deep feeling of identification, sympathy, and affection" for humankind, something that enhanced their capacity for civic engagement. Members of an elite based on character rather than race or color, they were friendlier than their less self-realized counterparts regardless of ethnicity, skin color, politics, or class. Moreover, unlike the ethnocentric authoritarian who displayed a "passive yielding to cultural shaping," self-actualized people evidenced a healthy "inner detachment from the culture in which they are immersed," something that made individuals "a saving remnant . . . especially important for American society." As the historian of science Nadine Weidman has made clear, for Maslow there was an "explicit connection between the healthy person and the healthy society." Although a heart attack cut short his life at age 62, Maslow's influence was immense, both during his lifetime and after. He served as president of the American Psychological Association, and his writings were among the most frequently cited in professional journals. His work influenced therapeutic approaches, corporate management practices, the study of student development, and how the general public understood human experiences and aspirations.[27]

JAMES OLDS AND THE SEARCH FOR THE BRAIN'S PLEASURE CENTER

If social and behavioral scientists in the postwar world articulated one approach to happiness, neuroscientists offered another. For eons, the brain's pleasure center was the object of philosophers' speculation, but a key discovery occurred in the mid-1950s. In his 1956 "Pleasure Centers in the Brain," the psychologist James Olds reported on a transformative experiment that stands as one of the foundational, albeit eventually contested, studies of neuroscience. "His discovery of the 'reward' system in the brain," a colleague reported in 1999, "is the most important single discovery yet made in the field concerned with brain substrates of behavior." Long interested in motivation, on his postdoc at McGill University following a PhD at Harvard, Olds discovered, somewhat by accident, that stimulating the brains of rats could lead them to pursue pleasure. According to his findings, when rats pressed a lever that activated an electrode to stimulate a portion of their brains, they ceased chasing after food, deriving pleasure instead from brain stimulation itself. "A hungry animal often ignored food in favor of the pleasure of stimulating itself electrically. Some rats with electrodes," he observed, "stimulated their brains more than 2,000 times for 24 consecutive hours!" Writing in *Scientific American* as he appealed to the broad scientific community, Olds finished his article by speculating on the larger implications of his study. He announced that his findings contradicted the notion that brain stimulation meant punishment and hoped future studies might locate nerve cells whose stimulation by electrodes or drugs could satisfy other basic drives such as the quest for hunger and sex. Ultimately, the hope was that his results "can very likely be generalized eventually to human beings—with modifications, of course."[28]

Scientists did indeed apply what Olds learned to human subjects— taking his discovery in many directions, not all of them benign. In the 1950s Tulane psychiatrist Robert Heath began to shift attention from rats to humans, as he attempted to show that an electrode implanted in the brain could cure people of serious neurological conditions. In one case he helped a twenty-four-year-old depressed man overcome his yearning for love and sex with other men. The patient's repeated self-stimulation by electrical currents, Heath reported, produced "feelings of pleasure, alertness, and warmth (goodwill)." In the 1973 movie *Sleeper*, Woody Allen accidentally enters an orgasmatron, an electromechanical device that uses an electrode implanted in the lower spine to produce the sensation of an orgasm. A third of a century later, a North Carolina physician, seeking to alleviate pain by inserting electrodes into human brains, discovered that a slightly off-kilter implant enabled women to achieve orgasms that had heretofore eluded them. "You're going to have to teach my husband to do that," one experimental subject remarked. Soon after, the physician sought an investor who could help him bring his discovery to market. Such experiments, imagined and real, were controversial. However, Olds's original discovery was transformative. He was able to identify what he thought was a verifiable pleasure center in the brain. His investigations were transformative because they revealed it was possible to study pleasure in the laboratory and opened up the possibility of how to increase it through scientific interventions.[29]

FRANK BERGER AND HAPPINESS IN A BOTTLE OF PILLS

In the 1950s, scientists discovered that not only electrical stimulation but also pills could make people happy. This made clear, they insisted, that emotions were rooted in neurochemistry or neurobiology, not in character or personal history. Exactly how chemicals affected the brain took a long time to verify, but before 1970 some scientists made headway in proving that a chemical element or a pill could rectify or ameliorate a neurological disorder. In 1949, John F. J. Cade discovered that lithium salts helped treat manic depression. During the 1950s, prescription drugs came to market that made it possible to produce, if not bliss, then at least lower levels of anxiety, proving that drugs could influence emotions.[30] Drug companies, advertising agencies, scientists, doctors, and consumers asserted that the symptoms psychotropic drugs alleviated varied widely—including social problems and a range of medical and psychological ones. However, central to understanding their power was the insistence that pills could reduce anxiety and promote happiness and equanimity, especially among those to whom they were frequently targeted. Known as "happy pills," they were the subject of "articles giving the impression that the elixir of happiness has been found," wrote an observer in a Canadian medical journal in 1958. An "eager and gullible public," he noted, "puts physicians under pressure to supply happiness." Historians Andrea Tone and David Herzberg make clear that psychotropic drugs, like suburban homes, television sets, and automobiles, were central to postwar consumer culture: they all promised a better life. Mood-altering medicines, Herzberg has written, "became part of a new consumerist 'American Dream' that reconfigured conceptions of what a good middle-class life—what happiness itself—ought to be like."[31]

Already in the late 1950s some writers had painted a picture of a pharmacological utopia. In 1957, the physician Nathan Kline talked of a time when anti-depressants, serving as "psychic energizers," might achieve "something more than mere surcease of sorrow" and thus help enhance pleasure. "The exaltation of heightened awareness, strong positive affective relationships and the pride of useful accomplishment may, at this moment, be in our grasp." At the same time Robert S. de Ropp, a biochemist who increasingly turned to spiritualism, predicted that "soon the specter of care will be banished from your world, the burden of anxiety and guilt will be lifted from your souls. The restoration of your primeval innocence, your re-entry into the Garden of Eden, will now be accomplished through the agency of a pill."[32]

Miltown was the first in a series of moderately powerful tranquilizers that promised relief from social, medical, and psychological misery. The story of Miltown's development reveals how a research scientist who had overcome miserable circumstances produced a pill that eventually lessened anxiety and enhanced happiness. Dr. Frank Berger, a mild-mannered, scholarly scientist who accidentally discovered its properties, was "a left-leaning humanist whose principles were hedged by a pragmatism culled from decades of struggle," Andrea Tone has written. He "never abandoned his belief in humanity's capacity to eradicate suffering." And decades of suffering is what he had faced. Born in 1913 in the Austro-Hungarian Empire, he struggled as a child against the discrimination he experienced as a

German-speaking lad in a Czech world. While in medical school in Prague, he saw his future calling, he noted retrospectively, as helping him uncover the "great mysteries of life such as birth and death, suffering, sex, and love." When he realized that a Nazi-occupied Prague would not be a safe place for a socialist and a Jew, he fled with his wife to London, where he ate at soup kitchens and slept on park benches. Eventually authorities rounded him up with the other homeless people and sent them to prison. Out of prison, he worked first in a camp for refugees from the war-torn continent and then as a bacteriologist in a government laboratory. All this he managed to endure, but the death of his infant son was something he said he never completely overcame.[33]

An accidental byproduct of his work on making penicillin widely available was his discovery of mephenesin, a compound that relaxed mice but left them fully conscious. This was a tranquilizing effect unheard of in modern medicine, reported on in 1946 and first tested on humans a year later. Problems associated with the use of the resulting drug limited its commercial success. In 1947, Berger and his wife moved to the United States, determined to make new lives for themselves after learning of the deaths of many of his friends and family members in Nazi camps and of the Communists' seizure of his family's property. By 1949 he had become president and director of medical research for a subsidiary of Carter Products in New Jersey, a company whose laxative, Carter's Little Liver Pills, had come under increasing attack after having long sustained the company's corporate well-being.

Berger's success as a scientist working for this pharmaceutical company came quickly. In 1950 he and an associate synthesized a meprobamate (later commercially known as Miltown), which turned vicious monkeys into calm, friendly, and alert ones. They had discovered a muscle relaxant that worked effectively with talk therapies but also appeared to reduce the suffering of psychotics and epileptics. Yet commercial success took a while because of corporate timidity, regulatory uncertainty, and the doubts doctors expressed about a pill that they could prescribe to treat anxiety in seemingly run-of-the-mill patients. By 1955 additional testing, reported in the influential *Journal of the American Medical Association,* eroded resistance. Unable to patent a drug named after the quiet village Milltown, located a few miles from the lab, the company dropped one letter and called it Miltown. Searching for a way to classify the drug without fully understanding the precise mechanism that made it effective, Berger settled on the notion that Miltown produced tranquility, not sedation. After a slow start, meprobamate, marketed as Miltown by Carter and as Equanil by Wyeth Laboratories (to which Carter licensed it), became the nation's first blockbuster psychotropic drug. One year after it came on the market in 1955, 5 percent of Americans had tried it. By 1957, a billion pills of Miltown had been manufactured, and it was the third most commonly prescribed drug in America. Early work on psychotropic medicines raised the question of whether they eliminated depression or actually increased happiness.

FROM MENTAL ILLNESS TO WELL-BEING

A very different connection between science and happiness came in the first sustained social science studies of people's sense of well-being, ones that originated out of concerns about mental illness but soon led to the exploration of well-being.[34] The authors of *Americans View Their Mental Health: A Nationwide Interview Survey* (1960) worked under the auspices of a congressionally authorized commission funded by twenty-one foundations, professional associations, and corporations, including the American Legion, the American Medical Association, and the pharmaceutical company that in 1952 had developed the first antipsychotic drug, chlorpromazine. The Survey Research Center at the University of Michigan carried out the study. Its researchers interviewed 2,460 American adults for an average of two hours each. "How well or badly adjusted do they consider themselves to be?" they asked. "Are they happy or unhappy, worried or unworried, optimistic or pessimistic in their outlook?" They aimed to determine how people felt about their lives and, if they had problems, whether and from whom they would seek help. The project then turned its focus to how legislators and mental health professionals might develop policies and resources that would increase people's happiness. This was professional help, not self-help.[35]

In a way that reflected how important domesticity and stability were in the 1950s, the study concluded that "well over half the population finds its greatest happiness in the home, a state that is conditioned strongly by feelings of economic security." What was involved was "comfort and adequacy and limited aspirations, rather than luxury." In contrast, fewer than 10 percent of those surveyed were very concerned with anything beyond the domestic sphere, including politics or the possibility of nuclear annihilation. The researchers could only speculate on why there was such a contrast between a sense of domestic well-being and a lack of concern with the wider world. Perhaps, they wondered, so many of the respondents focused on realities that were most pressing or had a "sense of helplessness" or a "political immaturity combined with a persistent undercurrent of isolationism, resulting in a renunciation of social responsibility."[36]

Overall, they concluded, about 90 percent of Americans reported that they were very or pretty happy. This was true even though most people worried a great deal, especially about their financial situations. Those with less education were less happy; the more educated people reported being happier but also worrying more. Women were more distressed than men about home life, marriage, and parenting. In contrast, highly educated men who had good jobs and substantial incomes not only derived more satisfaction from their work but also found jobs "a source of greater worry and distress." Older people were both more unhappy and worried less, perhaps, the researchers speculated, because of "a resignation, apathy, and passive acceptance of life and oneself."[37]

Five years later came a report that more clearly shifted the focus of social surveys from mental health to subjective well-being. Compared with *Americans Viewed Their Mental Health*, what was important about *Reports on Happiness: A Pilot Study of Behavior Related to Mental Health* was neither its methods nor its conclusions about the correlates of happiness. Rather, the social psychologist Norman M. Bradburn and the sociologist David Caplovitz broke fresh ground by focusing on the mental well-being of what they called "normal" people and urged researchers to pay more attention to "positive satisfactions" and less to mental problems. Based in part on brain science, their work emphasized that although the balance of positive and negative feelings was central to people's happiness, the two impulses often operated independently of one another, with a person's sense of well-being determined by the balance between the two. They emphasized the association between "high positive feelings" and "a greater degree of involvement in the world . . . and a higher rate of social interaction"—phenomena more common among people of higher socioeconomic status than those of lower status who attended fundamentalist churches "which frown on many sorts of social activity." Finally, with their survey fortuitously taking place at the time of the Cuban Missile Crisis, they studied how a major public event impacted the lives of citizens psychologically. To their surprise, they found scant evidence that people's "psychological state was particularly affected" by the confrontation between the United States and the USSR.[38]

INTERNATIONAL SURVEYS

At the same time that researchers provided innovative studies of happiness among Americans, in his 1965 *The Patterns of Human Concerns*, Hadley Cantril offered a pathbreaking examination that shifted the focus to the study of human aspirations abroad. He and his colleagues interviewed almost 20,000 people around the world. The analysis of the data convinced Cantril of "the truth of Aristotle's observation that happiness comes from 'the exercise of vital powers along lines of excellence in a life according them scope.'" Reflecting mid-1960s modernization theory, he remained confident that developed nations in the West served "as models by means of which people in less-developed nations learn to define and expand their wants." In the first phase of his historical model, one he labeled as pre-mobilization and he claimed as characteristic of much of India, people fatalistically acquiesced to their circumstances. Next came a period when people began to awaken to the potential for new lives, as was true not only of "some of the more backward Negroes" in America but also of the poorest among the Brazilians and Yugoslavians. The third era, visible in contemporary Nigeria, occurred when people sensed that what was potential could become real. The fourth, one of "assurance and self-reliance" visible in Israel, came when people began to experience the fruits of their action. Then at last, as was true of most Americans, people, generally satisfied with their lives, anticipated the fruits of further development.[39]

At the end of the book, Cantril sketched out what he saw as genetically determined "demands human beings everywhere impose on any society or political culture." Without mentioning Maslow's hierarchy of needs, he articulated a series of steps—beginning with survival, proceeding through a desire for security and order, developing a sense of hope, freedom, and personal dignity. Finally came a search for values and beliefs worthy of an individual's commitment, along with the confidence that their society would make it possible for them to fulfill their aspirations. Whatever the weaknesses of its universalism and its reliance on Western values and patterns of development, Cantril had nonetheless revealed the fruitfulness of a comparative study of aspirations and happiness across national borders.[40]

ALAN WATTS AND THE COUNTERCULTURE

The counterculture of the 1960s and early 1970s bequeathed to later studies of happiness experimentation with drugs, LSD especially; an interest in Eastern religions; the practice of meditation; a commitment to humanistic psychology; and a belief that experiences, especially intense ones, provided more pleasure than goods, especially highly commercial ones.[41] Before the 1960s, these elements had come together in the life and writings of Alan Watts, a central figure in America's romance with Asian religions, part of what the historian of science Anne Harrington called "Eastward Journeys" that Westerners took to find solutions and inspirations they felt their own worlds did not provide.[42]

The British-born and Anglican-raised Watts discovered Asian religions at an early age, and by the time he was fifteen, he had decided he was a Buddhist. In 1938, at age twenty-three, he moved to the United States. His commitment to Zen Buddhism and Taoism stood in unresolved tension with a life that was far from peaceful and harmonious. "My existence is, and has been, a paradox, or better, a coincidence of opposites," he wrote in his memoir. Or as his biographer put it, what "seemed incongruous" about Watts was "the combination of spiritual insight and naughtiness, of wisdom and childishness, of joyous high spirits and loneliness." Seeking pleasure, he never fully freed himself from the strictures of his Christian education. "A shameless egotist," Watts acknowledged that "the ego named Alan Watts is an illusion." He remarked that he was "an unrepentant sensualist" and "an immoderate lover of women and the delights of sexuality," including sado-masochism. Yet he spoke of a liberated consciousness, of transcendence of the here and now, and of freedom from earthly cravings. Seeking to transcend the limitations of the physical body, he nonetheless used alcohol in excessive amounts to achieve an altered state of consciousness. Though he espoused simplicity, he had to support ex-wives, a current one, and seven children. This required rounds of writing and lecturing and seemingly endless travel.[43]

Watts understood that life's tensions were inevitable, and he was hardly the first or last person whose own life stood in uneasy contradiction to his beliefs. Yet it was his writings more than his life that had an impact on ample audiences. Central to his outlook, as he wrote in 1961, was "the transformation of consciousness, of the inner feeling of one's own existence" and of "the release of the individual from forms of conditioning imposed upon him by social institutions." Achieving happiness involved reconnecting what modern life disconnected, not only man and nature but also, as he remarked in *The Meaning of Happiness*, "the individual and the unknown Self, the unconscious, inner universe." He wrote of finding "a center of relaxed balance and poise in man's individual life." Central to this quest were ways of achieving Nirvana. In his immensely popular *The Way of Zen* (1957), he described meditation as "simply a quiet awareness, without comment, of whatever happens to be here and now. This awareness is attended by the most vivid sensation of 'nondifference' between oneself and the external world, between the mind and its contents . . . it just comes by itself when one is sitting and watching without any purpose in mind—even the purpose of getting rid of purpose." Initially skeptical of the use of drugs, by 1962 he hailed LSD as an entry point to a "Joyous Cosmology," enabling people to reach "the deeper, or higher, levels of insight . . . when accompanied by sustained philosophical reflection by a person who is in search, not of kicks, but of understanding."[44]

If meditation and drugs led to happiness, what impeded that quest were "external events" and "the whirl that goes on around" them. Centering life in inner experiences led in two directions. The first was skepticism about if not antipathy to efforts to change the world by movements to achieve peace and expand the welfare state. "The more these heroic and admirable enterprises succeed," he remarked in 1966 as Lyndon Johnson shifted from expanding the Great Society to expanding America's intervention in Vietnam, "the more they provoke new and increasingly horrendous problems." What good is it, he asked at a time when starvation more than entry into the middle class affected hundreds of millions in the Third World, "to convert Hindus and Africans into a huge *bourgeoisie*, where every Bengali and every Zulu has the privilege of joining our special rat-race, buying appliances on time and a television set to keep him running?" The second impediment to knowing oneself was the whirl of consumer culture closer to home, which involved Americans in what Watts saw as a constant, vicious, and frustrating struggle to satisfy insatiable desires. This quest, he wrote in 1951, kept people "in a sort of orgasm-without-release through a series of teasing glimpses of shiny automobiles, shiny female bodies, and other sensuous surfaces," all designed "to tease without satisfaction, to replace every partial gratification with a new desire." Such "cravings," he insisted, "drive us to do work which is of no interest save for the money it pays—to buy more lavish radios, sleeker automobiles, glossier magazines, and better television sets, all of which will somehow conspire to persuade us that happiness lies just around the corner if we buy one more."[45]

CONCLUSION

By 1970, many of the elements that would later shape happiness studies and positive psychology were already in place. In addition to the major contributions already discussed, scattered in scholarly journals were important studies whose implications would later emerge as important in a more expansive body of research. In 1954, Leon Festinger's "A Theory of Social Comparison Processes" focused on people's abilities and opinions, although it would take time before scholars deployed the concept of social comparison in order to explain how people developed a sense of wellbeing. Studies like Robert B. White's 1959 "Motivation Reconsidered: The Concept of Competence" would later undergird an emphasis on the importance of competence as a character strength and support the idea that pursuing a goal was more important than achieving it. In a similar manner, in this case pointing forward to how positive psychologists emphasized the importance of giving to the person who offered help rather than received it, in 1965 Frank Riesmann articulated "The 'Helper' Therapy Principle," one that made clear that the giver of aid benefited as much as its recipient. Similarly, a group of psychologists explored conditions under which a person would act altruistically by aiding a stranger. Moreover, several studies of the 1950s and early 1960s examined the biological bases of emotions, typically but not always negative ones. These studies, and many of those this chapter has focused on, represent new ways researchers engaged with their subjects—such as experiments, surveys, and drugs—revealing a certain fluidity in subjectivity that underwrote new possibilities of subjective well-being.[46]

Positive psychologists would draw on what came before, often in ways their predecessors could not have anticipated or approved of. Positive psychologists echoed Peale's emphasis on the power of positive thinking even as they kept their distance from what he wrote and insisted they grounded his analysis and recommendations in science. Frankl suggested how people could turn traumatic events into opportunities for personal growth. Peale and Frankl demonstrated how significant was the potential audience for books that showed the way toward satisfaction with life. Scholars who developed attachment theory revealed the importance of intense personal relationships, even as John Bowlby's larger social vision would go largely unrecognized. Aaron Beck was among those who developed cognitive behavioral therapy as an alternative to Freudianism and behaviorism and pointed the way toward the shift from mental illness to psychological well-being. Abraham Maslow underscored the importance of self-realization and peak experiences. James Olds's discovery of the pleasure center of the brain, despite the challenges that later work posed, was a critical step in the development of the link between neuroscience and pleasure. Early work on psychopharmacology did more to relieve the misery of patients than it did to shape positive psychology, a field that preferred alternative avenues to mental health. The years before 1970 provided key precedents in attempts to measure subjective well-being of large populations: seen in how social scientists shifted their attention from mental illness to well-being and how investigators explored global dimensions of happiness. Moreover, at the end of the quarter century following World War II, the study of happiness remained largely if not exclusively an American enterprise. The writings of Allan Watts represent an important starting point in the popularization of Eastern spirituality, even as his personal excesses remind us of the distance most positive psychologists wanted to keep from the counterculture.[47]

Though precedents were obvious, there were limits to their scope, integration, and grounding. It would be years before happiness studies or positive psychology emerged as self-conscious fields with their presence fostered by major public and private organizations and by entrepreneurial academics. Although some advocates of a more pleasurable future understood (but rarely articulated in a full manner) that there was a relationship between the personal and political, an individualistic emphasis dominated discussions. Neuroscience and an understanding of how various chemical substances exerted their effects on the brain were in their infancy. To a considerable extent, approaches grounded in spirituality, religion, psychology, and science existed on separate tracks.

With the exception of Peale's facile optimism, what shaped most of the discussions before 1970 was a rich combination of deeply felt personal misery and the equally powerful traumas of social dislocation and violence so common in the 1940s—especially concentration and refugee camps, the separation of loved ones from each other, and the slaughter of tens of millions of people worldwide. Ironically, all this drove key observers not to despair but in the opposite direction. What would eventually become happiness studies and positive psychology thus found their origin in people determined to see in miserable circumstances the possibility of a more pleasure-filled world. The shift from misery and pessimism to happiness and optimism had begun, but there was plenty of ground left to cover.

NOTES

1. Wladyslaw Tatarkiewicz, *Analysis of Happiness* (The Hague: Martinus Nijhoff, 1976), xi. Written from 1939 to 1943, published in Polish in 1962 and in English fourteen years later, this book did not have the impact that others under discussion here had. Although they might have influenced later theorists, I found few if any references in the literature to works by Herbert Marcuse, Wilhelm Reich, Paul Tillich, or Norman O. Brown. For an early exploration of happiness and media, see Elihu Katz, "The Happiness Game: A Content Analysis of Radio Fan Mail," M.A. thesis, Columbia University, 1950.
2. On how World War II led to funding of research on mental illness, see Shelly L. Gable and Jonathan Haidt, "What (and Why) Is Positive Psychology?" *Review of General Psychology* 9 (June 2005): 106.
3. Norman Vincent Peale and Smiley Blanton, *The Art of Real Happiness* (New York: Prentice-Hall, 1950), 3. The best source on the New Thought tradition remains Donald Meyer, *The Positive Thinkers: A Study of the American Quest for Health, Wealth and Personal Power from Mary Baker Eddy to Norman Vincent Peale* (Garden City, NY: Doubleday, 1965). For a biography of Peale, see Carol V. R. George, *God's Salesman: Norman Vincent Peale and the Power of Positive Thinking* (New York: Oxford University Press, 1993). See also Eva S. Moskowitz, *In Therapy We Trust: America's Obsession with Self-Fulfillment* (Baltimore: Johns Hopkins University Press, 2001) and Christopher Lane, *Surge of Piety: Norman Vincent Peale and the Remaking of American Religious Life* (New Haven, CT: Yale University Press, 2016).
4. R. C. Murphy, "Think Right: Reverend Peale's Panacea," *Nation*, May 7, 1955, 399; Norman Vincent Peale, *The Power of Positive Thinking* (New York: Prentice-Hall, 1952), vii, 258–95.
5. Peale, *Positive*, 72, 75, 154–55, 181; Meyer, *Positive*, 259, 261.
6. Peale, *Positive*, vi-viii, 27–28, 41.
7. William Lee Miller, "Some Negative Thinking About Norman Vincent Peale," *Reporter*, Jan. 13, 1955, 21.
8. Joshua L. Liebman, *Peace of Mind* (New York: Simon & Schuster, 1946), xi, 65. Andrew R. Heinze, *Jews and the American Soul: Human Nature in the Twentieth Century* (Princeton, NJ: Princeton University Press, 2004) discusses many of the writers under consideration

here, including Joshua Liebman, Abraham Maslow, and Viktor Frankl. Jonathan Haidt, *The Happiness Hypothesis: Finding Modern Truth in Ancient Wisdom* (New York: Basic, 2006), 138, fn. 6, p. 257, credits Frankl as a pioneer in developing this idea. For the longer history of the topic, see Allan Young, *The Harmony of Illusions: Inventing Post-Traumatic Stress Disorder* (Princeton, NJ: Princeton University Press, 1995).

9. Viktor Frankl, *Man's Search for Meaning: An Introduction to Logotherapy,* trans. Ilse Lasch (1959; rev. ed.; Boston: Beacon, 1962). The title of the 1959 edition was *From Death-Camp to Existentialism: A Psychiatrist's Path to a New Therapy.* On Frankl's importance to positive psychology, see Emily Esfahani Smith, "There's More to Life than Being Happy," *Atlantic,* Jan. 9, 2013.

10. Frankl, *Meaning,* 73.

11. Frankl, *Meaning,* 36, 42, 43, 65, 66, 72, 77.

12. Frankl, *Meaning,* 105, 120, 132, 136–37. For his view of logotherapy, see Frankl, *Meaning,* 97–137.

13. Timothy Pytell has published a book on Frankl in German and a number of articles in English, including "Extreme Experience, Psychological Insight and Holocaust Perception: Reflections on Bettelheim and Frankl," *Psychoanalytic Psychology* 24 (Oct. 2007): 641–57; "Transcending the Angel Beast: Viktor Frankl and the American Humanistic Psychology Movement," *Psychoanalytic Psychology* 23 (Summer 2006): 490–503; "The Missing Pieces of the Puzzle: a Reflection on the Odd Career of Viktor Frankl," *Journal of Contemporary History* 35 (April 2000): 281–306; for critiques by Karlheinz Biller and Jay I. Levinson and Pytell's response, see "Viktor Frankl—Opposing Views," *Journal of Contemporary History* 37 (Jan. 2002): 105–13. Pytell shows how Frankl's critique of humanistic psychology reflects a preference for transcendence over immanence; exaggerated how much time he spent in Auschwitz; cooperated with the Nazis, even by carrying out medical experiments on fellow Jews; developed his approach to therapy before he entered the camps; minimized the horrors of the camps; in writing his book worked through his own experiences; and provided Americans with inspiring lessons about the Holocaust. In a 1971 video, *The Humanistic Revolution,* Frankl talked of the pursuit of happiness. For a take on concentration camp experiences and more generally traumas very different from that of Frankl, see Henry Krystal, ed., *Massive Psychic Trauma* (New York: International University Press, 1968).

14. On Bowlby, see Frank C. P. van der Horst, *John Bowlby—From Psychoanalysis to Ethology: Unravelling the Roots of Attachment Theory* (Chichester, UK: Wiley-Blackwell, 2011); Suzan van Dijken, *John Bowlby: His Early Life, A Biographical Journey into the Roots of Attachment Theory* (London: Free Association Books, 1998); Lenny van Rosmalen, Frank C. P. van der Horst, and René van der Veer, "From Secure Dependency to Attachment: Mary Ainsworth's Integration of Blatz's Security Theory into Bowlby's Attachment Theory," *History of Psychology* 19 (Feb. 2016): 22–39.

15. John Bowlby, *Maternal Care and Mental Health* (Geneva: World Health Organization, 1951), 11; John Bowlby, "Separation Anxiety," *International Journal of Psycho-Analysis* 41 (March–June, 1960): 89–113; John Bowlby, "The Nature of the Child's Tie to His Mother," *International Journal of Psycho-Analysis* 39 (Sept.–Oct., 1958): 350–73. Bowlby drew on the work of others, especially Harry F. Harlow and Mary Ainsworth; Haidt, *Happiness Hypothesis,* 109–117 explores these connections. See also Harry F. Harlow and Robert R. Zimmerman, "Affectional Responses in the Infant Monkey," *Science,* Aug. 21, 1959, 421–32; Mary D. Salter Ainsworth et al., *Patterns of Attachment: A Psychological Study of the Strange Situation* (Hillsdale, NJ: Erlbaum, 1978).

16. John Bowlby, *Attachment,* vol. 1, *Attachment and Loss* (New York: Basic, 1969), 4.

17. John Bowlby, *A Secure Base: Parent-Child Attachment and Healthy Human Development* (New York: Basic, 1988). Marga Vicedo, *The Nature and Nurture of Love: From Imprinting*

to Attachment in Cold War America (Chicago: University of Chicago Press, 2013), 36–43, which considers the work of Bowlby, Harlow, and Ainsworth, emphasizes how fully Bowlby's work reflected and shaped the contemporary emphasis on the quality of emotional mothering, despite questionable scientific evidence. Donna Haraway, *Primate Visions: Gender, Race, and Nature in the World of Modern Science* (New York: Routledge, 1989), 234–43, explores dynamics—gendered and human/animal—of the experiments of Harry Harlow. For the gendered nature of Bowlby's emphases, see Frank C. P. van der Horst and René van der Veer, "The Ontogeny of an Idea: John Bowlby and Contemporaries on Mother-Child Separation," *History of Psychology* 13 (Feb. 2010): 25–45. In Bowlby, *Maternal Care*, there was some discussion of mother substitutes but virtually none about fathers. For her discussion of the role of fathers elsewhere, see Ainsworth et al., *Patterns of Attachment*, 190–95, 271–73. For a summary of later research on attachment, see Jonah Lehrer, *A Book About Love* (New York: Simon & Schuster, 2016). On Bowlby's other commitments, see Ben Mayhew, "Between Love and Aggression: The Politics of John Bowlby," *History of the Human Sciences* 19 (Nov. 2006): 19–35.

18. Aaron T. Beck and Sigmund Valin, "Psychotic Depressive Reactions in Soldiers Who Accidentally Killed Their Buddies," *American Journal of Psychiatry* 110 (Nov. 1953): 352; see also Aaron T. Beck, "Successful Outpatient Psychotherapy of a Chronic Schizophrenic with a Delusion Based on Borrowed Guilt," *Psychiatry* 15 (Aug. 1952): 305–12. If Beck, along with Albert Ellis and others, was the father of cognitive behavioral therapy, then Ulric Neisser was the father of cognitive psychology: see Albert Ellis, *How to Live with a Neurotic* (New York: Crown, 1957); Ulric Neisser, *Cognitive Psychology* (New York: Appleton-Century-Crofts, 1967). Ellis is also important as a writer who emphasized the importance of sexual pleasure: Albert Ellis, *Sex Without Guilt* (New York: Lyle Stuart, 1958). Cognitive behavioral therapy, with its focus on the individual, emerged at the same time that others, such as R. D. Laing, saw psychological disorders as social in origin: Michael E. Staub, *Madness Is Civilization: When the Diagnosis Was Social, 1948–1980* (Chicago: University of Chicago Press, 2011).

19. Aaron T. Beck, *Depression: Causes and Treatment* (published since 1967 with various titles; Philadelphia: University of Pennsylvania Press, 1972), 21, 231, 236, 238, 290, 321. Rachel I. Rosner, "The 'Splendid Isolation' of Aaron T. Beck," *ISIS* 105 (Dec. 2014): 734–58 cogently chronicles Beck's development, which involved on his part not a replacement of Freudianism with cognitive behavioral therapy but a series of elaborate building of bridges between various fields.

20. For biographical information, see Edward Hoffman, *The Right to Be Human: A Biography of Abraham Maslow* (Los Angeles: Tarcher, 1988). For a summary of views on happiness by postwar psychologists, including Maslow, see V. J. McGill, *The Idea of Happiness* (New York: Praeger, 1967), 321–47. There is a considerable body of scholarly literature on Maslow, including Ian A. M. Nicholson, "'Giving Up Maleness': Abraham Maslow, Masculinity, and the Boundaries of Psychology," *History of Psychology* 4 (Feb. 2001): 79–91; Nadine Weidman, "Between the Counterculture and the Corporation: Abraham Maslow and Humanistic Psychology in the 1960s," in *Groovy Science: Science, Technology, and American Counterculture*, ed. David Kaiser and W. Patrick McCray (Chicago: University of Chicago Press, 2016), 124–63; Ellen Herman, "Being and Doing: Humanistic Psychology and the Spirit of the 1960s," in *Sights on the Sixties*, ed. Barbara L. Tischler (New Brunswick, NJ: Rutgers University Press, 1992), 87–101. Carl Rogers is the other humanistic psychologist who influenced positive psychology, although perhaps not as much as did Maslow: see Carl Rogers, *On Becoming a Person: A Therapist's View of Psychotherapy* (Boston: Houghton Mifflin, 1961).

21. Hoffman, *Maslow*, 148; A[braham]. H. Maslow and Béla Mittlemann, *Principles of Abnormal Psychology: The Dynamics of Psychic Illness* (New York: Harper & Brothers, 1941), 35.

22. A[braham] H. Maslow, "The Authoritarian Character Structure," *Journal of Social Psychology* 18 (Nov. 1943): 401–11.

23. A[braham] H. Maslow, *Motivation and Personality* (New York: Harper, 1954), 89.

24. Maslow, *Motivation*, 87, 89, 90–91, 214.

25. Maslow, *Motivation*, 207, 213–14, 218, 234, 245. On Maslow's engagement with the counterculture, see Weidman, "Maslow," 140–48.

26. Maslow, *Motivation*, 176, 178.

27. Maslow, *Motivation*, 217, 224; Weidman, "Maslow," 130.

28. Richard F. Thompson, "James Olds," in *Biographical Memoirs* 77 (Washington, DC: National Academy Press, 1999), 247; James Olds, "Pleasure Centers in the Brain," *Scientific American* 195 (Oct. 1956): 114–16. Cathy Gere of University of California San Diego is working on Olds and on the history of neuroscience more broadly.

29. The Heath story comes from Morten Kringelbach and Kent C. Berridge, "The Joyful Mind," *Scientific American* 307 (August, 2012): 40–45. On Heath's experiments, see Robert G. Heath, "Electrical Self-Stimulation of the Brain in Man," *American Journal of Psychiatry* 120 (Dec. 1963): 571–77. Gary Stix, "Turn It Up, Dear" [also published as "A Sex Chip? Targeting the Brain's Pleasure Center with Electrodes"], *Scientific American* 300 (May 1, 2009): 22–23.

30. In this discussion of early psychotropic medicines, I am relying on Andrea Tone, *The Age of Anxiety: A History of America's Turbulent Affair with Tranquilizers* (New York: Basic, 2009) and David Herzberg, *Happy Pills in America: From Miltown to Prozac* (Baltimore: Johns Hopkins University Press, 2009). There is a distinction between barbiturate sedatives, available in the early twentieth century; amphetamine stimulants, available commercially as Benzadrine beginning in 1933; lithium salts, first proposed for use in 1949; major tranquilizers or antipsychotics, such as Thorazine (chlorpromazine), synthetized in 1950 with use spreading in the mid-1950s; minor tranquilizers or antianxiety drugs (such as Miltown and its twin Equanil), widely used after 1955, followed by Librium and Valium (approved in 1960 and 1963); and antidepressants such as Prozac and Paxil, on the market in the early 1980s. David Healy, *The Creation of Psychopharmacology* (Cambridge, MA: Harvard University Press, 2002), 4 calls the discovery of chlorpromazine in 1952 "one of the seminal events in human history," whose importance drugs such as Prozac and Valium had overshadowed and obscured; the key issue is that the science of chlorpromazine made it possible to develop precise measures of the effectiveness of drugs. In addition, Americans made a persistent distinction, rooted in history, between prescription medicines aimed at "respectable people" and illegal or street drugs (such as marijuana, cocaine, heroin, and LSD) used by marginalized groups. However, the discovery beginning in late 1950s of how Miltown could become addictive could have undermined this distinction. See also David Healy, *The Antidepressant Era* (Cambridge, MA: Harvard University Press, 1997). Healy's approach is more technical, while that of Herzberg and Tone is cultural. For a more general discussion, which nonetheless focuses very little on drugs, see Martin Halliwell, *Therapeutic Revolutions: Medicine, Psychiatry, and American Culture, 1945–1970* (New Brunswick, NJ: Rutgers University Press, 2013).

31. T. F. Rose, "The Use and Abuse of the Tranquilizers," *Canadian Medical Association Journal* (Jan. 1958): 146, quoted in Herzberg, *Happy Pills*, 45; Herzberg, *Happy Pills*, 4.

32. Nathan Kline, Foreword to Robert S. de Ropp, *Drugs and the Mind* (New York: St. Martin's Press, 1957), x; Ropp, *Drugs and the Mind*, 283.

33. Tone, *Age of Anxiety*, 29; the discussion of the development of Miltown relies heavily on Tone, *Age of Anxiety*, 27–52; Frank Berger, unpublished autobiography, quoted in Tone *Age of Anxiety*, 30.

34. Gerald Gurin, Joseph Veroff, and Sheila Field, *Americans View Their Mental Health: A Nationwide Interview Survey* (New York: Basic, 1960). The commission also

sponsored the research that resulted in the publication of Marie Jahoda, *Current Concepts of Positive Mental Health* (New York: Basic, 1958), which discussed a wide range of conceptions of the book's subject, including ideas about "happiness, well-being, and contentment" (19). On how surveys helped create a public and a sense of the normal or average, see Sarah E. Igo, *The Averaged American: Surveys, Citizens, and the Making of a Mass Public* (Cambridge, MA: Harvard University Press, 2007). As early as 1930, social and behavioral scientists had relied on self-reporting questionnaires to measure the "avowed" happiness of people in United States and abroad: Warner Wilson, "Correlates of Avowed Happiness," *PB* 67 (April 1967): 294.

35. Jack R. Ewalt, "Staff Review," in Gurin, Veroff, and Field, *Americans View*, ix.

36. Ewalt, "Staff Review," xii–xiii; and Gurin, Veroff, and Field, *Americans View*, 48.

37. Ewalt, "Staff Review," xvii.

38. Norman M. Bradburn and David Caplovitz, *Reports on Happiness: A Pilot Study of Behavior Related to Mental Health* (Chicago: Aldine, 1965), 2, 19–20, 42–43, 49, 127. The National Institute of Mental Health funded this study, which the University of Chicago's National Opinion Research Center carried out.

39. Hadley Cantril, *The Pattern of Human Concerns* (New Brunswick, NJ: Rutgers University Press, 1965), 231, 273, 304, 307. The first comparative international study appeared in 1948; for a historical survey of international studies, see Ruut Veenhoven, "Inequality of Happiness in Nations," *JHS* 6 (Dec. 2005): 351–55. On modernization theory more generally, see Nils Gilman, *Mandarins of the Future: Modernization Theory in Cold War America* (Baltimore: Johns Hopkins University Press, 2003).

40. Cantril, *Pattern*, 315–21.

41. On humanistic psychology and the counterculture, and their impact on positive psychology and happiness studies, see Jessica Grogan, *Encountering America: Humanistic Psychology, Sixties Culture and the Shaping of the Modern Self* (New York: HarperCollins, 2013).

42. Anne Harrington, *The Cure Within: A History of Mind-Body Medicine* (New York: W. W. Norton, 2008), 205–42. Useful coverage of Watts and more generally of the history of Buddhism is in Richard H. Seager, *Buddhism in America* (rev. ed.; New York: Columbia University Press, 2012); Rick Fields, *How the Swans Came to the Lake: A Narrative History of Buddhism in America*, 3rd ed. (Boston: Shambhala, 1992); Jeff Wilson, *Mindful America: The Mutual Transformation of Buddhist Meditation and American Culture* (New York: Oxford University Press, 2014); Peter N. Gregory, "Describing the Elephant: Buddhism in America," *Religion and American Culture* 11 (Summer 2001): 233–63. For a discussion of the practice of Zen in the Bay Area beginning in the late 1950s, see Steven M. Tipton, "Antinomian Rules: The Ethical Outlook of American Zen Students," in *Getting Saved from the Sixties: Moral Meaning in Conversion and Cultural Change* (Berkeley: University of California Press, 1982), 94–175. See also Shunyru Suzuki and Trudy Dixon, *Zen Mind, Beginner's Mind* (New York: Weatherhill, 1970).

43. Alan Watts, *In My Own Way: An Autobiography, 1915–65* (New York: Pantheon, 1972), 45–45; Monica Furlong, *Zen Effects: The Life of Alan Watts* (Boston: Houghton Mifflin, 1986), xi.

44. Alan Watts, *Psychotherapy East and West* (New York: Pantheon, 1961), 25; Alan Watts, *The Meaning of Happiness: The Quest for Freedom of the Spirit in Modern Psychology and the Wisdom of the East* (1940; London: Rider, 1978), xxi; Alan Watts, *The Way of Zen* (New York: Knopf, 1957), 155–56; Alan Watts, *The Joyous Cosmology: Adventures in the Chemistry of Consciousness* (New York: Pantheon, 1962), book title and xvii.

45. Watts, *Happiness*, xxi; Alan Watts, *The Book: On the Taboo Against Knowing Who You Are* (New York: Pantheon, 1966), 110; Alan Watts, *The Wisdom of Insecurity* (1951; New York: Pantheon, 1961), 61–62.

46. Leon Festinger, "A Theory of Social Comparison Processes," *Human Relations* 7 (May 1954): 117–40; Robert B. White, "Motivation Reconsidered: The Concept of Competence," *Psychological Review* 66 (Sept. 1959): 297–333; Frank Riesmann, "The 'Helper' Therapy Principle," *Social Work* 10 (April 1965): 27–32; Harvey A. Hornstein, Elisha Fisch, and Michael Holmes, "Influence of a Model's Feeling About His Behavior and His Relevance as a Comparison Other on Observers' Helping Behavior," *JPSP* 10 (Nov. 1968): 222–26; Stewart Wolf, "Effects of Suggestion and Conditioning on the Action of Chemical Agents in Human Subjects: The Pharmacology of Placebos," *Journal of Clinical Investigation* 29 (Jan. 1950): 100–9; Jack E. Hokanson and Michael Burgess, "The Effects of Status, Type of Frustration, and Aggression on Vascular Processes," *Journal of Abnormal and Social Psychology* 65 (Oct. 1962): 232–37; Stanley Schachter and Jerome Stringer, "Cognitive, Social, and Physiological Determinants of Emotional State," *Psychological Review* 69 (Sept. 1962): 379–99.

47. For efforts in the 1920s and 1930s to measure subjective well-being, see Erik Angner, "The Evolution of Eupathics: The Historical Roots of Subjective Measures of Well-Being," *International Journal of Wellbeing* 1 (Jan. 2011): 4–41.

CHAPTER 3

Crisis of Confidence?

1970–1983: Providing the Groundwork for
the Study of Positive Happiness

On July 15 1979, President Jimmy Carter delivered his "Crisis of Confidence" speech, commonly known as the malaise address. This came against a background of dramatic and depressing stories that marked the 1970s as a turning point—the degraded position of America in the world so evident in the Arab oil embargo and the Vietnam War, years of stagflation, and the Watergate scandal. These events provided what Martin Seligman in 1995 called "ample fodder for the growth of American pessimism," making them years that, at first glance, were not especially fertile for the study of happiness to flourish. Yet while in the 1970s and early 1980s these fields had not fully emerged, there were nonetheless many elements that were both important in themselves and critical components of positive psychology in the future. This was true despite the fact that observers from varied fields wrestled with questions of personal satisfaction during a period of tremendous national and global turmoil.[1]

Five years later, in 1984, when the Dutch sociologist Ruut Veenhoven surveyed research on happiness, he noted 245 studies and a recent "slight upsurge" in attempts to measure people's sense of well-being. Despite "stray investigations" that had produced a "sizeable body of data," he nonetheless recognized that the "promised systematic study of happiness was never produced." Alas, he concluded, "the subject is still the Cinderella it always was." However, if happiness studies and positive psychology as defined, self-conscious fields were not on the scholarly horizon in the early 1980s, this chapter makes clear that before 1984 there were plenty of books, approaches, and studies upon which writers would later draw; that positive psychology grew from several, often disparate streams. Yet at key moments scholars did not articulate the implications of the findings for happiness studies or positive psychology later observers would explore. Even as the quality of data collection and analysis grew apace, what surveys revealed underscored the pall cast by the nation's mood that hindered the emergence of a robust, integrated field. Timing did not make the situation ripe for ebullient or even moderate hope—something clear when an optimistic book failed to attract much of an audience, while a pessimistic one captured widespread attention.[2]

HEDONIC TREADMILL

In the dozen or so years after 1970, behavioral and social scientists carried out a series of experiments and studies that would later shape the fields of happiness studies and positive psychology. In order of appearance, first was the influential concept of the "hedonic treadmill," stated most clearly in the classic 1971 article "Hedonic Relativism and Planning for the Good Society" by Philip Brickman and Donald T. Campbell. They drew on the earlier work of Harry Helson on adaptation level theory, which theorized that how we judge an outcome depended on how constancy, contrast, and adaptation influenced the ways we understood our past experiences and expectations of future ones. In the background was the evidence from surveys that America's growing prosperity was not accompanied by a significant increase in reports of personal well-being. Reacting more explicitly to the expansion of social welfare programs and the social turmoil of the 1960s, the authors wondered how to prevent unmet but rising levels of aspiration from causing adverse social consequences. Congratulating the Founding Fathers for recognizing the transient nature of happiness when, in the Declaration of Independence, they spoke of the pursuit of happiness rather than its achievement, Brickman and Campbell emphasized the key principle of the adaptation level theory, that "even as we contemplate our satisfaction with a given accomplishment, the satisfaction level fades, to be replaced finally by a new indifference and a new level of striving."

Although the authors were principally concerned with what happened when a society committed itself to providing better social conditions for its citizens, the implications of what they wrote for the social and individual pursuit of happiness were clear: as people achieved higher income levels, the happiness they anticipated faded because they dreamed of even greater levels of affluence. Just as Brickman and Campbell hailed society's commitment to improve the lives of people, they also emphasized the pessimistic conclusion that the dynamics of adaptation level theory condemned "men to live on a hedonic treadmill, to seek new levels of stimulation merely to maintain old levels of subjective pleasure," without ever achieving "any kind of permanent happiness or satisfaction."[3]

As the psychologist Daniel Kahneman later wrote perceptively, this is a "deeply troubling notion" because "if people adapt to improving circumstances to the point of affective neutrality, the improvements yield no real benefits." Consequently, increases in the standard of living "do little to improve the human lot, at least above a threshold of adequate per-capita income." Better conditions "could cause people to require even more frequent and more intense pleasures to maintain the same level of satisfaction with their hedonic life." If people are on a hedonic treadmill, they keep their eyes out for those above and below them in socioeconomic terms, something explained by a theory of social comparison, first proposed by Leon Festinger in 1954.[4]

The article by Brickman and Campbell is important in at least two respects. The concept of the hedonic treadmill went a long way in explaining key dynamics of the relationship between happiness and rising incomes. Moreover, here were two psychologists venturing into public policy, territory that is typically occupied by economists, political scientists, and politicians. "They have taken some findings from laboratory psychology," an observer noted, expressing hope that other psychologists would follow suit, "and shown how they illuminate problems of society" even as he and they had "a nagging doubt . . . as to whether what we have to say is all that useful." In some ways the urban violence Brickman and Campbell saw stemming from a revolution of rising expectations in the 1960s provided the emotional undertow for their essay. They rejected the possibility of society embracing continually higher levels of wealth and social welfare because "limited resources, declining marginal utilities for goods, and social comparison complexities" made this an impossible goal—though their article reflected the more general malaise abroad in the nation in the late 1960s and early 1970s, one that may have drawn on a crisis of masculinity. Comparative adaptation levels, they cautioned, "should be lowered by reducing people's perceptions of what they deserve," something made more urgent as "our own egalitarian media—especially movies and television" enhanced the impact of social comparison, increasing the potential for "highly explosive" social expectations. Although they carefully avoided offering specific public policy recommendations and did not reveal which social groups they were counseling to accept their fate, they nonetheless made it clear that what they proposed involved preventing the restless striving from "wreaking its most destructive consequences" by acquiring "new, human means of controlling rising" adaptation levels.[5]

If Brickman and Campbell's concept of the hedonic treadmill would influence later generations of positive psychologists, the shift among scholars from cognition and behaviorism to emotion would reverberate for decades in the social and behavioral sciences and served as a foundational contribution to the emerging fields of sociobiology or evolutionary psychology that would later permeate happiness studies.[6] A key figure in the psychology of emotions was Paul Ekman. Interested in the study of non-verbal communications as early as 1957, he soon turned his focus to facial expressions and by the mid-1970s had developed tests to measure and codify them. Ekman's *Darwin and Facial Expression: A Century of Research in Review* appeared in 1973, just missing by one year the centennial of the publication of Charles Darwin's *The Expression of Emotions in Man and Animal* (1872). Although his predecessor had argued that emotional expressions were both universal and innate, Ekman concluded that some facial expressions were universal but not necessarily innate. As he had written in 1971, although the specific events that activated facial expressions were "socially learned and culturally variable," a "neuro-cultural theory" explained the universal nature of emotions revealed in facial expressions. Over a long and distinguished career, Ekman has continued to influence scholarship, public policy, and people's lives. For our purposes what is important is that though he focused considerable attention on negative emotions such as anger, fear, and disgust, especially beginning in the 1990s Ekman's work inspired key figures to emphasize the transformative power of positive emotions.[7]

At roughly the same time as Ekman's homage to Darwin appeared, and also having broad and potent impact over the long term, was the work by Robert L. Trivers in evolutionary biology. In his 1971 "The Evolution of Reciprocal Altruism," Trivers asked why people sometimes cooperated even if they were engaged in battles for the survival of the fittest. Because of his assertion that cooperation operated as a key element in such struggles, his work helped highlight the importance of sociobiology to people interested in the power of positive feelings.

Although Trivers began his article by focusing on two instances where animals practiced reciprocal altruism, he quickly turned to human behavior. In a careful and nuanced way he drew on pre-history, biology, anthropology, and sociology to analyze the conditions under which people did and did not help others. As an example of reciprocity, he explored why one person would save another from drowning, even though they were not kin and the act carried some risk. He concluded that such heroic acts are performed in anticipation of the person saved reciprocating with a similar act of kindness in the future. Trivers focused on natural selection and genetic factors as explanations for such reciprocity. "Under certain conditions," he insisted, "natural selection favors these altruistic behaviors because in the long run they benefit the organism performing them." He went on to remark that while "there is no direct evidence regarding the degree of reciprocal altruism practiced during human evolution nor its genetic basis today," it was nonetheless "reasonable to assume that it has been an important factor in recent human evolution and that the underlying emotional dispositions affecting altruistic behavior have important genetic components." If in their 1972 cookie and dime study, discussed below, Alice M. Isen and Paula F. Levin would insist that people experienced the warm glow of happiness when they acted kindly, for Trivers altruism was a matter of cold cost/benefit calculations in a world governed by the laws of evolution and genetics. Such an approach even influenced the operation of sympathy, which motivated "altruistic behavior as a function of the plight of the recipient of such behavior; crudely put, the greater the potential benefit to the recipient, the greater the sympathy and the more likely the altruistic gesture, even to strange or disliked individuals."[8]

Of course when people think of evolutionary theory of the postwar period, the first name that comes to mind is Edward O. Wilson, author of *Sociobiology: The New Synthesis* (1975). Years later, Trivers remarked that Wilson's contribution was mostly a semantic one: Wilson, he asserted, was not the field's father, but "the father of the name of the discipline." That is an unfair assessment; Wilson's work in the field antedated his 1975 book, and the book itself was original, commanding, and influential. Moving easily from the study of non-humans (ants were his specialty) to humans, Wilson emphasized how genetics, evolution, and the process of natural selection shaped human behavior. In a book filled with a focus on conflict, he nonetheless remarked that "the central theoretical problem of sociobiology" was "how can altruism, which by definition reduces personal fitness, possibly evolve by natural selection?" He found the answer in the dynamics of kinship. "If the genes causing the altruism," he commented, "are shared by two organisms because of common descent, and if the altruistic act by one organism increased the joint contribution of these genes to the next generation, the propensity to altruism will spread through the gene pool."[9]

The eventual incorporation by positive psychologists of evolutionary biology would not be without its problems. While it might be possible to test some its specific findings in a laboratory, when scholars made the transition from biological data to social theory, they often wandered from the scientifically verifiable to the philosophically speculative. The historian of science Vassiliki Betty Smocovitis pointed to "the power of narratives to lend coherence to intellectual and scientific projects . . . especially with grand narratives—all-embracing, universalizing, originary stories told about the universe, life and humanity, and about the construction of the grandest narrative of Western culture, the modern story of evolution." To the extent that it helped shape the vision positive psychologists offered, the use of evolutionary biology buried messiness, multiplicity, and contingency under the veneer of neatness, unity, and certainty that evolutionary theory ostensibly offered. These impulses may help explain the thinness of the field's social analysis, including lack of attention to race, class, sexuality, and gender, as well as its relative insensitivity to cultural differences.[10]

COOKIES AND KINDNESS

The question of how helping others made a person feel happier was at the heart of an influential 1972 study, "Effect of Feeling Good on Helping: Cookies and Kindness" by Alice M. Isen and Paula F. Levin. These authors carried out two experiments. In the first, they distributed cookies to one group of students but not to another. They then asked the subjects whether and for how long they would volunteer to help or hinder as confederates in a future experiment by either assisting or distracting the experimental subjects. The results showed that those subjects who unexpectedly received a cookie were more likely to volunteer to help than to distract their fellow students and were willing to do so for a longer period of time than their counterparts who had not received a cookie. Isen and Levin tentatively concluded that their study supported the "'warm glow' hypothesis" that "people who feel good themselves are more likely to help others." Still, they felt it necessary to rule out a possible explanation that those who received a cookie were more inclined to help because of having just encountered some kind, modeling behavior and because they had been explicitly solicited to do so. To address these issues, the authors conducted a second study that tested whether feeling good led to unsolicited helpfulness in the absence of a role model. In this, their "dime" study, they left a coin in the return slot of a pay phone and observed whether someone who found the coin would be more likely to help a person who walked by afterward, "accidentally" dropping some papers. The results showed that "differential unsolicited helping occurs even when good mood is induced in an impersonal manner," leaving Isen and Levin confident that the "'warm glow' hypothesis" was correct—when people feel good, they are more likely to help others with not-so-random acts of kindness.[11]

SEASON'S GREETINGS

The subject of altruism, reciprocity, and subjective well-being stood more implicitly at the heart of another classic study—this one carried out in

1974 by the sociologist Phillip Kunz. He sent out almost 600 Christmas cards to people whose names he picked randomly from two published directories. Twenty percent of recipients responded, rarely inquiring about who the sender was, usually by sending their own Christmas greetings in return, and less frequently by writing a personal note that assumed the recipient knew the sender. "We miss your father," wrote one, pulling a reference out of thin air, "They were such grand friends." Only six respondents puzzled over Kunz's identity. Kunz was also interested in how the social status of both sender and recipient affected the rate and nature of reactions, with responses to cards from a high-social-status sender (indicated by signing the card "Dr. and Mrs. Kunz" as opposed to "Phil and Joyce") prompting higher rates of return, especially from blue-collar recipients. Recipients of fancy cards were more likely to answer than those who got simpler ones. People from a small town in South Dakota were more likely to respond than those living in Omaha, Nebraska's largest city.

Graphs, statistics, and tables filled the scholarly article, and Kunz drew no larger conclusion from the study. However, in an interview with a reporter, he was a bit more expansive. "Our society is interested in upward mobility," he remarked, "and it is more appropriate to reply to an authority figure, especially for those in the rural community." In contrast, other aspects revealed by Kunz's study garnered the attention of later generations of social and behavioral scientists. In 1995, in an article titled "The Need to Belong: Desire for Interpersonal Attachments as a Fundamental Human Motivation," two psychologists, drawing on Kunz's experiment, noted that "many social institutions and behavior patterns seem to serve a need to preserve at least the appearance of social attachment in the absence of actual, continued interaction." Others focused on what the study revealed about how people derive pleasure from reciprocity in ways that tied social relationships to personal well-being. "Interestingly," noted a social psychologist in 2015, "this study is often used as an example of the norm of reciprocity, but the original paper" did not "use this term—or even claim to be testing it."[12]

DOES MONEY BUY HAPPINESS?

The authors of some of these studies did not at the time make the broader implications of what they wrote very explicit, but this cannot be said of the economist Richard Easterlin. In 1974, he articulated what came to be known as the Easterlin (or the income-happiness) Paradox. There were two parts to this. The first was that while despite the complications of culturally different standards there were often small differences in reported happiness between people in rich and poor nations, within nations well-to-do people were happier than poor ones. The second was that while higher incomes do correlate with more happiness at one point in time, over the long term increased incomes do not correlate with increased happiness. As Easterlin wrote in 1973 in a way that reflected the period's pessimism about the state of the economy and the prospects of economic policy, "in the United States, the average level of happiness in 1970 was not much different from what it had been in the late 1940's, though average income, after allowance for taxes and inflation, could buy 60 per cent more." Relying on ample data others had collected since the end of World War II, he looked at the situation within a nation and comparatively between nations. He concluded that within the United States, there was a positive correlation between higher incomes and greater happiness, but across national borders, there was no clear relationship. Focusing on the lack of convincing evidence within the United States to support commensurate increases in happiness over time, he reported that despite the economic boom in the quarter century after 1945, people's reported happiness actually declined in the 1960s. Turning to the reasons why this was so, he underscored the impact of changing social norms such that "an escalation in human aspirations . . . negates the expected positive impact on welfare." In others words, Americans were on a hedonic treadmill.[13]

While Easterlin's 1974 essay was highly technical, six years later he produced *Birth and Fortune: The Impact of Numbers on Personal Welfare*, a book written for a general audience and one in which demographic determinism ruled. Here he argued that the size of one's generational cohort fundamentally shaped well-being. For members of a small generation, such as those born between the beginning of the Depression and America's entry into World War II, "life is—as a general matter—disproportionately good," with the obverse being true for members of the postwar baby boom generation. The former faced better economic prospects reflected in healthy economic growth rather than stagflation; higher rates of employment, career advancement, and incomes; higher rates of marriage and lower rates of illegitimate births and divorce; a greater ability of married women to stay at home to take care of their children; a more ample sense of emotional well-being reflected in lower rates of crime, suicide, and "feelings of alienation." Although not without its problems, Easterlin's analysis was richly suggestive of the changes that swept across America after World War II. It helped account for the good fortune of those born in the 1930s, as well as the malaise or crisis of confidence of the 1970s, a period when the baby boom generation came to maturity.[14]

A very different but equally influential take on the dynamics of happiness emerged in Mihaly Csikszentmihalyi's 1975 examination of flow, the pleasure people experience in work and play, a phenomenon that had intrigued him for more than a decade. His sustained work on the concept of flow marks him as one of the most influential and imaginative precursors of positive psychology. Csikszentmihalyi grew up in an aristocratic Hungarian family uprooted during World War II. He came to the United States in 1956 with $1.25 in his pocket but determined to understand how the mind worked. He began to think about flow as early as 1963 when, in researching his dissertation, he observed artists working in a trance-like state. He first fully articulated the concept of flow in his 1975 *Beyond Boredom and Anxiety*, a title that played upon and critiqued that of the behavioral psychologist B. F. Skinner's 1971 *Beyond Freedom and Dignity*. Like other founders of positive psychology, Csikszentmihalyi was reacting not only against behaviorism and Freudianism but also against those who emphasized the primacy of the pursuit of money and power. He approached the study of flow through an examination of adult play informed by phenomenology. He relied on a number of investigative methods, including the Experience Sampling Method (ESM), a technique he developed in the early 1970s that strove to capture people's everyday experiences naturalistically by using new technology. Researchers gave subjects beeps at random times throughout the day, prompting them to report on their thoughts and feelings in the moment.[15]

Examining a spectrum of people experiencing flow states, from chess and basketball players to dancers, rock climbers, artists, daydreamers, and surgeons, Csikszentmihalyi sought "to understand enjoyment, here and now—not as compensation for past desires, not as preparation for future needs, but as an ongoing process which provides rewarding experiences in the present." People involved in flow, he insisted as he described something akin to Zen mindfulness, "concentrate their attention on a limited stimulus field, forget personal problems, lose their sense of time and of themselves, feel competent and in control, and have a sense of harmony and union with their surroundings." For him, the stakes were considerable. Like others, he saw alcoholism, depression, and gambling making it difficult for Americans to achieve happiness. Moreover, "if the trend toward increased mechanization of life is to be reversed—and social alienation and individual meaninglessness thereby reversed—the first step must be the recognition that there is such a thing as positive enjoyment"—achievable by the experience of flow. If "alienated children in the suburbs and bored housewives" do not experience flow, he wrote at the book's end without being very specific about the relationship between individual flow and commitments to social action, they will turn to "substitutes in the form of escape or consumption. The task is awesome, bristling with the oldest problems of economic and social justice. . . . [I]f human evolution is to go on, we shall have to learn how to enjoy life more thoroughly."[16]

Csikszentmihalyi's book was both intriguing and influential. His approach involved a mixture of styles. On the one hand, it was clearly the work of an empirically oriented scholar, relying as it did on carefully executed research whose results he and his colleagues presented through a combination of first-person accounts, description, analysis, charts, graphs, and statistics. Yet he also revealed his indebtedness to humanistic psychology and more broadly to the counterculture. He acknowledged the influence of Abraham Maslow (especially the notion of peak experiences), Carl Rogers, Ivan Illich, Paul Goodman, William Blake, Herbert Marcuse, and Carlos Castaneda—as well as the practice of Zen and yoga. For him, flow involved transcendent experiences, often religious in nature—they were, he wrote, "a going beyond the known." In the ensuing years, the concept of flow had immense impact around the world and in myriad fields—including politics, sports, therapy, organizational behavior, and education.[17]

PARAPLEGICS AND LOTTERY WINNERS

A 1978 study of how people who in midlife became paraplegics or lottery winners would also have tremendous implications for the relationship between happiness studies and social theory. Philip Brickman, Dan Coates, and Ronnie Janoff-Bulman drew on Harry Helson's classic 1947 study of adaptation level theory and Brickman's more recent discussion of hedonic adaptation. They posited that in the short run, for winners the "contrast effect" would diminish "the pleasure found in mundane events," while over a longer period of time the "process of habituation" would chip away at the impact of good news. In a parallel way, for people like paraplegics who experienced such terrible loss, they assumed that over the short term "their unhappiness should be mitigated by a contrast effect that enhances the impact of mundane pleasures, which are now contrasted with the extreme negative anchor of the accident." Over a longer period, "their unhappiness should be mitigated by a process of habituation that erodes the impact of the accident itself."[18]

What their study actually found was both somewhat more ambiguous and significantly more revealing. Adaptation level theory was more convincingly relevant for lottery winners than for accident victims. Compared with members of a control group, lottery winners did not rate themselves significantly different in their level of happiness, but they derived less plea-sure from ordinary events. Sudden good fortune made ordinary events seem less pleasurable, and as time passed, the pleasure of winning the lottery wore off. Adaptation level theory worked less persuasively for paraplegics who remembered having been happier in the past due to what the scholars called "a nostalgia effect" but felt they were less happy in the present time than were members of a control group even though they did not seem to be as unhappy as expected. The three psychologists found it ironic that the paraplegics, by drawing nostalgically on an idealized past that helped them derive pleasure from ordinary events in the present, "had just as strong a positive anchor as the lottery winners, which worked to make current mun-dane events seem less pleasurable by contrast." In the end, the researchers remained somewhat puzzled over what they found as they emphasized "how observers overestimate the extent to which winning a lottery or being crippled affects the psychological state of participants."[19]

Scholars later hailed and somewhat simplified what Brickman, Coates, and Janoff-Bulman found. Kahneman called the study an "instant clas-sic" that has "retained its status" and revealed that people "exposed to life-altering events ultimately return to a level of well-being that is characteristic of their personality." This leads many to the conclusion, as he states it, that "happiness . . . is a personality trait with a large heritable component," which others called a happiness set point. Put somewhat differently, the conclu-sion drawn from this study, which went beyond what the three scholars actually found and opened the possibility of exaggerating the conclusions drawn from one study, could reinforce the observation that objective con-ditions had relatively little impact on people's sense of well-being, whereas temperament or heredity appeared to weigh more heavily. Earning more money, living in a more egalitarian society, joining a social movement, or having the good fortune to be born a white male seemed to matter little.[20]

MAKING DECISIONS WHEN THE FUTURE IS UNKNOWN

Like the study of lottery winners and paraplegics, the emphasis on pros-pect theory relied on what economists call anchoring—the way distinctive life experiences shape how people make choices and evaluate their deci-sions, often in ways shaped by emotions. Two essays—one from 1979 and one published a year later—over time helped build toward the connec-tion between behavioral economics and positive psychology. In their 1979 article "Prospect Theory: An Analysis of Decision Under Risk," Daniel Kahneman and Amos Tversky emphasized how the power of emotional, social, and cognitive factors undercut the assumption of many economists that people make decisions on a rational basis. Determined to improve how people evaluated their prospects or options, they underscored the role emotions played in decision-making in ways that often undermined the quest for happiness. Prospect theory thus relied on a study of how people responded to hypothetical choices where the likelihood of an outcome was known, such as buying insurance or gambling with their money. Examining how people assessed risk as they made decisions, they proposed replacing utility theory with an approach in which people assigned value to what they might gain or lose rather than to what the final outcomes would be. And they replaced probabilities with weighted implications. Their essay, which made no reference to happiness, at the time marked a major advance in the study of the relationships between behavioral economics and decision making.[21]

In 1980, Richard Thaler published "Toward a Positive Theory of Consumer Choice," an essay that Kahneman hailed, when speaking of his own Nobel Prize–winning work in economics for his work on prospect theory, as "the founding text of behavioral economics." Here Thaler followed Kahneman and Tversky in critiquing those who relied on the notion that people made decisions in a rationality-maximizing way. In many instances, Thaler asserted, the normative model failed to predict people's behavior. Relying on questionnaires, laboratory experiments, and market data, discussions with friends and colleagues, and above all on what Kahneman and Tversky had written on prospect theory, Thaler explored a range of situations in which consumers did not act in the utility-maximizing ways orthodox economists might predict—such as when consumers made foolish decisions about their health care or when they voluntarily limited their choices by opting for packaged vacations. He concluded that orthodox economists, in assuming consumers were "robot-like experts," provided a problematic explanation of how consumers actually behaved. Some might be mavens in the marketplace, but most, far from being stupid, made a rational decision not to expend excessive time and psychic energy when they shopped.[22]

SURVEYS

Although surveys of people's sense of satisfaction began in the late 1950s with concern over mental illness, by the early 1970s attention had shifted decisively to measuring well-being. Discussions about the consequences of affluence helped drive this change, with presidents from Dwight Eisenhower through Richard Nixon calling on the nation to ponder the meaning of American life in an age of affluence—and by the presidency of Lyndon Johnson to develop national measurements of social progress. None of the resulting efforts was successful in devising ways of determining with any precision the impact of public policy on elusive goals, not the least among them how happy people were. For a wide spectrum of people what was at issue was a feeling, sometimes vague and sometimes articulate, that increasing affluence in the postwar world had not produced commensurate non-economic gains. Nixon in 1970 identified as "a fundamental truth" that the nation "can be the best clothed, best fed, best housed people in the world . . . but we could still be the unhappiest people in the world."[23]

With these contexts in the political background, from the mid-1960s until the early 1980s America witnessed a boom in the business of measuring life satisfaction. Private foundations, corporations, and the federal government supported many studies, which were useful to scholars, public policy experts, and businesses. The most important of these were done at University of Michigan's Institute for Social Research.[24] Carried out for two decades beginning in the late 1950s, they relied on one-hour in-home interviews of several thousand adults, selected by sophisticated probability sampling techniques. "Taking all things together," surveyors asked, for example, "how would you say things are these days—would you say you're very happy, pretty happy, or not too happy?"[25]

This was the key question Michigan's Angus Campbell reported in *The Sense of Well-Being in America: Recent Patterns and Trends* (1981), as he summed up two decades of research. In contrast with the overwhelming sense of happiness reported in the mid-1960s, Campbell now lamented that a decreasing percentage of Americans described themselves as very happy. Americans had lost confidence in their ability to walk safely in their streets, in their sense of attachment to their communities, in the satisfaction they derived from their jobs, in their belief in the coherence of their families, and in their trust in elected officials. Consequently, "as economic welfare increased . . . psychological well-being declined," he remarked, drawing on Maslow's hierarchy of needs, with people coming to rely less on increasing income and more on what money could not buy—"equity, participation, respect, challenge, and personal growth." Other findings are worth mentioning. When he looked at the relatively thin data on international comparisons, he noted that while Americans had among the world's strongest sense of well-being, research revealed irregular patterns, with the relationship between national affluence and happiness hardly at all consistent.[26]

Within the United States, the pattern that struck Campbell was the same one Easterlin had discovered in the 1970s—a weakening link between income, education, and occupation and a sense of well-being. Although people with high incomes were more likely to describe themselves as very happy, these factors accounted for a low and declining influence in promoting happiness and satisfaction. As he disaggregated the data for the United States, he noted that affluent citizens were more satisfied with their lives, while the unemployed, divorced, and disabled were less positive about theirs. Yet regardless of social status, a satisfying marriage, effective relationships with family and friends, and good health powerfully shaped people's satisfaction with their situation. Being married, and to a lesser extent having children, was the factor that most powerfully enhanced people's sense of well-being, despite the awareness of how often couples divorced, of increased questioning of family life, and of a burgeoning women's movement. Less important though nonetheless influential was a satisfying job, which most men reported having despite the claims of those who emphasized how alienating work was. Similarly, even with the dramatic increase in numbers of women working outside the home and the widely accepted idea that those who stayed at home were miserable, women expressed levels of satisfaction similar to those of men despite their lives being more strained. African Americans, even those with higher levels of education and income, did not have a sense of well-being comparable to their white counterparts. Unlike what earlier studies had found, the evidence indicated that older people were more content with their lives than younger ones. Being in good health, physically attractive, in control of one's life, having a strong sense of self—all these were powerful influences largely independent of one's economic situation.[27]

In short, avoiding race and class situations where his generalization did not fit, Campbell insisted life's "objective circumstances" were relatively weak determinants of people's sense of well-being, accounting for no more than 10 percent of people's responses. At every level of income there were very happy and very unhappy people. Over time, as the link between well-being and objective conditions weakened and levels of happiness did not increase, he insisted, the nation became less happy but more just. With increasing affluence, at some point that Campbell did not specify, greater income lost its "preeminence" and higher needs took over, especially for those pertaining to relationships with other people and what Maslow had called self-actualization or self-fulfillment.[28]

Criticism of Campbell's approach intensified over time. Already in 1963 the humanist Joseph Wood Krutch, in an article titled "Through Happiness with Slide Rule and Caliper," remarked that "the sociologist seems . . . to pretend to define the undefinable and measure the unmeasurable." Eventually critiques flooded in from social and behavioral scientists as well. As it turned out, people's responses to surveys were exceedingly sensitive to context, such as features as minor as finding a dime or watching a soccer game, but even more important the order in which questions were asked. In retrospect, the perspectives offered by the surveys were limited: they did not establish many international comparisons, had no grounding in cognitive or brain science, and were designed to develop information for public policy (initially in the field of mental health and eventually for a wide range of social policy issues) rather than serve as advice for popular consumption that would guide individuals on how to increase their happiness. Yet the studies Campbell drew on and carried out in the two decades beginning in the late 1950s were important in themselves and historically. They deployed immense resources—financial and intellectual—in a state-of-the art but not always fully successful attempt to measure happiness. They explored the relationship between well-being and major public events such as the assassination of JFK, the race riots of the 1960s, the war in Vietnam, the movements for liberation of women and African Americans, and the stagflation of the 1970s. The social scientific measurement of life satisfaction, which had begun in the 1950s, had by the early 1980s shifted its focus from mental health to well-being but did not yet amount to part of a self-conscious field of happiness studies.[29]

BETTER LIVING THROUGH RELAXATION

A very different approach to well-being came from the marriage of Eastern religion and Western science, one that reveals how people in disparate fields that would eventually come together in a full-blown positive psychology were starting to communicate with one another. A key moment in this story happened in the mid-1950s, when the Asian Indian Maharishi Mahesh Yogi founded what came to be known as Transcendental Meditation® (TM). In 1968, as part of his world tour, he traveled to Boston and met with Dr. Herbert Benson of Harvard Medical School to see if he could persuade Benson to undertake studies that might reveal that TM provided medical benefits. Initially reluctant because the medical establishment associated TM with the counterculture, Benson soon agreed: a cardiologist, he had already begun research on the relationship between stress and blood pressure in monkeys. Three years after meeting the Maharishi, Benson published a scientific paper in the prestigious journal *Science* in which he explored the positive impact of meditation on health, an important step in the way meditation was becoming medicalized.[30]

Then in 1975, Benson published his popular and pathbreaking book *The Relaxation Response*, in which he made clear the larger contexts of his writings. Abroad at the time were deep uncertainties about the nation's destiny, as well as threats to Americans' dream of success in terms of money and advancement. Despite the nation's unprecedented level of affluence, unhappiness plagued many people—dissatisfaction affected both those who succeeded and those who failed to increase their income and experience upward social mobility. Across the board, Americans "want more and want it faster," an attitude that did "not leave time for relaxation or for appraising problems." He also acknowledged tensions closer to his world—especially the deep rift between medical doctors and scientists, on the one hand, and most psychologists, on the other—a condition that hampered understanding of the connections between physiological and psychological aspects of stress.[31]

Benson relied on a major shift in the scientific understanding of emotions. He observed that the fight-or-flight response, which physicians had seen as an evolutionary-based survival mechanism, caused physiological changes that in turn were responsible for a significant percentage of ailments that drove patients to see doctors. He and his colleagues had discovered a different evolutionary-based physiological mechanism, the relaxation response, which helped people rejuvenate their bodies by slowing down and breathing deeply in order to dramatically decrease their heart rate and blood pressure. He drew on a number of approaches, including operant conditioning, biofeedback, evolutionary biology, and scientific experiments with animals and humans. What Benson recommended was easy to follow. All people needed was a mental device (such as a word or sound) that focused the attention of the practitioner and a calm attitude that prevented distractions; helpful but not necessary were a peaceful environment and a comfortable posture.

Relaxation Response reflected the urgency of a central issue with which Benson wrestled—the roles of religion, spirituality, medicine, and science in underwriting the relaxation response. While he recognized that he was going against commonly accepted medical knowledge, scientific evidence robustly supported his recommendations. As he later wrote, in the early 1970s "it was considered scientific heresy for a Harvard physician and researcher to hypothesize that stress contributed to health problems and to publish studies showing that mental focusing techniques were good for the body." From the time the Maharishi came to see him onward, Benson knew that any association of his work with alternative medicine would taint or destroy his reputation among virtually all serious medical professionals, though publishing proof of the effectiveness of the relaxation response in *Science* helped somewhat.[32]

To ensure that what he discovered would be widely adopted, Benson worked to make a religious-based yoga acceptable to Westerners. He discussed how all religious traditions (and many secular ones as well) involved some version of going beyond day-to-day existence to transcendent experiences: Christian and Jewish mysticism, Buddhist meditation, or writers in the Romantic tradition. While he made it clear that just as religious people could repeat Hail Mary, Shema Yisrael, Our Father Who Art in Heaven, Om, or Insha'Allah, secularists could use key words such as peace or love. He acknowledged that his form of meditation involved reaching what others had called an altered state of consciousness, even as he distanced himself from what he saw as cult-like countercultural or religiously specific claims. To use the relaxation response, "you don't have to engage in any rites or esoteric practices," he said, instead reassuring his peers and readers. In other words, you did not have to be Jewish, which Benson was (or Christian, Buddhist, Muslim, Taoist, or secular), to benefit from the relaxation response.[33]

Benson's selective borrowing from Buddhism reminds us of the nature of American adaptations of both Buddhism and mindful meditation. The religious studies scholar Jeff Wilson has tracked this story, making clear that most American practitioners adopted and adapted a range of traditions. Although Alan Watts and others had earlier introduced many Americans to Buddhism, it was really in the 1970s that it arrived and spread more fully. Making it more accessible and palatable, much as Benson had done, advocates connected it with medicine and psychology. They reduced or eliminated the importance of striving for nirvana in ways that transcended the pulls of daily life, of going to retreats, and of engaging in religious rituals— and instead emphasized practical benefits, lay leadership, and the minimal effort needed. Wilson has demonstrated several things that happened to Buddhism and mindfulness in America over time for which Benson's work was an important turning point: by becoming medicalized, it fulfilled psychological and therapeutic impulses; it was transformed into a commercial product in robust marketplaces; it was connected to moral values; and, distanced from its Asian origins and practitioners, it was whitened. Ironically, in America Jews and Protestants played major roles in the development of positive psychology and its predecessors, with one perhaps unintended consequence being the transformation of Asian culture from the strange other to the source of peace and wisdom, albeit in ways that could make the exotic commonplace.[34]

Few books have matched the impact of *Relaxation Response*. A literary agent who represented a host of best-selling authors suggested Benson turn his scientific research into a book for general audiences. Once published, people read about it in *Time, Good Housekeeping,* and *Family Circle* and heard about it on *The Today Show, Good Morning America,* and *Nightline*. Research revealed that his program counteracted the adverse effects of a long list of conditions, including anxiety, mild depression, hypertension, menopausal hot flashes, and irritable bowel syndrome. Tens of millions used the approach he advocated—in the quarter century after the book's publication, the percentage of Americans practicing some forms of the techniques he recommended went from 7 to 33. *Relaxation Response* quickly reached the top of the *New York Times* list of bestsellers and stayed there for months. Eventually it sold more than 5 million copies and was translated into more than a dozen languages. Laurence Rockefeller sponsored workshops for members of the clergy. And Sir John Templeton, long interested in finding ways to reconcile science and religion, invited Benson to advise his foundation. As Benson wrote on the 25th anniversary of the book's publication, "many different groups, from churches to corporations, from spas to professional associations, began to clamor for information" he and his colleagues had developed. Benson and the Dalai Lama became friends, and in the 1980s Benson and his associates traveled to India several times to study how Tibetan monks practiced meditations that enabled them to perform remarkable mind–body feats.[35]

In time, the medical establishment overcame much of its skepticism. In 1988, Benson and his colleagues established the Mind/Body Medical Institute at the Harvard-affiliated Deaconess Hospital in Boston. Two years later, to honor the work Benson and his colleagues had done, Harvard established the Mind/Body Medical Institute Professorship. In 1995, the National Institutes of Health held a conference to assess mind–body work. Four years later, the federal government set aside $10 million in order to create Centers for Mind/Body Interactions and Health across the United States. In addition, almost every medical school developed programs on the relationship of mind, body, and spirituality.[36]

Nonetheless, despite its many strengths and abundant impact, Benson's book makes clear that a psychology based on positivity was in the future. His emphasis remained more on alleviating the problems of mental and physical illness than on the promotion of happiness. Though he used words such as pleasure and transcendence, his real focus was on "the huge personal suffering and social costs" inflicted on people by a range of illnesses.[37]

BETTER LIVING THROUGH CHEMISTRY

Benson offered one example of how physiology and emotions interacted, and Andrew Weil offered another: shifting how people understood the ways drugs—legal and illegal—might influence people's positive emotions. In the last third of the twentieth century and well into the twenty-first, he was among the most influential writers on the mind–body relationship, someone who in 1972 advocated the embrace of altered states of consciousness that would bring humanity "toward equilibrium, balance and harmony." With an interest in psychopharmacology that began with his familiarity with the LSD experiments of Richard Alpert and Timothy Leary, by the time Weil earned his MD from Harvard Medical School in 1968 he had already shifted his focus to holistic medicine and multiple ways of achieving higher and expanded modes of consciousness. In *The Natural Mind: A New Way of Looking at Drugs and the Higher Consciousness* (1972), he expressed two overlapping concerns: countering widely held assumptions about the deleterious effects of illegal drugs such as marijuana, mescaline, and LSD and making the case that many people achieved altered states of consciousness, from young children whirling "themselves into vertiginous stupor," to teenagers getting high by sniffing volatile solvents, to adults consuming alcohol or drugs, to those practicing yoga or meditation.[38]

Weil argued for the existence of an innate drive to expand consciousness. This led, he asserted, to the "potential for strongly positive psychic development . . . to more effective and fuller use of the nervous system, to development of creative and intellectual faculties, and to attainment of certain kinds of thought that have been deemed exalted by all who have experienced them." To focus on the legality of drugs, as did federal government agencies, college administrators, and most physicians, was to confuse means and ends. For Weil, drugs were just one, and in his mind not necessarily the preferred avenue to expanded, more ebullient mental states. This was so, he wrote, because "they can keep people from reaching the goal of consciousness developed to its highest potential" by fostering "the illusion that these states of consciousness arise from external reality rather than internal reality." Widening the scope of how people could achieve more integrative and fulfilled lives, he insisted on the importance of synthesizing Eastern and Western traditions, body and mind, feeling and intellect. Writing at a time when the counterculture of the 1960s was ascendant and the traumas of the 1970s such as rampant inflation, Watergate, the end of the war in Vietnam were just beyond the horizon, Weil was optimistic about the future. The United States, he wrote, would be "the focus of a revolution in consciousness that will transform human society."[39]

TOWARD A SCIENTIFIC BASIS OF HAPPINESS

Oddly enough, given the widespread use of Miltown in the 1950s and then Valium beginning in the 1960s, Weil paid no attention in his book to research into how the brain worked and virtually none to how prescription drugs changed moods.[40] Yet the period from 1970 to 1984 was an important one in the development of neuroscience (often called psychobiology at the time) and psychotropic drugs. In the mid-1970s, psychologists and psychiatrists critiqued Freudian skepticism about the possibility of abundant pleasure.[41] The scientific exploration of the brain yielded important insights. In 1977, Robert Heath, a neuropsychologist at Tulane interested in the science of violence and psychosis, reported on how stimulation of the septal region of the human brain by implantation of cerebellar pacemakers produced pleasurable sensations. This furthered the ability to map the brain in ways that helped locate its pleasure center, in the process revealing the connection between the limbic areas that affect emotion (hippocampus, amygdala, and septal regions) and the cerebellum. Important changes in these years also occurred in the world of prescription drugs. Valium displaced Miltown and then Librium as the drug of choice, with Prozac, already in development, not yet ready for the market.[42]

Research into how drugs operated on the brain intensified in the 1960s, but it was not until the early 1970s that scientists, relying on what they considered rigorous studies, demonstrated exactly how psychotropic drugs such as Miltown and Valium operated, affecting the brain to produce emotional changes. The key discovery was neurotransmitter receptors. As a historian of psychopharmacology has put it, these receptors "were to be the targets of the magic bullets of modern pharmacotherapy" that would, in turn, challenge the belief in the effectiveness of talk therapy. Before long, prescription drugs underwrote "a philosophy of how all therapies should work" and did so in ways with consequences for what insurance companies would and would not reimburse. With the increasing power of the *Diagnostic and Statistical Manual* (DSM) confirming for many the practical effect of these changes, the shift from the psychological to the biological, underway in the late 1960s and clear in the publication of DSM-III in 1980, was proceeding apace by the 1990s.[43]

It turned out that benzodiazepines such as Valium worked on the neurotransmitter gamma-aminobutyric acid (GABA) by mimicking naturally occurring substances in the brain, in the process lowering the excitability of the nerve's membrane and resulting in a sedative effect. Further research located the greatest concentration of benzodiazepine receptors in the amygdala, a subcortical brain region essential to detecting and responding to threats. This helped explain how the drugs attenuated anxiety. These discoveries, writes the historian Andrea Tone, "helped reposition anxiety from a problem bequeathed by one's past," as Freudians and others had posited, "to a neurobiological disorder responsive to pharmacotherapy."[44] "For the first time we may have a reasonable understanding of the biochemistry of anxiety," reported a scientist at the National Institute of Mental Health in 1982. Scientific advances provided relief for millions from depression and other miseries, helped erode the power of Freudianism, and enhanced that of neuroscience. "Having strayed from the enticing abstractions of Freud," wrote one observer, "we find ourselves in a molecular universe as rigorous yet accessible as astronomy and physics." Or, as a writer in 1979 put it with fewer restraints, the day was coming when brain researchers would help you "Improve your memory! Increase your sexual potency! Relieve your anxiety! Banish your depression!"[45]

Others also painted a picture of a psychopharmacological utopia. In 1981, the psychiatrist Seymour Rosenblatt and the writer Reynolds Dodson provided the best example in their *Beyond Valium: The Brave New World of Psychochemistry*. Although they acknowledged the legitimacy of some fears that scientists could bring about the sort of dystopia Aldous Huxley had predicted, they nonetheless went ahead. "Might it not be possible that there will be a groundswell of research to try to undo this anatomical injustice," they wrote as they referred to the "cerebral handicap" caused by differences between the brains of men and women that had not sat "well with some feminist ideology." Although some of the new drugs posed problems for men's sexual performance, they looked forward to a time when "the use of chemicals could sustain the libido, turning the act of coitus into an Olympic marathon!" In other ways, they sought to shift the focus of psychology from illness to well-being. "We are approaching the age of 'mental face-lifting,' and . . . we will be dealing with the question of whether the methods we have developed should be restricted to sick people." Perhaps, they speculated, further understanding of how the brain works will lead not just to cures for depression but to ways of enhancing creativity.[46]

POPULARIZATION

Already in this period, the notion of studying happiness and applying the resulting findings had gained popularity beyond the confined world of scholarly research. However, the fate of three books revealed the clear limits to the extent to which happiness, as a self-conscious field of study, had by the late 1970s entered into popular discussions. A series of books aimed at wide audiences, which few achieved despite the naive optimism of some, provided evidence of the gap between authors writing for the general public and serious scholars who focused on addressing their peers.[47]

Moreover, one careful book that tried to bridge that gap—*Happy People: What Happiness Is, Who Has It, and Why* (1978) by Jonathan L. Freedman, a social psychologist who did his best to reach a non-academic audience—failed to attract much attention. In answering the questions asked in the subtitle, he offered conclusions that were hardly surprising. Americans remained "wonderfully optimistic about their lives," despite facing difficult times. No single factor determined personal happiness. People involved in sustained, intimate relationships were more satisfied with their lives than their more lonely counterparts; married women expressed more dissatisfaction than their husbands; unhealthy people were less content than healthy ones; poor people were less happy than rich ones, but above a relatively low income level more money did not have much effect on happiness; and cynical people were less satisfied than their more trusting ones. Despite being written in an accessible style, containing personal stories about how respondents did and did not achieve happiness, and being published by a major commercial press, there were meager sales and few reviews. Nor did Freedman, as positive psychologists would do later, jump genre boundaries that then confined most social and behavioral scientists. "This is not a 'how-to' book," he told his readers. "It offers no easy ways to find happiness."[48] The time was not ripe for a popular book on happiness.

In contrast, nowhere was the sober mood that blocked reception of an optimistically happy work clearer than with two influential books of the period—Tibor Scitovsky's *The Joyless Economy: An Inquiry into Human Satisfaction and Consumer Dissatisfaction* (1976) and Christopher Lasch's *The Culture of Narcissism: American Life in an Age of Diminishing Expectations* (1978). Trained as an economist, beginning in the late 1950s Scitovsky had grown dissatisfied with his discipline's inability to grapple with "the puzzling relation—or lack of it—between income and satisfaction." So he turned to works by psychologists, which gave him the ammunition to challenge economists' assumptions that consumers were rational beings who achieved their goals through the operation of an efficient market. Instead, he showed, psychologists had emphasized the importance of arousal that avoided the extremes, the need for stimulation and novelty, and the importance of pleasure over comfort.[49]

Scitovsky then applied these insights to contemporary America. He underscored the role of externalities in curtailing satisfaction by pointing out the nation's reckless militarism, environmental degradation, and reliance on technology. He compared mainstream American consumption patterns with those of Western Europe and the homegrown counterculture, both of whose choices he found preferable. As befitting a democratically inclined émigré from a noble Hungarian family, he found problematic what he called the impact of the "Puritan Ghost," which caused Americans to prefer comfort over stimulation and to self-righteously impose their beliefs on others by passing laws that curtailed the use of drugs or that proscribed sexual activity. Moreover, the puritan heritage made Americans work too hard and overemphasize making money instead of pursuing culture, pleasure, or public goods. *Joyless Economy*, a timely but densely written book, did not achieve a wide readership. Nonetheless, the book effectively captured what many experienced as the gloomy mood of the 1970s and pointed the way forward to how a later generation could combine economics and psychology to explore the conundrums Americans experience as they chased after a higher standard of living.[50]

One book that captured the same mood but reached a more-than-ample audience was Lasch's *Culture of Narcissism*. He painted a depressing picture of life in America, a nation ravaged by the erosion of savings by inflation, filled with people who no longer hoped to prosper and instead struggled to survive. With tragic consequences, the liberal welfare state, media, corporations, and experts had transformed the society and in the process all but destroyed genuine forms of work, love, and community. Consumer culture, capitalism, and affluence, Lasch argued, were among the many causes of the rise of narcissism to such a powerful position in society in ways that failed to produce genuine satisfaction. The self itself became a saleable good, as if the individual's "own personality were a commodity with an assignable market value." Advertising, by fostering unquenchable appetites for goods and experiences, made consumers "perpetually unsatisfied, restless, anxious, and bored." The "propaganda of commodities" offered purchasable goods and experience as substitutes for political protest, turned politics into spectacle, made alienation a commodity, institutionalized envy, and fostered in women and young people a false sense of emancipation. Moreover, it freed "women and children from patriarchal authority, however, only to subject them to the new paternalism of the advertising industry, the industrial corporation, and the state." "The ideology of personal growth, superficially optimistic, radiates a profound despair and resignation," he lamented at a time when a wildly popular book told readers to say *I'm OK, You're OK*.[51]

CONCLUSION

I placed a question mark after "Crisis of Confidence" in the title of this chapter because not everything from the period points in one direction. There were some relatively unambiguous signs of movement toward new visions of happiness. In 1972 the king of Bhutan replaced the Gross Domestic Product (GDP) with a Gross National Happiness (GNH) Index, one that stressed the importance of protecting the environment, preserving cultural values rooted in Buddhism, reconciling the spiritual and the material, improving the quality of family life, and enhancing spiritual life.[52] A series of publications appeared whose authors would later help shape positive psychology. In the late 1970s Norman Cousins offered two versions of *Anatomy of an Illness (as Perceived by the Patient)* that were milestones in how the medical community and the more general public accepted the power of positive thinking—one in the prestigious *New England Journal of Medicine* and another in an immensely popular and influential book.

He told of how, having been diagnosed with an apparently incurable illness, he searched for an alternative to hyper-medicalization of his body, an alternative that relied on the relationship between the brain, emotions, and the body.[53] In addition, a series of books appeared that over time would become canonical works of positive psychology.[54] A few examples will suffice. In 1979 Daniel Goleman and Richard J. Davidson edited *Consciousness, Brain, States of Awareness, and Mysticism*. Alasdair Macintyre's 1981 *After Virtue: A Study in Moral Theory* revived an Aristotelian focus on the connection between morality and character. In 1983, Howard Gardner's work on multiple intelligences, *Frames of Mind*, explored human potential as viewed from a psychological perspective.[55]

In addition, scholarly articles had begun to pay attention to other elements that would form the basis of happiness studies and positive psychology. Neuroscientists were enhancing how we understood the science of pleasure.[56] Davidson and Goleman explored whether meditation could yield long-term changes in the brain.[57] Scholars turned their attention to the importance of character and virtues—resilience, social connectedness, and generosity—in promoting happiness.[58] Studies revealed numerous aspects of the dynamics of subjective well-being with one exploring how "positive affective states enhanced learning." Another demonstrated how giving people a greater sense of choice and responsibility increased their sense of well-being. A critical link between Viktor Frankl's *Man's Search for Meaning* and the post-1984 flowering of the field of posttraumatic studies appeared in a 1980 study of repatriated prisoners captured in Vietnam. Two research projects of Ellen J. Langer were compelling. Her 1977 study, which quickly became a classic, demonstrated how giving residents of nursing homes responsibility for their environment intensified their sense of pleasure and extended their lives. In a similar vein that suggested how the mind could counteract the effects of aging, her 1981 experiment revealed that men in their late seventies benefited psychologically and physically from re-experiencing the world they had earlier known. Finally, in 1977 the psychologist Michael Fordyce conducted research that led to specific recommendations on how people could increase their level of happiness, which would eventually undergird his Personal Happiness Enrichment Program.[59]

Yet there is plenty of evidence for the years from 1970 to 1984 of the impediments to the birth or robust development of happiness studies and positive psychology. For example, several investigations that focused on the dynamics of pleasure were more interested in negative states of well-being than happy ones.[60] Moreover, the implications of studies that would later emerge as classics in the field—of reciprocity, the hedonic treadmill, paraplegics and lottery winners, evolutionary biology, and prospect theory—remained unclear at this time. Work on the concept of the hedonic treadmill and surveys of the relationship between income and happiness nationally and internationally reflected the period's pessimism that Watergate, inflation, and an inglorious end to the war in Vietnam engendered. Despite Weil's optimism, the scourge of heroin and the crack epidemic, increasingly dominant in the 1980s, outweighed whatever benefits marijuana and LSD provided.

Moreover, many scholars did not communicate across disciplinary boundaries and published their findings in specialized journals, precluding opportunities for cross-pollination between different fields. Many of them evidenced little interest in writing in ways that would make their insights available to a wider public. More typically, work in the field privileged opaque over accessible prose. A few examples will suffice. Trivers began his essay on reciprocal altruism with complex language hardly designed to reach a wide audience as he noted that "altruistic behavior can be defined as behavior that benefits another organism, not closely related, while being apparently detrimental to the organism performing the behavior, benefit and detriment being defined in terms of contribution to inclusive fitness." Kahneman, who in 2011 would write an international bestseller, summarized what he and Tversky revealed in their 1979 article this way: "The value function is normally concave for gains, commonly convex for losses, and is generally steeper for losses than for gains." They illustrated one of their findings by remarking that "decision making under risk can be viewed as a choice between prospects or gambles. A prospect $(x1, Pi; \ldots; xn, pn)$ is a contract that yields outcome xi with probability Pi, where $Pl + P2 + \cdots + pn = 1$."[61]

Finally, there was one relatively lone but influential voice that readers took as questioning the pursuit of happiness as a goal. In his 1974 *Anarchy, State, and Utopia*, the libertarian political philosopher Robert Nozick included a brief section titled "The Experience Machine." In this thought experiment, Nozick asked readers to ponder whether they wanted to be plugged into such an apparatus that would give them whatever experience they desired. Perhaps, he remarked as he drew on his knowledge of contemporary experiments, "super-duper neuropsychologists could stimulate your brain so that you would think and feel you were writing a great novel, or making a friend, or reading an interesting book." Moving from speculation to criticism, Nozick asked what people wanted other than the experience of feeling something. The answer seemed clear: we want to do things, not just have the experiences we would have if we were doing them; we want to be a certain kind of person; and we want to go beyond "man-made reality, to a world no deeper or more important than that which people can construct," such as that represented by transcendent religious experiences.[62]

What many observers take as Nozick's questioning of hedonism and utilitarianism resonated powerfully. It emerged as a theme in the 1999 movie *The Matrix*. He was the professor who most influenced Seligman as an undergraduate. Teachers used Nozick's experiment in many classrooms around the world. Yet even though Nozick used the word experience or experiences more than two dozen times, he did not use the word happy or happiness in his discussion of the Experience Machine.[63] In experiments carried out decades later, out of thousands surveyed, about 5 percent said they preferred the happiness machine, while the remaining 95 percent "opt for work, social connections, and pain over orgasmic bliss."[64]

NOTES

1. Martin E. P. Seligman et al., *The Optimistic Child* (Boston: Houghton Mifflin, 1995), 51. Elizabeth Telfer, *Happiness* (London: Macmillan, 1980), published in this period, is a philosophical consideration of the difference between hedonistic and eudaimonic concepts of happiness.
2. Ruut Veenhoven, *Conditions of Happiness* (Dordrecht, Netherlands: D. Reidel, 1984), ix, 2–3, 119, 122.
3. Philip Brickman and Donald T. Campbell, "Hedonic Relativism and Planning the Good Society," in *Adaptation-Level Theory: A Symposium*, ed. M. H. Appley (New York: Academic Press, 1971), 287, 289. For later revisions to the theory, see Ed Diener, Richard E. Lucas, and Christie Napa Scollon, "Beyond the Hedonic Treadmill: Revising the Adaptation Level Theory of Well-Being," *AP* 61 (May–June 2006): 305–14. On adaptation level theory or hedonic adaptation, the key texts are Harry Helson, *Adaptation-Level Theory: An Experimental and Systematic Approach to Behavior* (New York: Harper & Row, 1964), with the original article as Harry Helson, "Adaptation-Level as Frame of Reference for Prediction of Psychophysical Data," *American Journal of Psychology* 60 (Jan. 1947): 1–29.
4. Daniel Kahneman, "Objective Happiness," in *Well-Being: Foundations of Hedonic Psychology*, ed. Daniel Kahneman, Ed Diener, and Norbert Schwarz (New York: Russell Sage Foundation, 1999), 13–14.
5. David C. McClelland, "Comment," in Appley, *Adaptation-Level Theory*, 303; Brickman and Campbell, "Hedonic Relativism," 290, 296–97, 300. For another study of social comparison in the period, see Howard S. Friedman and Ronald E. Riggio, "Effect of Individual Differences in Nonverbal Expressiveness on Transmission of Emotion," *Journal of Nonverbal Behavior* 6 (Winter 1981): 96–104.
6. For others who fostered the shift from cognition to emotion, see Donald R. Griffin's *Animal Minds: Beyond Cognition to Consciousness* (Chicago: University of Chicago Press, 2001) and the work of the sociobiologist Edward O. Wilson.
7. Paul Ekman, "Universals and Cultural Differences in Facial Expressions of Emotion," in *Nebraska Symposium on Motivation, 1971*, ed. James K. Cole (Lincoln: University of Nebraska Press, 1972), 277–79; Paul Ekman, ed., *Darwin and Facial Expression: A Century of Research in Review* (New York: Academic Press, 1973), including his "Introduction" (1–10) and "Cross-Cultural Studies of Facial Expression" (169–222). Among those Ekman influenced were Dacher Keltner, who had a postdoc with Ekman in the early 1990s and soon after began to publish articles with him on what smiles revealed of emotions; Richard J. Davidson, who prefers to call himself an affective neuroscientist rather than a positive

psychologist; and Barbara Fredrickson, whose transformative broaden and build theory of emotions drew on Ekman's pioneering work on emotions: see Dacher Keltner, conversation with author, March 29, 2016, and Dacher Keltner, email to author, Sept. 15, 2016; http://richardjdavidson.com/research/; and Barbara J. Fredrickson, "Positive Emotions Broaden and Build," in *Advances in Experimental Social Psychology* 47, ed. Patricia Devine and Ashby Plant (New York: Academic Press, 2013), 1–53.

8. Robert L. Trivers, "The Evolution of Reciprocal Altruism," *Quarterly Review of Biology* 46 (March 1971): 35, 48, 49. Steven Pinker called Trivers "one of the great thinkers in the history of Western thought": Steven Pinker, quoted in Drake Bennett, "The Evolutionary Revolutionary," *Boston Globe*, March 27, 2005. In "Influence of Extraversion and Neuroticism on Subjective Well-Being: Happy and Unhappy People," *JPSP* 38 (April 1980): 668–78, Paul T. Costa and Robert R. McCrae provided others with the material that made it possible to suggest the existence of a happiness gene. For such a use, see Michael W. Eysenck, *Happiness: Facts and Myths* (Hove, UK: Erlbaum, 1990), 20–22.

9. Robert Trivers, quoted in Bennett, "Evolutionary"; Edward O. Wilson, *Sociobiology: The New Synthesis* (Cambridge, MA: Harvard University Press, 1975), 3–4. Trivers and Wilson were hardly the first postwar writers to emphasize the impact of evolution on human behavior: see, for example, Konrad Lorenz, *On Aggression*, trans. Marjorie K. Wilson (New York: Harcourt, Brace, and World, 1966); Robert Ardrey, *African Genesis: A Personal Investigation into the Animal Origins and Nature of Man* (New York: Atheneum, 1961); Robert Ardrey, *Territorial Imperative: A Personal Inquiry into the Animal Origins of Property and Nations* (New York: Atheneum, 1966); Desmond Morris, *Naked Ape: A Zoologist's Study of the Human Animal* (New York: McGraw-Hill, 1967).

10. Vassiliki Betty Smocovitis, *Unifying Biology: The Evolutionary Synthesis and Evolutionary Biology* (Princeton, NJ: Princeton University Press, 1996), xi. The work of Smocovitis is but one example of scholarship on science that reveals trends parallel to the emergence of positive psychology: see, for example, Marga Vicedo, *The Nature and Nurture of Love: From Imprinting to Attachment in Cold War America* (Chicago: University of Chicago Press, 2013); Erika L. Milam, *Looking for a Few Good Males: Female Choice in Evolutionary Biology* (Baltimore: Johns Hopkins University Press, 2010); and Robert M. Sapolsky, *A Primate's Memoir* (New York: Scribner's, 2001).

11. Alice M. Isen and Paula F. Levin, "Effect of Feeling Good on Helping: Cookies and Kindness," *JPSP* 21 (March 1972): 384–88.

12. Phillip R. Kunz and Michael Woolcott, "Season's Greetings: From My Status to Yours," *Social Science Research* 5 (Sept. 1976): 271; "People Answer Strangers' Christmas Cards," *The Spokesman-Review*, Dec. 19, 1975; Roy F. Baumeister and Mark R. Leary, "The Need to Belong: Desire for Interpersonal Attachments as a Fundamental Human Motivation," *PB* 117 (May 1995): 502; Melanie Tannenbaum, "I'll Show You My Holiday Card If You Show Me Yours,"*Psysociety* (online publication of *Scientific American*), Jan. 2, 2015, https://blogs.scientificamerican.com/psysociety/i-8217-ll-show-you-my-holiday-card-if-you-show-me-yours/. Among the other studies that would influence positive psychology and happiness studies were those that focused on how social comparison affected self-esteem: see, for example, Stan Morse and Kenneth J. Gergen, "Social Comparison, Self-Consistency, and the Concept of Self," *JPSP* 16 (Sept. 1970): 148–56; Thomas A. Wills, "Downward Comparison Principles in Social Psychology," *PB* 90 (Sept. 1981): 245–71. For an essay that brought together social comparison, the hedonic treadmill, and policy issues, see Richard Layard, "Human Satisfactions and Public Policy," *Economic Journal* 90 (Dec. 1980): 737–50.

13. Richard Easterin, "Does Money Buy Happiness?" *Public Interest* 30 (Winter 1973): 7; Richard A. Easterlin, "Does Economic Growth Improve the Human Lot? Some Empirical Evidence," in *Nations and Households in Economic Growth: Essays in Honor of Moses*

Abramovitz, ed. Paul A. David and Melvin W. Reder (New York: Academic Press, 1974), 89–125, with the quote on p. 90.

14. Richard E, Easterlin, *Birth and Fortune: The Impact of Numbers on Personal Welfare* (New York: Basic Books, 1980), 40.

15. Mihaly Csikszentmihalyi, *Beyond Boredom and Anxiety* (San Francisco: Jossey-Bass, 1975); five other scholars made contributions to this book. For biographical information, I draw on Mihaly Csikszentmihalyi, conversation with author, Feb. 6, 2015, but especially on Mihaly Csikszentmihalyi, "Preface to the 25th Anniversary Edition," in Mihaly Csikszentmihalyi, *Beyond Boredom and Anxiety* (San Francisco: Jossey-Bass, 2000), ix–xxx, where he made clear his intellectual indebtedness to a wide range of people including Edmund Husserl, Carl Rogers, and Abraham Maslow.

16. Csikszentmihalyi, *Beyond Boredom*, 9, 182, 196, 206.

17. Csikszentmihalyi, *Beyond Boredom*, 33.

18. Philip Brickman, Dan Coates, and Ronnie Janoff-Bulman, "Lottery Winners and Accident Victims: Is Happiness Relative?" *JPSP* 36 (August 1978): 918. Martin E. P. Seligman, *Flourish: A Visionary New Understanding of Happiness and Well-Being* (New York: Simon & Schuster, 2011), 280–81 points out that the study revealed that it was more difficult to increase than decrease happiness. In *The Pools Winners* (London: Caliban Books, 1975), Stephen Smith and Peter Razell examined the lives of lottery winners and found that the windfall made most of them undramatically happier. Although paraplegics did recover, there were several events that tested people's ability to adapt—the loss of a job or a spouse, and the long-term intensive care for a loved one who suffered from dementia. For a recent review and critique of the theory of how lottery winners adapted, see "Keeping Up with the Karumes," *Economist*, Oct. 31, 2015.

19. Brickman, Coates, and Janoff-Bulman, "Is Happiness Relative?" 921, 924, 926.

20. Kahneman, "Objective," 14, 16. For another classic study, see David Schkade and Daniel Kahneman, "Does Living in California Make People Happy? A Focusing Illusion in Judgments of Life Satisfaction," *PS* 9 (Sept. 1998): 340–46.

21. Daniel Kahneman and Amos Tversky, "Prospect Theory: An Analysis of Decision under Risk," *Econometrica* 47 (March, 1979): 263–91. Michael Lewis, *The Undoing Project: A Friendship That Changed Our Minds* (New York: W.W. Norton, 2017) chronicles the relationship between Kahneman and Tversky.

22. Daniel Kahneman, "Daniel Kahneman-Biographical," on the Nobel Prize web site, http:// www.nobelprize.org/nobel_prizes/economic-sciences/laureates/2002/kahneman-bio. html; Richard Thaler, "Toward a Positive Theory of Consumer Choice," *Journal of Economic Behavior and Organization* 1 (Feb. 1980): 58. See also Richard H. Thaler, *Misbehaving: The Making on Behavioral Economics* (New York: W.W. Norton, 2015). Tversky died in 1996, and six years later Kahneman won the Nobel Prize in economics for the work on which they had collaborated.

23. Richard M. Nixon, "State of the Union Address," Jan. 22, 1970, http://www.infoplease. com/t/hist/state-of-the-union/183.html. The key documents are Raymond A. Bauer, ed., *Social Indicators* (Cambridge, MA: MIT Press, 1966); U.S. Department of Health, Education, and Welfare, *Toward a Social Report* (Washington, DC: GPO, 1969); Report of the National Goals Research Staff, *Toward Balanced Growth: Quantity with Quality* (Washington, DC: GPO, 1970). On the effort in Bhutan to measure Gross National Happiness, see http://www.grossnationalhappiness.com/wp-content/uploads/2012/ 04/Short-GNH-Index-edited.pdf. In 2013, that nation turned away from committing itself to measure progress by a happiness index: http://www.nytimes.com/2013/10/05/ world/asia/index-of-happiness-bhutans-new-leader-prefers-more-concrete-goals.html. In this period, as in many others, there were relatively few studies that focused on the relationship between happiness, politics, and society.

24. In the United States and abroad, the 1970s saw the launching of major surveys, though, unlike the University of Michigan's efforts, most of them did not initially focus directly or primarily on subjective well-being. Such a list would begin with the University of Chicago's General Social Survey of 1972.

25. Angus Campbell, *The Sense of Well-Being in America: Recent Patterns and Trends* (New York: McGraw-Hill, 1981), 27. Among the other pre-1982 studies I have relied on are Norman M. Bradburn and David Caplovitz, *Reports on Happiness: A Pilot Study of Behavior Related to Mental Health* (Chicago: Aldine, 1965); Norman M. Bradburn and C. Edward Noll, *The Structure of Psychological Well-Being* (Chicago: Aldine, 1969); Angus Campbell, "Aspiration, Satisfaction, and Fulfillment," in *The Meaning of Social Change*, ed. Angus Campbell and Philip E. Converse (New York: Russell Sage Foundation, 1972), 441–66; Frank M. Andrews and Stephen B. Withey, *Social Indicators of Well-Being: Americans' Perceptions of Life Quality* (New York: Plenum, 1976). There is a robust debate among scholars about whether any single question provides a proper evaluation of subjective well-being. Like those involved with the Oxford Happiness Inventory or Satisfaction with Life Scales, most investigators rely on multiple questions. For the debate over this issue, see Arthur H. Goldsmith et al., "Adult Happiness and Prior Traumatic Victimization In and Out of the Household," *Review of Economics of the Household*, https://www.research-gate.net/publication/302981038_Adult_happiness_and_prior_traumatic_victimization_in_and_out_of_the_household.

26. Campbell, *Sense*, 6, 9, 11, 37. In *Britain on the Couch: Why We're Unhappier Compared With 1950 Despite Being Richer: A Treatment for the Low-Serotonin Society* (London: Century Random House, 1997), Oliver James argued that what explained the decline in satisfaction despite the increase in national wealth was that advanced capitalism, by emphasizing dissatisfactions that stemmed from social comparisons, created a low-serotonin society.

27. Campbell, *Sense*, 50, 69–70.

28. Campbell, *Sense*, 224, 225. It is possible that Campbell's emphasis on the impact of tumultuous events of the 1970s influenced his findings.

29. Joseph Wood Krutch, "Through Happiness with Slide Rule and Caliper," *Saturday Review*, Nov. 2, 1962, quoted in Campbell, "Aspiration," 463. For a summary of critiques, see Norbert Schwarz and Fritz Strack, "Reports of Subjective Well-Being: Judgmental Processes and Their Methodological Implications," in Kahneman, Diener, and Schwarz, *Well-Being*, 61–84. For discussions at the time, see T. W. Smith, "Happiness," *Social Psychology Quarterly* 42 (March 1979): 18–30; Brickman and Campbell, "Hedonic Relativism," 287–302; Otis D. Duncan, "Does Money Buy Satisfaction?" *SIR* 2 (Dec. 1975): 267–74.

30. Herbert Benson et al., "Decreased Systolic Blood Pressure Through Operant Conditioning Techniques in Patients with Essential Hypertension," *Science*, Aug. 20, 1971, 740–42.

31. Herbert Benson, *The Relaxation Response* (New York: Morrow, 1975), 124; Herbert Benson, "Foreword: Twenty-fifth Anniversary Edition Update," in *Relaxation* (New York: HarperCollins, 2000), ix–liv. In the following footnotes, all references using roman numerals are to the Foreword; all others, to the original book. Benson was one of the few writers who, in contributing to the development of happiness studies, paid much attention to women's liberation: see, for example, Benson, *Relaxation*, 3. References to meditation in scientific journals began to take off in 1975, plateaued later on, and then began to climb rapidly: see chart in Jon Kabat-Zinn, Richard J. Davidson, and Zara Houshmand, eds., *The Mind's Own Physician: A Scientific Dialogue with the Dalai Lama on the Healing Power of Meditation* (Oakland, CA: New Harbinger, 2011), 7. On the way the Dalai Lama, beginning in 1979, made it possible for Benson to study the scientific dimensions of meditation practice by Tibetian Buddhists , see Anne Harrington, *The Cure*

Within: A History of Mind-Body Medicine (New York: W.W. Norton, 2008), 231–34; see Harrington, Cure Within, 214–20 for her discussion of Benson.

32. Benson, Relaxation, x.

33. Benson, Relaxation, 123.

34. This section relies heavily on Jeff Wilson, Mindful America: The Mutual Transformation of Buddhist Meditation and American Culture (New York: Oxford University Press, 2014), which tracks the arrival and adaptation of Buddhism and mindfulness in America. Among other key events of the 1970s were the publication of Shunryu Suzuki and Trudy Dixon's Zen Mind, Beginner's Mind in 1970, Thich Nhat Hahn, The Miracle of Mindfulness! A Manual on Meditation in 1976, the opening of Naropa University in 1974, and the launching of Jon Kabat-Zinn's Stress Reduction Clinic at the University of Massachusetts Medical School in 1979.

35. Benson, Relaxation, xxxi.

36. On the book's impact, see Benson, Relaxation, "Foreword," ix–liv; http://www.mind/body.harvard.edu.

37. Benson, Relaxation, 110.

38. Andrew Weil, The Natural Mind: A New Way of Looking at Drugs and the Higher Consciousness (Boston: Houghton Mifflin, 1972), 19, 204.

39. Weil, Natural Mind, 17, 36, 72, 202.

40. For a rare and brief mention, see Weil, Natural Mind, 41.

41. Paul Meehl, "Hedonic Capacity: Some Conjectures," Bulletin of the Menninger Clinic 39 (July, 1975): 295–307; Donald F. Klein, "Endogenomorphic Depression: A Conceptual and Terminological Revision," Archives of General Psychiatry 31 (Oct. 1974): 447–54; Peter Kramer, Listening to Prozac (New York: Viking Penguin, 1993), 228–33. Darrin M. McMahon, Happiness: A History (New York, Atlantic Monthly Press, 2005), 442–51 discusses Sigmund Freud's deep pessimism about the prospect of achieving happiness, expressed in Civilization and Its Discontents (1930), a book originally titled "Unhappiness in Civilization."

42. Robert Heath, "Modulation of Emotion with a Brain Pacemaker: Treatment for Intractable Psychiatric Illness," Journal of Nervous and Mental Disease 165 (Nov. 1977): 300–17; for a discussion of this and other studies, see Richard M. Restak, The Brain: The Last Frontier (Garden City, NY: Doubleday, 1979), 125–33.

43. David Healy, The Creation of Psychopharmacology (Cambridge, MA: Harvard University Press, 2002), 6. For his detailed history of the discovery of receptors, see 178–228. For a critique of the narrative that chronicles a decisive shift from the psychological to the biological, see Jonathan Michel Metzl, Prozac on the Couch (Durham, NC: Duke University Press, 2003).

44. This section relies heavily on Andrea Tone, The Age of Anxiety: A History of America's Turbulent Affair with Tranquilizers (New York: Basic, 2009), 166–68, with the quote on 167, and on David Herzberg, Happy Pills in America: From Miltown to Prozac (Baltimore: Johns Hopkins University Press, 2009), 170–72. A transformative moment in neuroscience came in 1973 when Solomon Snyder and Candace Pert discovered the opioid receptor in the brain.

45. Steven M. Paul quoted in Harold M. Schmeck Jr., "The Biology of Fear and Anxiety: Evidence Points to Chemical Triggers," NYT, Sept. 7, 1982, C1; Seymour Rosenblatt and Reynolds Dodson, Beyond Valium: The Brave New World of Psychochemistry (New York: G.P. Putnam, 1981), 23; Rita Christopher "The Mystery of Moods—It's All in the Mind," Maclean's, Oct. 1, 1979, 46–49, quoted in Herzberg, Happy Pills, 171. For a later, more technical, and somewhat more tentative assessment, see Solomon H. Snyder, Drugs and the Brain (New York: Scientific American Books, 1986).

46. Rosenblatt and Dodson, Beyond Valium, 237–39, 242.

47. Wayne W. Dyer, *Your Erroneous Zones* (New York: Funk and Wagnalls, 1976), which assumed true and full happiness was possible by overcoming self-destructive behavior, was the only of these books that was immensely successful. Walt Menninger, *"Caution: Living May be Hazardous": Debunking the Happiness Myth* (Kansas City, KS: Sheed Andrews and McMeel, 1978) deployed a series of brief stories to insist that we can learn from painful experiences and that life is not just about happiness. Florence Littauer's *The Pursuit of Happiness* (Eugene, OR: Harvest House, 1978) offered a series of personal stories that reveal how Christians can achieve satisfaction in their lives. Drawing on both Abraham Maslow's self-actualizing theories and Aaron Beck's cognitive behavioral therapy, Albert Ellis and Irving M. Becker's *A Guide to Personal Happiness* (North Hollywood: Wilshire Book Company, 1982) used materials from therapeutic sessions to demonstrate how an emphasis on putting oneself first leads to personal happiness. Paul Watzlawick, *The Situation Is Hopeless, But Not Serious* (New York: W.W. Norton, 1983) provided a witty and quirky critique of how people make themselves miserable, resulting in the achievement of happiness being more elusive. In 1982 two psychologists published a book that resembled much of what scholars in happiness studies and positive psychology would later emphasize, but the book appeared from a minor press and garnered no reviews in either psychological or general interest publications: E. M. Suarez and Roger C. Mills, *Sanity, Insanity, and Common Sense: The Missing Link in Understanding Mental Health* (West Allis, WI: Med-Psych Publications, 1982).
48. Jonathan L. Freedman, *Happy People: What Happiness Is, Who Has It, and Why* (New York: Harcourt Brace Jovanovich, 1978), 9, 37, 64–72. One important innovation was the inclusion of data on the relationship between homosexuality and happiness: Freedman, *Happy People*, 64–72. Additional proof that happiness studies had not yet emerged as a field comes from Freedman referring to very few works available then that over time would achieve canonical status in the field.
49. Tibor Scitovsky, *The Joyless Economy: An Inquiry into Human Satisfaction and Consumer Dissatisfaction* (New York: Oxford University Press, 1976), ix.
50. Scitovsky, *Joyless*, 4, 151, 204, 206, 208.
51. Christopher Lasch, *The Culture of Narcissism: American Life in an Age of Diminishing Expectations* (New York: W.W. Norton, 1978), 51, 63–64, 71–74; Thomas A. Harris, *I'm OK, You're OK: A Practical Guide to Transactional Analysis* (New York: Harper & Row, 1969). For a critique of Lasch's book, see Elizabeth Lunbeck, *The Americanization of Narcissism* (Cambridge, MA: Harvard University Press, 2014).
52. For later reconsiderations in Bhutan, see http://www.nytimes.com/2013/10/05/world/asia/index-of-happiness-bhutans-new-leader-prefers-more-concrete-goals.html?_r=0.
53. Norman Cousins, "Anatomy of an Illness (as Perceived by the Patient)," *New England Journal of Medicine* 295 (Dec. 23, 1976): 1458–63; Norman Cousins, *Anatomy of an Illness as Perceived by the Patient: Reflections on Healing and Regeneration* (New York: W.W. Norton, 1979), 34–35. See also Harrington, *Cure Within*, 122–26.
54. Among the books that were harbingers of the future were Csikszentmihalyi's *Flow* and two others—James J. Lynch, *The Broken Heart: the Medical Consequences of Loneliness* (New York: Basic, 1977), and Lionel Tiger, *Optimism: The Biology of Hope* (New York: Simon & Schuster, 1979)—that explored the scientific basis of positivity.
55. Daniel Goleman and Richard J. Davidson, eds., *Consciousness, Brain, States of Awareness, and Mysticism* (New York: Harper & Row, 1979); Daniel Goleman, *Varieties of Meditative Experience* (New York: Irvington, 1977), a discussion of traditions from a variety of religious traditions; Howard Gardner, *Frames of Mind: The Theory of Multiple Intelligences* (New York: Basic, 1983), x.
56. In Michael Argyle, *The Psychology of Happiness* (London: Methuen, 1987), a summary of current findings, the author devoted a few pages (134–37) to "The Physiological Basis of

Positive Emotions." For examples, see Michael Cabanac, "Physiological Role of Pleasure," *Science*, Sept. 17, 1961, 1103–07; Richard Squires and Claus Braestrup, "Benzodiazepine Receptors in Rat Brain," *Nature* 266 (April 21, 1977): 732–34; Robert Karasek et al., "Job Decision Latitude, Job Demands, and Cardiovascular Disease: A Prospective Study of Swedish Men," *American Journal of Public Health* 71 (July 1981): 694–705.

57. Richard J. Davidson and Daniel J. Goleman, "The Role of Attention in Meditation and Hypnosis: a Psychobiological Perspective on Transformations of Consciousness," *International Journal of Clinical and Experimental Hypnosis* 25 (Oct. 1977): 291–308.

58. Ann S. Masten, "Ordinary Magic: Resilience Processes in Development," *AP* 56 (March 2001): 227–38 discusses how in the 1970s psychologists discovered resilience among at-risk children.

59. John C. Masters, R. Christopher Barden, and Martin E. Ford, "Affective States, Expressive Behavior, and Learning in Children," *JPSP* 37 (March 1979): 380; William H. Sledge, James A. Boydstun, and Alton J. Rabe, "Self-Concept Changes Related to War Captivity," *Archives of General Psychiatry* 37 (May 1980): 430–43; Judith Rodin and Ellen J. Langer, "Long-Term Effects of a Control-Relevant Intervention with the Institutionalized Aged," *JPSP* 35 (Dec. 1977): 897–202; Ellen J. Langer, *Mindfulness* (Reading, MA: Addison-Wesley, 1989), 81–113; Michael W. Fordyce, "Development of a Program to Increase Personal Happiness," *Journal of Counseling Psychology* 24 (Nov. 1977): 511–21.

60. Peter Lewinsohn and Julian Libet, "Pleasant Events, Activity Schedules, and Depressions," *Journal of Abnormal Psychology* 79 (June, 1972): 291–95; Fred B. Bryant and Joseph Veroff, "The Structure of Psychological Well-Being: A Sociohistorical Analysis," *JPSP* 43 (Oct. 1982): 653–73.

61. Trivers, "Reciprocal Altruism," 3; Kahneman and Tversky, "Prospect Theory," 263.

62. Robert Nozick, *Anarchy, State, and Utopia* (New York: Basic, 1974), 42–43. Fred Feldman, "What Do We Learn from the Experience Machine?" in *Cambridge Companion to Nozick's Anarchy, State, and Utopia*, ed. Ralph M. Bader and John Meadowcroft (Cambridge, UK: Cambridge University Press, 2011), 59–86 points out the common misunderstanding of Nozick's position and that the evidence he presents does not support such claims.

63. Sissela Bok, *Exploring Happiness: From Aristotle to Brain Science* (New Haven, CT: Yale University Press, 2010), 25.

64. Ed Diener and Robert Biswas-Diener, *Happiness: Unlocking the Mysteries of Psychological Wealth* (Malden, MA: Blackwell, 2008), 249.

CHAPTER 4

Morning in America, 1984–1998

Assembling Key Elements in the Study of Happiness and Positivity

I choose 1984 as a turning point in the history of happiness studies for several reasons. To begin with, this was around the time the Library of Congress established BF 204.6 as the call number for books on happiness, acknowledging its status as a bona fide subfield in psychology. In addition, as discussed in the previous chapter, in that year the Dutch scholar Ruut Veenhoven reported in his *Conditions of Happiness* that, despite the 245 studies he reviewed in the field of happiness studies and long-standing promises of a burgeoning new field, programmatic research remained in the distance with the subject "still the Cinderella it always was." Eleven years later, still the leading figure in globalizing of happiness studies, he returned to examine the topic once again. Now he reported that his "World Data Base of Happiness" referenced 2,472 studies on "the subjective appreciation of life." He concluded that although "this stream of research has not yet crystallized into a sound body of knowledge on happiness" and "the understanding of processes and conditions involved in determinants and consequences of happiness is still very incomplete and tentative," scholars had largely resolved key issues of how to conceive and measure happiness. He went on to explore the reasons all the scholarly attention had "not yet brought the expected break-through." The subject matter was highly complex, the scholarship uncoordinated, terms poorly defined, correlations only loosely examined, and international comparisons rarely explored with any rigor. Nonetheless, despite his cautionary notes, an examination of scholarly research on happiness carried out between the mid-1980s and the late

1990s reveals more considerable progress and visibility than Veenhoven acknowledged. On the eve of Martin Seligman's announcement of the birth of positive psychology, happiness studies and the as-yet-unnamed positive psychology were beginning to flourish, spurred in part by the recovery from the national traumas of the 1970s and signs of renewed optimism in the ensuing decade.[1]

In important ways, morning in positive psychology dovetailed with "Morning in America," the title of a legendarily effective advertisement for Ronald Reagan's 1984 campaign. Avoiding negative attacks on the challenger Walter Mondale, just as positive psychologists sought to take attention away from negativity, the advertisement offered feel-good, positive images and words. Picturing a middle-class, mostly if not entirely white world and one that referenced farms but not factories, it emphasized jobs, marriages, suburban domesticity, and patriotism.[2]

This came at a time when the leadership of presidents Ronald Reagan, George H. W. Bush, and William Clinton were promoting conservative and neoliberal policies that eroded the social safety net and exposed people to market forces in a world shaped by globalization and technological change. After the traumas of the 1970s, it was morning in America, although the culture wars, multiple recessions, and wrenching economic changes caution us not to offer sweeping, positive assessments of these years. To be sure, academic fields develop through an internal logic all their own and the relationship between national mood and scholarly advances is not always strong or consistent; indeed in some cases advances in the field were at odds with political currents. Nonetheless, a number of aspects of positive psychology a-birthing bore some connection to the moods and policies engendered by national politics. Among them were a weakening of fights for social justice, an attack on big government, the emphasis on personal as opposed to social factors in explaining subjective well-being, the focus on mind–body relationships that emphasized the brain and meditation rather than social policy as critical in fostering happiness, definitions of happiness that stressed character and virtue, and the preference in drug policy for pharmaceuticals that promised rebirth rather than illegal ones that led to jail. If the end of the Soviet Union heralded an end to the Cold War, inner peace achieved through a wide range of methods was also at hand.

DR. HAPPINESS SURVEYS THE FIELD

If Veenhoven in 1995 reported both a ten-fold increase in the number of studies in a little over a dozen years and somewhat disappointing progress in turning disparate studies into a cohesive field, 1984 nonetheless offered reason for hope, even though in some quarters the nature of advances in research may have confirmed George Orwell's vision in *Nineteen Eighty-Four* of a dystopian world where threats to privacy and excessive social engineering were abundant. Moreover, many social and behavioral economists remained skeptical about claims by positive psychology that they were closing in on fully convincing scientific conclusions. In some quarters observers wondered about the causes and consequences of happiness. Economists focused on problems of endogeneity—problems associated with confusing correlation with causation. Did happiness lead to marriage, or did marriage foster happiness? Were some variables mistakenly emphasized or others simply ignored? Given that many psychologists have an easier time evaluating the well-being of individuals, what happens when they shift their attention to judgments of collective well-being? What problems emerged from the tendency of positive psychologists to rely too heavily on convenient samples such as readily available college students rather than broader, randomly selected populations, which would make their conclusions more generalizable?[3]

Nonetheless, the most important piece of evidence of scholarly advances in the field of positive psychology, published more than a dozen years before Seligman's presidential address, was a major article titled "Subjective Well-Being" that appeared in the American Psychological Association's *Psychological Bulletin*, written by University of Illinois professor Ed Diener. If Seligman was the entrepreneur who had a knack for both original scholarship and for bringing the work of himself and others to large audiences, then among Americans, Diener was the founding scholar in the modern study of happiness. Later called by *Time* "Dr. Happiness" in an essay marking the tenth anniversary of Seligman's presidential address, for more than forty years beginning in the 1970s Diener produced foundational, pathbreaking scholarship.[4]

Diener's 1984 contribution was one of those scholarly efforts that both summarized where a field was and suggested where it might go. Diener announced that he was reviewing the literature on subjective well-being (SWB), a term that included happiness, life satisfaction, and positive affect. For a long time, he announced at the outset, "psychologists largely ignored positive subjective well-being," focusing instead on "human unhappiness." Only in the last decade had social and behavioral scientists begun to rectify this situation, with "theoretical and empirical work . . . emerging at an increasingly faster pace."[5]

The first of three topics Diener focused on was defining and measuring SWB, where he identified considerable recent advances. Researchers continued to rely on self-report data gathered through interviews and questionnaires. Students in the field had paid little attention to Aristotle's emphasis on eudaimonia as virtue or flourishing, focusing instead on hedonics or high-arousal positive affect. Diener noted the striking and controversial conclusion that negative and positive assessments seemed independent of one another, which suggested that they might be two distinct aspects of SWB, a possibility, he noted, that humanistic psychologists such as Carl Rogers and Abraham Maslow had emphasized as evidence that the profession had neglected the positive dimension and focused "too exclusively on the negative." Although Diener hailed the current state of scholarship on defining and measuring SWB, he identified areas that needed attention: whether happiness was a trait or a state; the ambiguities in the concept of happiness; and whether self-reporting provided accurate data.[6]

Diener then turned to his second topic, the causal factors that influenced people's happiness. When he looked at subjective ones, he noticed that self-esteem had a major and positive impact on happiness. Moreover, "satisfaction with standard of living and with family life were also highly correlated with life satisfaction, whereas the correlation for satisfaction with work" was only moderate and with "health and community" even lower. He pointed out the abundant evidence of a positive relationship between income and SWB within nations, though the relationship was weaker across national boundaries. As Richard Easterlin and others had noted, however, over time, real—as opposed to nominal—increases in income did not seem to produce significantly greater happiness, especially among people above the poverty level. Moreover, by the late 1970s, Diener, relying on the University of Michigan surveys, reported that the impact of higher incomes may have leveled off or even decreased. Affluence may have produced negative consequences of pollution and stress. Studies revealed weak correlations between happiness and both age and health. Intense friendships, love, and marriage increased the sense of satisfaction, while having children had a negative impact. People who were socially active and engaged were happier, but the relationship between cause and effect remained unclear. Education counted for relatively little, and the results for religion were far from clear. Diener revealed that social comparisons influenced the relationship between income and life satisfaction. "People may only know how satisfied they should be," he noted, "by comparing their situation with that of others."[7]

Even though by 1984 the civil rights and women's movements had claimed national attention for well over a decade and a half, Diener paid relatively little attention to race and gender in his essay, despite the fact that the extensive bibliography referred to many articles on these topics. He did note that because studies revealed that women experienced both greater joys and more negative affect, gender did not account for much overall difference in the experience of happiness. Younger women reported being happier than younger men, a situation that reversed itself around age 45. Married women reported being more stressed than their single counterparts, but they also reported higher levels of satisfaction. More than twenty years after the publication of Betty Friedan's *The Feminine Mystique* in 1963, the word "housework" did not appear in Diener's report. Nor did the phrase "social class." He duly noted the disastrous effects of unemployment, yet the word "poverty" appeared only once, with the announcement that once "basic needs are met," income did not affect levels of happiness.[8]

Diener also remarked that African Americans reported lower levels of SWB than their white counterparts, though factors such as age, income, marital status, and geographical location complicated the results. Moreover, the numbers of blacks surveyed was very small, which also compromised the ability to draw conclusions. "Despite apparent political advances made by blacks in the U.S. in the decades following World War II," he concluded, "there was no concomitant increase in happiness." Indeed, the blacks who might have most derived the greatest benefit from increased equality "were those who became most unhappy." He hypothesized that "with the political awakening of more educated blacks, their aspirations and hopes exceeded the gains that were actually made." In short, much of what he wrote—the emphasis on marriage and the family, along with the inattention to social class, gender, race, and poverty—dovetailed with major shifts in public policy.[9]

Having noted all the factors that influenced the levels of happiness Americans experienced, Diener nonetheless concluded that demographic forces appeared to have relatively little impact on happiness, again a perspective consistent with a shift from social conditions to personal circumstances. He called for further experimental, international, and longitudinal data, as well as greater focus on the role of temperament and personality—especially self-esteem, extraversion/introversion, and optimism/pessimism. He admitted that he would not focus on "biological (including heritability) or sociological theories." He made no mention of how the study of biochemistry, the nervous system, or evolutionary biology might enrich what remained his and the field's primary focus, psychology, with other aspects of the social sciences a distant second. Finally, Diener turned to the role of theories in explaining life satisfaction—and here he expressed disappointment. "Thus far," he reported, "few theories have received rigorous propositional development or probing empirical analyses. In addition, there has been no attempt to integrate the theories," he concluded in an otherwise generally upbeat essay.[10]

Six years after Diener's essay, President George H. W. Bush signed a presidential proclamation declaring the 1990s the Decade of the Brain. He hailed what scientists had already done and looked forward to future advances that would help "millions of Americans [who] are affected each year by disorders of the brain ranging from neurogenetic diseases to degenerative disorders such as Alzheimer's, as well as stroke, schizophrenia, autism, and impairments of speech, language, and hearing." The president's announcement came well after significant achievements in neuroscience, albeit relatively few of them at the time directly connected to happiness studies or positive psychology. Between 1977 and 1997, eight Nobel Prizes had been awarded for brain research. Universities had established and then expanded programs in neuroscience. The science of how the brain worked moved away from simplistic models to more complex ones that incorporated genetics, biology, chemistry, and conscious experiences. Among the technologies for studying how the brain worked especially promising was functional magnetic resonance imaging (fMRI). In contrast to the standard MRI technology typically used in medical settings to diagnose structural brain abnormalities while a patient is at rest, the fMRI enabled researchers to present emotionally evocative experimental stimuli in the scanner—such as images, sounds, or even performance tasks—and to observe change in the blood flow to various brain regions associated with the subject's response to them. First developed in the early 1990s, fMRI offered a way to carry out research on emotions.[11]

By the time Bush issued his proclamation, researchers had already begun to carry out the studies that over the long term would provide a scientific basis for well-being, yet its dissemination beyond specialized journals remained in the future. Many scientists, fearful of being compared to Frankenstein, had long confined their findings to scientific publications. "We are now beginning to understand what or 'who' the brain is," wrote two psychologists in 1984 in a book aimed at a wide audience, "but a great deal remains to be discovered in the neurosciences." Yet aside from the general issue of what remained to be found out, the most significant roadblock to promoting happiness through science was the focus on using neuroscience to elucidate problems rather than to promote well-being, something evident in the president's list of challenges. To be sure, the 1988 PBS series *The Mind*, and the accompanying book, did explore some of the reciprocal relationships between the brain and positive emotions, though most of the attention was on negative aspects such as pain, depression, and violence. To an even greater extent, in the Pulitzer Prize–winning *Molecules of the Mind: The Brave New Science of Molecular Psychology* (1987), the science writer Jon Franklin focused almost all of his attention on how neuroscience might cure addiction, schizophrenia, criminal behavior, depression, and phobias, only briefly mentioning how it might enhance the lives of relatively healthy people.[12]

Representing one of those pivotal moments when people took the risky leap across what seemed like fixed boundaries between fields, a key incident in the transition from negative to positive came with the Dalai Lama's 1992 visit to the University of Wisconsin–Madison campus to urge the psychologist Richard J. Davidson to use science to study kindness and compassion, not just depression. Beginning in the early 1970s Davidson had been involved in Eastern contemplative practice, which, in order to protect his reputation as a scientist, he had not made widely known. He was already well known for pathbreaking work on frontal asymmetry, which distinguished associations between the left and right sides of the brain and their relationships with positive and negative emotions, respectively. Soon after the visit Davidson shifted the focus of his lab. With his Wisconsin colleague Carol D. Ryff, he became one of a handful of prominent scholars who built the foundation for connecting science, particularly neuroscience, and positivity from the mid-1980s on, but especially in the 1990s.[13]

In a small but growing number of journal articles, researchers explored many connections between health and happiness. They discovered associations between changes in the body's brain and chemistry—whether brought on by laughter, watching a funny movie, or receiving support from friends and family—and positive health outcomes. They revealed that optimism and positivity were associated with reduced stress, shortened recovery time for major illnesses, a stronger immune system, and enhanced cognitive abilities. Slowly and haltingly, and paralleling what Herbert Benson had revealed earlier about the impact of meditation, the realization was emerging that interventions such as writing down positive thoughts, drawing support from social networks, or gaining more control at work enhanced physical well-being. In addition, scientists were coming to realize that not only were the relationships between emotions and the body bidirectional, but also that that there might be some connection between a sense of well-being and the brain's plasticity.[14]

Building on this foundation, for a decade beginning in the late 1980s, Ryff combined the hard science of happiness with capacious explorations of the philosophical implications of the meanings of what psychologists were discovering in the science of happiness. She drew on psychologists such as Gordon Allport, Erik Erikson, Marie Jahoda, and Abraham Maslow. As positive psychologists would do after the turn of the century, she made it clear that she rejected a limited view of happiness, which relied on a short-term sense of well-being. Instead, she preferred to emphasize "self-acceptance, positive relations with others, autonomy, environmental mastery, purpose in life, and personal growth." Countering the conclusion that demographic factors counted for so little in accounting for life satisfaction, something that could undercut attempts to work for social change though public policy, in a 1989 article in the *Journal of Personality and Social Psychology*, she stressed "more enduring life challenges such as having a sense of purpose and direction, achieving satisfying relationships with others, and gaining a sense of self-realization." Such commitments, she continued, "harken back to the deliberations of the Greeks regarding the difference between feeling good at the moment and the more demanding task of realizing one's true potential" and provided "guiding ideals that afford vitality and an ever-expanding source of standards for defining psychological well-being." As she wrote in 1995, it was clear that such emphases "point to aspects of positive functioning that are missing in current scientific studies of subjective well-being, and offer conceptually rich alternatives to the emphasis on negative functioning in mental health research."[15]

Then in early 1998, with Burton Singer, Ryff published a scholarly article that argued, at least as fully as Seligman would in his presidential address, for what would soon come to be known as positive psychology. "The refrain that positive health is 'more than the absence of illness' has long been heard," they remarked at the opening, pointing to statements by the World Health Organization in 1948 and Marie Jahoda ten years later. They then went on to advocate a bold, positive vision, emphasizing that "human wellness is at once about the mind and the body and their interconnections." They termed the chemical, physiological, and neurological dimensions of existing scientific research as "the physiological substrates of 'positive states on mind,'" and remarked that additional work on that topic constituted "key future directions for explication of mechanisms that underlie positive human health." They insisted on the importance of a broadly conceived vision of what comprised the good life. They urged scholars to move beyond a focus on fleeting pleasures connected with increased consumption and to instead focus on developing purpose and meaningful relationships with others and only secondarily concentrating on "greater self-regard." Following Viktor Frankl's writings, they insisted on not banishing negative emotions because "traumatic experience may, in some instances, be the route to achieving deeper meaning and purpose, closer ties to others, greater self-regard, and heightened mastery." Focusing on African cultures, Singer's specialty, they called into question whether there was a universal vision of the good life. Unlike individualistic Western approaches, the African ones were collectivistic and defined the good life in terms of beneficence, forbearance, practical wisdom, improvisation, forgiveness, and justice. Finally, emphasizing the importance of diet, exercise, medications, volunteer and paid work, and greater social equality, they suggested how scientists and health care professionals could develop agendas for improving people's lives.[16]

Nonetheless, despite these considerable gains, by 1998, researchers had not always or often made explicit the connections between changes in the body, health, and positivity. Scientific advances were not yet integrated into a comprehensive field.[17]

EVEN BETTER LIVING THROUGH CHEMISTRY

Over time, advances in brain science transformed psychopharmacology— and people's lives—in ways that dovetailed with the emerging fields of happiness studies and positive psychology. These gains also coincided with shifts in national drug policy and with the turn from social policy to personal transformation seen as well in increasing emphasis on neuroscience and meditation. Beginning in the 1950s, scientists and pharmaceutical companies worked to find an antidepressant wonder drug—for decades to no avail as side effects plagued discoveries. In the 1970s, anti-anxiety drugs like Valium, whose sales peaked in 1978, had come under increasing attack for having adverse side effects and especially a negative impact on women's aspirations. Although Valium and other anti-anxiety drugs had discredited the notion that they that would simultaneously transform the industry and peoples' lives, writers, scientists, and pharmaceutical companies were developing what the historian David Herzberg called a "vision of technologically crafted drugs emerging from the newly sophisticated brain science" that would eventually "permit control of the brain so precise that it would move doctors beyond curing illness to providing a nearly unlimited range of consumer choices for custom-built selves." As Herzberg has written, antidepressants would become a means "for popularizing the new brain sciences and the revolutionary consumer good they would soon provide: the 'designer brain.'" As an antidote to depression, they promised to accomplish more than simply making people less depressed; rather, Herzberg has observed, "they would enhance, augment, and otherwise improve normal mental and emotional states as desired."[18]

Prozac was the transformative, blockbuster drug that many patients, corporations, and scientists had long waited for. On the market in 1987 as a selective serotonin reuptake inhibitor (SSRI), it quickly emerged as one of a handful of prescription pills that annually registered more than $1 billion in sales. As opposed to the sedating effects of other drugs, it promised to empower women. It appeared during the Reagan administration when a renewed war on street drugs targeted crack cocaine users in the nation's inner cities. The distinction between legal and illegal drugs enhanced the respectability of pills like Prozac and the profits of corporations that made them. Further elevation came in March 1990, when *Newsweek* featured Prozac on its cover. The article inside quoted Providence, Rhode Island, psychiatrist Peter Kramer, who remarked that eventually there might be a drug that could "change people in ways they want to be changed—not just away from illness but toward some desirable psychological state." In 1990 Kramer had coined the phrase "cosmetic psychopharmacology." Three years later, he published *Listening to Prozac*, a book that transformed the drug and Kramer's life.[19]

Kramer came to combine the careers of writer and psychiatrist by routes that at least in retrospect seem overdetermined, in a life he characterized as "up from melancholy." His parents and some of his relatives escaped the Holocaust by coming to America, where his father pursued a career as a pharmacist. As an undergraduate at Harvard in the class of 1970, he majored in History and Literature, which deepened his interest in and command of literature and philosophy. Writing for the *Harvard Crimson* in response to the student takeover of an administrative building, he explored, more as an observer than as a participant, the ways student radicals wove together politics and emotions. On a Marshall Fellowship in London, he began a course of Freudian psychoanalytic therapy, during which he realized he wanted to become a psychoanalyst. His analyst made it clear to him, in Kramer's words, that what shaped his career choice was a "desire to protect my relatives—the need to ward off depression and to conquer disease." He then entered Harvard Medical School, where he earned his MD and continued his engagement with Freudianism. During his residency at Yale, he studied community mental health and the biological dimensions of mental illness. By 1985, as a writer he had begun to reach a wider audience among mental health professionals through a regular column in *Psychiatric Times*. Those essays helped him gain access to an even wider readership. Writing in the morning and seeing patients in the afternoon, Kramer authored a series of books, both fiction and non-fiction, that focused on how to understand happiness.[20]

In *Listening to Prozac* Kramer presented an informed, nuanced, probing, and accessibly written presentation of the drug's impact. He mixed discussions of brain science, evolutionary biology, stories from canonical literature, insights from philosophers, distinctions between prescribed and illegal drugs, and tales of patients, mostly middle-class white professionals, many of them women whom the drug had helped to become more effectively assertive. He pondered what it meant to have a drug that, without serious side effects, helped transform its consumers into people who, as one patient put it, were "better than well."[21] He focused on "fairly healthy people who show dramatic good responses to Prozac, people who are not so much cured of illness as transformed." Kramer carefully explored the benefits of treatment that integrated psychotherapy and drugs, offering a suggestive analysis of the interaction of biology and personal history. Above all, he helped readers think about what a drug that altered moods and personality meant for our understanding of the self, personality, character, authenticity, and identity. Kramer examined the profound ethical issues that transformations by medication raised: not only how Prozac challenged our understanding of human nature but also whether "we are using medication in the service of conformity to societal values." He also suggestively wondered about the cultural and historical context in which Prozac had become so compelling. "The success of Prozac," he wrote as he described one consequence of neoliberalism, "says that today's high tech capitalism values a very different temperament," one characterized by "confidence, flexibility, quickness, and energy."[22]

Kramer found his perspective shaped and reshaped by the experiences of his patients. What distinguished the narratives he presented were the transformative power and "the immediacy of the metamorphosis" they reported. This contrasted with how Freudians, philosophers, and novelists thought of "self-image as something accreted over time, acquired through living, subject mostly to incremental change." Kramer also critiqued what Gerald Klerman in 1972 called "pharmacological Calvinism," a tendency of critics to oppose drugs, legal or illegal, that gave people pleasure. Yet Kramer did distinguish among the effects of substances, asserting that among what differentiated the impact of Prozac from LSD, alcohol, and marijuana was that it "induces pleasure in part by freeing people to enjoy activities that are social and productive" and did "so without being experienced as pleasurable in itself and without inducing distortions of perception." Thus it "simply gives anhedonic people access to pleasures identical to those enjoyed by other normal people in their ordinary social pursuits." Kramer went on to explore the neurobiology of pleasure and to list all the experiences and traits it enhanced. Prozac, he noted, "both elevates mood and increases emotional resilience, perhaps because these two qualities are biologically represented by the same neurotransmitters." "It reaches broadly into every aspect of personality through enthusiasms, passion, aesthetic sensibility, and feelings of self-satisfaction."[23]

Listening to Prozac turned Kramer into one of America's most famous psychiatrists and an important cultural observer. As he wrote in a 1997 "Afterword," a "serious book by an unknown writer" had become "a best-seller and, more than a best-seller, the talk of the nation," claiming attention from *People* to the *New York Times*, from *Oprah* to National Public Radio. The *New Yorker* published cartoons linking his book to over-the-counter medicines and to famous figures. Comedians told Prozac-inspired jokes, and the *New York Times* used "Listening to 1993" as its headline summarizing events at year's end. People at cocktail parties, therapy sessions, and in casual conversations used terms Kramer had highlighted such as "better than well," "cosmetic psychopharmacology," and "pharmacological Calvinism."[24]

MEDITATION, EASTERN RELIGIONS, SCIENCE, AND HEALTH

While Prozac promised one path to greater well-being, another came from the continuing investigation into the connections between religion, science, and health. The contributions of Jon Kabat-Zinn parallel Herbert Benson's *The Relaxation Response* (1975) and were at least as important as his work in emphasizing both the scientific basis of the mind–body connection as the key to a healthy life and the power of personal transformations. Like Benson, Kabat-Zinn wrestled with the relationship between science and religion. However, more so than Benson, Kabat-Zinn, at least initially, emphasized the contribution of spirituality that was in turn indebted to Eastern religions.[25]

Like many of those who influenced positive psychology, Kabat-Zinn worked to reconcile the two cultures of scientific and humanistic learning. Born in 1944 into a secular Jewish household in Manhattan, he wove together art and science, the careers of his mother and father, respectively. Married to the daughter of the radical historian Howard Zinn and in the late 1960s protesting against the war in Vietnam while pursuing a PhD in molecular biology at MIT, he nonetheless focused on transforming the world not by radical politics but through a combination of medicine and meditation. He first learned about meditation at a talk by Zen missionary Philip Kapleau and continued his education with other Buddhists, such as the Vietnamese monk and Zen master Thich Nhat Hanh. "Mindfulness is the miracle by which we master and restore ourselves," wrote Hahn in 1976, emphasizing the central importance of simple attention to breathing. Then at the University of Massachusetts Medical School in 1979, Kabat-Zinn founded the Stress Reduction Clinic, where he built the Stress Reduction and Relaxation Program—which over time spawned Mindfulness-Based Stress Reduction (MBSR) programs across the nation and around the world. By the mid-1980s Kabat-Zinn had begun to publish articles in highly respected journals demonstrating that science supported the medical benefits of mindfulness. His work garnered national attention in 1993, when Bill Moyers featured it on a PBS special, *Healing and the Mind*. On either side of that appearance came two books that brought Kabat-Zinn's work to increasingly large audiences: *Full Catastrophe Living: Using the Wisdom of Your Body and Mind to Face Stress, Pain, and Illness* in 1990 and *Wherever You Go, There You Are: Mindfulness Meditation in Everyday Life* in 1994.[26]

In *Full Catastrophe Living*, Kabat-Zinn focused on strategies derived from hatha yoga that would help medical patients deal with serious illnesses. "Based on ten years of clinical experience with over four thousand" patients, he relied on the emerging field of behavioral medicine whose practitioners believed that "mental and emotional factors" could have a "significant effect" on "physical health and on our capacity to recover from illness and injury." His book, he remarked, was "a practical guide for anyone, well or ill, who seeks to transcend his or her limitations and move toward greater levels of health and well-being." To do so, they would learn how to practice "mindfulness, a form of meditation originally developed in the Buddhist traditions of Asia." Mindfulness, which is both "the heart of Buddhist meditation" and beyond any particular spiritual tradition and therefore potentially universal, referred to maintaining present-moment awareness of thoughts, feelings, body sensations, and the environment without labeling anything right or wrong. The practice enabled people to discover "deep realms of relaxation, calmness, and insight" within themselves. Helping people tune in fully to the present, rather than getting lost in rehashing the past or imagining a future, taught them "how to make time for yourself, how to slow down and nurture calmness and self-acceptance in yourself, learning to observe what your own mind is up to from moment to moment." Offering abundant and specific guides on how to achieve mindfulness through yoga, body scans, and breathing, Kabat-Zinn also filled his book with words and phrases that signaled what practitioners could achieve: simplicity, present-mindedness, non-judgmental attitudes, letting go, self-discipline, self-knowledge, self-efficacy, and harmony. For him mindfulness was a lifelong journey that eventually led only to where one was as a person.[27]

Kabat-Zinn also underscored the scientific basis for his conclusions. He presented evidence from behavioral medicine that relying on "the fundamental unity of mind and body" and on patients as "active participants" in their health care revealed the interconnectedness and interactions of physical conditions and emotional ones, operating as they did through the neurotransmitters, hormones, and immune system. New medical advances, he reported, had shown how "life-style, patterns of thinking and feeling, relationships, and environmental factors all interact to influence health." Moreover, in its insistence on unlearning patterns of self-destructiveness, his approach owed much to cognitive behavior therapy and more specifically to the work of Martin Seligman, whose studies of helplessness and optimism, Kabat-Zinn wrote, had demonstrated that people with "a highly pessimistic attributional style are at significantly higher risk for becoming depressed when they encounter a bad event than are people who have the optimistic way of thinking," which in turn made them more susceptible to illness. Yet like Seligman's early work, Kabat-Zinn's focused more on overcoming helplessness than on achieving happiness. At the end of the eight weeks at the clinic, he wrote, patients had learned to better cope with what ailed them and more generally were "less anxious, less depressed, and less angry." Indeed, in *Full Catastrophe Living*, he devoted more than 40 percent of his attention to dealing with pain, anxiety, fear, suffering, panic, and stress.[28]

Kabat-Zinn focused almost all of his attention on people's inner world and almost none at all on the external one. To be sure, he noted that we read daily of "human suffering and misery in the world, much of it inflicted by one human being or group of human beings on another," with environmental degradation and nuclear war as the two most frightening threats he mentioned. And he stressed the importance of seeing "that affiliative trust and seeing the basic goodness in others and in ourselves" fostered "basic healing powers." He lamented the way the media focused so much attention in depressing stories. "*The more complicated the world gets and the more intrusive it becomes on our own personal psychological space and privacy,*" he observed, "*the more important it will be to practice non-doing.*" He briefly acknowledged that what humans had wrought in the world they could, individually and collectively, remedy. Yet overall, his focus was individualistic, not collective. Having devoted almost his entire book on mindfulness as a practice individuals could pursue, near the book's end he focused in only one paragraph on political approaches. "Try to identify specific issues that you care about," he advised in ways that seemed to emphasize the personal benefit of activism, "that if you worked on, might help you to feel more engaged and more powerful." In a chapter titled "World Stress," he wrote "to have a positive effect on the problems of the larger environment, we will need continually to tune and retune to our own center, cultivating awareness and harmony in our individual lives."[29]

After the publication of *Full Catastrophe Living*, Kabat-Zinn executed a number of changes in his approach. He shifted his focus from people who suffered full catastrophes to those who encountered less dramatic situations in their everyday lives. Like others who wanted to avoid the fuzziness of spiritualism and instead rest their case on scholarly research, over time he minimized his debt to Buddhism and increased his claims that he relied on scientific information. Moreover, he Americanized and tamed what he had taken from Eastern religions. Writing in *Wherever You Go*, he remarked that meditation "is not some weird cryptic activity, as our popular culture might have it. It does not involve becoming some kind of zombie, vegetable, self-absorbed narcissist, navel gazer, 'space cadet,' cultist, devotee, mystic, or Eastern philosopher." While Thich Nhat Hanh had written the preface to his first book, in his second Kabat-Zinn insisted that mindfulness "has nothing to do with Buddhism per se or with becoming a Buddhist, but it has everything to do with waking up and living in harmony with oneself and with the world." When he turned to emphasize the American legacy on which mindfulness drew, he associated his approach with that of Henry David Thoreau and emphatically distanced himself from Norman Vincent Peale. Kabat-Zinn insisted his view was "neither particularly 'Eastern' nor mystical," offering as evidence that "Thoreau saw the same problem with our ordinary mind state in New England in 1846." He titled one of his chapters "Meditation: Not to Be Confused with Positive Thinking," and in it discussed how the "so-called positive thinking . . . can be confining, fragmented, inaccurate, illusory, self-serving, and wrong." As others did, Kabat-Zinn was keeping his distance from both Buddhism and positive thinking in an attempt to broaden his audience, make clear that meditation was scientifically legitimate, and avoid being associated with quackery.[30]

A critic later noted that Kabat-Zinn had learned to "scrub meditation of its religious origins." Writing in the *New York Times* in 2015, Virginia Heffernan asserted that he "believed that many of the secular people who could most benefit from meditation were being turned off by the whiffs of . . . religious esoterica." Then, "undercover of this innocuous word, Buddhist meditation nosed its ways into a secular audience bent on personal growth and even success strategies." Americanizing meditation selectively helped enable Kabat-Zinn to emerge by the late 1990s as a major figure in positive psychology. Through books, televisions appearances, CDs, MP3s, web sites, seminars, talks, workshops, and over 200 stress-reduction clinics worldwide, his work reached hundreds of thousands if not millions of people interested in pursuing a mindful life. Indeed, as the religious studies scholar Jeff Wilson has argued for mindfulness and Buddhism in America more generally, Kabat-Zinn significantly contributed to the Americanization of these traditions. He minimized the connections between these two elements. As did many others, Kabat-Zinn made clear their connection to either no religion or all religious traditions, and both medicalized and psychologized world views and practices. Moreover, he located the pursuit of mindfulness not at a retreat but in a hospital, where it relied less on religious teachers than on lay, professional ones, and emphasized practical results in daily life as opposed to transcendence.[31]

At least comparable to the work of Kabat-Zinn in message, influence, and personalism but more insistent on the importance of Eastern religion was *The Art of Happiness: a Handbook for Living*, by the Dalai Lama and the psychiatrist Howard C. Cutler. Struck by how the Dalai Lama "had learned how to live with a sense of fulfillment and a degree of serenity" he had never seen in others, Cutler set out to identify the principles that made this possible, all the while acknowledging that they could improve the lives of Buddhists and non-Buddhists alike. In planning to write the book, Cutler had "envisioned a conventional self-help format in which the Dalai Lama would present clear and simple solutions to all life's problems."[32]

As he listened, however, he learned that the Dalai Lama's message was richer, more nuanced, and more complex than he had anticipated. Nonetheless, Cutler distilled what he heard: that "the single note" the Dalai Lama "constantly sounded" was "one of hope . . . based on the belief that while attaining genuine and lasting happiness is not easy, it neverthe-less can be done." That message rested in turn on "a belief in the funda-mental gentleness and goodness of all human beings, a belief in the value of compassion, a belief in a policy of kindness, and a sense of commonality among all living creatures." Like others who prized meditation, the Dalai Lama emphasized using a disciplined mind to engage the world. "Identify and cultivate positive mental states; identify and eliminate negative" ones, Cutler wrote, as he both conveyed the Dalai Lama's message and drew on the American tradition of mind control that harkened back to the nine-teenth century and found expression in the work of Norman Vincent Peale. Like mainline scholars in happiness studies who, benefiting from multiple privileges, minimized the power of race, gender, and class, Cutler concluded that whether "we are feeling happy or unhappy at any given moment often has very little to do with" the external conditions of our lives. In something of a departure from what other, similar books offered, Cutler and the Dalai Lama emphasized that happiness radiated out from the person, to those around him or her, and then to the society at large— through means by which the compassion on the individual level perme-ated to the social level remained vague.[33]

Although much of the book was spiritual, Cutler did report on recent academic studies that revealed a connection between health and positive emotions. He pointed to how George Vaillant's *Adaptation to Life* (1977), part of the longitudinal Grant Study of adult development that followed the lives of several hundred Harvard graduates from the classes of 1939–1944, showed that altruistic behavior improves mental well-being. Cutler mentioned how a 1988 article by David McClelland and Carol Kirchnit demonstrated the power of the so-called Mother Teresa Effect. When Harvard students watched a film on Mother Teresa's work helping orphans in Calcutta, saliva tests showed that they had a significant increase in immu-noglobulin A (S-IgA), an antibody that helped strengthen the immune system. And Cutler pointed to Allan Luks's *The Healing Power of Doing Good: The Health and Spiritual Benefits of Helping Others* (1992), in which the executive director of New York City's Big Brothers Big Sisters programs underscored how the work of volunteers helped provide them with relief from stress disorders.[34]

Like the books of Kabat-Zinn and Benson, *The Art of Happiness* reflected both the accommodation and tension between religion and science, although in this case the tension was less within the mind of one author than within the interaction between two even as the book evidenced a greater willingness to talk across the lines that have sometimes separated the spiritual and the scientific. The book's format combined long quotes from the Dalai Lama with discussions by Cutler of his own ideas. All the while, Cutler struggled, he noted, "to reconcile our different perspectives: his as a Buddhist monk, and mine as a Western psychiatrist." Cutler combined discussions of the experiences of his patients with conclusions drawn from scholarly studies of happiness, of lottery winners and identical twins, of neuroscientists who used fMRI to reveal the brain's plasticity, and of Bowlby's work on attachment. Again and again, he commented on the difference between his skepticism or unease and the Dalai Lama's combination of humor, naturalness, and calm. Trained as a Freudian and as someone whose work as a therapist focused on depression and anxiety, Cutler found it hard to accept the Dalai Lama's belief that happiness was achievable. Knowing that scholarly studies revealed that married people were happier than their unmarried counterparts, Cutler shied away from asking the Dalai Lama how a presumably celibate monk could achieve happiness. Seeing a new car that he had longed for while knowing how studies showed that beyond a minimal level, more goods did not make someone happy, Cutler listened intently as the Dalai Lama discussed how some desires led to misery rather than happiness. This prompted Cutler to remind himself that "working on our mental outlook is a more effective means of achieving happiness than seeking it through external sources such as wealth, position, or even physical health."[35]

Translated into fifty languages, *The Art of Happiness* remained on the *New York Times* bestseller list for almost two years. The dynamic of the book, and perhaps the basis of its appeal to American audiences, was the dialogue between East and West, Buddhism and unchurched spiritualism, faith and science. The book mediated between the Dalai Lama's and Cutler's sense of how to achieve happiness. The *Art of Happiness* appealed precisely because readers could sense (and understand in themselves) the tension between the individualism and materialism of Cutler and the more temperamentally calm responses of the Dalai Lama, between Cutler's hesitations and his subject's peaceful but often implicit reassurances. Reflecting some of the factors that underlay the emergence of positive psychology, the book promised its readers that they too could be spiritual without being religious, that practical longings had higher meanings, and that the struggle to achieve happiness ended up somewhere between Cutler's uncertainties and the assurances that His Holiness conveyed.

If the Dalai Lama achieved prominence and influence for an Eastern version of mindfulness, the Harvard psychologist Ellen J. Langer did so from a version she labeled as "almost entirely within the Western scientific perspective." In her *Mindfulness* (1989), Langer translated the findings of experimental psychology into easily intelligible and implicitly practical ways to live more effectively. She urged people to create new categories of understanding, be open to new information, assume control of their living environment, embrace creative uncertainty, welcome the unexpected, and value process over outcomes—all of which would help them solve problems, resolve conflicts, be more effective at work, and attain healthier lives. Although not, strictly speaking, a positive psychologist, akin to those who offered a version of mindfulness influenced by Eastern religions, Langer and her teachings had immense impact on the field. Moreover, she taught at least one student, Tal Ben-Shahar, who in the new century would emerge as a major player in the field of positive psychology.[36]

HEDONIC PSYCHOLOGY AND BEHAVIORAL ECONOMICS

Although psychology was the foundational field of the positive psychology movement, over time economics, and particularly behavioral economics, came to play an increasingly prominent role. Reacting against how many economists assumed that human beings made decisions based on rational calculations and that consequently markets operated more or less perfectly, behavioral economists emphasized the power of psychological and social forces. A key figure bridging psychology and economics is the psychologist Daniel Kahneman, whom we met earlier in the discussion of prospect theory.[37] In a series of scholarly articles published in the 1990s, Kahneman and his colleagues reported on findings that promised to fundamentally challenge and reshape happiness studies and positive psychology, both by suggesting new ways of measuring experiences and by calling into question how accurately we can predict the impact of experiences on our sense of pleasure. He carried out a series of pathbreaking studies on how people experienced and remembered pleasure and pain: by exploring how patients responded to colonoscopies, how students reacted to aversive and pleasant film clips, and how subjects felt when they immersed their hands in cold water of varying temperatures. Though like survey researchers these behavioral economists relied on self-report questionnaires, they also broke fresh methodological ground. Without mentioning Csikszentmihalyi's Experience Sampling Method (ESM), a similar technique available decades earlier, they drew on methods developed by market researchers that enabled people to report their responses multiple times throughout the day by manipulating a knob on a meter or by recording their reactions when prompted by a programmed beeper. This led Kahneman to insist that the experiencing self (measured by responses recorded at the time) provided a more accurate assessment of well-being than the remembering self (measured by answering questions later).[38]

Over time, the contributions of Kahneman and others had a significant impact on both psychology and economics. Coming at a time when happiness studies had settled into comfortable, popular modes and when positive psychology was still in formation, the combination of behavioral economics and psychology helped make the study of emotions more sophisticated and more fully connected to the hard sciences. Having published a major piece in the *Quarterly Journal of Economics*, Kahneman was extending psychology's reach.

Kahneman, Ed Diener, and Norbert Schwarz brought the field's findings together in *Well-Being: The Foundations of Hedonic Psychology* (1999), which built on papers presented at a conference held several years before. Although most of the contributors taught in the United States, the inclusion of essays by scholars from Great Britain, Canada, the Netherlands, Venezuela, and Germany reflected the growing internationalization of the field. Similarly, though psychologists wrote most of the essays, the book included contributions from professors of neuroscience, economics, physiology, biology, and business management.[39]

In the book's preface, the editors dramatically announced "the existence of a new field of psychology" called "Hedonic psychology," which was "the study of what makes experiences and life pleasant or unpleasant," at almost the same time that Seligman was announcing the birth of the new field of positive psychology. They noted that introductory psychology textbooks contained "a few pages about pain, a mention of pleasure centers and the pleasure principle, but little else." Usually, there were "no entries at all for happiness or well-being," and past research evidenced a "remarkable accentuation of the negative." They called for breaking new ground in other ways. Unlike most of those involved in happiness studies or positive psychology at the time, they brought biochemical and physiological approaches into the fold, as means of measuring both positive and negative emotions. In contrast to the usual methods of evaluating people's sense of well-being, they wanted to focus on real-time or momentary evidence, shifting attention away from both retrospective and generalized evaluations and often problematic predictions of the choices people would make in future.[40]

Finally, they ambitiously called for positive psychology to influence public policy. In that context, they critiqued the dominant role of traditional economics, which could not evaluate the importance of more emotional and less materialistic factors such as love or stress. In addition, they critiqued economists for focusing too exclusively on market exchanges and assuming people were utility-seeking rational actors. They remarked that traditional economists were not centrally interested in how people experienced pleasure and pain over time or in discovering what situations promoted "enduring pleasures." Vague on what might be the policy implications of hedonic psychology, the three writers ended their preface with a call on nations to "begin monitoring pleasure and pain through on-line experience recording among samples of respondents to complement existing social indicators, and to provide a more direct assessment of the final outcome about which people are most concerned."[41]

Kahneman's essay "Objective Happiness," the first in the book, made clear the dimensions of his work. He summarized past research and set an ambitious agenda for the future. Although he began with issues surrounding how to measure happiness, the implications of his contribution were wide-ranging and transformative. His language was often dense: "Independent of whether or not it is implemented by recalling instant utility," he wrote at one point, "the principle of temporal integration highlights the importance of duration." As discussed earlier, he shifted attention in measuring happiness or misery from the remembering self to the experiencing self. [42]

Kahneman argued that in evaluating a person's sense of well-being, duration mattered little. Instead, what weighed heavily was the most intensely experience (the Peak Effect) and final moments (the End Effect). He emphasized the distinction between what people reported at the time ("instant utility") and what they recalled retrospectively (a more subjective "remembered utility"). He criticized economists' reliance on the assumption that people could wisely maximize their utility. He introduced the concept of the focusing illusion: how people commonly overestimated a specific anticipated aspect of what might make them happy, making it difficult for them to predict the pleasure or pain they might derive from the consequences of actual decisions. Anticipating the concept of affective forecasting, he observed that people were poor judges of how various events would influence their emotional lives. Studies based on prospect theory made clear that people experienced losses more intensely than gains. In some respects like those who emphasized the importance of mindfulness, Kahneman wanted to keep the focus on the experiences not of the past or future but of the present. Thus, "the present is fleeting, but memories and evaluations of the past endure and populate the mind." Scholars could take advantage of and work to improve methodologies that captured momentary responses. Measuring emotions in real time and diminishing the impact of retrospective reports would make it possible to measure objective well-being, "to determine the true nature of adaptation to new circumstances, to assess enjoyment and suffering in new settings, and to provide a criterion for the evaluation of economic and social policy."[43]

In political terms, the contributions of Kahneman and his colleagues pointed in multiple directions: consonant with contemporary trends was the emphasis on the unpredictability of actions on future emotions that undermined social planning while their critique of traditional economics challenged market-based conservatism or neoliberalism. Nonetheless, to reduce what they wrote to an element of political ideology is problematic. It is hard to underestimate the importance of what Kahenman and his colleagues contributed, which lay less along political grounds than along methodological ones.

EXPERIMENTS AND INVESTIGATIONS INTO CONDITIONS FOSTERING POSITIVITY

Other, somewhat more minor contributions made between the mid-1980s and the late 1990s reflected the national political mood and helped shape the future of happiness studies and positive psychology. Although social critics such as Thorstein Veblen had long ago paid attention to how people compared themselves to others, the breakthrough article on the topic was Leon Festinger's 1954 "A Theory of Social Comparison Processes."[44] As important as were his findings, it took years for social and behavioral scientists to explore and recognize the relationship between social comparisons and happiness. Scholars working on the topic in the late 1980s and early 1990s made clear the relativistic nature of how people evaluated their own happiness, as such judgments were largely contingent on contextual comparisons. Relying on Festinger's ideas, scholars explored how people felt better about themselves if they thought they were more prosperous or successful than those with whom they compared themselves, and the opposite was true as well. When thinking about their health, wealth, work, and relationships, they looked at others above and below themselves socially. In most cases, favorable comparisons enhanced a sense of well-being, while unfavorable ones had the opposite effect. Depending on mood and personality, a comparison could make an individual despondent or hopeful; happy people with a high sense of self-esteem could more readily resist the consequences of social comparisons. Beyond such specific focal points, the main conclusion was how fluid and relative was the impact of comparisons, how the way people viewed their social location shaped their perspectives on the relationship between the conditions of their lives and their evaluation of their well-being. The implications of social comparison theory were many, but one that became more important later on in ways that were both liberating and conservative was that because it could be especially hurtful to compare oneself with someone in a more fortunate circumstance, it might be better to be satisfied with one's own lot.[45]

Another area of investigation that informed happiness studies in this period centered on the issue of whether people's genetic makeup influenced their levels of happiness. Reacting against how Diener and others emphasized people's adaptability, David Lykken and Auke Tellegen emphasized the power of genetics, which, similar to Diener's insistence that external circumstances did not matter, suggested how predetermined was human happiness. Relying on an examination of the reported happiness of several thousand middle-aged twins (both identical and fraternal) from the Minnesota Twin Registry database, they concluded that demographic factors such as religion, education, marital status, or income accounted for no more than 3 percent of people's sense of well-being. In comparing identical and fraternal twins, they reported that 44 to 52 percent of the variance in personal satisfaction was accounted for by genes. When Lykken and Tellegen retested a smaller sample years later, they estimated the heritability of the "stable component of subjective well-being" to be closer to 80 percent. Much as the earlier studies of lottery winners and paraplegics had indicated, people seemed to have a genetically determined happiness or emotional "set point." Indeed, at one point the authors remarked that "it may be that trying to be happier is as futile as trying to be taller." The article generated tremendous interest, including stories in newspapers in the United States, Canada, and Western Europe. Yet Lykken reconsidered his pessimistic comparison about trying to become happier if not taller. Retracting his earlier claim, he proceeded "to illustrate some of the ways in which one can raise one's happiness 'set point' . . . above the level that one's genetic steersman would be likely to achieve if left in complete control."[46]

Looking back fifteen years later on studies from the 1980s that were confident about the significant impact of genetics on temperaments, two sociologists found themselves more cautious than Lykken and Tellegen in asserting the connection between heredity and happiness in what they called the "post-genomic age." Retrospectively, they remarked, they could understand how the temper of the times had shaped scientific advances. The "enormous confidence" of an "era of Reagan's 'morning in America' . . . the 'Washington consensus' that open markets and budget austerity" could fix so many social problems had "extended to human behavioural science . . . nowhere better embodied than in the promises made by researchers . . . that we could unravel the Gordian knot of nature and nurture."[47]

Another area that commanded extensive attention in the 1990s was how trauma could promote psychological growth. In *Man's Search for Meaning*

(1946), Viktor Frankl had offered powerful examples of how he had benefited from adverse conditions. Now, as part of the more general trend of
shifting from the damaging effects of stress to resilience and from transformative social events to life-changing individual ones, psychologists focused
on posttraumatic growth and development. In 1998, three psychologists—
Richard G. Tedeschi, Crystal L. Park, and Lawrence G. Calhoun—discussed
the origins of and recent research on posttraumatic growth (PTG), a term
they coined. They located the origins of the concept in ancient mythology
and religions, and more recently in the work of Frankl and in existential and
humanistic psychology generally, but noted it was not until the 1980s that
researchers had really focused on PTG. Until then, most of those who studied reactions to traumas mainly emphasized "the most negative outcomes"
and when they considered "the experience of growth in the aftermath of
crisis," they saw it "primarily as defensive or illusory."[48]

Although these three authors paid some attention to collective and political experiences such as the Holocaust, most researchers, rooted in the discipline of psychology which often emphasized the individual more than
the social, focused almost entirely on events experienced individually or
in small groups, such as bereavement, serious illness, and childhood abuse.
Summarizing recent findings, they emphasized how people "not only bounce
back from trauma, but use it as a springboard to further individual development or growth, and the development of more humane social behaviors and
social organization." Experiments and therapeutic interventions revealed
how the tremendous loss and confusion people experienced during traumatic events provided some of them with an opportunity to rebuild "a way
of life that they experience as superior to their old one in important ways."
Moreover, "they appreciate their newly found strength and the strength of
their neighbors and their community." Consequently, they "may value what
they now have, and the process of creating it, although the process involved
loss and distress." They reported how, in the face of traumatic encounters,
people transformed themselves from victims into survivors, inoculated
themselves against stress and adversity, gained a sense of hardy toughness,
enhanced their self-esteem, committed themselves to being more altruistic,
and understood their lives in deeper, more spiritual, and wiser terms.[49]

Altruism, which would play a key role in twenty-first-century positive
psychology, was another topic that was gaining traction in the late twentieth century, often in ways that revealed evidence of a "Helper's High,"
the way helping not only improved the situation that others faced but also
enhanced the positive mood of the helper. Perhaps giving was as important,
if not more important, to the benefactor than to the recipient.[50] At least
as early as 1982, epidemiologists had shown that whatever effect volunteer
work had on its recipients, it also increased the life expectancy of volunteers

themselves. Several books from the late 1990s summed up the relationships between altruism and positivity. In *The Altruism Question: Toward a Social-Psychological Answer* (1991), C. Daniel Batson, after reviewing philosophical discussions and psychological experiments, concluded that there seemed "to be clear evidence that an empathy-helping relationship can exist even among individuals anticipating a mood-enhancing experience." In his 1997 *The Origins of Virtue*, Matt Ridley drew on natural selection, genetics, and sociobiology to argue that it was also natural—and virtuous—for animals to cooperate. Then a year later Elliott Sober and David Sloan Wilson came out with their *Unto Others: The Evolution and Psychology of Unselfish Behavior*, in which they argued that evolutionary biology and psychology pointed in the same direction. "Altruism," they announced, "can be removed from the endangered species list in both biology and the social sciences."[51] Nonetheless, as of 1998, the connection between altruism and positivity remained incomplete. In scholarly articles, a handful of psychologists had provided evidence for the idea of a "Helper's High," but authors of books that reached a wider audience did not specifically connect their arguments that altruism enhanced happiness, instead resting their case on evidence that animals and humans tended to cooperate.[52]

Another important finding that emerged between 1984 and 1998 underscored the importance of social relationships, albeit on an intimate scale involving connections to family, friends, and co-workers. Building on attachment theory, psychologists were paying more (but a still modest amount of) attention to how the fundamental need for belonging and social connections enhanced psychological well-being, physical health, and effectiveness in interpersonal relationships and the work place.[53] Although studies revealed that happy people tended to exaggerate how skillful they were and even more rarely discussed the downside of positive emotions, they were nonetheless more effective in working at their jobs, solving problems, and developing personal relationships.[54] People with positive outlooks helped promote diversity in groups.[55] People who pursued their goals optimistically had higher levels of life satisfaction than their peers.[56] By the late 1990s, these studies impelled Barbara Frederickson to offer her broaden-and-build theory of positive emotions. Calling into question how psychologists had marginalized positive emotions, she talked of "joy creating the urge to play, interest the urge to explore, contentment the urge to savor and integrate, and love a recurrent cycle of each of these urges." As a result, "these broadened thought-action repertoires can have the often incidental effect of building an individual's personal resources, including physical resources, intellectual resources, and social resources." In short, the title of a 1993 scholarly article pointed to "The Power of Positive Thinking: The Benefits of Being Optimistic."[57]

After 1998, the relationships between character, religion, and happiness would command significant attention from positive psychologists. Until then, many psychologists had mostly stayed away from topics like character and virtue, which they felt should remain the purview of those like philosophers who focused on the morality of what we should do. Yet a few psychologists had ventured forth. They studied virtues such as courage. They counseled people to concentrate on their greatest strengths. They cautioned people to recognize the downside of both a belief in willpower and excessive concentration on positive emotions. One book, important for its origins and in itself, exemplifies the importance of the 1990s for the emergence of character as an issue: Christopher Peterson and Lisa M. Bossio's *Health and Optimism* (1991). This book emerged from a study Seligman and Peterson carried out with George Vaillant. In their book Peterson and Bossio showed how optimism, grounded in realism and further developed through social connections, positively affected health in myriad ways, including enhancing survival rates for cancer and strengthening the immune system.[58]

Similarly, overcoming the skepticism of a mostly secular field like psychology, many of whose members found religion and science incompatible, and reflecting the increasing prominence of religion in American public life, scholars set out to show how people with strong spiritual or religious orientations and/or affiliations tended to have an enhanced quality of life, sense of well-being, and mental and physical health.[59] The findings of more than a decade's worth of investigation came together in Kenneth Pargament's 1997 *The Psychology of Religion and Coping: Theory, Research, Practice.* Applying Bowlby's attachment theory to one's relationship to God, he showed that people imbued with a sense of the sacred, whether achieved through formal religious affiliation or spirituality, were better able to cope with life's adversities and attain "greater life satisfaction and well-being." "Armed with the knowledge that protection can always be found in God's loving arms," he wrote, "the religious individual may feel greater confidence venturing out into the world, searching for other forms of significance." Like other findings in the period, these reflected contemporary concerns—in this case the increasing and increasingly acknowledged power of religion in public life.[60]

INTERNATIONAL COMPARISONS

The dozen or so years beginning in 1984 also saw the flourishing of studies on subjective well-being and happiness across national borders. Scholars had begun to collect relevant data for the United States in the mid-1960s.

What broadened the focus was information from countries around the world—gathered by the European Commission's Eurobarometer (launched in 1973); the European Values Study and World Values Survey (both originating in 1981); the German Socio-Economic Panel (from 1984 on); and the General Social Survey at the University of Chicago's NORC, which co-founded the International Social Survey Program in 1985. All this enabled scholars to draw on the responses of hundreds of thousands of people who represented up to 90 percent of the world's population. Happiness was hardly the only focus of such data collection, but by the 1990s there was enough material to make possible sophisticated, rigorous international comparisons, and by late in the decade a consensus had begun to emerge. A nation's per capita income had a positive impact on the sense of well-being among its citizens, although how much this mattered decreased once a nation reached a more prosperous level of wealth. Supposedly individualist nations (such as the United States or Austria) differed from collectivist ones (such as Japan or Bangladesh) in terms of how their citizens defined and achieved life satisfaction. In individualist ones friendships and self-esteem were more important, while in collectivist ones social norms mattered more. Moreover, there was a weak correlation between cultural homogeneity and national subjective well-being; stronger factors were how ample were human rights, access to knowledge, social equality, interpersonal trust, and political freedom in a country. Ronald Inglehart, director of the World Values Survey, suggestively described one dimension of the change in the dynamics of well-being in nations as involving the change from modernization to postmodernization. One process with a strong generational component involved the shift in cultural values among advanced industrial societies in the postwar world, away from materialism and economic rationality and toward democratic institutions, more egalitarian gender roles, and non-economic aspects of the quality of life.

Yet if some things were clearly explainable and testable, others were not. In Western Europe, over a long period of time and perhaps reflecting different religious traditions, the French and Italians consistently reported low levels of satisfaction, while the Danes and Dutch stood at the opposite end of the spectrum—objective conditions did not explain either case. The most troubling puzzle was evidence of paradoxical relationships between life satisfaction and per capita GDP. It turns out that there are enduring anomalies. The data reveal a higher degree of life satisfaction among the Irish and Mexicans than among the Germans and Japanese—results also not explicable by purely economic conditions, but perhaps by cultural and historical ones that are admittedly harder to test and verify. Scholars did not often fully explore the policy implications of international comparisons, which rarely seemed to point in any one direction.[61]

By 1998, when Seligman delivered his presidential address, most of the key elements of a robust positive psychology were in place, some of them hidden from the public in recondite scholarly publications. But in the period prior to this, some authors (those discussed already and others who will be introduced in subsequent chapters) had already worked to offer findings from the fields of happiness studies and positive psychology to broader audiences by writing popular books.

Of course, it is rare to find a perfect fit between changes in an academic discipline and a nation's political mood, principally because fields like happiness studies and positive psychology develop under logics internal to what scholars consider important enough to pursue. It is important not to reduce advances in scholarship to mere reflections of changes external to a field. And indeed, there are exceptions to the generalization that links these academic fields and larger changes, among them Ryff's emphasis on social equality, the ambiguous implications of Kahneman's arguments, the multiple and often conflicting implications of international comparisons, and the relative silence or vagueness among scholars about the political implications of their findings. Still, even with these cautions, the parallels between these two mornings in America are striking.

NOTES

1. Ruut Veenhoven, *Conditions of Happiness* (Dordrecht, Netherlands: D. Reidel, 1984), 119; Ruut Veenhoven, "World Data Base of Happiness," *SIR* 34 (March 1995): 299–300. Ruut Veenhoven and Michael Argyle, eds., *How Harmful is Happiness?* (Rotterdam: Universitaire Pers, 1989), offered a series of essays, mostly by Dutch scholars, that focused not, as many did, on the determinants of happiness but on the consequences. Positive psychology as a Library of Congress category seems to have originated in 2006. One of the first items with a Library of Congress happiness call number was Desmond Morris's lecture, *Happiness* (Birmingham, UK: University of Birmingham, 1984). Lynne McFall, *Happiness* (New York: Peter Lang, 1982) is one of those philosophical considerations of the meaning of happiness that has had, as far as I can see, little impact on the main lines of inquiry.
2. The ad pictured two children of ambiguous ethnicity.
3. I am grateful to Art Goldsmith for emphasizing these points.
4. Ed Diener, "Subjective Well-Being," *PB* 95 (May 1984): 542–75; Claudia Wallis, "The Science of Happiness Turns Ten. What Has It Taught?" *Time*, July 8, 2009.
5. Diener, "Subjective," 542. For a later and important book on SWB, see Fritz Strack, Michael Argyle, and Norbert Schwarz, eds., *Subjective Well-Being: An Interdisciplinary Perspective* (Oxford, UK: Pergamon Press, 1991).
6. Diener, "Subjective," 547. For the idea of separate positive and negative reactions, see Norman M. Bradburn and C. Edward Noll, *The Structure of Philosophical Well-Being* (Chicago: Aldine, 1969).

7. Diener, "Subjective," 552, 553.

8. Diener, "Subjective," 553.

9. Diener, "Subjective," 555. In *Britain on the Couch: Why We're Unhappier Compared with 1950 Despite Being Richer: A Treatment for the Low-Serotonin Society* (London: Century Random House, 1997), 84, Oliver James claimed that women and African Americans did not experience greater satisfaction as their conditions improved because they saw their situations in unfavorable terms compared with that of men and whites. In *Contempt and Pity: Social Policy and the Image of the Damaged Black Psyche, 1880–1966* (Chapel Hill: University of North Carolina Press, 1997), Daryl M. Scott explores the discussions that underlay Diener's observations on race.

10. Diener, "Subjective," 562, 569.

11. George H. W. Bush, "Presidential Proclamation 6158," issued July 17, 1990. On the fMRI, see http://www.apa.org/research/tools/fmri-adult.pdf. For an example of some work on the historical background of this field, see Anna Kathryn Schoefert, "Neither Physician Nor Surgeons: Whither Neuropathological Skill in Post-War England," *Medical History* 59 (July 2015): 404–20.

12. Robert E. Ornstein and Richard F. Thompson, *The Amazing Brain* (Boston: Houghton Mifflin, 1984), 1; Richard M. Restak, *The Mind* (New York: Bantam, 1988), 158–95; Jon Franklin, *Molecules of the Mind: The Brave New World of Molecular Psychology* (New York: Atheneum, 1987), 37–38, 72, 278–79. Another book that discusses advances in neuroscience but does not connect them with happiness is Richard M. Restak, *The Modular Brain: How New Discoveries in Neuroscience Are Answering Age-Old Questions About Memory, Free Will, Consciousness, and Personal Identity* (New York: Simon & Schuster, 1994).

13. Richard J. Davidson, "Well-Being: Perspectives from Affective and Contemplative Neuroscience," talk at Fourth World Congress on Positive Psychology, Lake Buena Vista, FL, June 26, 2015.

14. For a sampling of this very considerable literature, see K. M. Dillon, B. Minchoff, and K. H. Baker, "Positive Emotional States and Enhancement of the Immune System," *International Journal of Psychiatry in Medicine* 15 (March 1986): 13–18; Richard J. Davidson et al., "Approach-Withdrawal and Cerebral Asymmetry: Emotional Expression and Brain Physiology: I," *JPSP* 58 (Feb. 1990): 330–41; Alice Isen, "The Influence of Positive and Negative Affect on Cognitive Organization: Some Implications for Development," in Nancy Stein, Bennett Leventhal, and Tom Trabasso, eds., *Psychological and Biological Approaches to Emotion* (Hillsdale, NJ: Erlbaum, 1990), 75–94; W. P. Smith, W. C. Compton, and W. B. West, "Meditation as an Adjunct to a Happiness Enhancement Program," *Journal of Clinical Psychology* 51 (March 1995): 269–73; B. S. McEwen, "Protective and Damaging Effects of Stress Mediators," *New England Journal of Medicine* 338 (Jan. 15, 1998): 171–79; Suzanne Segerstrom et al., "Optimism Is Associated with Mood, Coping, and Immune Change in Response to Stress," *JPSP* 74 (June 1998): 1646–55; Barbara L. Frederickson and Robert W. Levenson, "Positive Emotions Speed Recovery from the Cardiovascular Sequelae of Negative Emotions," *Cognition and Emotion* 12 (March 1998): 191–220.

15. Carol D. Ryff, "Happiness Is Everything, or Is It? Explorations on the Meaning of Psychological Well-being," *JPSP* 57 (Dec. 1989): 1069, 1077, 1080; Carol D. Ryff, "Psychological Well-Being in Adult Life," *Current Directions in Psychological Science* 4 (Aug. 1995): 100. In 1995, Ryff established MIDUS, a center to study, among other issues, well-being in mid-life: http://www.midus.wisc.edu/.

16. Carol D. Ryff and Burton Singer, "The Contours of Positive Human Health," *Psychological Inquiry* 9 (Jan. 1998): 1, 2, 10. The accompanying bibliography, with approximately 250 entries, contains references to many researchers prominent, then and in the future, in happiness studies and positive psychology including Roy Baumeister, Herbert Benson, John

Bowlby, and Richard J. Davidson but not to Mihaly Csikszentmihalyi, Ed Diener, Martin Seligman, or Ruut Veenhoven.

17. Evolutionary biology was a second scientific approach that in the 1990s enriched the emerging field of positive psychology. David T. Lykken, *Happiness: What Studies on Twins Show Us about Nature, Nurture, and the Happiness Set-Point* (New York: Golden Books, 1999) offered one example; for an idiosyncratic but influential and declensionist book, see Lionel Tiger, *The Pursuit of Pleasure* (Boston: Little, Brown, 1992).

18. David Herzberg, *Happy Pills in America: From Miltown to Prozac* (Baltimore: Johns Hopkins University Press, 2009), 151, 169, 170. Herzberg, *Happy Pills*, 150–52 and 175–91 is an indispensable source on changes in brain science and psychopharmacology. On the controversy surrounding the efficacy of Prozac, and more generally on the testing of antidepressants, see Linsey McGoey, "Profitable Failure: Antidepressant Drugs and the Triumph of Flawed Experiments," *History of the Human Sciences* 23 (Feb. 2010): 58–78.

19. Geoffrey Cowley et al., "The Promise of Prozac," *Newsweek*, March 26, 1990, 38–42. Among the other important books on Prozac are David Healy, *The Antidepressant Era* (Cambridge, MA: Harvard University Press, 1997) and the more personal and sanguine Elizabeth Wurtzel, *Prozac Nation: Young and Depressed in America* (Boston: Houghton Mifflin, 1994). On the impact of Prozac, see Herzberg, *Happy Pills*, 175–81.

20. Peter D. Kramer, "I Am Frightened (Yellow); I am Saddened (Blue)," *Harvard Crimson*, April 26, 1969; Arline Kaplan, "Through the Times with Peter Kramer, M.D.," *Psychiatric Times*, Dec. 1. 2005, and Peter Kramer, quoted in same. Full disclosure: I knew Kramer in the late 1960s when he was an undergraduate at Harvard and have kept in touch with him since. For his later defense of antidepressants, see Peter D. Kramer, *Ordinarily Well: The Case for Antidepressants* (New York: Farrar, Straus and Giroux, 2016). For a review that discusses Kramer's work and the controversies over antidepressants, see Scott Stossel, review of *Ordinarily Well, NYTBR*, July 10, 2016, 12–13.

21. "Sam," a patient, quoted in Peter Kramer, *Listening to Prozac* (New York: Viking Penguin, 1993), x.

22. Kramer, *Listening*, xix, 41, 292, 297.

23. Kramer, *Listening*, 208, 227, 258, 265, 274.

24. Kramer, "Afterword" to 1997 edition of *Listening* (New York: Penguin, 1997), 315–16.

25. On Kabat-Zinn, see Anne Harrington, *The Cure Within: A History of Mind-Body Medicine* (New York: W.W. Norton, 2008), 220–22; Jeff Wilson, *Mindful America: The Mutual Transformation of Buddhist Meditation and American Culture* (New York: Oxford University Press, 2014), 35–40 and 84–103. In the bestselling *Love, Medicine, and Miracles* (New York: HarperCollins, 1986), the pediatric surgeon Bernie S. Siegel insisted that positive emotions, working through the immune system, improved physical health.

26. Thich Nhat Hahn, *The Miracle of Mindfulness: A Manual on Meditation*, trans. Mobi Ho (1976; rev. ed.; Boston: Beacon Press, 1987), 14. On the familial dimensions of the tension between science and religion in his life, see http://www.onbeing.org/program/opening-our-lives/138. On his early publications in scientific journals, see, for example, Jon Kabat-Zinn, "An Outpatient Program in Behavioral Medicine for Chronic Pain Patients Based on the Practice of Mindfulness Meditation: Theoretical Considerations and Preliminary Results," *General Hospital Psychiatry* 4 (April 1982): 33–47, and Jon Kabat-Zinn, Leslie Lipworth, and Robert Burney, "The Clinical Use of Mindfulness Meditation for the Self-Regulation of Chronic Pain," *Journal of Behavioral Medicine* 8 (June 1985): 163–90. Among his books are Jon Kabat-Zinn, *Full Catastrophe Living: Using the Wisdom of Your Body and Mind to Face Stress, Pain, and Illness* (Garden City, NY: Doubleday, 1990) and *Wherever You Go, There You Are: Mindfulness Meditation in Everyday Life* (New York: Hyperion, 1994). See also Myla and Jon Kabat-Zinn, *Everyday Blessings: The Inner Work of Mindful Parenting* (New York: Hyperion, 1997).

27. Kabat-Zinn, *Catastrophe*, 1, 2, 12, 20.

28. Kabat-Zinn, *Catastrophe*, 8, 150, 151, 200.

29. Kabat-Zinn, *Catastrophe*, 6, 218, 418, 420. Elsewhere he remarked that "in the mindful cultivation of generosity, it is not necessary to give everything away, or even anything. Above all, generosity is an inward giving, a feeling state, a willingness to share your own being with the world": Kabat-Zinn, *Wherever*, 63.

30. Kabat-Zinn, *Wherever*, xv–xvii, 3, 4, 93, 95.

31. Virginia Heffernan, "The Muddied Meaning of 'Mindfulness,'" *NYTM*, April 14, 2015; Wilson, *Mindful America*, 35–40, 60–61, 84,103, 167–68, 170–79. For relevant web sites, see http://www.umassmed.edu/cfm/about-us/people/2-meet-our-faculty/kabat-zinn-profile/; http://www.mindfulnesscds.com/.

32. The Dalai Lama and Howard C. Cutler, *The Art of Happiness: A Handbook for Living* (New York: Penguin Putman, 1998), 3, 7–8. Yi Fu Tuan, *The Good Life* (Madison: University of Wisconsin Press, 1986) and Daniel Goleman, ed., *Healing Emotions: Conversations with the Dalai Lama on Mindfulness, Emotions, and Health* (Boston: Shambhala, 1997) mixed contemporary scholarship and Eastern philosophy. Although not usually considered part of happiness studies or positive psychology, Deepak Chopra combines many elements central to these fields, even as he represents a position closer to spirituality than science.

33. Cutler, *Happiness*, 8, 22, 41. The Dalai Lama advised readers that as soon as you got up in the morning, "you can develop a sincere positive motivation, thinking 'I will utilize this day in a more positive way'": Dalai Lama, *Happiness*, 42.

34. David C. McClelland and Carol Kirshnit, "The Effect of Motivational Arousal Through Films on Salivary Immunoglobulin A," *Psychology and Health* 2 (Jan. 1988): 31–52.

35. Cutler, *Happiness*, 4, 30. For some of the places where Cutler acknowledged these tensions, see Cutler, *Happiness*, 73, 189.

36. Ellen J. Langer, *Mindfulness* (Reading, MA: Addison-Wesley, 1989), 78.

37. Among the other works relevant here are Joop Hartog and Hessel Oosterbeek, "Health, Wealth and Happiness: Why Pursue a Higher Education," *Economics of Education Review* 17 (June 1998): 245–56, and Robert Frank, *Passions within Reason: The Strategic Role of the Emotions* (New York: Norton, 1988). Frank, one of the few economists who made significant contributions to positive psychology, critiqued the excessive emphasis on self-interest among social and behavioral scientists and insisted that at times moral behavior benefited those who practiced it. Though he summarized the findings of happiness studies, he did not really connect his critique of pursuit of alternatives to self-interest to happiness, though he did briefly suggest (201–02) that pursuit of materialistic self-interest produced less happy marriages.

38. Barbara L. Fredrickson and Daniel Kahneman, "Duration Neglect in Retrospective Evaluations of Affective Episodes," *JPSP* 65 (July 1993): 45–55; Daniel Kahneman et al., "When More Pain Is Preferred to Less: Adding a Better End," *PS* 4 (Nov. 1993): 401–05; Daniel Kahneman, Peter P. Wakker, and Rakesh Sarin, "Back to Bentham? Explorations of Experienced Utility," *Quarterly Journal of Economics* 112 (May 1997): 375–406; David Schkade and Daniel Kahneman, "Does Living in California Make People Happy? A Focusing Illusion in Judgments of Life Satisfaction," *PS* 9 (Sept. 1998): 340–346; Donald L. Redelmeier and Daniel Kahneman, "Patients' Memories of Painful Medical Treatments: Real-Time and Retrospective Evaluations of Two Minimally Invasive Procedures," *Pain* 66 (July 1996): 3–8. For a philosopher's critique of Kahneman's contribution, see Fred Kaplan, *What Is This Thing Called Happiness?* (New York: Oxford University Press, 2010), 46–52.

39. Daniel Kahneman, Ed Denier, and Norbert Schwarz, eds., *Well-Being: The Foundations of Hedonic Psychology* (New York: Russell Sage Foundation, 1999).

40. Kahneman, Diener, and Schwarz, "Preface," in Kahneman, Diener, and Schwarz, eds., *Well-Being*, ix.
41. Kahneman, Diener, and Schwarz, "Preface," xii.
42. Kahneman, "Objective," in Kahneman, Diener, and Schwarz, eds., *Well-Being*, 3, 6. In the bibliography following his article, Kahneman referred to Csikszentmihalyi's *Flow* but not at all to the work of Seligman.
43. Kahneman, "Objective," 22.
44. Leon Festinger, "A Theory of Social Comparison Processes," *Human Relations* 7 (May 1954): 117–40.
45. Richard H. Smith, Ed Diener, and Douglas H. Wedell, "Intrapersonal and Social Comparison Determinants of Happiness: A Range-Frequency Analysis," *JPSP* 56 (March 1989): 317–25; Joanne V. Wood, "Theory and Research Concerning Social Comparisons of Personal Attributes," *PB* 106 (Sept. 1989): 231–48; Lisa G. Aspinwall and Shelley E. Taylor, "Effects of Social Comparison Direction, Threat, and Self-Esteem on Affect, Self-Evaluation, and Expected Success," *JPSP* 64 (May 1993): 708–22; Sonja Lyubomirsky and Lee Ross, "Hedonic Consequences of Social Comparison: A Contrast of Happy and Unhappy People," *JPSP* 73 (Dec. 1997): 1141–57. Most of the scholars in happiness studies or positive psychology paid relatively little attention to larger social and political events and institutions; for an important exception, see Marsha Richings, "Social Comparison, Advertising and Consumer Discontent," *American Behavioral Scientist* 38 (Feb. 1995): 593–607. For a later, important study, see Sonja Lyubomirsky, *The How of Happiness: A Scientific Approach to Getting the Life You Want* (New York: Penguin, 2007), 115–19.
46. David Lykken and Auke Tellegen, "Happiness Is a Stochastic Phenomenon," *PS* 7 (May 1996): 186, 189; Lykken, *Happiness*, 1–3. For an earlier study that deemphasized the importance of the family environment for child reading of twins, see Auke Tellegen and David Lykken et al., "Personality Similarity in Twins Reared Apart and Together," *JPSP* 54 (June 1988): 1031–39.
47. Dalton Conley, "Commentary: Reading Plomin and Daniels in the Post-Genomic Age," *International Journal of Epidemiology* 40 (June 2011): 596–98. They were referring to Robert Plomin and Denise Daniels, "Why Are Children in the Same Family So Different from Each Other?" *Behavioral and Brain Sciences* 10 (March 1987): 1–16, but their remarks can be extended to the work of Lykken as well.
48. Richard G. Tedeschi, Crystal L. Park, and Lawrence G. Calhoun, "Preface," in *Posttraumatic Growth: Positive Changes in the Aftermath of Crisis*, ed. Richard G. Tedeschi, Crystal L. Park, and Lawrence G. Calhoun (Mahwah, NJ: Erlbaum, 1999), vii; Richard G. Tedeschi, Crystal L. Park, and Lawrence G. Calhoun, "Posttraumatic Growth: Conceptual Issues," in Tedeschi, Park, and Calhoun, *Posttraumatic Growth*, 1–22. Three years earlier two of them had considered these issues and ended their book with self-help advice to those who suffered from traumas: Richard G. Tedeschi and Lawrence G. Calhoun, *Trauma and Transformation: Growing in the Aftermath of Suffering* (Thousand Oaks, CA: Sage, 1995). In *Positive Illusions: Creative Self-Deception and the Healthy Mind* (New York: Basic, 1989), Shelley E. Taylor emphasized how, when faced with traumatic or tragic events, people could respond effectively with less than accurate reasoning. A key text on this topic is Judith L. Herman, *Trauma and Recovery* (New York: Basic Books, 1992).
49. Tedeschi, Park, and Calhoun, "Conceptual," 1, 2.
50. Gail M. Williamson and Margaret S. Clark, "Providing Help and Desired Relationship Type as Determinants of Changes in Moods and Self-Evaluations," *JPSP* 56 (May 1989): 722–34; Robert B. Cialdini et al., "Reinterpreting the Empathy-Altruism Relationship When One into One Equals Oneness," *JPSP* 73 (Sept. 1997): 481–94.

51. J. S. House, C. Robbins, and H. L. Metzner, "The Association of Social Relationships and Activities with Mortality: Predictive Evidence from the Tecumseh Community Health Study," *American Journal of Epidemiology* 116 (July 1982): 123–40; C. Daniel Batson, *The Altruism Question; Toward a Social Psychological Answer* (Hillsdale, NJ: Erlbaum, 1991), 173; Matt Ridley, *The Origin of Virtue: Human Instincts and the Evolution of Cooperation* (New York: Viking, 1997); Elliott Sober and David Sloan Wilson, *Unto Others: The Evolution and Psychology of Unselfish Behavior* (Cambridge, MA: Harvard University Press, 1998), 337.

52. All this hardly exhausts the list of topics to which psychologists were paying attention. Scholars clarified, qualified, and extended how subjective well-being developed and could be measured or defined: see, for example Ed Diener, Eunkook Suh, and Shieghiro Oishi, "Recent Findings on Subjective Well-Being," *Indian Journal of Clinical Psychology* 24 (March 1997): 25–41. Attention continued to shift toward the Aristotelean view of happiness: Sarah Broadie, *Ethics with Aristotle* (New York: Oxford University Press, 1991), 50. Others focused on the importance of smiles to positivity (Fritz Strack, Leonard L. Martin, and Sabine Stepper, "Inhibiting and Facilitating Conditions of the Human Smile: A Nonobtrusive Test of the Facial Feedback Hypothesis," *JPSP* 54 [May 1988]: 768–77); on writing about emotional experiences (James W. Pennebaker, "Writing About Emotional Experiences as a Therapeutic Process," *PS* 8 [May 1997]: 162–66); and on how satisfaction increased as workers shifted from job, to career, to calling (Amy Wrzesniewski et al., "Jobs, Careers, and Callings: People's Relations to Their Work," *Journal of Research in Personality* 31[March 1997]: 21–33).

53. Cindy Hazan and Phillip Shaver, "Romantic Love Conceptualized as an Attachment Process," *JPSP* 52 (March 1987): 511–24; James S. House, Karl R. Landis, and Debra Umberson, *Science*, July 29, 1988, 540–45; Roy F. Baumeister and Mark R. Leary, "The Need to Belong: Desire for Interpersonal Attachments as a Fundamental Human Motivation," *PB* 117 (May 1995): 497–529.

54. See, for example, D. Watson and L. A. Clark, "Extraversion and Its Positive Emotional Core," in *Handbook of Personality Psychology*, ed. R. Hogan, J. Johnson, and S. Briggs (San Diego, CA: Academic Press, 1997), 767–93; Alan M. Saks, "Longitudinal Field Investigation of the Moderating and Mediating Effects of Self-Efficacy on the Relationship Between Training and Newcomer Adjustment," *Journal of Applied Psychology* 80 (April 1995): 211–25.

55. John F. Dovidio et al., "Group Representations and Intergroup Bias: Positive Affect, Similarity, and Group Size," *Personality and Social Psychology Bulletin* 21 (Aug. 1995): 856–65.

56. Robert A. Emmons, "Personal Strivings: An Approach to Personality and Subjective Well-Being," *JPSP* 51 (Oct. 1986): 1058–68.

57. Barbara L. Frederickson, "What Good Are Positive Emotions?" *Review of General Psychology* 2 (Sept. 1998): 315; Michael F. Scheier and Charles S. Carver, "On the Power of Positive Thinking: the Benefits of Being Optimistic," *Current Directions in Psychological Science* 2 (Feb. 1993): 26–30.

58. Stanley J. Rachman, *Fear and Courage* (San Francisco: W.H. Freeman, 1978); Daniel Putnam, "Psychological Courage," *Philosophy, Psychiatry, and Psychology* 4 (March 1997): 1–11; Donald O. Clifton and Paula Nelson, *Soar with Your Strengths* (New York: Delacorte, 1992); Roy F. Baumeister and Todd F. Heatherton, "Self-Regulation Failure: An Overview," *Psychological Inquiry* 7 (Jan. 1996), 1–15; Lisa G Aspinwall, "Rethinking the Role of Positive Affect in Self-Regulation," *Motivation and Emotion* 22 (March 1988): 1–32; Ed Diener et al., "The Psychic Costs of Intense Positive Affect," *JPSP* 61 (Oct. 1991): 492–502; Christopher Peterson and Lisa M. Bossio, *Health and Optimism* (New York: Free Press, 1991).

59. Robert A. Witter et al., "Religion and Subjective Well-Being in Adulthood: A Quantitative Synthesis," *Review of Religious Research* 26 (June 1985): 332–42; Robert A. Emmons, Chi Cheung, and Keivan Tehrani, "Assessing Spirituality Through Personal Goals: Implications for Research on Religion and Subjective Well-Being," *SIR* 45 (Nov. 1998): 391–422; Christopher G. Ellison and Jeffrey S. Levin, "The Religion-Health Connection: Evidence, Theory, and Future Directions," *Health Education and Behavior* 25 (Dec. 1998): 700–20.

60. Kenneth I. Pargament, *The Psychology of Religion and Coping: Theory, Research, Practice* (New York: Guilford Press, 1997), 355.

61. Ed Diener, Marissa Diener, and Carol Diener, "Factors Predicting the Subjective Well-Being of Nations," *JPSP* 69 (Nov. 1995): 851–64; Ed Diener and Marissa Diener, "Cross-Cultural Correlates of Life Satisfaction and Self-Esteem," *JPSP* 68 (April 1995): 653–63; Ruut Veenhoven, *Happiness in Nations: Subjective Appreciation of Life in 56 Nations, 1946–1992* (Rotterdam: RISBO, 1993); Ronald Inglehart, *Cultural Shift in Advanced Industrial Society* (Princeton, NJ: Princeton University Press, 1990), esp. 25–43, 212–26; Ronald Inglehart, *Modernization and Postmodernization: Cultural, Economic, and Political Change in 43 Societies* (Princeton, NJ: Princeton University Press, 1997), esp. 86–88.

CHAPTER 5

Drawing (and Crossing) the Line

Academic and Popular Renditions of

Subjective Well-Being, 1984–1998

What emerged in books written from the mid-1980s to near the end of the next decade was a shifting, sometimes hard-to-distinguish, and complex relationship between approaches by scholars and professional writers. Those by both academics and freelancers did not incorporate many of the most important findings offered in specialized journals. Yet what marked the popular for both groups was a highly accessible style, the ambition to reach general audiences, a wide range of promotional tools, and the presentation of advice to "you" the reader. Books published by academics such as Mihaly Csikszentmihalyi and Martin Seligman, soon to emerge as among the most important leaders in the field, melded the scholarly and popular how-to approaches. In contrast, non-academic popularizers, though at times drawing on recent scholarship, tended to offer even more breathlessly optimistic self-help books.

In the context of an explosively expanding marketplace for books that told members of an eager audience how to enhance their sense of well-being, writers claiming the mantle of science therefore faced a series of challenges. National book store chains, publishing houses, and literary agents seeking bestsellers and a reading public eager for help in uncertain times together created potentially lucrative opportunities for writers who could offer evidence and advice in accessible prose. Clinical psychologists had always written self-help books, but less common were ones by academic researchers. Serious scholars, seeing a glut of books by their freelance counterparts who often put forward exaggerated claims, felt they had to correct the record. In addition, they watched as respected scholars in other fields wrote popular books that succeeded in the marketplace. In such contexts, professional psychologists policed the border between the pure and the impure, the soberly verifiable and the boisterously exaggerated. They had to do so because there were often no clear differences between books by academic scholars and those by freelance writers. Yet as writers, too, professional psychologists who were convinced they had truths that would improve the lives of millions had to figure out how far they could go in adopting or adapting the tricks of the trade so as to have the impact they were convinced their findings merited. Indeed, it would not be surprising to find that some in the profession worried that their peers rushed too swiftly from scholarly articles to popular books, presenting findings in the process that may have been exaggerated or premature.

The move by academics to cross the border into the popular, especially when this involved how-to advice, engendered both opportunities and dangers. On the one hand, popular books promised to enhance professorial influence. On the other, moving into the breach too quickly was potentially troublesome. Offering experimentally based findings to people other than one's peers threatened nuance and opened up possibilities of misunderstandings and misapplications. Journalists often sensationalized and simplified scientific findings when presenting them to readers who lacked the statistical knowledge to appreciate the caveats and limitations inherent in making inferences about a population based on samples, particularly in the case of novel findings that have not been replicated. Moreover, a lay public eager for health and happiness based on what seemed like scientifically validated solutions risked the danger of embracing fads promoted, perhaps inadvertently, by academics eager to enhance the influence of their research agendas. "There is probably little that true positive psychologists can do to defend the science from the more vulgar marketers," Todd B. Kashdan and Michael F. Steger remarked in a state-of-the-field essay published in *Designing Positive Psychology: Taking Stock and Moving Forward* (2011). "The first data on rigorously tested positive psychology have only recently begun to show up in journals," they continued, "yet people have been offering to 'apply' positive psychology for several years already. What kind of message does this convey about the scientific endeavor of positive psychology? Is it any wonder that positive psychology is often dismissed as 'happiology' or the equivalent of accepting a Dixie cup of Kool-Aid from Jim Jones?"[1]

Beginning in the mid-1980s scores of books on happiness appeared, few more important than those by two among a handful of major figures in the field, Csikszentmihalyi and Seligman. In a series of books published in the late 1980s and 1990s, they continued to present empirical findings while they experimented with reader-friendly approaches with which populariz-ers had reached broad lay audiences.

Csikszentmihalyi continued his work on flow, how people achieved hap-piness through immersion in what they did, and, as he did so, he moved beyond the scholarly formulations he relied on in his 1975 *Beyond Boredom and Anxiety*. As the person most responsible for making flow central to the understanding of positive psychological experiences, he had carefully tracked the enormous impact of that book, in the process realizing what it meant to gain a wide audience. Scholars and practitioners built on his insights in multiple directions. In the United States and elsewhere, they applied flow to the domains of education, business, sports, leisure, therapy, advertising, and museum design.[2]

In central ways, what Csikszentmihalyi wrote after 1975 followed what he had earlier laid out. He continued to focus on the importance of flow in fostering meaningful and happy lives. He described and analyzed the conditions that fostered creativity—and did so in sophisticated, prob-ing ways; indeed, among those who contributed to happiness studies, he was the most deeply learned and philosophical. He persisted in drawing on and contributing to humanistic psychology. He made clear his debt to Abraham Maslow by noting the resemblance between Maslow's emphasis on peak experiences and his own on flow. He continued to see work more than leisure as the principal locus of flow, even as he made clear the often paradoxical relationships between the two realms. He acknowledged the influence of Eastern religions. He envisioned flow as mystical, most notably when he spoke of psychic energy, inner harmony, and transcendence. Thus he ended *Flow: The Psychology of Optimal Experience* (1990) by stating that "the problem of meaning will then be resolved as the individual's purpose merges with the universal flow."[3]

Yet Csikszentmihalyi kept his distance from the excesses of the power of positive thinking and of the counterculture, even as he embraced an expan-sive vision of a pleasurable life. Having a good life was not a question of winning friends and influencing people, he remarked as he countered the language of Dale Carnegie. "The human potential and other New Age move-ments of the past thirty years," he wrote in *The Evolving Self: A Psychology for the Third Millennium* (1993), "have tried to restore to men and women the dignity lost to scientific reductionism. In doing so, however, they have often overshot the mark and fallen into the opposite sort of excess." These narcissistic movements, he insisted, offered a romanticism that proffered shallow and false hopes. Nonetheless, he spoke again and again of optimal (and presumably more genuine) experiences that gave pleasure, happiness, enjoyment, joy, and exhilaration. On the back cover of one of his books appeared a quote from the *New York Times* saying that Csikszentmihalyi "is a man obsessed by happiness." If so, he distinguished shallow happiness from deep and sustained pleasure: flow produced a very special kind of subjective well-being, a profound and lasting one.[4]

Even as he continued to focus on flow, there were important differences between what Csikszentmihalyi wrote in 1975 and toward the century's end. He increasingly drew similarities between flow and meditation. Like many scholars in other fields, he paid more and more attention to genetics, neuroscience, and cultural and biological evolution, while insisting that it was important to break "out of the fatalistic acceptance of genetic or historical programming" by controlling consciousness. He placed a greater emphasis on the idea that people could achieve flow-based happiness even when external circumstance militated against such a possibility. The key to life, he wrote in *Flow*, is how "*people manage to enjoy life despite adversity.*" Counseling people that neither wealth nor power mattered, he advised them to avoid the "frustrating treadmill of rising expectations" and instead to live in the present. "If a person learns to enjoy and find meaning in the ongoing stream of experience, in the process of living itself," he concluded, "the burden of social controls automatically falls from one's shoulders." Although not a major focus in his writing, he nonetheless explored how to develop strategies and public policies that could enhance people's lives, even going so far as to suggest that more equitable distribution of flow experience in a population was central to achieving social justice. In the end, however, he felt that changing individual consciousness both was more important and would come more quickly than a fundamental transformation of society.[5]

Another important way his later books differed from his 1975 one was in style and approach. Csikszentmihalyi's 1975 book had combined ethnographies of groups of people, such as rock climbers and basketball players, who fully immersed themselves in what they did, with complicated statistics and charts that might have put off some readers. In contrast, in the late 1980s and 1990s, as he reached out to broader audiences, he wrote in ways less encumbered by scientific apparatus. Instead, he told human interest stories, writing in highly accessible prose and offering lucid summaries of research he and others had conducted. Yet the most interesting change in the trajectory of Csikszentmihalyi's writing is his increasing shift toward the genre of how-to books. In his 1990 *Flow*, he remarked that writing for a general audience is "somewhat dangerous, because as soon as one strays from the stylized constraints of academic prose, it is easy to become careless or overly enthusiastic about such a topic." So he insisted that his was "not a popular book that gives insider tips about how to be happy" because "a joyful life is an individual creation that cannot be copied from a recipe." Instead, he presented "general *principles*, along with concrete examples of how some people have used these principles." He remarked that he was not offering "easy short-cuts" but "enough information to make possible the transition from theory to practice." In contrast, three years later, at the end of each chapter of his next book, *The Evolving Self*, he listed questions to be answered and provided space for readers to answer them. "Can you recognize when your body interferes with control over consciousness—e.g. when being hungry makes you nervous and snappy?" he asked readers before going on to suggest they record "ways of regaining control."[6]

In *Creativity: Flow and the Psychology of Discovery and Invention* (1996), Csikszentmihalyi expressed none of the defensiveness about writing a how-to book that was present in his 1990 *Flow*. On the very first page, he remarked that though his book offered "no simple solutions," it ended "with ideas about how to make your life more like that of the creative exemplars" he studied, a strategy that could involve offering easy solutions to difficult problems. The key words here were "you" and "your," something that soon became evident when he commented on "the message that the creative person is sending us: You, too, can spend your life doing what you love to do." At several points, he built on his evidence to offer a homily, for example, ending one chapter by remarking that "the lives of these creative individuals reassure us that it is not impossible" for readers' children and grandchildren to experience more "joy in writing poetry and solving theorems than in being passively entertained." Then in the last chapter he turned from "description to prescription," informing his readers that he would "extract some useful ideas from the lives of a few creative persons about how to enrich the lives of everybody" as he offered "explicit suggestions for how to apply" the insights gained from a look at individuals "to everyday life."[7]

What followed were almost a score of recommendations, such as "*try to surprise at least one person every day*," wake up daily thinking about a specific goal, "*make time for reflection and relaxation*," and look at your work from "*as many viewpoints as possible*."[8] A year later the back cover characterized *Finding Flow: The Psychology of Engagement in Everyday Life* (1997) as "part psychological study, part self-help book . . . a prescriptive guide that helps us reclaim ownership of our lives." Although his suggestions were hardly as trite, naïve, or in most cases as simplistic as those Norman Vincent Peale offered in *The Power of Positive Thinking*, Csikszentmihalyi had nonetheless added to his studies about the relationship between flow and fulfillment by making explicit recommendations about how to achieve a sense of well-being through creativity.[9]

Seligman, similarly aware of the dangers and opportunities the market rewarded, was also beginning to offer books designed to reach wider audiences. Three of them mark his movement toward the positive psychology he articulated in his 1998 presidential address to the American Psychological Association and, like his colleague's work, toward a more popular how-to approach. Seligman shifted from *Helplessness: On Depression, Development and Death*, the title of his 1975 book, to *Learned Optimism: How to Change Your Mind and Your Life*, the title of one that appeared fifteen years later. This shift toward optimism and the self-help genre becomes clear in this and two other books he authored in the 1990s: *What You Can Change and What You Can't: The Complete Guide to Successful Self-Improvement* (1994) and *The Optimistic Child* (1995).

Seligman lamented that psychologists had focused too much on negativity. While acknowledging the importance of improving the lives of unhealthy people, he sought "to make the lives of well people even better." Pessimists could learn to be optimists "not through mindless devices like whistling a happy tune or mouthing platitudes ('Every day, in every way, I'm getting better and better'), but by learning a new set of cognitive skills." Following a central insight of cognitive behavioral therapy, Seligman emphasized the importance of choosing a positive explanatory style that would undermine self-fulfilling negative beliefs and lead people not just to think optimistically but to act optimistically. How we explain to ourselves why events happened was critical, as people learned to balance a flexible optimism with a realistic pessimism. In turn what mattered was not falling into the belief that adversity was permanent, pervasive, and of one's own making.[10]

In addition, Seligman offered both analysis and suggestions of how "to speak to yourself about your setbacks from a more encouraging viewpoint." He relied on an acronym to help people remember what they had to do: ABCDE, standing for Adversity, Belief, Consequences, Disputation, and Energization, illustrating this five-step process with easily understood stories. "Tune into your own negative dialogue," he advised, "by writing down the beliefs you have when adversity strikes" and then challenge your pessimistic outlook. Then find a way of externalizing this dialogue by going over it with a friend or colleague. All this, he proposed, would help create greater levels of physical health and achievement, at work and play, in schools and in the family, on sports fields and in corporate settings.[11]

At the end of *Learned Optimism*, Seligman turned from psychology to social criticism, broadening his perspective and the roles he envisioned for himself. Seeking to explain why he believed depression had reached epidemic proportions in developed nations since World War II, he focused on how affluence and advertising had helped create "the deciding, choosing, hedonistically preoccupied individual." Here he relied on Christopher Lasch's *Culture of Narcissism* as he described the emergence of "a new kind of self, a 'maximal' self" that focused on gratification and control. This raised expectations of what was possible in love and work to unrealistic levels. Given that the tumultuous events of the 1960s and 1970s fostered a shrinking of what Seligman called the "commons"—"a belief in the nation, in God, in one's family, or in a purpose that transcends our lives"—people had increasingly turned to look inside themselves. These forces intensified personal depressions. As Seligman peered into the future, he considered the possibility of the maximal, self-exhausting self and of the nation surrendering its freedoms to authoritarianism.

In contrast, he offered two more positive solutions. The first was that people could develop greater commitments to the commons and more meaningful lives. Although his specific recommendations implied that "the community at large" was largely local and involvement in it highly personal, he nonetheless supported reaching outside the self, not so much by developing government-funded social welfare programs or joining protest movements as by giving to charities in a more thoughtful, generous, and engaging manner; sacrificing an everyday pleasure such as eating out for the sake of helping others by working in a soup kitchen, visiting with AIDS patients, or helping out on a local school board campaign; writing letters to people who have acted heroically or despicably and then contacting politicians and others who could follow up. His second solution to the overbearing power of the maximal self was through a realism and flexibility. "We must be able to use pessimism's keen sense of reality when we need it," he remarked in the second-to-last sentence, "but without having to dwell in its dark shadows. The benefits of this kind of optimism," he wrote in the final sentence, were "without limit."[12]

While hardly abandoning scholarship, Seligman was moving toward programmatic self-help. The title of his 1994 book, *What You Can Change and Can't: The Complete Guide to Successful Self-Improvement*, fully captured this shift. The other two books reflected this familiar approach, absent from much of his earlier work. The cover of the hardback of *Learned Optimism* made the promise that the book could reveal how to obtain "a good and successful life," a sentiment echoed on the book's back cover by Aaron Beck's statement about optimism—"you can measure it, you can teach it, and you will be healthier and happier for it." Similarly, in *The Optimistic Child*, Seligman promised "a practical, concrete plan of action."[13]

In these three books, Seligman relied on a combination of powerful stories of illness and recovery, questionnaires readers could fill out, practical advice (often presented in bullet-point form), and summaries of scientific findings. He made clear that he rejected as counterproductive the ascendant power of the self-esteem movement among teachers, parents, and pop psychologists and promoted by what he called "an enormous, and profitable, self-improvement industry" that emphasized how children felt rather than what they could do by meeting challenges. "FEELING GOOD VERSUS DOING WELL" ran a boldface subheading in one chapter. He called Norman Vincent Peale, Robert Schuller, and, more problematically, Abraham Maslow "bootstrappers" who believed that the individual self was the agent of change. As others in positive psychology did, here Seligman was both critiquing and adopting the techniques that his popularizing predecessors had offered in even more exaggerated ways.[14]

Learned optimism, he insisted as he made clear his opposition to what Peale offered, "is not a rediscovery of the 'power of positive thinking'" that emerged "from the pink Sunday-school world of happy events" and involved repeating positive self-affirmations. Decades of research had revealed the importance of an approach more profound than "repeating boosterish phrases to ourselves." To test his theories of depression and optimism, Seligman drew on data collected in laboratories, schools, therapy, and corporations. He directed large-scale and well-funded studies in school systems and major business organizations. He acknowledged the power of genetic, pharmacological, evolutionary, and biochemical factors in shaping human personality but also made clear that these factors had limited power, operating more forcefully in some realms than in others. Consequently, as the title of one of these three books underscored, there were things people could control (learning optimism and influencing mood states) and things they could not (curing alcoholism or undoing deeply rooted problems caused by childhood traumas).[15]

Even though the end of *Learned Optimism* could be taken as a criticism of neoliberalism, elsewhere in the 1990s he offered a positive vision of what contemporary capitalism had wrought. "Most American children," he remarked, "are now born into a time of enormous opportunity: they live in a very powerful and wealthy country, where people enjoy unprecedented individual liberties and choices; as the shadow of nuclear war recedes, science and medicine continue to make major advances; and communications networks span a global village of books, music, games, trading, and knowledge." The stakes were high: unless Americans shifted from pessimism to optimism, he wrote in ways that invoked hopes for nationalism and an unexplored interest in positive social change, "our liberty, our wealth, and our power will be of little use. . . . We will lack the initiative to achieve justice at home, and our children will come to adulthood in a country crippled by sterile self-absorption."[16]

Although Seligman's theory of learned optimism broke fresh ground, in *Learned Optimism*, but elsewhere as well, he spent more energy describing and killing pessimism than explaining optimism. In this respect he differed from happiness popularizers. Significantly, as of the early to mid-1990s, the positive psychology he was beginning to develop lacked the unbound sense of possibility conveyed by many authors who had never written a book on helplessness and who now used the word "happiness" instead of optimism in their book titles.

The relationship of Csikszentmihalyi and Seligman to highly popular and wide-eyed books on happiness was complicated. After all, as scientists who had achieved professional prominence and authors of books designed to be commercially successful, they were attempting to straddle scholarly rigor and lay accessibility, even though in such books they might tell readers not to worry about status and success. Csikszentmihalyi may have initially been wary of entering the chase after popularity with offerings of self-help, but he wound up doing so nonetheless. Seligman objected to what he had called the "profitable, self-improvement industry," but by the mid-1990s he too was working to figure out his relationship to what he opposed through a mixture of caution against simple optimism and movement toward a popular self-help genre. Here were cases of serious academics engaging in strategies that operated on somewhat conflicting fronts. Aware of both the success and distorted exaggerations of unbridled popularizers, Csikszentmihalyi and Seligman sought to differentiate themselves from them. At the same time, as leaders of positive psychology as a cultural movement, they were figuring out how to develop approaches that would enable them to reach broader audiences.

POPULARIZING HAPPINESS

From the mid-1980s until the late 1990s, books on happiness that were aimed even more unapologetically at popular audiences appeared in droves, in the process giving scientifically oriented academics much to imitate—and worry about.[17] Some, like *Gay Happiness: How to Get It* or *For Black Women Only: A Complete Guide to Successful Life-Style Change, Health, Wealth, Love and Happiness*, targeted specific audiences. Books more general in their focus varied considerably in how they approached the topic. In *Are You Happy? Some Answers to the Most Important Question in Your Life* (1986), the recovering alcoholic and TV show host Dennis Wholey gathered the responses of more than fifty famous people. In the same year,

William A. Miller, a pastoral counselor at a Minneapolis hospital and author of several previous advice books, with *The Joy of Feeling Good: Eight Keys to a Happy and Abundant Life* offered what the jacket copy called "A Treasury of Practical Wisdom for Your Journey to Christian Maturity!" At the book's end he announced that "I take God to mean that that superadded, exceedingly abundant life includes the joy of feeling good." In *15 Principles for Achieving Happiness* (1988), Archibald D. Hart, a Christian psychologist at Fuller Theological Seminary, wrote that readers could use his book and "God's grace" to raise their "happiness score." With the "profound union of creature and Creator, real happiness simply cannot be disrupted!" With *Happiness Is an Inside Job* (1989), the Jesuit John Powell, one of the relatively rare Roman Catholics to write on happiness, talked of a moment in his novitiate when, filled with God's *"undeniable presence,"* he thought *"If this is what happiness is, I have never been happy before. This,"* he concluded, *"is a taste of new wine."* Verena Kast's *Joy, Inspiration, and Hope* (1991) and Robert Johnson's *Ecstasy: Understanding the Psychology of Joy* (1987) relied on Jungian perspectives, the former philosophical and the latter both philosophical and practical. Barry Neil Kaufman's *Happiness Is a Choice* (1991), an inspirational book by a therapist that received considerable media attention, posited a will to believe in happiness that resulted in quick and easy transformations: "the first best way" to happiness, he insisted, "would be to decide right now to be happy." The psychotherapist Richard Carlson's inspirational, motivational *You Can Be Happy No Matter What: Five Principles Your Therapist Never Told You* (1992) appeared five years before his *Don't Sweat the Small Stuff . . . and It's All Small Stuff: Simple Ways to Keep the Little Things from Taking Over Your Life* (1997), which rocketed to the top of the bestseller list where it remained for two years—and was translated into thirty languages. In *Happiness Is a Serious Problem: A Human Nature Repair Kit* (1998), observant Jew and talk show host Dennis Prager advocated for the central role of the mind in the passionate and moderate pursuit of happiness, something he deemed a moral obligation.[18]

Popular books provided Seligman and other scholars proof that there was a huge audience ready to buy books that offered accessible guides to happiness. More specifically, at least two authors made clearly explicit what it would mean to shift focus from mental illness to well-being. More than fifteen years before Seligman's call for a positive psychology, E. M. Suarez and Roger C. Mills published *Sanity, Insanity and Common Sense: The Missing Link in Understanding Mental Health* (1982), which offered mental health professionals a diagnosis and prognosis similar to that which Seligman articulated in his 1998 presidential address. Standing in opposition to both Freudianism and behaviorism, they lamented that psychology focused so much on mental illness and so little on mental health. They insisted that "mental health in all individuals is the most natural, ordinary and accessible condition in life." Emphasizing what they called "The Power of Positive Feelings" achieved through common sense and wisdom, they asserted that "the route to mental health" was "through positivity, happiness and feelings of enjoyment."[19]

The tone of most of these popular books varied from sober to enthusiastic. They also differed in terms of the traditions relied on—from canonical works on Western philosophy and literature to the Bible, to Eastern religions, to various strands of psychology. Though some of them drew on empirical findings from psychology, few of them referenced advances in biochemistry, genetics, neuroscience, or evolutionary biology. Their publishers ranged from obscure to major houses and their sales varied from hundreds to hundreds of thousands or even millions. Some were religious, but most were secular. Although most of the authors were American, books originating around the same time in the Netherlands, Switzerland, and Britain signaled the internationalizing of the field, albeit still largely limited to Western, highly developed nations. Many of these books had little impact on the lives of their authors; others brought fame, riches, and influence through sales, appearances on the lecture and talk show circuit, workshops, and additional publishing deals. In 1990 a British psychologist unintentionally captured the promise and limits books on happiness underscored. On the one hand, he warned that many popular books on happiness "make all kinds of weird and wonderful claims about how your life can be transformed as a result of reading their books, since they have discovered the secret (or secrets) of constant happiness." On the other hand, near the book's end, he exemplified the formulaic approach by offering "A Program for Happiness" that, relying on scientific research, suggested fourteen paths to a happier life.[20]

Together, these popularizing authors offered remarkably similar views of happiness and how to achieve it. They emphasized the importance of self-esteem and of abandoning personal judgments. They commonly relied on personal anecdotes; stories of how therapy, meditation, or spirituality healed people; and clichéd, hopeful assertions. They emphasized self-help, sometimes implicitly through the telling of life histories or offering homilies. Often they gave explicit advice through a series of formulaic instructions that relied on checklists, exercises, and routines: for example, Powell with ten "Practices," Miller with eight "Keys," Carlson with five principles, and Hart with fifteen. They usually steered people away from the future and, more insistently, the past, urging them to concentrate on the present. As Carlson wrote, although most therapists encouraged patients to focus on the past, he urged his readers to adopt "The Principle of the Present Moment."[21]

These popular books focused almost entirely on the inner self and remarkably little on the relation between the individual and the outside world, with friends and family members usually providing the only external touchstones. This was a broadening that still had sharp limits that sustained people's attention to others not very different in background from themselves. Lamenting how much the media focused on the tragedies of war and poverty, Kaufman insisted that "the irony is that for ourselves individually and for the planet collectively there perhaps is no more pressing issue than personal happiness." They denied that happiness involved hedonistic pleasure or materialistic success. They viewed the relationships of mind, emotions, spirit, and body as reciprocal and entwined. To varying degrees and implicitly drawing on the findings of cognitive psychologists, they emphasized to readers that they could learn to stop thinking negatively and begin thinking positively. As Kast wrote, "the emotions of anxiety, grief, and rage have been investigated much more thoroughly" than "the emotions of elation." They all agreed that people could both accept their fate (often expressed in terms of having realistic expectations and a moderate income) and achieve happiness. As Hart wrote, "happiness grows out of choosing to live harmoniously with your life circumstances—whatever they are." "A major cause of unhappiness," he continued as he cautioned against envy, "is *not valuing what we already have.*"[22]

Reflecting the storied tradition of New Thought's mind control that reached one culminating point in the work of Peale, these authors assumed that happiness was the natural and inevitable state, something people could choose, and so they called on their readers to think positively. "It's *our thinking*," Carlson emphasized as he followed others in minimizing the importance of factors such as race, class, and gender, "not our circumstances that determines how we feel." It was possible to learn, and easier than most people assumed, Hart wrote, to achieve "long-lasting, deep-seated, personal happiness." These authors were confident that they could help put people on the path to happiness: as Carlson wrote enthusiastically, the principles he enunciated, "once understood," would "allow you to feel happy and contented regardless of your problems—really!" Wholey echoed such a belief, remarking that happy people "seem to operate on a philosophy of positive thoughts, positive expectations, positive action, positive results. They always look at a half-full, not half-empty glass. Happy people accept life and see it as an adventure."[23]

Driving home the formulaic simplicity of some popularizers, one book in the period that made no pretense of being serious exemplifies the naiveté and simplicity of other, more pretentious ones. Barbara Ann Kipfer's *14,000 Things to Be Happy About* was published in 1991 by Workman, the hugely successful producer of zippy how-to books. According to a web site,

Kipfer's book was an "obsessive, quirky, and utterly captivating compendium with over 950,000 copies in print." Without analysis or commentary, she randomly listed thousands of things that could make a person happy, from paper cups of cinnamon-flavored apple sauce to snow picnics, to ironing hair.[24] By 2009 her book even inspired a negative copycat, *11,002 Things to Be Miserable About: The Satirical Not-So-Happy Book*, which included among its negative counterparts to Kipfer's lists dust mites, student loans, and imitation crabmeat.[25]

If one book fully captures the popularizing direction in which even academic psychologists were moving, it was Robert Holden's *Happiness Now! Timeless Wisdom for Feeling Good Fast*. By the time the book appeared in 1998, Holden had already worked at the BBC as a "personal performance trainer," established both a Laughter Clinic and a Stress Busters Clinic under the aegis of the National Health Service, and founded the Happiness Project that held seminars to help people achieve personal fulfillment. With a PhD in psychology and in his early thirties at the time, Holden went on to become one of Britain's most famous happiness experts: the author of a series of bestselling books, a regular figure on *Oprah*, and featured in two BBC documentaries, *The Happiness Formula* and *How to Be Happy*, which according to his web site were "shown in 16 countries to more than 30 million television viewers." His web site offers for sale a wristwatch that replaces the hours of the day with the words "NOW." The book itself offered ample evidence of what lay ahead: from the exclamation point in the title, to the praise printed on the first page ("Profound wisdom neatly packaged" and "Offers a passport, map and compass to true joy"), to Holden's dedication "to those who dare to sprinkle kindness, radiate love and scatter joy," to his cats, Great and Wonderful.[26]

He made clear that his formal education in psychology had taught him "a lot about our potential, in particular, our potential for unlimited amounts of misery." In six years while earning his doctorate, he continued, he had not heard even one lecture on "our potential for joy, peace, unity, wholeness and success." Then, he reported, one day he "realised the absolute necessity of being able to see the Light of the unconditional Self in healing."[27]

Well versed in writings by other professional psychologists, Holden also drew on canonical British writers, humanistic psychologists, social scientists, Protestant ministers, and Asian religious figures and their Western interpreters. Holden wove together stories of people he had encountered as a therapist, the findings of spiritual leaders, aphorisms derived from the traditions of mind cure, and the bromides of positive thinking. Ordinary people can learn what Schuller called "'possibility thinking,' *children can make anything out of anything.*" Throughout the book he highlighted his points by inserting punchy boldface headings for short sections: "*we all* 'suffer' from a highly critical condition of C.S.J.—constant self-judgment"; "everything—absolutely everything—is available to you 'now'"; "true happiness is an inner power, natural, healing, abundant and always available"; "Like a fragrance to a flower, true happiness is an expression of your unconditional Self—the real You"; "your intention to love, no matter what, is the absolute key to happiness." In sum, the message was clear: banish negative thoughts; recover your true self; choose happiness rather than search for it; and achieve abundant happiness by embracing your own destiny, the source of which is inside yourself not in the external world.[28]

As was true of most positive thinkers, Holden's was a self-contained universe that offered little evidence of the outside world in what he wrote and did. A 1994 article in London's *Independent* captured this well. Referring to his book *Living Wonder-fully* and his Laughter Clinic, the journalist wondered about the relevance of Holden's work to the life of a middle-aged Yorkshire miner who had lost his job. The journalist furnished his point with an imaginary dialogue between the two. The miner, watching TV with his kids while his wife worked at McDonald's, was "shouting at the kids and the wife and drinking too much." The writer went on to wonder what it meant for the miner to lose an industrial job and experience "intolerable stresses" in his family life. "No," the journalist responded, assuming Holden's view and capturing some of the blind spots in positive thinking, "you're suffering from a bad case of low self-esteem," which had become "an explanation for many of the social ills of the Nineties."[29]

Positive psychology academic researchers rarely spoke in a direct and evaluative manner about popularizers. One exception occurred in 1991 when the social psychologist Roy Baumeister, who in the next century would contribute several articles to *Journal of Positive Psychology*, argued that books like Peale's *Power of Positive Thinking* and its more contemporary equivalents promoted optimism, self-esteem, and a can-do attitude that corresponded "rather closely to what researchers have found as predictors of happiness." Although those who wrote popular self-help books "might be reluctant to acknowledge that they are designed to teach self-deception," nonetheless "that may in fact be their best bet for helping people to become happy." After all, researchers had consistently shown that "the happiest and healthiest people may be those who show systematic distortions and illusions in their perceptions of reality." Baumeister's comments make clear that as much as academics did their best to distance themselves from naïve popularizers, the conclusions both groups reached and the approaches they relied upon were often remarkably similar. However, his remarks also reveal that within the field of positive psychology there were well-respected scholars capable of critiquing the field for its blind spots. However, as two scholars have noted about an earlier period in the history of psychology, "popularization served as much to erode the fragile boundaries between common sense and science as to create them, which had been the original intention."[30]

SCHOLARLY CONSENSUS

Building on decades of research, scholars had reached a consensus akin to what Ed Diener had reported in 1984 and with emphases that both resembled and differed from their popularizing counterparts. Happiness is measurable and transparent, they confidently insisted, even though key issues remained contested. Surveys based on subjective evaluations of well-being revealed that most people were reasonably happy. Definitions of happiness avoided the simple and ecstatic, focusing instead on a meaningful and fulfilling and self-perceived well-being. As the British psychologist Michael Argyle put it in his 1987 book, happiness is "not entirely the opposite of unhappiness," but could "be understood as a reflection on satisfaction with life, or as the frequency and intensity of positive emotions." Levels of satisfaction varied within nations and across national borders. People in some nations, such as the Danes, were happier than those in others, such as the Greeks. The correlation between national well-being and affluence was positive but only moderately and not always consistently so. Within the United States, the richer you were the happier you were, though once a relatively moderate level of personal wealth was reached, the gains from additional wealth were modest. Particularly adverse or favorable events influenced people's sense of satisfaction, but only temporarily, with one's level of happiness shaped by a number of factors, including prior experiences (adaptation level theory) and one's comparison to how others were doing.[31]

When they did focus on demographic factors, scholars concluded that age, race, parental status, residential location, and education had a less-than-significant influence in determining a person's sense of well-being. Their research may have justified such conclusions but considered as social theory, what they confidently concluded problematically narrowed their vision and undermined commitments to social change that relied on collective action. Not surprisingly, while Americans generally avoided a focus on social class, British studies reported that working-class people faced greater trials in terms of "anxiety, depression, and minor forms of mental disorder" than did their middle- or upper-class counterparts. Gender had relatively little impact on the levels of happiness people reported, though the situation here was complicated. As Argyle wrote, "there is little gender difference in satisfaction with life as a whole or in positive affect, but women have more negative affect and more intense feelings." Unlike what Diener had reported earlier, Argyle concluded that women experienced more conflict than men: they felt more anxious and depressed in part because they more quickly decided that "they are ill, or have emotional problems" because of conflicts between housework, child care, and work outside the home and because of the ways girls were socialized—though he added that such gender differences seem to have diminished in recent years. The relationship between health and happiness was reciprocal. Biology, chemistry, and genetics influenced people's sense of well-being but only to a moderate degree, in part because the relationship between happiness and our brains was reciprocal and in part because attitudes often follow behavior, rendering what we did with our temperaments, talents, and opportunities somewhat more important.[32]

The factors affecting people's sense of satisfaction, they reported, had consequences for how they should lead their lives. Given that genetics, as well as many social indicators such as income and education, were fixed or had relatively little impact, attention focused on other domains where there was much people could do to enhance their happiness: live healthy lives; set realistic goals; foster a sense of self-esteem and optimism; gain a sense of control over one's life; connect with other people, especially friends and a partner in marriage; carefully balance a commitment to meaningful work and leisure with adequate rest, especially by cultivating flow in what one did.[33]

Some studies revealed specific interventions that could enhance how people felt about themselves. It helped to keep a log of what provided pleasure and then to develop a commitment to increasing such activities. Meditation reduced anxiety. Watching funny movies, listening to happy music, hearing a joke, drinking alcohol in moderation, encouraging people to smile, or offering them good news all aided. Argyle drew on the 1968 work by Emmet Velten that revealed it was possible to induce a positive mood by having experimental subjects read and ponder statements such as "I feel cheerful and lively" or "I've certainly got energy and self-confidence to share." Although the impact of this modern, scientific version of Norman Vincent Peale's power of positive thinking was short-lived, the method nonetheless opened up for later researchers the investigation of ways of producing more long-lasting results. Indeed Argyle relied on a 1973 study to offer a list of forty-nine "pleasant activities which affect mood for the whole day," from being in the company of happy people, to offering compliments or praise, to experiencing the presence of God, to learning how to do something new, to going out for a good meal.[34]

While positive psychology revealed the importance of individual acts of altruism, most people who wrote about happiness, including scholars, paid little to no attention to the role of engagement in or awareness of domestic or international politics. In this period, people from outside the ranks of what would become positive psychology—especially a small group of economists—were more likely to connect happiness with political and economic issues.[35] Indeed in Argyle's list of forty-nine pleasure-giving activities, there was no hint of a world outside friends, co-workers, and family. In some hands, the literature on happiness was reminiscent of the mind-control movement represented in an earlier generation by Norman Vincent Peale. Although scholars insisted that happiness studies and positive psychology owed little to the power of positive thinking or to humanistic psychology, the parallels across generations were striking—among them mind control, individualism, disengagement from politics, and confidence.[36]

Moreover, in some hands happiness studies led to conclusions consonant with America's and Britain's increasing turn to more conservative or centrist policies, whether in the conservatism of Reagan/Thatcher years or in the neoliberalism of the Clinton/Blair ones. As David Myers wrote in his 1992 *The Pursuit of Happiness*, the recognition that there was no inextricable connection between wealth and well-being "liberates us from envying the life-styles of the rich and famous" and in turn to being more satisfied with the material dimensions of our given lot in life. Because once above the poverty level, additional wealth brought relatively little and temporary happiness, he continued, "we needn't be so envious of the wealthy." Indeed, in a 1993 study two psychologists concluded that "when goals for financial success exceeded those for affiliation, self-acceptance, and community feeling, worse psychological adjustment was found." So the advice of many happiness writers was to accept external conditions, be satisfied with your station in life, and exercise mind control.[37]

Such recommendations fit well with the mood many Americans experienced at the time. Events such as the end of the war in Vietnam in 1975, the Iran hostage crisis of 1979, and the killing of 241 American servicemen in Beirut in 1983 had called into question America's hegemony abroad. President Bill Clinton's 1996 declaration that the United States was "ending welfare as we know it," the shift in pensions from defined benefits to defined contributions, and the federal government's weakening support for organized labor made clear that domestic public policy no longer evidenced a commitment to government's role in enhancing social welfare. The stagnation or slow growth of the living standards of low- and moderate-income Americans beginning in the early 1970s, and at the same time the widening gap between the incomes and wealth of the rich and most other Americans, meant that broad swaths of American society were stuck in place, or worse.

Although popular books by lay writers and those by academic psychologists had a great deal in common, as summaries in this chapter make clear, there were important differences. To some extent, books by academics paid more attention to scientific advances and international comparisons, evidenced more interest in measuring happiness, differentiated between what it was possible and impossible to control, and made clear which factors did and did not cause variations in how different groups experienced a sense of well-being. Although academics had come to embrace accessibility and how-to advice, compared with their even more commercially oriented peers, their tone was more sober; their view of happiness, more nuanced.

CONCLUSION

A maturing field of happiness studies and an about-to-emerge positive psychology had developed considerably by the late 1990s. A full complement of writings ranged from thousands of highly technical scholarly articles to summations that ran the gamut from soberly scholarly to breathlessly popular. If there was still a distinction between happiness studies and positive psychology, then the former was far ahead of the latter in terms of visibility and consensus.

Three senior founders of the field that would soon come to be known as positive psychology—Ed Diener, Mihaly Csikszentmihalyi, and Martin Seligman—each made vitally important contributions, as did members of a younger generation. With his 1984 commanding discussion of research on happiness, Diener had emerged as a leading figure in the study of subjective well-being. Csikszentmihalyi's emphasis on flow, made available in books that marked his abundant productivity, had among others things deepened the understanding of what true happiness was and provided a way that both scholars and ordinary people could get off the hedonic treadmill. Both had focused on well-being from the outset of their careers. In contrast, Seligman had begun with depression and mental illness, and then, from *Helplessness* in 1975 to *Learned Optimism* fifteen years later, he had made a change critical to the flourishing of positive psychology. Along with others scholars, including those who emphasized resilience in face of traumatic events, Seligman had shifted attention away from mental illness and depression to well-being and optimism.[38]

A self-professed grouch, Seligman had a temperament and approach different from those of his two senior colleagues. The Live Happy web site reports that Seligman "had little regard for the science-worthiness of something as 'soft' as happiness, and he wasn't personally all that big on it, either." He remarked that "the feelings of happiness, good cheer, ebullience, self-esteem and joy all remained frothy for me." Conversely, unlike Seligman's work, that of Csikszentmihalyi and Diener had little of the mental illness baggage. However, Seligman's organizational and entrepreneurial skills, force of personality, and ambition carried the day as the time for his presidential address approached.[39]

The flood of popular self-help books in the late 1980s and into the 1990s made clear that there was a market for positive psychology. Popularization also made it clear how problematic for serious scholars were overconfident, unscientific, and often superficial approaches that threatened to leave little room for a more rigorous and empirically driven positive psychology. In the 1990s academic psychologists interested in making the shift from mental illness to mental well-being—most notably Csikszentmihalyi and Seligman—had themselves produced more optimistic, popular books that embraced the self-help mode. The creation of a self-conscious field called positive psychology helped make sure that carelessly ebullient versions of happiness studies did not totally dominate public consciousness.

By the time of Seligman's presidential address to the American Psychological Association, virtually all the elements of happiness studies and positive psychology were in place. A field that originated in psychology now also drew on behavioral economics, Eastern religions, psychopharmacology, and, to a lesser extent, neuroscience and evolutionary biology. Beginning mostly in the United States and still remaining largely American, positive psychology had become increasingly international, with scholars from Britain, the Netherlands, Germany, and Japan making important contributions. Scholars had begun mapping out connections among dimensions of resilience, international comparisons, posttraumatic growth, altruism, character, and scientific evidence of the way the mind–body connections shaped subjective well-being. Proof of what the field might become could be seen in Daniel Goleman's influential 1995 book *Emotional Intelligence*, where he drew on a wide range of research, including neuroscience, and brought together multiple strands of positive psychology— optimism, character, virtue, flow, empathy, and social connections—as central building blocks of emotional intelligence.[40]

Yet the development of a coherent, fully articulated and integrated field remained in the future. Proof of how the field had to develop in a more capacious and integrated way came in Seligman and Csikszentmihalyi's lead article on positive psychology in the special 2000 issue *American Psychologist*. They covered many of the key aspects of the emerging field, such as character, posttraumatic growth, religion and spirituality, as well as the distinction between short-term happiness and a deeper sense of well-being. Yet though they asked "Can psychologists develop a biology of positive experience and positive traits?" they failed to mention the work of Richard J. Davidson and Carol D. Ryff.[41] They referred to the work of Daniel Kahneman but not to that of Richard Easterlin. They paid no attention to mindfulness—not Ellen Langer's secular version, Jon Kabat-Zinn's spiritual one, or the religious one of the Dalai Lama. They did not mention the importance of international comparisons. In sum, advances in linking science and happiness were available but not yet integrated into a comprehensive view of the ground from which positive psychology, still over the horizon, would soon emerge as a field.[42]

At the same time, positive psychologists were coming to learn that there was a vast audience for their findings, that they could translate their findings from the laboratory and classroom to bestselling books. As they cast their eyes over the shelves of bookstores, scholars could see that there were immensely popular books whose excesses and lack of scientific backing they had to counter, books such as Barry Neil Kaufman's 1991 *Happiness Is a Choice*, Robert Holden's 1998 *Happiness Now!*, and the Dalai Lama's *The Art of Happiness* in the same year. If journalists, clinicians, and spiritual leaders could write popular books, they began to ask themselves, why can we not do the same but more accurately? Seligman's three books—*Learned Optimism* in 1990, *What You Can Change and What You Can't: The Complete Guide to Successful Self-Improvement* in 1993, and *The Optimistic Child* in 1999, along with David G. Myers's *The Pursuit of Happiness* in 1992— had helped reveal how to balance science and popularity. At least equally important in doing so were not only literary agents (such as John Brockman and Tina Bennett) and editors who encouraged professors to write books that reached broad audiences, but also bestselling books by other highly respected, serious authors—Tom Peters's *In Search of Excellence* in 1982, Robert B. Cialdini's *Influence: How and Why People Agree to Things* in 1984, Bernie S. Siegel's *Peace, Love & Healing: Bodymind Communication and the Path to Self-Healing: An Exploration* in 1989, James W. Pennebaker's *Opening Up: The Healing Power of Confiding in Others* in 1990, Steven Pinker's *The Language Instinct* in 1992, Stephen Jay Gould's *The Mismeasure of Man* in 1996, and Howard Gardner, *Intelligence: Multiple Perspectives* in 1996.[43]

To coin a phrase offered by Malcolm Gladwell in the *New Yorker* in 1996 and in a runaway bestselling book four years later, a more positive—and popular—psychology had reached a "tipping point."[44] The consequences for positive psychologists were enormous, even beyond the additional income some of them reaped. Popular books transformed the dynamics of professionalization. If in the late twentieth century deans, department chairs, and peers cast a skeptical eye on colleagues who became famous, the situation soon changed. Moreover, publishing popular books brought in their wake more talented graduate students, funding from private foundations and government agencies, and the opportunities to reach broad publics through op-ed essays and television appearances. Popular positive psychology helped enhance the positivity of its proponents.

NOTES

1. Todd B. Kashdan and Michael F. Steger, "Challenges, Pittfalls, and Aspirations for Positive Psychology," in *Designing Positive Psychology: Taking Stock and Moving Forward*, ed. Kennon M. Sheldon, Todd B. Kashdan, and Michael F. Steger (New York: Oxford University Press, 2011), 18.
2. See the following books by Mihaly Csikszentmihalyi: with Isabella Selega Csikszentmihalyi, ed., *Optimal Experience: Psychological Studies of Flow in Consciousness* (New York: Cambridge University Press, 1988); as sole author *Flow: The Psychology of Optimal Experience* (New York: Harper & Row, 1990); *The Evolving Self: A Psychology for the Third Millennium* (New York: HarperCollins, 1993); *Creativity: Flow and the Psychology of Discovery and Invention* (New York: HarperCollins, 1996); and *Finding Flow: The Psychology of Engagement with Everyday Life* (New York: Basic Books, 1997).
3. Csikszentmihalyi, *Flow*, 240.
4. Csikszentmihalyi, *Flow*, 16, 45; Richard Flaste, "The Power of Concentration," *NYTM*, Oct. 8, 1989, quoted on back cover of *Finding Flow*.
5. Csikszentmihalyi, *Flow*, 7, 10, 14, 19.
6. Csikszentmihalyi, *Flow*, xi; Csikszentmihalyi, *Evolving Self*, 54.
7. Csikszentmihalyi, *Creativity*, 1, 106, 126, 343.
8. Csikszentmihalyi, *Creativity*, 347, 349, 353, 365.
9. Back cover of Csikszentmihalyi, *Finding Flow*.
10. Martin E. P. Seligman, *Learned Optimism* (New York: Knopf, 1991), 5, 96.
11. Seligman, *Optimism*, 207, 225, 279.
12. Seligman, *Optimism*, 282–83, 284, 289, 292.
13. Back jacket, Seligman, *Optimism*; Martin E. P. Seligman, *The Optimistic Child* (Boston: Houghton Mifflin, 1995), 9.
14. Martin E. P. Seligman, *What You Can Change and What You Can't: The Complete Guide to Successful Self-Improvement* (New York: Knopf, 1994), 16, 27; Seligman, *Child*, 33.
15. Seligman, *Optimism*, 15; Seligman, *Child*, 52.
16. Seligman, *Child*, 6, 8.
17. Among the other popular books on happiness, some of them over-the-top in optimism, are John Pepper, *How to Be Happy* (Boston: Arcana, 1985), with a preface by the Dalai Lama; Liah Kraft-Kristane, *30 Days to Happiness: Setting Yourself Up to Win in Life* (Walpole, NH: Stillpoint, 1987); Penelope Rusianoff, *When Am I Going to Be Happy? How to Break the Emotional Bad Habits That Make You Miserable* (New York: Bantam Books, 1988); Ken Keyes Jr., *Prescriptions for Happiness* (St. Mary, KY: Living Love, 1981); Robert Holden, *Laughter: The Best Medicine* (San Francisco: Thorsons, 1993); Jonathan Robinson, *Shortcuts to Bliss: The 50 Best Way to Improve Your Relationships, Connect with Spirit, and Make Your Dreams Come True* (Berkeley: Conari, 1998); Alain De Botton, *How Proust Can Change Your Life* (London: Picador, 1997).
18. Lee Dodé, *Gay Happiness: How to Get It* (Key West, FL: Arete, 1998); Ingrid D. Hicks, *For Black Women Only: A Complete Guide to a Successful Life-Style Change: Health, Wealth, Love, and Happiness* (Chicago: African American Images, 1991); Dennis Wholey, ed., *Are You Happy? Some Answers to the Most Important Question in Your Life* (Boston: Houghton Mifflin, 1986); William A. Miller, *The Joy of Feeling Good: Eight Keys to a Happy and Abundant Life* (Minneapolis: Augsburg, 1986), back jacket and 187; Archibald D. Hart, *15 Principles for Achieving Happiness* (Dallas: Word Publishing, 1988), xii, 180; John Powell, *Happiness Is an Inside Job* (Allen, TX: Tabor, 1989), 134; Verena Kast, *Joy, Inspiration, and Hope*, trans. Douglas Whitcher (College Station: Texas A&M University Press, 1991); Robert Johnson, *Ecstasy: Understanding the Psychology of Joy* (New York: Harper & Row,

1987); Barry Neil Kaufman, *Happiness Is a Choice* (New York: Fawcett Columbine, 1991), 70; Richard Carlson, *You Can Be Happy No Matter What: Five Principles Your Therapist Never Told You* (Novato, CA: New World Library, 1992); Richard Carlson, *Don't Sweat the Small Stuff—and It's All Small Stuff: Simple Ways to Keep the Little Things from Taking Over Your Life* (New York: Hyperion, 1997); Dennis Prager, *Happiness Is a Serious Problem: A Human Nature Repair Kit* (New York: Regan, 1998).

19. E. M. Suarez and Roger C. Mills, *Sanity, Insanity and Common Sense: The Missing Link in Understanding Mental Health* (West Allis, WI: Med-Tech, 1982), [13], 122, 124. Unlike almost any other psychologist writing on the problems with diagnoses of mental illness, Suarez and Mills referred to the classic 1973 study of how false labeling of entrants into mental hospitals influenced professionals who ran such institutions: David Rosenhan, "On Being Sane in Insane Places," *Science*, Jan. 19, 1973, 250–58.

20. Michael W. Eysenck, *Happiness: Facts and Myths* (Hove, UK: Erlbaum, 1990), ix, 106.

21. Carlson, *Happy*, 56.

22. Kaufman, *Choice*, 64; Kast, *Joy*, 3; Hart, *Happiness*, 5, 33.

23. Carlson, *Happy*, 2, 6; Hart, *Happiness*, xi; Wholey, "The Question," in Wholey, *Happy*, 6.

24. Barbara Ann Kipfer, *14,000 Things to Be Happy About* (New York: Workman, 1991); Goodreads.com entry for *14,000 Things to Be Happy About*.

25. Leo Romeo and Nick Romeo, *11,002 Things to Be Miserable About: The Satirical Not-So-Happy Book* (New York: Harry N. Abrams, 2009).

26. Robert Holden, *Happiness Now! Timeless Wisdom for Feeling Good Fast* (London: Hodder and Stoughton, 1998, v, viii, 31; http://www.robertholden.org/about-robert.aspxa; Eddie and Debbie Shapiro and Jerry Jampolsky, in Holden, *Happiness*, i.

27. Holden, *Happiness*, 9, 11, 34.

28. Holden, *Happiness*, 2, 4, 15, 40, 74, 224.

29. Linda Grant, "Positive Thinking Doesn't Work: Don't Be Fooled: Just 'Feeling Good About Yourself' Won't Solve Your Problems," *Independent*, May 7, 1994.

30. Roy Baumeister, *Meanings of Life* (New York: Guilford Press, 1991), 222, 230; Jill G. Morawski and Gail A. Hornstein, "Quandary of the Quacks: The Struggle for Expert Knowledge in American Psychology, 1890–1940," in *The Estate of Social Knowledge*, ed. JoAnne Brown and David K. van Keuren (Baltimore: Johns Hopkins University Press, 1991), 108.

31. Michael Argyle, *The Psychology of Happiness* (London: Methuen, 1987), 13. This summary relies on Argyle, *Happiness* and David G. Myers, *The Pursuit of Happiness: Discovering the Pathway to Fulfillment, Well-Being, and Enduring Personal Joy* (New York: William Morrow, 1992). Argyle's book, by an Oxford psychologist, carefully summarized current scholarship and contained no hint of a how-to approach. Myers, a psychologist at Hope College, offered both the standard summation and a Christian perspective that emphasized, more so than most scholars, the importance of religion and heterosexual marriage to happiness. Moreover, with its easily accessible style and direct-to-the-reader offer of advice, his book comes closer to the how-to genre. Among other books of the period by psychologists that focused on the pursuit of happiness was Allen Parducci, *Happiness, Pleasure, and Judgment: The Contextual Theory and Its Applications* (Hillsdale, NJ: Erlbaum, 1995).

32. Argyle, *Happiness*, 110, 174.

33. Argyle, *Happiness*, 31.

34. Emmett Velten, "A Laboratory Task for Induction of Mood States," *Behaviour Research and Therapy* 6 (Nov. 1968): 473–82; http://www.wellbeingwizard.com/index.php?option=com_content&task=view&id=503&Itemid=98; Argyle, *Happiness*, 204; Peter M. Lewinsohn and Michael Graf, "Pleasant Activities and Depression," *Journal of Consulting and Clinical Psychology* 41 (Oct. 1973): 261–68.

35. In "Why Act for the Public Good: Four Answers," *Personality and Social Psychology Bulletin* 20 (Oct. 1994): 603–10, psychologist C. Daniel Batson established a framework

that positive psychologists would later find useful. For the arguments that, although at any point in time there was a positive correlation between increases in wealth and happiness, this was not true over time and that the hedonic treadmill and the proliferation of consumer choices would undercut efforts to spread wealth more evenly, see these publications by Richard Easterlin: "Will Raising the Incomes of All Increase the Happiness of All?" *Journal of Economic Behavior and Organization* 27 (June 1995): 35–47; *Growth Triumphant: The Twenty-First Century in Historical Perspective* (Ann Arbor: University of Michigan Press, 1996), 105–40. In "Happiness and Economic Performance," *Economic Journal* 107 (Nov. 1997): 1815–31, Andrew J. Oswald argued that reducing unemployment would increase happiness more than would a broad increase in national income. Note also that in 1987, the State of California established a Task Force on Self-Esteem and Personal and Social Responsibility.

36. Myers, *Happiness*, 87–104 both historicized and replicated this tradition.

37. Myers, *Happiness*, 46, 68; Tim Kasser and Richard M. Ryan, "A Dark Side of the American Dream: Correlates of Financial Success as a Central Life Aspiration," *JPSP* 65 (Aug. 1993): 421. On the other hand, in ways that may reflect differences between British and American attitudes to social class, in 1990 a British psychologist lamented inequality in the United States and suggested that a more egalitarian society might be a happier one: Eysenck, *Happiness*, 96.

38. Especially in the mid-1990s it is possible to detect a growing literature on resilience: see, for example, Alexander C. McFarlane and Rachel Yehuda, "Resilience, Vulnerability, and the Course of Posttraumatic Reactions," in *Traumatic Stress: The Effects of Overwhelming Experience on Mind, Body, and Society*, ed. Bessel A. Van der Kolk, Alexander C. McFarlane, and Lars Weisaeth (New York: Guilford, 1996), 155–81.

39. John David Mann, "Happiness Revolution," *livehappy*, Oct. 11, 2013, http://www.live-happy.com/science/positive-psychology/happiness-revolution.

40. On the limits to the integration of neuroscience, physiology, and psychopharmacology, see Ruut Veenhoven, "Questions of Happiness: Classic Topics, Modern Answers, Blind Spots," in *Subjective Well-Being: An Interdisciplinary Perspective*, ed. Fritz Strack, Michael Argyle, and Norbert Schwarz (Oxford, UK: Pergamon Press, 1991), 16. On the history of neurosciences, see the Feb. 2010 issue of *History of the Human Sciences* on "Neuroscience, Power and Culture." Daniel Goleman, *Emotional Intelligence* (New York: Bantam, 1995).

41. Martin E. P. Seligman and Mihaly Csikszentmihalyi, "Positive Psychology: An Introduction," *AP* 55 (Jan. 2000): 12.

42. This is true also of Strack, Argyle, and Schwarz, *Subjective Well-Being*. Jon Kabat-Zinn, *Full Catastrophe Living: Using the Wisdom of Your Body and Mind to Face Stress, Pain, and Illness* (Garden City, NY: Doubleday, 1990) did not mention work of Ryff or Davidson; Eysenck, *Happiness* paid no attention to the emerging field of neuroscience; Csikszentmihalyi, *Evolving*, 22–23 did mention neuroscience.

43. I am relying on the following discussions of the move to the popular: Sonja Lyubomirsky, telephone conversation and email with author, May 8, 2016; Kim Cameron, telephone conversation with author, May 31, 2016. Martin E. P. Seligman, conversation with author, May 19, 2016 mentioned the importance of the literary agent Richard Pine in encouraging him, in 1988, to write popular books.

44. Malcolm Gladwell, "The Tipping Point," *New Yorker*, June 3, 1996 and *The Tipping Point: How Little Things Can Make a Big Difference* (Boston: Little, Brown, 2000).

CHAPTER 6

Building a Positively Happy World View

In 2005, *Time* magazine featured a story on happiness studies and positive psychology in ways that announced to a wide audience that the fields had arrived, something that occurred gradually between Martin Seligman's 1998 presidential address and the *Time* story. An early January issue contained an article titled "The New Science of Happiness." Beginning the story with news of the meeting of positive psychologists at the Mexican resort Akumal, Claudia Wallis noted "an explosion of research on happiness, optimism, positive emotions, and healthy character traits. Seldom has an academic field been brought so quickly and deliberately to life." Though momentarily casting a skeptical eye on what happiness scholars were discovering, overall the journalist's assessment was positive. "The most fundamental finding from the science of happiness," she reported, was that nearly all happiness exercises that positive psychologists developed pointed in one direction: that personal connections between people were the key to a sense of well-being. She paused for a moment, asking "can a loner really become more gregarious through acts-of-kindness exercises? Can a dyed-in-the-wool pessimist learn to see the glass as half full?" Then came the clincher, drawn as much from popular culture as from serious scholarship. "I'll quote Oprah here, which I don't normally do," remarked the prominent positive psychologist Sonja Lyubomirsky. "She was asked how she runs five miles a day, and she said, 'I recommit to it every day of my life.' I think happiness is like that. Every day you have to renew your commitment. Hopefully, some of the strategies will become habitual over time and not a huge effort."[1]

Eight years later, in the summer of 2013, *Time* elevated the study of happiness to the coveted place on its cover, which featured the silhouette of a drawing of a woman's profile with the words "The Pursuit of Happiness" in the center of her head. Surrounding those words were cartoon drawings that suggested the ingredients that fostered people's sense of well-being were affluence, inventiveness, and connections with friends and family (including those followed on of social media). The cover also announced the double issue's feature story: "Why Americans Are Wired to Be Happy—and What That's Doing to Us." Inside, the journalist Jeffrey Kluger focused on "The Happiness of Pursuit" in a long essay that combined historical generalizations, reports on recent research, and colorful statements about the nation's prospects.

Reviewing the long sweep of American history in an anachronistic way, Kluger found reason for optimism at a time when the Great Recession and political gridlock had taken their toll. Again and again in the nation's history, when faced with disruptive crises, Americans had found their way to better lives. "If the settler gazing out over 1,000 pristine acres felt that delicious frisson of neurotransmitters churning a century or two ago," he intoned, "why shouldn't the entrepreneur drafting a business plan or the Web designer preparing to launch a site experience the same thing?" History, genetics, natural selection, and an abundant environment operated in the future's favor, providing the nation a historically based national happiness set point. Early on, America had replaced the Old World's "savor-the-moment contentment" with "an almost adolescent restlessness, an itch to do the Next Big Thing." From early in the seventeenth century on, self-selective patterns of immigration had brought to our shores ambitious, restless risk takers, making Americans "heirs to a genetically optimistic temperament."

Kluger went on discuss the relationships between affluence and subjective well-being. Despite dramatic gains in real income in the postwar world, people reported no increase in subjective well-being, and the data may even have shown a decrease. Recent studies, he reported, had revealed that in wealthy nations subjective well-being rose more swiftly with increased income than in poor countries. Yet he had to admit that recognition of the power of the hedonic treadmill and social comparison meant that on the individual level, rising incomes brought rising levels of happiness "only if a person's wealth and aspirations keep pace" with one another. The problem was that in the good old days, the beggar had little exposure to the lives of millionaires; in contrast, in the early twenty-first century, celebrity culture, reality television, and social media exposed everyday Americans to people who seemed more attractive, affluent, and happy than themselves.

So now, in 2013, Americans faced a crisis. "Consumptive happiness, the happiness that comes not from sowing but from reaping," no longer brought the satisfactions that pioneers had experienced. Few Americans declared themselves very happy, optimism was plummeting, and the incidence of psychological depression was rising. Nowhere were the problematic results clearer than in international comparisons—with the United States ranking twenty third out of fifty nations, way behind leaders Ireland, New Zealand, and Denmark and trailing even Vietnam and Tanzania. Indeed, "the gap between our optimistic expectations and the reality that a significant portion of the population is, of late, cranky and dissatisfied may be what has spawned the vast happiness industry," one that offered up pills, food, and a full panoply of self-help strategies ranging from yoga to smartphone apps. Nonetheless Kluger ended with the requisite upbeat conclusions, which left unexplored the tension between biological determinism and self-determination. "If there's an upside to America's down mood," he insisted, "it's that happiness and the ways we pursue it are so wonderfully adaptive." Moreover, "if you're an American and you're not having fun, it just might be your own fault." The nation's "happiness set point," which for generations was "high and healthy," relied on "a simple gift of biology, history and environment" that "may be but a gift all the same. In our own loud and messy way, we've always worked to make the most of it, and we probably always will."[2]

Time magazine's articles brought happiness studies and positive psychology to the attention of millions of Americans, although by the time they did so, tens of millions of people had already encountered some aspects of these burgeoning fields. If, as we have seen, almost all pieces were in place by 1998, then what changed in the ensuing years? From the very end of the twentieth century until the end of the new century's first decade and a half, social and behavioral scientists built the infrastructure necessary to highlight and advance scholarship that included scholarly journals, databases, and laboratory experiments; professors and popularizers produced scores of books, many of them reaching coveted places on bestseller lists; scholars continued to refine their findings and to give added emphasis to a handful of topics; both kinds of authors more fully integrated the many strands that comprised the field; and critics began to find their voices. To be sure, many of the claims, especially those offered in popular books, involved propositions that needed to be qualified and verified. Yet within less than twenty years after Seligman's 1998 speech, happiness studies and positive psychology had produced a robust vision of where America and other nations of the world stood and where they were headed, a topic under consideration earlier but one that now increasingly received attention.

BUILDING A PROFESSIONAL INFRASTRUCTURE

In the years after 1998, positive psychologists took the lead in developing the institutions, programs, and publications essential to the establishment of a legitimate field. Although there had been some pre-1998 organizational precedents, they hardly matched those that would come afterwards.[3] In 1999 at Harvard, Phillip Stone taught the nation's first positive psychology course—to twenty undergraduates; eight years later, American universities hosted more than 200 such courses with more than 10,000 students enrolled. Then in 2006 Tal Ben-Shahar offered a course at Harvard on positive psychology which, with 855 students, had the highest enrollment in the university's history. It was a class, the Boston Globe reported, with an unexamined juxtaposition of popularization and science, "whose content resembles that of many a self-help book but is grounded in serious psychological research."[4] Scholarly journals increasingly published articles; beginning in 2002 the number of scholarly articles on positive psychology took off—initially in the United States and abroad very soon after.[5] Well before 1998, the Journal of Personality and Social Psychology had presented scores of articles that contributed to the two fields. The new century saw publications with a sharper focus: Journal of Happiness Studies in 2001; Applied Research in Quality of Life five years later; and Journal of Positive Psychology one year after that. More articles containing the key word "happiness" appeared in psychology journals in the first fifteen years of the twenty-first century than in the entire century before.[6]

Newspapers and magazines increasingly offered familiar discoveries as well as new ones. In 2006 the BBC broadcast a six-part series titled "The Happiness Formula." Textbooks and handbooks codified the latest findings.[7] Moving increasingly away from political polling by focusing on new areas of inquiry, including happiness, in 1997 the Gallup Organization established the Gallup International Positive Psychology Summit. Government agencies and private foundations played key roles in supporting the field. the Templeton Foundation, eager to place positive values on a firm scientific basis, provided lavish funding to scholars who worked in that vineyard. In 2000 Princeton University launched its Center for Health and Wellbeing; a year later, also with funding from the Templeton Foundation, came the Institute for Research on Unlimited Love at SUNY–Stony Brook. The year 2001 also saw the inauguration of the University of Pennsylvania's Positive Psychology Center, with a $2,200,000, 6½-year grant from the Templeton Foundation. The same year University at California–Berkeley founded the Center for the Development of Peace and Well-Being, later renamed the Greater Good Science Center.

Professional societies sprung up everywhere: around 2000 the International Society for Quality-of-Life Studies, followed soon after by the International Positive Psychology Association, and then the European Network of Positive Psychology. Programs in positive psychology grew in the United States and in scores of nations on every continent. These included online and in-residence courses, short-term workshops, and graduate degree programs at major universities and pop-up sites. Outcomes ranged from the experience itself to certificates and degrees. By 2015, there were more than fifty TED talks on happiness. Rarely had an academic field risen so quickly to such prominence.[8]

MOUNT RUSHMORE ICONS: ONCE AGAIN POLICING (AND CROSSING) THE BORDER BETWEEN SCIENCE AND POPULARIZATION

In October 2013, the magazine *Live Happy* offered up a version of Mount Rushmore that replaced the one depicting George Washington, Thomas Jefferson, Abraham Lincoln, and Theodore Roosevelt with the editor's choice of five founders of positive psychology—Martin Seligman of the University Pennsylvania, Barbara Fredrickson of the University of North Carolina, Sonja Lyubomirsky of the University of California–Riverside, Ed Diener of the University of Illinois, and Mihaly Csikszentmihalyi of the Claremont Graduate University.[9] In the first decade and a half of the twenty-first century, each of them published at least one book, an oeuvre that both made distinctive contributions and brought the field's finding to ample audiences. "Powerful cultural anxieties," the historian of science Anne Harrington has written in a way applicable to how positive psychologists entered the public arena, function on many levels and evoke "unstable status as both a mainstream/professional and an alternative/popular body of knowledge and practice." She goes on to characterize the "therapeutic self-help industry" in ways appropriate to the self-help, popularizing turn in positive psychology as "one of the most important mediators between elite and popular, mainstream and alternative versions of different narrative traditions."[10] Moreover, she notes that in the late twentieth century a new "populist strand of self-help has been increasingly superseded by a new kind of therapeutic self-help culture in which scientific experts . . . tell everyone else how to live happier, healthier, and more productive lives."[11]

Seligman's distinctive contributions came in his emphasis on character strengths and offering of formulations of what it meant to be happy in ways that went against the grain of books by popularizers who, he felt, often put forward a simplified and incautiously optimistic sense of what readers could achieve. Seligman made his case for a complex understanding of subjective well-being in two books that combined the popular and professional: *Authentic Happiness: Using the New Positive Psychology to Realize Your Potential for Lasting Fulfillment* (2002) and *Flourish: A Visionary New Understanding of Happiness and Well-Being* (2011).[12]

In *Authentic Happiness,* as others would do, Seligman not only criticized unscientific hucksters and Pollyannas but also stepped over the boundaries that once separated them from rigorously scientific academics. "Why," he remarked at the outset, "is a book about Positive Psychology about anything more than 'happiology' or *hedonics*—the science of how we feel from moment to moment?" So he focused on differentiating what he did from what Norman Vincent Peale had offered earlier. "Is Positive Psychology just positive thinking warmed over?" he asked. His answer was that Peale and positive psychology were connected philosophically but not methodologically. They both relied on the "Arminian heresy" that led to one's election to grace and a belief in "the individual freely choosing." Yet they differed in several important respects. If positive thinking was for amateurs, then positive psychology relied on systematic, empirically based, and replicable science, he noted in ways that reflected the higher prestige often accorded to fields that could claim the mantle of science. Moreover, unlike what Peale and his ilk advocated, Seligman and his compatriots, rather than holding "a brief for positivity," carefully balanced it with and addressed negativity. Yet as with other popular books Seligman's promised readers, as the book's subtitle indicated, "your potential for lasting fulfillment." Similarly, he offered questionnaires for readers to fill out, specific exercises they might do, and a catchy set of formulas.[13]

Central to *Authentic Happiness* was a distinction between hedonic, short-term pleasures and eudaimonic, long-term gratifications, that in turn rested on the differentiation between superficial personality characteristics and enduring character ones. "I am a dyed-in-the-wool pessimist," Seligman remarked. "I believe that only pessimists can write sober and sensible books on optimism." Yet he insisted at the outset that his "book takes you through the countryside of pleasure and gratification, up into the high country of strength and virtue, and finally to the peaks of lasting fulfillment: meaning and purpose." On the onc hand were inauthentic, fleeting but intensely felt pleasures that came from eating chocolate or getting a back rub. On the other were deeper, stabler, and more authentic gratifications that led not to the pleasant life but to the good one. Authentic gratifications, he insisted, drawing on the concept of flow, "engage us fully, we become immersed and absorbed in them, and we lose self-consciousness." Attempting to provide an alternative to the American Psychiatric Association's pathology-focused *Diagnostic and Statistical Manual of Mental Disorders* with a well-being approach, he insisted on "focusing on what is right about people and specifically about the strengths of character that make the good life possible." He and his colleagues offered a catalogue of healthy virtues. Six in number, they were wisdom and knowledge, courage, love, justice, temperance, and spirituality and transcendence. If the pleasures were "about the senses and the emotions," then the gratifications were "about enacting personal strengths and virtues." In turn he broke these six virtues into twenty-four character strengths such as curiosity, judgment, valor, integrity, humility, playfulness, and passion. To achieve "the good life," Seligman insisted, use "your signature strengths every day in the main realms of your life to bring abundant gratification and authentic happiness."[14]

Seligman cast his advocacy of character strengths and virtues in a specific framework. Social science, he asserted, had long ago turned its back on "Victorian moralizing" and replaced it with an emphasis on "egalitarianism" by emphasizing environmental causation rather than character. In doing so, social science allowed us to "escape from the value-laden, blame-accruing religiously inspired, class oppressing notion of character, and get on with the monumental task of building a heathier 'nurturing' environment." Consequently, "in this age of postmodernism and ethical relativism, it has become commonplace to assume that virtues" were "merely a matter of social convention, peculiar to the time and place of the beholder." Now, he insisted as he reflected his admiration for Puritan theology, "the time has come to resurrect character as a central concept to the scientific study of behavior."[15]

In important ways, Seligman's *Authentic Happiness* was an extended meditation on 9/11, as well as an extension of his earlier work on ethnopolitical conflict. In 2003, Seligman remarked that although "the civilized world" was engaged in a "war with Jihad Islamic terrorism," it took "a bomb in the office of some academics to make them realize that their most basic values are now threatened." Shortly after 9/11 Seligman and a colleague studied how that event affected Americans' character strengths. They discovered that "seven character strengths showed increases: gratitude, hope, kindness, leadership, love, spirituality, and teamwork." There was, however, a more controversial aspect to Seligman's response to 9/11. In December 2001 the APA adopted a "Resolution on Terrorism" that encouraged psychologists to help in the fight again terrorism. In the same month, Seligman hosted at his home in a suburb of Philadelphia a meeting that brought together psychologists and representatives from the intelligence communities. The head of the FBI's Behavioral Science Unit remarked that "Seligman's 'gathering' produced an extraordinary document that is being channeled on high (very high)." Present at the meeting were government officials who, drawing on Seligman's theory of learned helplessness, would play key roles in the development of the CIA's torture or enhanced interrogation programs.[16]

As part of a more general investigation of the APA's code of ethics and involvement in the federal government's use of techniques of "enhanced interrogation," the APA commissioned a prominent law firm to study such matters. Seligman maintained that his intention was to have his theory of learned helplessness used to help captured American service members resist torture, while critics insisted that Seligman and the APA were complicit in the development of techniques of torture in the wake of 9/11. The resulting report, issued in 2015 and known as the Hoffman Report, concluded that "on balance, it seems difficult to believe that Seligman did not at least suspect that the CIA was interested in his theories, at least in part, to consider how they could be used in interrogations. However, we found no evidence to support the critics' theory that Seligman was deeply involved in constructing or consulting on the CIA's interrogation program."[17]

In his second book during this period, *Flourish*, Seligman announced that he had changed his mind about what positive psychology was trying to achieve. He told readers that against his wishes, the publisher of his earlier book insisted he use the words "happiness" and "authentic" in the title. People took the first word to mean "buoyant mood, merriment, good cheer, and smiling" and the latter "as a close relative of the overused term *self*, in a world of overblown selves." A self-confessed grumpy man, the title had burdened him "with that awful smiley face whenever positive psychology made the news." Moreover, he wanted to distinguish his book from that of "pop psychology and the bulk of self-improvement" works. If the goal of authentic happiness was to increase life satisfaction by focusing on positive emotion, engagement, and meaning, he now embraced "well-being theory," composed of five elements demarcated by PERMA: Positive emotion, Engagement, Relationships, Meaning, and Accomplishment. This shift, he argued, moved the discussion beyond the monism of feeling good to higher ground: flourishing was more profound than happiness.[18]

Seligman distinguished himself from Mihaly Csikszentmihalyi, whose *Good Business: Leadership, Flow, and the Making of Meaning* appeared a year after *Authentic Happiness*—and did so in ways that highlighted the dynamics of straddling the boundary between the scholarly and the popular. Csikszentmihalyi, he wrote, was someone from a European aristocratic background who nowhere "directly" told "his readers how to acquire more flow." Unlike him, Seligman insisted, "I come unapologetically from the American tradition, and I believe enough is known about how gratifications come about to give advice about enhancing them." Although in some of his pre-1998 work Csikszentmihalyi had crossed the line between scientific description and how-to advice, in *Good Business* he refrained from doing so.[19]

Good Business, based on work that the Templeton Foundation supported, represents the ways in which a leading figure in positive psychology moved to apply findings to a specific field; in his case business, but with others, education or counseling. Csikszentmihalyi gave special praise to "visionary leaders" who saw "their jobs as entailing responsibility for the welfare of the wider community" and called on them to foster happiness by enabling all employees to experience "*soul*—the energy a person or organization devoted to purposes beyond itself." Thus corporations should it make possible for employees and citizens "seeking new challenges and developing new skills" to unfold their selves "across increasingly complex lines." Executives could do this by making sure "the objective conditions of the workplace" were "as attractive as possible"; by imbuing "the job with meaning and value," in the process increasing the likelihood that workers would experience flow; and by supporting leaders who "can steer the morale of the organization as a whole in a positive direction." The corporate leaders he most admired had capacious visions that extended far beyond maximizing profits. They had "the calling *to build a better world*"—to develop "a sense of responsibility that reaches out to the community in which they work, to democracy as the best upholder of civic institutions, and to the environment that allows us to survive and prosper."[20]

Rather than a how-to book relying on exercises for readers to pursue, bullet points that highlighted what to do, or injunctions for "you," the reader, to act, *Good Business* mixed philosophical discussions with stories drawn from interviews Csikszentmihalyi carried out with corporate leaders that more implicitly than explicitly provided guidance "for a way of conducting business that is both successful and humane."[21]

Others, especially those in organizational behavior programs in business schools, would be bolder in connecting positive psychology, business, and a how-to formula. Indeed, in the same year that *Good Business* appeared, Jane E. Dutton, a professor of business administration and psychology at the University of Michigan, published *Energize Your Workplace: How to Create and Sustain High-Quality Connections at Work*, a book markedly less philosophical and more practical than Csikszentmihalyi's. As proof that flow was possible for even the most menial employees to experience, Dutton and Amy Wrzesniewski had elsewhere revealed how janitors working in a hospital doing menial and unpleasant tasks could in some instances see their jobs in harmony with the goals of their organization, helping to heal people. Taking the initiative before doctors asked them to do something or trying to make the lives of seriously ill patients more pleasant, they turned their potentially nasty jobs into a rewarding calling.[22]

The distinctive contribution of Sonja Lyubomirsky's *The How of Happiness: A Scientific Approach to Getting the Life You Want* (2008) was the perfection of the genre of a how-to book that relied on up-to-date academic findings and popularized the notion of the 40 percent solution, the idea that such a percentage represented the extent of what we could control in enhancing our happiness. At several key points, she acknowledged that what she wrote resembled popular clichés, even as she distanced herself from them. Happiness had become "a fad, like hula hoops, big hairdos, and Fonzie." The prevalence of such expressions of "frenzy," "relatively uninformed by empirical data," drove researchers like herself both "to want to keep a distance" and to engage the public with discussions that abided "by strict scientific standards." She was, she insisted, "a research scientist," not a "self-help guru." "We're in a new era, each month witnessing hot-off-the-press publications about how to achieve and sustain happiness," but "unfortunately, these findings are typically disseminated formally or informally only among scientists or else published in technical journals ... beyond the reach of the nonexpert." Though many of the most important happiness strategies, like " 'smile!' " or " 'count your blessings,' " sounded hokey, "these strategies, when practiced in effortful and optimal ways, have been borne out in numerous studies to be incredibly effective."[23]

So in a book translated into nineteen languages, Lyubomirsky went ahead, carefully balancing science and what in some hands might have been considered clichés. She provided questionnaires that readers could fill out to identify the specific strategies that would work best to help "make yourself permanently happier and more fulfilled." She skillfully mixed personal stories, including self-disclosing ones, of how people achieved happiness, reports of positive psychology's latest findings, exercises and questionnaires to which readers could respond, and eye-catching lists enumerating what would make a difference in one's life. She reproduced one questionnaire that asked readers, using a six-point scale, to assess whether they were optimistic about the future or found it difficult to make decisions. She also provided twelve happiness activities that served as lessons for learning to express gratitude, cultivate optimism, avoid rumination, perform acts of kindness, develop social connections, find strategies for coping, practice forgiveness, increase the experience of flow, savor the joys of life, make commitments to goals, practice religion and spirituality, and take care of your body. With each one, she offered specific suggestions for developing happy-inducing habits. For example, for strengthening social relationships, she counseled readers to make time for friendship, express affection, and share their inner life with others. She ended that chapter by imploring people to hug more, something both popular web sites and scientific studies urged people to do.[24]

Lyubomirsky emphasized cultivating habits that could enhance individual happiness because research, she claimed, revealed that 40 percent of happiness is "in our power to change through how we act and how we think." Focusing on the other determinants—the 10 percent shaped by life circumstances such as wealth, health, marital status, and physical attractiveness and the 50 percent due to genetically based happiness set points—would yield few if any results. Near the end of the book she reported that working on it had "knocked me for a loop." For almost two decades she had carried out research in positive psychology, but writing *The How of Happiness* had "an unexpected impact on me, an impact that quickly became almost laughingly predictable." Her husband, she reported, "was pleasantly surprised when he found me practicing on him the techniques I wrote about in the section on nurturing relationships." And as "the least spiritual person I know," when writing on that topic she said she began "thinking about the larger questions on meaning and purpose and reading messages into some of the major events of my life." Although she claimed not to be the type of person who read self-help books or counted her blessings, this is exactly what had happened to her. "If I, the ultimate reluctant subject, can be transformed in her recognition of the power and efficacy of this book's suggestions, then some of you reluctant readers can be transformed too." She had completed the circle, connecting how-to books and scientific research; the personal and the professional.[25]

The father–son team Ed Diener and Robert Biswas-Diener's *Happiness: Unlocking the Mysteries of Psychological Wealth* (2008) arguably represents the most systematic and serious summary of findings. Yet they too embraced some of the kinds of catchy approaches used by bestselling popularizers.[26] As one observer remarked, the two of them were "scholars who do the research and not just journalists or pop psychologists reporting it second hand."[27] Their book was a unique collaboration, between a father who had been the most important American scholar of happiness well before the birth of positive psychology and a son known as the Indiana Jones of positive psychology because of his adventuresome investigations of happiness among slum dwellers of Calcutta, Inuit natives in Greenland, tribes living in the African savannah, and homeless people in American cities.[28]

While offering a careful and thorough survey of the most recent findings of academic researchers, they policed and overstepped the borders between scientific and popular approaches. Authors of self-help books, they remarked, along with "inspirational speakers seek to make you joyous: possibly because they want you to buy their products, perhaps because they have faith in their mission." In addition, positive psychologists "often motivated by empathy, want you to be happier." As a result of these and other efforts, a "large happiness industry has blossomed." Again and again, they criticized "self-help books and gurus" that had offered a "clever happiness method advocated" in the book's title, even as they confirmed that the most rigorous and up-to-date research often corroborated what popularizers claimed. Without mentioning Norman Vincent Peale or his 1952 book, they talked extensively of the "power of positive thinking" as "a mindset in which you recognize your blessings more than you pay attention to daily hassles." Even as they seemed to mimic what they criticized, they cautioned against magical cures, noted that "some self-help gurus and self-growth organizations suggest silly interventions for positive thinking that want us to be cheerful all of the time," and remarked that "we are not advocating psychological bubbliness or positivity that is devoid of reality." Yet they insisted that scientific research confirms that "a shift toward positive thinking can often lead to more gains in happiness than a change in life circumstances. This realization can enhance your psychological wealth!"[29]

For Diener and Biswas-Diener, who preferred a well-being level of eight rather than ten, the problem was that "all the well-intentioned meddlers" could make people unhappy by suggesting that the highest level of subjective well-being was both achievable and an ideal to strive toward. Even some academics had overemphasized the importance of happiness, making some "sick and tired of positive psychologists trying to make them happier." Father and son went so far as to caution "do not let others, including the authors of this book, dictate your level of positivity." Having policed the border and issued cautions about crossing the line between respected science and simple, popular formulations, they nonetheless plowed on. "No single secret is likely to make you or Cinderella happy forever; no Prince Charming can ensure eternal bliss," they cautioned in highly gendered language. While acknowledging that achieving happiness was a process, not a goal, they nonetheless insisted that "it takes a recipe to do the trick" and then offered a "list of fundamental ingredients that make up the delicious dish of happiness." They ended the chapter declaring "achieving psychological wealth is, ultimately, the most important goal in life. Now it is up to you."[30]

In other ways they adopted the tricks of the trade. Ed, who earlier studied the happiness levels of the wealthiest Americans, now offered his readers "measures of psychological wealth so that you can determine the net worth of your psychological wealth balance sheet." If *Fortune* could offer up its annual list of the financially wealthiest, then this book, relying on a balance sheet, presented a comparable way of listing those with good fortune of a different type. "You probably did not make the Forbes list of billionaires, but are you a billionaire when it comes to psychological wealth?" They also offered readers a series of self-tests to measure their level of happiness and the nature of their social relationships. In addition, like Seligman's PERMA, Lyubomirsky's trademark 40 percent solution, and Fredrickson's 3-to-1 ratio, they had their own catchy phrase: AIM, which referred to Attention, Interpretation, and Memory. "We walk you through the nuts and bolts of a happy mindset," they reassured readers, "by encouraging you to 'take AIM at happiness.'" This and other statements in the book relied on what both academic and non-academic writers drew upon—the use of "you" and "your," words that did not appear in the title of their book but frequently found their way inside the covers.[31]

Barbara Fredrickson's *Positivity: Top-Notch Research Reveals the 3-to-1 Ratio That Will Change Your Life* (2009) exemplifies how successfully and problematically an academic researcher could translate her findings into an effective, popular medium. To begin, the title combined the snappy word "Positivity," the formulaic ratio, and the ambitious promise that "Top-Notch" scientific research "Will Change Your Life." Fredrickson began the book with a discussion of multiple ways of looking at a personal story of her life as a mother, wife, colleague, and researcher. The book also offered boxes filled with highlighted points, highly personal stories of people's suffering and redemption, and specific advice on how to diminish negativity and increase positivity. The back jacket of the book reinforced her message: "Partly cloudy with a chance of rain . . . or partly sunny with the possibility of a rainbow? *You choose.*" Unintentionally echoing advocates of the power of positive thinking, at one point she remarked "Thinking Makes It So."[32]

Fredrickson's central message was that we all have a happiness birthright, one best developed by working toward a positivity ratio of three to one, with positivity and negativity offered in a balanced way. Her book skillfully mixed scientific evidence and self-help exercises, including tests to take and lists to fill out. We are skeptical when marketers say something will change your life, she remarked, but then went on to say "I'm a scientist, not a marketer" and "I say with cautious confidence: *positivity can change your life.*"[33]

Avoiding the word "happiness" because "it's murky and overused" and reacting against the insincerity of a Pollyanna, she insisted on "No Yellow Smiley Faces" even if one prominently appeared on the book's cover. Though "some of this may sound like the vocabulary of greeting cards," she insisted that positivity broadens and builds, deploying a phrase that had earlier made her work famous, because it helped a reader "see new possibilities, bounce back from setbacks, connect with others, and become the best version of yourself." Promising life-changing wisdom, she remarked "if you crave more in your life, this book is for you," insisting that positivity "can also *produce* success and health." Fredrickson proceeded to list "ten forms of positivity: joy, gratitude, serenity, interest, hope, pride, amusement, inspiration, awe, and love." For each of them she urged readers to gather mementos such as quotes, photos, and letters—and then assemble them in a portfolio. Apparently unaware of the similarity between what she and Norman Vincent Peale had recommended and instead relying on a Tibetan Buddhist meditation, she urged people to "repeat silently to yourself" statements of hope that a loved one will be happy. At the book's end, she offered "A New Toolkit" that included a dozen techniques, including her most distinctive contribution, "Loving-Kindness" meditation. A method that promised to help overcome the power of the hedonic treadmill, loving-kindness meditation differed from many other types by emphasizing the process of extending feelings of love and warmth from the self to others, even as this approach might risk avoidance of sustained engagement with a wider world by focusing so much on a relatively confined one.[34]

The 2013 decision by the editors of Live Happy to create an image of a Mount Rushmore for positive psychology with five figures was both arbitrary and consensus confirming. It was arbitrary because it left no room for a psychologist and neuroscientist like Richard J. Davidson; non-Americans such as the pioneering Dutch scholar Ruut Veenhoven or the Buddhist monk of French origin Mattieu Ricard, who exemplified the importance of Eastern spirituality; scholars like Daniel Kahneman who linked behavioral economics and the study of well-being; or, as explored in the following chapter, those clearly on the left (Richard Layard or Dacher Keltner) or right (Arthur Brooks) whose works broadened the sometimes more centrist or seemingly apolitical orientation of the Mount Rushmore five. Focusing on only five scholars also turns attention away from others, such as Robert Emmons and Michael McCullough, whose work was generative in the specific fields of gratitude and forgiveness, respectively.[35] Finally, Live Happy's decision to enshrine the Mount Rushmore five and my decision to adopt this approach as a heuristic but in some ways problematic device neglects two popular, serious, and compelling books published in 2006: Daniel Gilbert's Stumbling on Happiness and Jonathan Haidt's The Happiness Hypothesis: Finding Modern Truth in Ancient Wisdom.

Moreover, some of these major books by the Mount Rushmore five, along with some of the scholarship on which they drew, were problematic. To be sure, Diener's precision and carefulness and Csikszentmihalyi's more focused approach opened neither of them to serious challenges. Yet some scholars and lay readers have found some of these books, especially those by Fredrickson, Lyubomirsky, and Seligman, intellectually thin—rushed too quickly from specialized research to popularization, often not up to the scientific gold standard.

Specifically, researchers have subjected key assertions of Fredrickson and Lyubomirsky to convincing critiques in ways that suggest that the penchant for glib formulas and catchy popularization is troublesome. While taking a course on applied positive psychology at University of East London, Nick Brown, a retired British IT professional, growing skeptical of the math proffered by Marcial Lasoda that underlay Fredrickson's assertion of the critical, minimal positive ratio of 2.9103, began to explore her specific conclusion and its wider application. The result was a publication in the American Psychologist where Fredrickson's initial finding had appeared.[36] "The idea that any aspect of human behaviour or experience should be universally and reproducibly constant to five significant digits," Brown wrote, "would, if proven, constitute a unique moment in the history of the social sciences." Fredrickson admitted the problematic nature of the math but did not accept the more robust implications of the criticism of her work. Doubling down, she insisted that "ample evidence continues to support the conclusion that, within bounds, higher positivity ratios are predictive of flourishing mental health and other beneficial outcomes."[37] Lyubomirsky's pie chart of 50/40/ 10 (genetics, intentional activity, circumstance) encountered serious but somewhat less specifically grounded headwinds. Indeed, in a 1999 scholarly article Diener and some colleagues had explored just how variable were such figures. Then her in 2016 book, *America the Anxious; How Our Pursuit of Happiness Is Creating a Nation of Nervous Wrecks*, the lay writer Ruth Whippman offered a stinging critique. Lyubomirsky's "40 percent figure," she asserted, "represents the field's greatest marketing opportunity. This is the 40 percent that anyone with a book to sell, a course of coaching to offer, or a happiness technique to market is hoping to co-opt," of which, she noted, "Lyubomirsky has several."[38]

Nonetheless, the iconic image of the Mount Rushmore five did confirm a widely held but hardly universal consensus of who led and mattered in the field of positive psychology. Each of the three seniors among them had established himself as a leading figure: Diener by his early and then continuing publications; Seligman by his scholarship and leadership; Csikszentmihalyi by the importance of the concept of flow. The publication of popular books enabled them and their two younger, female colleagues to reach audiences far wider than did articles published in academic journals. Major scholars decided to write popular how-to books, something in the works since the 1990s, for multiple reasons. The nexus of literary agents, market-oriented editors, and supportive private foundations propelled scholars to enhance their incomes. However, more than money was at stake—most notably the desire to use this medium and others to transform the world through a cultural movement. Moreover, the decision to author books that often incorporated key elements of the self-help tradition meant entering the territory of a genre that is profoundly shaped by Protestant notions of salvation and redemption through character, hard work, and charity.

A POSITIVELY HAPPY CONSENSUS, CONTINUED

Books in the years after 1998 by the five Mount Rushmore authors, along with writings by other scholars, highlight, elaborate, modify, qualify, and extend what was available before that critical date. Every generalization has its qualification or opposition, but soon after 1998 a consensus had emerged. Much of it was apparent before, with changes noted later in this chapter and in the next.[39] More and more people used "lifestyle" drugs to enhance their sense of well-being, but long after the publication of *Listening to Prozac* in 1993, Peter Kramer in 2009 reported "scant progress in the development of psychotherapeutic drugs." Moreover, skeptics increasingly questioned the use of psychopharmaceuticals that once seemed to hold such promise.[40] In addition, deeply skeptical of the benefits of Freudian and behavioral therapies, positive psychologists cast their lot with various versions of cognitive behavioral therapy, which involved challenging unproductive ways of thinking and learning productive ones. Cosmetic drugs, as well as psychotherapy, Seligman wrote, were palliative, not curative, and often had only minor positive effects.[41]

Other themes, prominent before 1998, continued to receive emphasis, though not without controversy. To drive home their points, behavioral scientists continued to rely not only on rigorous experiments but also on the writings of major philosophers, poets, and novelists.[42] As discussed earlier, three factors commanded attention: a genetically determined happiness set point responsible for 50 percent of positivity, external circumstances for 10 percent, and intentional activity for 40 percent. External circumstances, including physical attractiveness, race (which remained the focus of relatively few studies), age, and gender mattered, but not very much. Most observers assumed that by focusing on what was amenable to change, people could increase their level of happiness. Among the most important realms deserving of attention were social relationships, goal orientation, and physical exercise.[43]

One influential treatment on social connectedness, which relied on the extraordinary, longitudinal data from the Framingham Heart Study, revealed the infectious nature of happiness. "People who are surrounded by many happy people . . . are more likely to become happy in the future." The Harvard Grant Study, which tracked the lives of several hundred male graduates from the classes of 1938–1944, confirmed the importance of social relationships. George Vaillant, who directed the study from 1972 to 2004, remarked in 2013 that love was the key to a happy and fulfilled life. "Joy is connection," he insisted, echoing earlier studies that emphasized the importance of social relationships and drawing on evidence that the strength of meaningful relationships was the best predictor of subjective well-being: "the more areas in your life you can make connection, the better."[44]

Happier people were more productive, creative, and effective; not only were they healthier, but they also lived longer.[45] One important experiment underscored the strong connection between happiness and health.

Researchers sequestered 334 volunteers under very controlled circumstances and then gave them nasal drops of rhinoviruses. Those with positive emotional styles had a significantly lower risk of developing a cold after exposure to the rhinovirus, suggesting a clear connection between positive attitudes, immune system function, and the likelihood of getting ill.[46] More generally, among the most influential concepts was Fredrickson's of broaden and build, a process that fostered a so-called "upward spiral of life style changes."[47] Similarly, flow remained productive of happiness in a wide range of activities. More recent on the scene was savoring, what Diener and Biswas-Diener called "the process of active enjoyment of the present, and of using active appreciation to enjoy a past success."[48] Posttraumatic growth, and resilience more generally, remained topics that commanded a great deal of attention.[49]

To a considerable extent, summary books by the Mount Rushmore five reflected positive psychology's commitment to the emphasis placed on the pro-capitalist, market-oriented values of neoliberalism that minimized the importance of the social welfare state and instead stressed the enterprising self. Thus, Diener and Biswas-Diener, in casting their argument as involving parallels between balance sheets of financial and psychological wealth, could state that "happiness is a cornerstone of psychological wealth in part because it is emotional currency that can be spent on other desirable goals." Lyubomirsky used a different metaphor when, having insisted that happy people earned more money than unhappy ones, she spoke of happiness bringing "multiple fringe benefits." Fredrickson described the entrepreneurial temperament when she spoke of an "open and curious" mindset, which, by making you open to new opportunities, "draws you out to explore, to mix it up in the world in unexpected ways." Similarly, she referred to resources as "any enduring part of yourself that you may draw on later, when you face challenges, setbacks, or new opportunities." Seligman emphasized the role of self-discipline in achievement and highlighted the link between wealth and well-being (as opposed to superficial happiness) under the umbrella of what he called "New Prosperity."[50]

Finally, Csikszentmihalyi's message in *Good Business* was clear. Under inspiring leadership, corporations could do good, in both spiritual and material terms. At a time when companies were outsourcing and downsizing, he offered a different view of corporate life by insisting that under visionary leadership such as that provided by Yvon Chouinard at Patagonia and J. Irwin Miller at Cummins, "work can be one of the most joyful, most fulfilling aspects of life." Speaking of Enron leaders who "use language only as a disguise" for evil-doing, he offered an alternative. With "the capitalist vision" standing "alone on the world stage," corporate leaders, by accepting "the responsibilities that come with the privileges they have been given," could make the welfare of employees, corporations, and society cooperate effectively. In the new century, positive psychologists seemed to be embracing a corporate system that others saw as exploitatively selfish and a social order that others saw as increasingly insecure and unequal.[51]

READERS RESPOND

An examination of responses on Amazon.com to books by the Mount Rushmore five illuminates important aspects of their reception.[52] Positive reviewers hailed their books for successfully making the shift from mental illness and pessimism to mental health and optimism. Their authors did so, some respondents remarked, by offering careful, scientific, empirically based evidence that encouraged a balanced approach to achieving happiness. "Most of the truckloads of happiness books out there try to make you as happy as possible," a Belgian reader remarked in response to Diener and Biswas-Diener's *Happiness*. "They embody an 'optimizer' view on happiness. This publication is different. It is OK to be, say, quite happy without incessantly jumping around for joy." Yet readers who offered positive assessments had a difficult time consistently locating these books in traditions. On the one hand, they lauded the way the authors relied on science and avoided the pitfalls of pop psychology and the power of positive thinking. "A person might be tempted to think that this is pop psychology by untrained lay persons who tell lots of 'feel-good' stories and encourage people to say 'I'm feeling fantastic' all day long," a male minister from a Chicago suburb commented after reading Fredrickson's *Positivity*, before going on to say "that's not the case" because the book reported the "findings of legitimate academic research from leading universities and credible scientists." Someone could make such an assessment even though others hailed these very same books for offering simple exercises and telling personal stories, all in order to enhance a reader's happiness.

Indeed, readers lauded the authors of these books for offering quizzes, exercises, and other kinds of practical, how-to suggestions that helped transform their lives, sometimes dramatically so. "I am naturally a pessimistic/negative-reacting person," wrote one person on Amazon's web site who had read and listened to Fredrickson's *Positivity*. "I am slowly changing into a more positive, upbeat, joy-filled person," this person from Modesto, California continued. "I am able to work through negative situations rather quickly and have changed some painful memories into good ones with helpful suggestions . . . I want to 're-wire' my brain towards positivity!" A similarly transformative report came from a "naturally . . . very happy person" from Stillwater, Oklahoma, who had read Lyubomirsky's *How of Happiness* and who could "say without reservation that this book has made me happier.

My friends have found it surprising that someone as happy as me would be reading a book on happiness. After hearing my profound respect for this book, they too purchased it and found it a life-changing experience."

Of course, not everyone found encountering books by the Mount Rushmore five life-changing or even positive. Many among the relatively small percentage of negative reviewers found these books not very helpful, often because they offered advice that was hard to follow or were either too scientific or insufficiently so. One reader said of Seligman's *Authentic Happiness* that it failed because it problematically involved subjectivity "in the hands of those who study objectivity? Come on," a male reader responded, "It's evident to me that these people in APA are either ignoring, or have never heard of the epistemic crises of the twentieth century." On the other hand, some felt these books lacked adequate grounding in science. *The How of Happiness*, complained "Ameliawizard" from Florida, was "nothing more than recycled psychobabble. You can sum it up in these words, 'you will feel happier if you just say you are.'" "Shame on Dr. Martin Seligman," commented a New York man who acknowledged he had an "argumentative bent." "Following in the footsteps of Stephen Covey, Deepak Chopra and Wayne Dyer, he has abandoned legitimate science and moved into the touchy-feely realm of self-help psychology, by appealing to people's thirst for easy answers to difficult life problems."

Other critics asserted that positive psychologists underestimated the possibility of achieving happiness in some instances and overestimated it in others. One respondent complained that by assigning too much power to genetics and too little to psychotherapy, they were unduly pessimistic in their assumptions about how much people could change. Others emphasized the limits to achieving happiness. In one case, in reference to Seligman's *Authentic Happiness*, a reader warned "STAY AWAY" if "you've ever been in therapy, have PTSD or were abused as a child." On a different but related note, several observers lamented the way some positive psychologists focused on people leading comfortable lives and neglected those struggling with objectively difficult social-economic situations. "In a paradoxical way," "GirlScoutDad" said of *Positivity*, "Fredrickson suffers from the lack of suffering in life, and it does come through at times in giving her exhortations ('meditate . . . savor the taste of good food . . . go on vacation') an air of elitism and superficiality." In a similar vein, "SurvivorGal" offered an extensive criticism of *The How of Happiness* for being "actively harmful in letting privileged people blame the unfortunate for their own misery." Lyubomirsky asserted that money and what it bought did not enhance people's happiness, remarked a woman from Minneapolis, "but negates to mention the fact that those without basic essentials, those struggling to keep a roof over their head, those struggling to buy food are going to have different needs than to simply 'show more gratitude.'" Consequently, "if you make more than $75,000 a year, have a husband, and have a huge, supportive social network—then this book might be right up your alley!" However, for others "her empty platitudes don't mean much . . . . I'm highly doubtful that if I was married to the love of my life, lived in a nice house, had a job I was passionate about, didn't struggle financially constantly, lived someplace without miserable winters, etc. that I would not be significantly happier! And, when I was happier than I am now—it wasn't because I thought differently—it was because my life circumstances were DRASTICALLY different and more in line with the life I crave."

How most readers responded to popular books by positive psychologists revealed how successfully these authors had accomplished their goals. In contrast, the negative reactions highlighted critical limitations of their findings some readers identified. Moreover, both positive and negative evaluations underscored how tricky it was to meld the scientific, popular, and how-to.

THREE FAMILIAR ISSUES, NOW ELABORATED ON: MONEY, MEASURING, AND THE MEANING OF HAPPINESS

In addition to all these commonly agreed-upon findings, three issues of long-standing interest to students of happiness commanded considerable attention, often marked by disagreement. The first was the relationship between money and happiness, a topic that generated disputed conclusions. There was among positive psychologists a skepticism, based in large measure on research, about the benefits of materialism. Csikszentmihalyi said it trenchantly, and others agreed: "*Our consumer culture has done much to devalue work* in general, by extolling the virtues of relaxation, material comfort, and pleasure." Or as Lyubomirsky put it, "you too could become a janitor of your possessions"; however, "not only does materialism not bring happiness, but it's been shown to be a strong predictor of *unhappiness*." Most scholars in the field believed that more money did make people happy but, as Daniel Gilbert put it, "we think money will bring lots of happiness for a long time, and actually it brings a little happiness for a short time." Central to why more money was problematic was that social comparisons, especially upward ones, and the hedonic treadmill served to undermine any gains that improved finances might otherwise bring.[53]

Recent scholarship, perhaps reflecting the upward redistribution of wealth and income, has challenged the Easterlin Paradox, which emphasized that increasing wealth did not yield comparably greater levels of satisfaction.[54] In 2008 Diener and Biswas-Diener proceeded cautiously, reporting that "it is difficult to sum up with a simplistic yes or no" to "answer the question of whether money buys happiness." On the one hand, they remained convinced, as happiness scholars had for decades, that "extra dollars often amount to modest gains in happiness." On the other hand, they suggested that "additional income can translate to greater social status, feelings of personal control, a sense of security, and unique opportunities to make a lasting contribution to society."[55] Another challenge to Easterlin came in 2008 from the economists Betsey Stevenson and Justin Wolfers. They worked to resolve the apparent contradiction Easterlin had exposed: that there is a correlation between high incomes and happiness to a point and over time the correlation between increased incomes and greater happiness diminished. Relying on an impressive array of datasets and sophisticated analytic tools, Stevenson and Wolfers examined the relationship between happiness and money both across national boundaries and within nations. They found "no evidence of a satiation point beyond which wealthier countries" plateau in happiness.[56] Both across national boundaries and within them, they concluded, "the relationship between wellbeing and income is roughly linear-log and does not diminish as incomes rise. If there is a satiation point, we are yet to reach it." The critique of the Easterlin Paradox by economists calls to mind the 2015 statement by Leon Wieseltier that "economic concepts go rampaging through noneconomic realms. Economists are our experts on happiness! Where wisdom once was, quantification will now be."[57]

This points not only to the high regard economists garnered in the postwar world but also to the second familiar topic that now commanded reformulation, how to measure happiness or subjective well-being. This issue involves two widely used and much admired ways of measuring individual happiness. For decades psychologists had relied on asking respondents, initially in interviews and eventually on line, how happy they were.[58] Advocates of relying on this remembering self insisted that focusing on memories elevates authentic satisfactions (engagement, meaning) and the pursuit of meaning over transient, superficial ones.[59] Later on the scene was the Day Reconstruction Method (DRM). Developed early in the twenty-first century by Daniel Kahneman and his colleagues, studies that used the DRM cast doubt on global self-reports of happiness.[60] To determine a person's happiness and arrive at an evaluation of "Objective Happiness," researchers used the DRM to ask respondents to systematically reconstruct how they felt on the previous day by completing a questionnaire that focused on what the experiencing self revealed. Respondents used a diary of their activities to record what they did—when, where, and with whom—and then how they felt about their experiences, evaluating each one on a seven-point scale. The results, supporters of the DRM claimed, rely on "the reality of present experience, not in fallible reconstructions and evaluations of the past."[61]

It turns out that global, retrospective reports of subjective well-being (How happy are you? What provides you with the most pleasure?) do not correlate well with records of specific, day-to-day experiences (Traffic on my commute was terrible). Kahneman contrasted actual experiences recorded at the time they occurred with more generalized, retrospective views and deemed the former more important, especially when it came to the implications of happiness research for public policy.

Related to how Kahneman and his colleagues developed new ways of measuring subjective well-being was the complexity they added to the ways people understood the implications of their decisions. His work on prospect theory was a major contribution to behavioral economics, a critique of economists who believed humans behaved as utility-maximizing rational actors when making decisions. By bringing behavioral economics and psychology together, he enriched and nuanced the ways we think about the decision-making process. One consequence of his careful analysis was that he cast a skeptical eye on how many positive psychologists claimed that a very high percentage of Americans reported they were happy or very happy. All this became clear in his *Thinking, Fast and Slow* (2011), a book that achieved a prominent and sustained place on the national list of bestselling books.

In a series of sophisticated, probing, and profound essays that drew on work he had done since the mid-1970s, often in collaboration with Amos Tversky, Kahneman focused on the role of irrationality and unpredictability in decision-making. "Considering how little we know," he remarked in a way that revealed how richly complicated was his understanding of human nature, "the confidence we have in our beliefs is preposterous—and it is also essential." He relied not on bullet points and exercises to follow, but on intriguing approaches that used visual, statistical, and semantic examples. A perceptive reader might rely on what Kahneman wrote to make more intelligent decisions, but no one could confuse his book with popular how-to ones written by academics.[62]

Kahneman distinguished between the two fictional types of thinking announced in the book's title: fast, which was automatic, impulsive, and confident; and slow, which was effortful, thoughtful, skeptical, and logical. Relying on concepts such as prospect theory, framing and anchoring effects, narrative fallacies, loss aversion, the law of small numbers, duration neglect, and focusing illusion, he recognized the pluses and minuses of both approaches and acknowledged how interestingly each interacted with its opposite. His aim, he wrote at the outset, was to "improve the ability to identify and understand errors of judgment and choice, in others and even in ourselves, by providing a richer and more precise language to discuss them."[63]

In the book's final section he distinguished between the experiencing and remembering selves and between decision utility ("wantability" or the benefits a rational person envisioned when making decisions) and experienced utility (how they actually encountered goods and services). The deployment of these concepts and the results of DRM studies drove Kahneman to a series of important conclusions. A small percentage of people experienced a disproportionate amount of suffering. For a sample of American women, commuting and child care were among the most unpleasant activities. One's sense of emotional satisfaction changed greatly over short periods of time. Attention was the key to subjective well-being; at work, special situations were more important than generalized job satisfaction—with opportunities for socializing yielding pleasure (confirming what others had discovered), and time pressure and the presence of a boss among the most unpleasant. He pointed to important policy implications of his findings, something positive psychologists did less frequently. "Improved transportation for the labor force, availability of child care for working women, and improved socializing opportunities for the elderly" were among the most efficient ways of diminishing unpleasant experiences. Initially skeptical about the importance of a generalized sense of well-being, Kahneman had come to "accept the complexities of a hybrid view" that acknowledged the importance of both the experiencing and remembering selves.[64]

Although the principal targets of Kahneman's work were economists who continued to insist that humans acted rationally, here and elsewhere he offered a critique of those, including some positive psychologists, who, governed by the illusion that we can reliably control behavior, confidently asserted that it was easy for people to train themselves to be happier and more effective. As Daniel Gilbert remarked in *Stumbling on Happiness* (2006), a book whose emphases resembled *Thinking, Fast and Slow*, "there is no simple formula for finding happiness." Central to Kahneman's attention to the unpredictability of life, and of attempts to successfully pursue happiness, was the "focusing illusion" that referred to what people concentrated on at the moment and played a greatly significant but inaccurate role in their global evaluation of their present and future. Though the fear of loss outweighed the hope of gain, the focusing illusion nonetheless led many to optimistic and false forecasts. Referring to the work of Daniel Gilbert and Timothy Wilson, Kahneman called attention to the phenomenon of *"miswanting"*—poor choices that stemmed from mistakes driven by affective forecasting or the focusing illusion. It turns out that people are poor judges of the impact on their well-being of purchases of goods and experiences, especially when they favored exciting ones that would turn out to offer only evanescent pleasures. They could compensate for such errors by learning how to make thinking fast and thinking slow work effectively together, including by relying on the experience of how others carefully understood the consequences of their decisions, often in ways that relied on statistical evidence.[65]

Kahenman's work laid down significant challenges to those who studied happiness and well-being, especially positive psychologists. He convincingly emphasized how difficult it was to think clearly about happiness and insisted on the importance of addressing complexity. He explored how the focusing illusion made it difficult to predict or understand the consequences of our decisions. He emphasized the distinction between the way the experiencing self and remembering self saw the world as especially important, with the latter exerting a stronger influence on how we make decisions. This distinction was especially important to one of the most important questions of positive psychology—whether greater income made people happier. For the experiencing self, an income above $60,000 made no difference. In contrast, for the remembering self, additional income made, and continued to make, a significant difference. The lessons for public policy might turn out to be significant. The challenge to positive psychologists was also weighty—the ability to measure and improve subjective well-being turned out to be more complicated than those who talked of precise ratios had assumed.[66]

Kahenman's work in turn leads us to another issue to which positive psychologists had long paid attention but now did so in more sophisticated ways: definitions of happiness itself. In the last ten years, Kahneman noted, we have learned "that the word *happiness* does not have a simple meaning and should not be used as if it does. Sometimes scientific progress leaves us more puzzled than we were before." As my review of books by the Mount Rushmore five made clear, positive psychologists who wrestled with how to define happiness offered more nuanced and complicated positions after 1998. To a greater extent than they had earlier, they emphasized negativity, giving it an important albeit subordinate position in their examination of how to measure and enhance subjective well-being. They used a variety of distinctions, the most common ones relying on the difference between hedonic and eudaimonic—between pleasure, happiness, and shallow and short-term satisfactions, on the one hand, and meaning, purpose, virtue, and long-term ones, on the other.[67]

A few studies revealed the various dimensions of these differences. In 2002, Carol Ryff and her colleagues distinguished between subjective well-being, the extent of satisfaction with life, and psychological well-being, which, relying on work by Abraham Maslow, Carl Rogers, Erik Erikson, and Marie Jahoda, involved "engagement with existential challenges of life." Then, in 2002, Barry Schwartz, Sonja Lyubomirsky, and their colleagues reported on experiments that distinguished between maximizers and "satisficers," a made-up word that combined satisfy and suffice. Compared with satisficers, maximizers chased after an enlarged list of choices and experienced more depression, regret, dissatisfaction with consumer decisions, and problems with upward social comparisons.[68] In 2008 Ryff and Burton H. Singer drew on Aristotle's *Nicomachean Ethics* and on empirical data to underscore two conclusions. First, they showed that "well-being, construed as growth and human fulfillment, is profoundly influenced by the surrounding contexts of people's lives, and as such, that the opportunities for self-realization are not equally distributed." Generally speaking, they concluded, higher socioeconomic status correlated with a greater sense of well-being. There was an important exception: relying on her earlier study of African Americans and Mexican Americans, Ryff pointed out that "minority status was found to be a positive predictor of eudaimonic well-being, underscoring themes of psychological strength in the face of race-related adversity." A second conclusion Ryff and Singer reached was that genuine satisfaction enhanced people's health by regulating "multiple physiological systems."[69] Finally, in 2010 Veronika Huta and Richard M. Ryan relied on experimental data to confirm what others had suggested, that the hedonic (maximizing pleasure) and eudaimonic (involving something more lasting and profound) versions of well-being were "both overlapping and distinct niches within a complete picture of well-being, and their combination may be associated with the greatest well-being."[70]

So, in the early twenty-first century, most positive psychologists cautioned against a myopic focus on hedonism and embraced eudaimonia. They would have agreed with what Diener and Biswas-Diener claimed: "if we pursue only happiness, for example, to the exclusion of spirituality and meaning, we may become hedonists who do not find true well-being."[71]

POPULARIZING HAPPINESS

After 1998 scores of popular books on happiness continued to capture the attention of an eager reading public—something *Time* magazine's coverage of the field made clear. The number of popular non-fiction books on happiness increased dramatically. As Ben-Shahar quipped in 2007, "the role of positive psychology" was to bring together "the ivory tower and Main Street, the rigor of academe and the fun of the self-help movement."[72]

The authors of these popular books included Zen practitioners, clinical psychologists, freelance writers from varied backgrounds, and well-credentialed academics. What made these books different from those discussed earlier by the Mount Rushmore five was that they did not combine thorough summaries of current research with extensive how-to suggestions.[73] Building their books with a series of short (often very short) chapters, they offered personal stories of rebirth (about themselves and others), homilies on often clichéd truisms, parables, discussions of canonical religious and humanistic texts, and practical suggestions on how to achieve happiness. Many of them paid little or no attention to academic research. Some contained an almost mystical sense of what happiness wrought and offered a religious, usually pan-religious, approach. Born a Jew and a clinician who studied both Western psychology and Eastern philosophy, Alan Gettis remarked that "the majority of my religious experiences have had little to do with religion; they've had more to do with awe, love, mystery, and transcending labels and categories." In *The Zen Commandments*, Dean Sluyter, a meditation teacher since 1970, captured the anti-theological and pan-religious spirit effectively when he remarked that "the light—the kingdom of heaven or nirvana or moksha or tawhid or shekina, depending on your preferred vocabulary—is within *you*." He drew "on any tradition that promotes compassionate outer behavior and enlightened inner awareness," insisting "I'm just interested in *what works*—a sort of dogma free spiritual street smarts."[74]

Inspirational and often individualistic (it is all up to you and you alone), these books offered solace, harmony, freedom, reassurance, and comfort. Although they acknowledged the importance of giving, their focus was on what jack-of-all-trades and author David Ambrose called "*self-time*," best achieved through meditation. As M. J. Ryan, raised as a Roman Catholic but now relying on a combination of Western psychology and Eastern wisdom, put it: "You're not responsible for anyone else's happiness." If academic research insisted on the importance of social networks and connections, popular writers, attuned to their audience's hunger for transcendence, tended to offer a narrower focus. As Ambrose stated in a way that minimized the importance of earthly social interactions, "all of us are connected on a spiritual level."[75]

These popularizers all insisted on the centrality of the present moment. "While we can get nostalgic for the past—oh, I used to be happy—or wistful about the future—someday I will be happy—it is *now*," Ryan insisted, "in this very moment, that we must create the only happiness we can count on." They encouraged readers to accentuate the positive and minimize the negative, relying on, among other techniques, cognitive behavioral therapy, meditation, and prayer.[76]

Unlike books by the Mount Rushmore five, these offered relatively few cautionary notes, optimistic as they were that genuine happiness was achievable, and with relatively little struggle. "The journey is the joy," remarked one author in what was a common note for others. In a somewhat similar vein, Ryan, while acknowledging the existence of a happiness set point, went on to say that "as of yet, no one has discovered an upper limit" of your happiness. Or as Gettis claimed in a way that made it all sound so easy and willful, "happiness is a choice and . . . you can make that choice right now." Confidence typically triumphed over doubt, in ways that seemed to reflect Peale's emphasis on positive thinking. It "may seem like overly inspirational hokum to some," remarked Shawn Achor, who relied on the insights of positive psychology in his role as a corporate trainer for Fortune 500 companies and whose TED talk commanded more than 4 million views and parodied the power of positive thinking more than relied on science, but "the more you believe in your own ability to succeed, the more likely it is you will."[77]

Theirs was an anti-materialistic vision. At times their criticism of consumer culture and the chase after the false gods represented by mammon led them to minimize the importance of external conditions to a far greater extent than did positive psychologists. As Ambrose wrote in a formulation typical of a simplistic, naïve, and problematic use of science for social analysis, "you can be happy whatever your lot in life" regardless of whether "you are living out on the streets or in a mansion." Similarly, Gettis wrote "happiness isn't so much about getting what you want as it is about wanting what you have." Or, as Ryan put it, "somehow we've gotten the message that happiness is out there, something to be sought after—in the right job, the mate who never annoys you, the $50,000 BMW—rather than inside ourselves." While they stressed the importance of some character strengths such as forgiveness, unlike Seligman's, theirs was a vision more reliant on commitments to expressive personality than on tough character.[78]

Focusing on one popular book helps us understand the genre. An ideal choice because of its popularity, its sophisticated use of multiple approaches, and its seductive style is Gretchen Rubin's 2009 *The Happiness Project: Or, Why I Spent a Year Trying to Sing in the Morning, Clean My Closets, Fight Right, Read Aristotle, and Generally Have More Fun*. After earning her BA and JD at Yale, where she served as editor-in-chief of the *Yale Law Journal*, Rubin clerked for Supreme Court Justice Sandra Day O'Connor. *The Happiness Project*, a learned and highly accessible book, remained on the national bestseller list for over two years. Overall Rubin's books have sold more than 2 million copies and have been translated into more than thirty languages. People in more than 192 nations listen to her weekly podcast, co-written with her sister Elizabeth Craft.[79]

The Happiness Project, Lyubomirsky said on the book's jacket, is "a cross between the Dalai Lama's *The Art of Happiness* and Elizabeth Gilbert's *Eat, Pray, Love*." In working on the book, Rubin read even more widely than do most popularizers—including canonical texts by Aristotle, William James, and Adam Smith; books by scholars of happiness; and works by Viktor Frankl, C. G. Jung, Jon Krakauer, and Henry David Thoreau. Among the works she singled out for having the greatest influence on her project were Benjamin Franklin's *Autobiography* and anything Samuel Johnson wrote. Yet although she read extensively in positive psychology, she told readers that she learned more from "one person's highly idiosyncratic experiences than I do from sources that detail universal principles or cite up-to-date studies." She hoped "the most compelling inspiration" for the reader's "happiness project is the book you hold in your hands." The book's jacket, using typical promotional language, claimed it was "illuminating yet entertaining, thought-provoking yet compulsively readable. Gretchen Rubin's passion for her subject," the writer's publisher claimed, "jumps off the page, and reading just a few chapters of this book will inspire you to start your *own* happiness project."[80]

Rubin began her book, as others had done, with a personal story of seeking redemption after wandering aimlessly in the desert. One day, as she looked out from the window of a Manhattan bus, she realized she "was in danger of wasting my life." While she acknowledged her good fortune in life, she knew she was "suffering from midlife malaise." So she set out on her happiness project, dedicating twelve months in an attempt to be happier. Though she had steeped herself in writings on happiness, she realized she "had to create a scheme to put happiness ideas into practice in my life."[81]

Inspired by Franklin's list of virtues to create a checklist of her own, validated by how contemporary scholarship confirmed the wisdom of tracking progress in a systematic way, Rubin structured her book around twelve projects, one for each month of the year centering on a particular facet of well-being identified by the philosophical, scholarly, and spiritual writers who informed her book: boosting energy (vitality), remembering love (marriage), aiming higher (work), lightening up (parenthood), being serious about play (leisure), making time for friends (friendship), buying some happiness (money), contemplating the heavens (eternity), pursuing a passion (books), paying attention (mindfulness), keeping a contented heart (attitude), and working toward what she called "Boot Camp Perfect" happiness.[82]

With the project for each month, she listed a few specific tasks. For example, under buying some happiness, she put down indulging in a modest splurge, buying necessities, and giving something up. With making time for friends, she listed remembering birthdays, being generous, showing up, and avoiding gossip. With each monthly project she mixed information about what academic studies revealed, personal stories of how she worked to achieve her goals, how-to advice, responses to her blogs, and insights from literary, religious, and philosophical figures. What she learned, and conveyed to the reader, was that the only person you can change is yourself, that wise spending could buy happiness, that having sufficient income made it more possible to focus on the transcendent, that small changes were as important as major ones, that passion was essential to performing well in work, that the unexpected as well as the familiar made us happy, that minimizing negativity was helpful, and that social connections were crucial. She ended the book with a personal affirmation that doubtlessly reassured readers. "I really am happier," she reported, after her year on the project was over. "After all my research, I found what I knew all along: I could change my life without changing my life. When I made the effort to reach out for them," she told readers, "I found that the ruby slippers had been on my feet all along; the bluebird was singing outside my kitchen window."[83]

Like Thoreau's journey to Walden Pond or Franklin's to virtuous perfection, Rubin's was a compelling literary construct. Whether she actually confined her search to a calendar year and devoted precisely one month to each specific project may or may not have been true, but for readers it was a useful approach. Her economic, cultural, and social capital surely helped launch the book into a literary stratosphere that none of the Mount Rushmore five achieved. She had savvy marketing muscle behind her. She drew engaging pictures of her own life, one peopled by family, friends, and colleagues. She was among the first to meld old and new media so extensively, breaking fresh ground by including reader's responses to her blogs and directing readers to her blogs and web sites. Her recipe was familiar enough, with its mixture of academic studies, personal stories, reflections on enduring themes, and examples that implicitly or explicitly offered practical advice to readers. Jonathan Haidt's *Happiness Hypothesis* had adopted the strategy of weaving classical questions about human nature with academic research. Fredrickson's *Positivity*, which appeared in the same year as Rubin's book, had a virtually identical mixture of approaches. As Lyubomirsky's blurb, cited earlier, makes clear, Rubin was exceptionally adept at drawing on and bringing together approaches other inquiries into happiness had offered.

Several things help account for the exceptional popularity of Rubin's book. She successfully melded seeming opposites. A skilled writer, she could refer to achievements as a law student and lawyer, and yet use anecdotes, humor, and simple language to make what she said relatable to readers whose lives were more common than hers. She combined an ambitious agenda with grounded, specific experiences; high culture and low; lofty inspirations and practical suggestions; skillful translations of conceptually sophisticated scholarship along with very accessible advice; references to her stratospheric legal career (a Supreme Court clerkship) with down-to-earth accomplishments (uncluttering by cleaning her closet).

An examination of the more than 1,300 reviews on Amazon.com, most of them from women, helps us understand the book's appeal.[84] Twelve percent of the readers gave the book a lowly one star. Their most common complaints were what they saw as Rubin's whininess, self-promotion, and privilege. These readers resented what they took to be gratuitous references to résumé-bragging about her Yale degrees and her Supreme Court clerkship. Even more annoying were the marks of her privilege, which for critical readers cast doubt on the authenticity and replicability of her experiences. Married to the son of Robert Rubin, Goldman Sachs executive and Secretary of the Treasury under President William Clinton, living in a triplex on Manhattan's Upper East Side, employing a nanny and a housekeeper, and having the wealth and income that the 99 percent envied or found offensive, gave her, one responder remarked, "lots of free time and disposable income to fund her 'happiness project'" and made it difficult for readers to take seriously her whining about the errands she had to run or "how hard it is for her to spend a week being nice to her husband."

In contrast, positive reviews (49 percent gave the book 5 stars and 19 percent 4) had no difficulty finding much to admire in what Rubin wrote. Some of the positive responders actually turned the tables on the negative ones by acknowledging that while they approached the book thinking Rubin's privilege would be off-putting, she convinced them otherwise. Thus one woman who said she would buy her hardback copy approached the book skeptically, "thinking that anyone like Gretchen Rubin, who isn't lacking money or work prestige, isn't really in touch with those of us who struggle with these things." Yet she concluded in a way that underscored the power of Rubin's book to convince and covert, "it turns out the subjects she works on are things any of us can master." Positive responders appreciated the liveliness and accessibility of her style—which one reader characterized as "open, engaging, often humorous." They also found helpful her discussion of "do-able actions" that "really transform the way you view happiness and your potential to achieve it." They admired Rubin's honesty, best seen in her willingness to make clear through stories the tensions she experienced with her husband and children. They appreciated that she did not seek perfection or tell them to expect they could do so. As one reader remarked, what made her book so appealing "is that she admits that she isn't perfect; she's not afraid to show her ugly side instead of painting a picture of sunshine and rainbows." Another woman remarked that "the vulnerability" Rubin displayed "was enough to bring me to tears several times while reading. (Tears only because I so thoroughly identified with her.)."

Her suggestions seemed down-to-earth: in what was perhaps an implicit reference to *Eat, Pray, Love*, one reader remarked that rather than recommending something "radical" like taking a trip around the world, Rubin focused on her effort "to change little things and to make resolutions that were concrete and manageable"—a "practical, achievable & customizable guide" as one person called them. "Making small changes that have a big impact," remarked another, characterizing Rubin's approach. *The Happiness Project* "may be life-altering," someone commented, "paradoxically by showing that these changes aren't designed to be life-altering at all, but simply life-enhancing." Readers found enormously helpful her ability to translate the findings of scholars and connect readers with the wisdom of great thinkers without herself being pedantic. Rubin, one reader wrote, "was not one of those wordy, dry experts in fields such as psychology or cognitive therapy. This means," she continued, "the book isn't crammed with tiny print, waffly language and tiresome graphs, tables and other statistics." By relying on memoir and anecdotes, which this reader found "far more readable and appealing," meant that "Rubin has done it for us, and made the path far easier to follow."

What is most striking about the Amazon.com reviews (and her blogs as well) is how readers who responded were engaged in a reciprocal, interactive dialogue with other readers and with Rubin herself. Many positive readers began their comments by making clear how they dissented from and criticized the negative reviews they had read, in the process revealing that they had read many Amazon.com responses. A frequent theme was that readers found Rubin approachable, one indication of how positive psychology evoked highly personal responses: one respondent remarked that the author was "pretty likeable and interesting—I wouldn't mind having a cup of coffee with her"; someone else put it that reading the book "felt more like a conversation with a friend than just another book." Moreover, social media and the Internet reinforced the personal connections readers felt they had with other readers and with Rubin. As one remarked, Rubin's blogs and podcasts provided "byte sized reminders" of the book's content. "Gretchen is also incredibly friendly and grateful to her readers," she continued. "If you write to her on Facebook, she'll respond! She's awesome. Definitely the best author ever. She'll also help you start your very own happiness project if you want to!"

CONCLUSION

Rubin's book, along with others by both professors and popularizers, made clear which ideas positive psychology had coalesced around in the early twenty-first century, relying as they did on concepts drawn from psychology itself, from Eastern spirituality, and from neuroscience. A robust professional infrastructure had emerged. The Mount Rushmore five policed and crossed the border between the academic and the popular. Professional psychologists and others explored issues surrounding the meaning of money, the challenges of measuring, and the meanings of happiness itself.

Observers with many backgrounds and diverse training emphasized the existence of a set point, the importance of social connections, and the connections between health and happiness. We turn now to other writings that revealed new issues that positive psychologists were emphasizing, as well as the political ideologies that undergirded the field and the critiques of its vision.

NOTES

1. Claudia Wallis, "The New Science of Happiness," *Time*, Jan. 9, 2005; Oprah Winfrey and Sonja Lyubomirsky quoted in same.
2. Jeffrey Kluger, "The Happiness of Pursuit," *Time*, July 8, 2013.
3. For the agenda in building a field, see Christopher M. Peterson and Martin E. P. Seligman, "Positive Organizational Studies: Lessons from Positive Psychology," in *Positive Organizational Scholarship*, ed. Kim S. Cameron, Jane E. Dutton, and Robert E. Quinn (San Francisco: Berrett-Koehler, 2003), 14–27.
4. D. T. Max, "Happiness 101," *NYTM*, Jan. 7, 2007; Carey Goldberg, "Harvard's Crowded Course to Happiness 'Positive Psychology' Draws Students in Droves," *Boston Globe*, March 10, 2006.
5. Meg Rao, "Overview of and Methods in Positive Psychology," Fourth World Congress on Positive Psychology, June 26, 2015, Buena Vista, FL (hereinafter cited as IPPA meeting); Heejin Kim, "Positive Psychology Across the World," June 26, 2015, IPPA meeting. For an analysis of the growth of interest in positive psychology as reflected in journals, see Reuben D. Rusk and Lea E. Waters, "Tracing the Size, Reach, Impact, and Breadth of Positive Psychology," *JPP* 8 (April 2013): 207–21. Using sophisticated statistical techniques, Christopher Kullenberg and Gustaf Nelhans, "The Happiness Turn? Mapping the Emergence of 'Happiness Studies' Using Cited References," *Scientometrics* 103 (May 2015): 615–30 charts the centrality of Ed Diener's 1984 article, the emergence of social indictors research in the 1970s, a takeoff in journal articles in the 1990s but without integration of seemingly disparate fields, and a more integrated and even steeper rise after 2000.
6. This is based on data in PsychInfo and Robert Biswas-Diener et al., "Positive Psychology as a Force for Social Change," in *Designing Positive Psychology: Taking Stock and Moving Forward*, ed. Kennon, 410–11.
7. Among the examples of newspaper coverage are David Leonhardt, "If Richer Isn't Happier, What Is?" *NYT*, May 19, 2001; Arthur C. Brooks, "A Formula for Happiness," *NYT*, Dec. 14, 2013. For textbooks and handbooks, see C. R. Snyder and Shane J. Lopez, eds., *Handbook of Positive Psychology* (New York: Oxford University Press, 2002); C. R. Snyder and Shane J. Lopez, *Positive Psychology: The Scientific and Practical Explorations of Human Strengths* (Thousand Oaks, CA: Sage Publications, 2007); Anthony D. Ong and Manfred H. M. van Dulmen, eds., *Oxford Handbook in Methods of Positive Psychology* (New York: Oxford University Press, 2007); Shane J. Lopez, ed., *Positive Psychology: Exploring the Best in People*, 4 vols. (Westport, CT: Praeger, 2008); Steve R. Baumgardner and Marie K. Crothers, *Positive Psychology* (Upper Saddle River, NJ: Prentice Hall, 2009); Shane J. Lopez, ed., *The Encyclopedia of Positive Psychology* (Malden, MA: Wiley-Blackwell, 2009); Susan A. David, Ilona Boniwell, and Amanda C. Ayers, eds., *The Oxford Handbook on Happiness* (Oxford: Oxford University Press, 2013); Michele M. Tugade, Michelle N. Shiota, and

Leslie D. Kirby, eds., *Handbook of Positive Emotions* (New York: Guilford Press, 2014). For a discussion of textbooks in the field, see Grant J. Rich, "Teaching Tools for Positive Psychology: A Comparison of Available Textbooks," *JPP* 6 (Dec. 2011): 492–98.

8. For a guide to programs, see http://positivepsychologyprogram.com/positive-psy-chology-courses-programs-workshops-trainings/. For some discussion of the building of an infrastructure, see Mihaly Csikszentmihalyi and Jeanne Nakamura, "Positive Psychology: Where Did It Come From, Where Is It Going?" in Sheldon, Kashdan, and Steger, *Designing Positive Psychology*, 3–8.

9. See http://www.livehappy.com/science/positive-psychology/happiness-revolu-tion. According to the web site Web of Science, Seligman, Fredrickson, Diener, and Csikszentmihalyi are authors of some the most frequently cited scholarly articles listed under positive psychology.

10. Anne Harrington, *The Cure Within: A History of Mind-Body Medicine* (New York: W.W. Norton, 2008), 247–48.

11. Harrington, *Mind-Body*, 249.

12. Martin E. P. Seligman, *Authentic Happiness: Using the New Positive Psychology to Realize Your Potential for Lasting Fulfillment* (New York: Free Press, 2002); Martin E. P. Seligman, *Flourish: A Visionary New Understanding of Happiness and Well-Being* (New York: Simon & Schuster, 2011).

13. Seligman, *Authentic*, 6, 288–89.

14. Seligman, *Authentic*, xiv, 24, 102, 112, 161; Christopher Peterson, "The Values in Action (VIA) Classification of Strengths," in *A Life Worth Living: Contributions to Positive Psychology*, ed. Mihaly Csikszentmihalyi and Isabella Selega Csikszentmihalyi (New York: Oxford University Press, 2006), 30.

15. Seligman, *Authentic*, 127–29, 291–92.

16. See http://edge.org/q2003/q03_seligman.html; Martin E. P. Seligman and Christopher Peterson, "Character Strengths Before and After September 11," *PS* 14 (July 2003): 381–84; Stephen Band, quoted in Tamsin Shaw, "The Psychologists Take Power," *NYRB*, Feb. 25, 2016.

17. Law firm of Sidley Austin, LLP, "Report to the Special Committee of the Board of Directors of the American Psychological Association: Independent Review Relating to APA Ethics Guidelines, National Security Interrogations, and Torture," July 2, 2015, 165. For more discussion of these controversies in the *New York Review of Books*, see Shaw, "Psychologists Take Power"; Jonathan Haidt and Steven Pinker, "Moral Psychology: An Exchange," April 7, 2016, and reply by Tamsin Shaw; " 'Learned Helplessness' and Torture: An Exchange"; Martin E. P. Seligman and reply by Tamsin Shaw, April 21, 2016. For more of Seligman's involvement, see Jane Mayer, *The Dark Side: The Inside Story on How the War on Terror Turned Into a War on American Ideals* (New York: Doubleday, 2008); Stacy Burling, "The Power of a Positive Thinker," http://www.philly.com, May 30, 2010.

18. Seligman, *Flourish*, 1, 10, 11–27.

19. Seligman, *Authentic*, 121.

20. Mihaly Csikszentmihalyi, *Good Business: Leadership, Flow, and the Making of Meaning* (New York: Viking, 2003), 10, 19, 82, 87, 199.

21. Csikszentmihalyi, *Good Business*, 3.

22. Jane E. Dutton, *Energize Your Workplace: How to Create and Sustain High-Quality Connections at Work* (San Francisco: Jossey-Bass, 2003); Amy Wrzesniewski and Jane E. Dutton, "Crafting a Job: Revisioning Employees as Active Crafters of Their Work," *Academy of Management Review* 26 (April 2001): 179–201.

23. Sonja Lyubomirsky, *The How of Happiness: A Scientific Approach to Getting the Life You Want* (New York: Penguin, 2008), 2, 3, 7. See also her *The Myths of Happiness: What*

Should Make You Happy But Doesn't; What Shouldn't Make You Happy, But Does (New York: Penguin, 2013).

24. Lyubomirsky, *How*, 38.

25. Lyubomirsky, *How*, 6, 282–83.

26. Ed Diener and Robert Biswas-Diener, *Happiness: Unlocking the Mysteries of Psychological Wealth* (Malden, MA: Blackwell, 2008). See also Todd B. Kashdan and Robert Biswas-Diener, *The Upside of Your Dark Side: Why Being Your Whole Self—Not Just Your "Good" Self—Drives Success and Fulfillment* (New York: Hudson Street, 2014); Robert Biswas-Diener, *Practicing Positive Psychology Coaching: Assessment, Activities, and Strategies for Success* (Hoboken, NJ: Wiley, 2010); Robert Biswas-Diener, ed., *Positive Psychology as Social Change* (Dordrecht, Netherlands: Springer, 2011); Robert Biswas-Diener, *The Courage Quotient: How Science Can Make You Braver* (San Francisco: Jossey-Bass, 2012).

27. Michael B. Frisch, quoted in Diener and Biswas-Diener, *Happiness*, ii.

28. Michael B. Frisch, blurb in Diener and Biswas-Diener, *Happiness*, ii. For an earlier study that focused on measuring large numbers of people's psyches worldwide, see Rebecca Lemov, "X-Rays of Inner Worlds: The Mid-Twentieth-Century American Projective Test Movement," *Journal of the History of the Behavioral Sciences* 47 (Summer 2011): 251–78.

29. Diener and Biswas-Diener, *Happiness*, 64, 182, 183, 188, 200, 207.

30. Diener and Biswas-Diener, *Happiness*, 208, 218, 220, 224, 233.

31. Diener and Biswas-Diener, *Happiness,* 11, 183, 243.

32. Barbara Fredrickson, *Positivity: Top-Notch Research Reveals the 3-to-1 Ratio That Will Change Your Life* (New York: MJF Books, 2009), book jacket, and 48. Her other book is *Love 2.0: How Our Supreme Emotion Affects Everything We Feel, Think, Do, and Become* (New York: Hudson Street, 2013).

33. Fredrickson, *Positivity*, 95.

34. Fredrickson, *Positivity*, 6, 12, 14, 18, 33, 37, 39, 199, 210.

35. Their scholarship is extensive, but good places to begin include Michael E. McCullough, Robert A. Emmons, and Jo-Ann Tsang, "The Grateful Disposition: A Conceptual and Empirical Topography," *Journal of Personality and Social Psychology, 82* (Jan. 2002): 112–27; Robert A. Emmons, *Thanks! How the New Science of Gratitude Can Make You Happier* (Boston: Houghton Mifflin, 2007); Michael E. McCullough, *Beyond Revenge: The Evolution of the Forgiveness Instinct* (San Francisco: Jossey-Bass, 2008).

36. Nicholas J. L. Brown, Alan D. Sokal, and Harris L. Friedman, "The Complex Dynamics of Wishful Thinking: The Critical Positivity Ratio," *AP, 68* (Dec. 2013): 801–13. For the ensuing controversy, see Andrew Anthony, "The British Amateur Who Debunked the Mathematics of Happiness," *The Guardian*, Jan. 18, 2014, and James Coyne, "Positive Psychology Is Mainly for Rich White People," PLOS Blogs, Aug. 21, 2013; http://www.thedailybeast.com/articles/2013/08/16/barbara-fredrickson-s-bestselling-positivity-is-trashed-by-a-new-study.html. The original article was Barbara l. Fredrickson and Marcial F. Lasoda, "Positive Affect and the Complex Dynamics of Human Flourishing," *AP* 60 (Oct. 2005): 678–86. For her reliance on Lasoda's work, see Fredrickson, *Positivity*, 120–38.

37. Nicholas Brown, quoted in Anthony, "British Amateur"; Barbara Fredrickson, "Updated Thinking on Positivity Ratios," *AP* 69 (Dec. 2013): 814.

38. Ed Diener, Eunkook M. Suh, Richard E. Lucas, and Heidi L. Smith, "Subjective Well-Being: Three Decades of Progress," *PB*, 125 (March 1999): 276–302; for a more recent review of the issues, see Joachim I. Krueger, "Happy Pie: Intend to Become Happier and Do Something About It," *Psychology Today*, March 4, 2015. Essential in casting a skeptical eye on Lyubomirky's formulation is epigenetics, the observation that experiences can switch genes off and on: for a review of recent work in this field, see George D. Smith, "Epigenetics for the Masses: More Than Audrey Hepburn and Yellow Mice?" *International*

Journal of Epidemiology 41 (Feb. 2012): 303–08. Ruth Whippman, *America the Anxious; How Our Pursuit of Happiness Is Creating a Nation of Nervous Wrecks* (New York: St. Martin's Press, 2016), 195.

39. Among the other books summarizing the field are Alan Carr, *Positive Psychology: The Science of Happiness and Human Strengths* (New York: Brunner-Routledge, 2004); Richard Layard, *Happiness: Lessons from a New Science* (New York: Penguin, 2005); Daniel Gilbert, *Stumbling on Happiness* (New York: Knopf, 2006); Ilona Boniwell, *Positive Psychology in a Nutshell: A Balanced Introduction to the Science of Optimal Functioning*, 2nd ed. (London: PWBC, 2008); Christopher Peterson, *A Primer in Positive Psychology* (New York: Oxford University Press, 2006); Tal Ben-Shahar, *Happier: Learn the Secrets to Daily Joy and Lasting Fulfillment* (New York: McGraw-Hill, 2007); Tal Ben-Shahar, *Even Happier: A Gratitude Journal for Daily Joy and Lasting Fulfillment* (New York: McGraw-Hill, 2010); Tal Ben-Shahar, *The Pursuit of Perfect: How to Stop Chasing Perfection and Start Living a Richer, Happier Life* (New York: McGraw-Hill, 2009); Shawn Achor, *Before Happiness: 5 Actionable Strategies to Create a Positive Path to Success* (New York: Crown Business, 2013); Elizabeth Dunn and Michael Norton, *Happy Money: The Science of Smarter Spending* (New York: Simon & Schuster, 2013); Jan D. Sinnott, *Positive Psychology: Advances in Understanding Adult Motivation* (New York: Springer, 2013); Shigehiro Oishi, *The Psychological Wealth of Nations: Do Happy People Make a Happy Society?* (Malden, MA: Wiley-Blackwell, 2012).

40. Peter Kramer, "Incidental Enhancement: Cosmetic Psychopharmacology Two Decades Out," lecture delivered in Tübingen, Germany, August 1, 2009, copy in author's possession; David Healy, *Let Them Eat Prozac: The Unhealthy Relationship Between the Pharmaceutical Industry and Depression* (New York: New York University Press, 2004). See also David Servan-Schreiber, *The Instinct to Heal: Curing Stress, Anxiety, and Depression Without Drugs and Without Talk Therapy* (Emmaus, PA: Rodale, 2004). For an evaluation of Kramer's idea of the relationship between drugs and authenticity, see Ineke Bolt and Maartje Schermer, "Psychopharmaceutical Enhancers: Enhancing Identity?" *Neuroethics* 2 (June 2009): 103–11.

41. Seligman, *Flourish*, 46.

42. Jonathan Haidt, *The Happiness Hypothesis: Finding Modern Truth in Ancient Wisdom* (New York: Basic, 2006) provides the most extensive juxtaposition of findings of positive psychologists, on the one hand, and humanistic writers, on the other. With little reference to the findings of psychologists, Alain de Botton used the humanities to explore how to achieve a fulfilled life: *How Proust Can Change Your Life: Not a Novel* (London: Picador, 1997); *The Consolations of Philosophy* (New York: Pantheon, 2000); *The Architecture of Happiness* (New York: Pantheon, 2006). For a philosopher's take on the field, see Fred Feldman, *What Is This Thing Called Happiness?* (New York: Oxford University Press, 2010).

43. Carol Gilligan, *The Birth of Pleasure* (New York: Knopf, 2002), while not a book informed by positive psychology, explores the gendered dynamics of happiness. For an important but relatively rare study of gender and well-being, see Gerhard Meisenberg and Michael A. Woodley, "Gender Differences and Subjective Well-Being and Their Relationships with Gender Equality," *JHS* 16 (Dec. 2015): 1539–55.

44. James H. Fowler and Nicholas A. Christakis, "Dynamic Spread of Happiness in a Large Social Network: Longitudinal Analysis Over 20 Years in the Framingham Heart Study," BMJ.com, Dec. 5, 2008, 1; George Valliant, quoted in Carolyn Gregoire, "The 75-Year Study That Found the Secrets to a Fulfilling Life," *Huffington Post*, Aug. 23, 2013.

45. See, for example, Jingping Xu and Robert E. Roberts, "The Power of Positive Emotions: It's a Matter of Life and Death—Subjective Well-Being and Longevity Over 28 Years in a General Population," *Health Psychology* 29 (Jan. 2010): 9–19.

46. Sheldon Cohen et al., "Emotional Style and Susceptibility to the Common Cold," *Psychosomatic Medicine* 65 (July-Aug. 2003): 652.

47. Barbara Fredrickson, "Individual Differences in Prioritizing Positivity: New Measures and Findings," IPPA meeting, June 25, 2015.

48. Diener and Biswas-Diener, *Happiness*, 198.

49. For the entry into public discussions of the notion that suffering is good for you, see David Brooks, "What Suffering Does," *NYT*, April 7, 2014.

50. Diener and Biswas-Diener, *Happiness*, 9; Lyubomirsky, *How*, 24–25; Fredrickson, *Positivity*, 23, 90–91; Seligman, *Flourish*, 237.

51. Csikszentmihalyi, *Business*, 3, 4, 9.

52. This analysis relies on responses in Amazon.com to Diener and Biswas-Diener, *Happiness*; Fredrickson, *Positivity*; Lyubomirsky, *How*; Seligman, *Flourish* and *Authentic* but not to Csikszentmihalyi, *Business*, because it did not fit the genre others exemplified.

53. Csikszentmihalyi, *Business*, 99; Lyubomirsky, *How*, 43; Daniel Gilbert, quoted in Carey Goldberg, "Materialism is Bad for You, Studies Say," *NYT*, Feb. 8, 2006. For a critique of the standard version of the hedonic treadmill theory, see Ed Diener, Richard E. Lucas, and Christie Napa Scollon, "Beyond the Hedonic Treadmill: Revising the Adaptation Theory of Well-Being," *AP* 61 (May–June 2006): 305–14.

54. For recent works that emphasize more positive correlations, above the poverty line, between money and subjective well-being, see Ryan T. Howell, Mark Kurai, and Wing Yin Leona Tam, "Money Buys Financial Security and Psychological Need Satisfaction: Testing Need Theory in Affluence," *SIR* 110 (Jan./Feb. 2013): 17–29; Joachim Weimann, Andreas Knabe, and Ronnie Schöb, *Measuring Happiness: The Economics of Well-Being* (Cambridge, MA: MIT Press, 2015).

55. Diener and Biswas-Diener, *Happiness*, 110–11. In 2003, Veenhoven had questioned the Easterlin Paradox as applied to international comparisons: Michael R. Hagerty and Ruut Veenhoven, "Wealth and Happiness Revisited: Growing National Income *Does* Go with Greater Happiness," *SIR* 64 (Oct. 2003): 1–27; for the response, see Richard A. Easterlin, "Feeding the Illusion of Growth and Happiness: A Reply to Hagerty and Veenhoven," *SIR* 74 (Dec. 2005): 429–43.

56. Betsey Stevenson and Justin Wolfers, "Economic Growth and Subjective Well-Being: Reassessing the Easterlin Paradox," NBER Working Paper, No. 14282, Aug. 2008. For the response see Richard A. Easterlin et al., "The Happiness-Income Paradox Revisited," *Proceedings of the National Academy of Sciences* 107 (Dec. 28, 2010): 22463–68.

57. Betsey Stevenson and Justin Wolfers, "Subjective Well-Being and Income: Is There Any Evidence of Satiation?" 2013, CESifo Working Paper, No. 4222, 3; Leon Wieseltier, "Among the Disrupted," *NYRB*, Jan. 7, 2015.

58. For a recent version, see https://www.authentichappiness.sas.upenn.edu/testcenter.

59. In *Memory: Fragments of a Modern History* (Chicago: University of Chicago Press, 2012), Alison Winter explores the larger story of problematic memories.

60. Daniel Kahneman et al., "A Survey Method for Characterizing Daily Life Experience: The Day Reconstruction Method," *Science*, Dec. 3, 2004, 1776–80. For his discussion of the DRM, see Daniel Kahneman, *Thinking, Fast and Slow* (New York: Farrar, Straus and Giroux, 2011), 392–97 and the accompanying notes. For a thorough history of ways of measuring subjective well-being, see Oishi, *Psychological Wealth*, 18–33.

61. Daniel Kahneman, "Objective Happiness," in *Well-being: Foundations of Hedonic Psychology*, ed. Daniel Kahneman, Ed Diener, and Norbert Schwarz (New York: Russell Sage Foundation, 1999), 22. See also Daniel Kahneman and Alan B. Krueger, "Developments in the Measurement of Subjective Well-Being," *Journal of Economic Perspectives* 20 (Winter 2006): 3–24; Bruno Frey et al., *Happiness: A Revolution in Economics* (Cambridge, MA: MIT Press, 2008). Arthur A. Stone and Christopher Mackie, eds.,

Subjective Well-Being: Measuring Happiness, Suffering, and Other Dimensions of Experience (Washington, DC: National Academies Press, 2013) distinguishes between kinds of subjective well-being: the experienced and the evaluative (representing what the remembering self recalls), and the eudaimonic (purpose, meaning). Similarly, Cass R. Sunstein, "Who Knows If You're Happy?" *NYRB*, Dec. 4, 2014, 20 distinguishes between "evaluative well-being," the generalized and somewhat retrospective evaluation, and "experienced well-being," reported on at the time.

62. Kahneman, *Thinking*, 209.

63. Kahneman, *Thinking*, 4.

64. Kahneman, *Thinking*, 395, 402.

65. Gilbert, *Stumbling*, 238; Kahneman, *Thinking*, 406.

66. Daniel Kahneman, "The Riddle of Experience vs. Memory," TED talk, March 1, 2010.

67. Kahneman, *Thinking*, 407. Among the many considerations of these issues are Ruut Veenhoven, "Hedonism and Happiness," *JHS* 4 (Dec. 2003): 437–57; Daniel Kahneman and Angus Deaton, "High Income Improves Evaluation of Life but Not Emotional Well-Being," *Proceedings of the National Academy of Sciences* 107 (Sept. 21, 2010): 16489–93; Carol D. Ryff, "Psychological Well-Being Revisited: Advances in the Science and Practice of Eudaimonia," *Psychotherapy and Psychosomatics* 83 (2014): 10–28; David Brooks, "The Problem with Meaning," *NYT*, Jan. 5, 2015. Samuel S. Franklin, *The Psychology of Happiness: A Good Human Life* (New York: Cambridge University Press, 2010) provides a thorough discussion of Aristotle, eudaimonia, and a values-based positive psychology.

68. Corey L. M. Keyes, Dov Shmotkin, and Carol D. Ryff, "Optimizing Well-Being: The Empirical Encounter of Two Traditions," *JPSP* 82 (June 2002): 1007–22; Barry Schwartz et al., "Maximizing Versus Satisficing: Happiness Is a Matter of Choice," *JPSP* 83 (Nov. 2002): 1178–97. For an influential application of this distinction, see Lori Gottlieb, *Marry Him: The Case for Settling for Mr. Good Enough* (New York: Dutton, 2010).

69. Carol D. Ryff and Burton H. Singer, "Know Thyself and Become What You Are: A Eudaimonic Approach to Psychological Well-Being," *JHS* 9 (Jan. 2008): 14–15; Carol D. Ryff, Corey L.M. Keyes, and Diane L. Hughes, "Status Inequalities, Perceived Discrimination, and Eudaimonic Well-Being: Do the Challenges of Minority Life Hone Purpose and Growth?" *Journal of Health Science Behavior* 44 (Sept. 2003): 275.

70. Veronika Huta and Richard M. Ryan, "Pursuing Pleasure or Virtue: The Differential and Overlapping Well-Being Benefits of Hedonic and Eudaimonic Motives," *JHS* 11 (Dec. 2010): 735–62. For a similar argument see Todd B. Kashdan, Robert Biswas-Diener, and Laura A. King, "Reconsidering Happiness: The Costs of Distinguishing Between Hedonics and Eudaimonia," *JPP* 3 (Jan. 2008): 219–33.

71. Diener and Biswas-Diener, *Happiness*, 8.

72. Ben-Shahar, *Happier*, x–xi. On the plethora of books on positivity, see Sam Binkley, *Happiness as Enterprise: An Essay on Neoliberal Life* (Albany: State University of New York Press, 2014), 29.

73. This discussion relies on relevant books in Amazon's "Top 10 Books on Happiness," especially Alan Gettis, *The Happiness Solution: Finding Joy and Meaning in an Upside Down World* (Norwood, NJ: Goodman Beck, 2008); Alan Gettis, *Seven Times Down, Eight Times Up: Landing on Your Feet in an Upside Down World* (Norwood, NJ: Goodman Beck, 2009); David Ambrose, *Your Life Manual: Practical Steps to Genuine Happiness* (Calgary, Canada: Revolution Mind Publishing, 2006); M. J. Ryan, *The Happiness Makeover: How to Teach Yourself to Be Happy and Enjoy Every Day* (New York: Broadway, 2005); Dean Sluyter, *The Zen Commandments: Ten Suggestions for a Life of Inner Freedom* (New York: Penguin Putnam, 2001). See also John F. Schumaker, *In Search of Happiness: Understanding an Endangered State of Mind* (Westport, CT: Praeger, 2007). I cite others in earlier chapters, since they appeared before 1998: Barry Kaufman's *Happiness Is a Choice*, Robert Holden's

Happiness Now!, and The Dalai Lama and Howard Cutler's *The Art of Happiness*. In addition, Seligman's *Authentic Happiness*, which I have already discussed, appears on the list, as does Ben-Shahar, *Happier*.

74. Gettis, *Solution*, 198; Sluyter, *Commandments*, 2, 4.
75. Ambrose, *Manual*, 129, 220; Ryan, *Makeover*, 74.
76. Ryan, *Makeover*, 6.
77. Ryan, *Makeover*, 6; Robert Hastings, "The Station," in Ambrose, *Manual*, 11; Gettis, *Solution*, 54; Shawn Achor, *The Happiness Advantage: The Seven Principles That Fuel Success and Performance at Work* (New York: Crown Business, 2010), 74.
78. Ambrose, *Manual*, 35; Gettis, *Solution*, 41; Ryan, *Makeover*, 4. In addition to those cited elsewhere, I count more than two dozen books of this period aimed at popular audiences, some of them by academics. Too numerous to cite all, a sampling includes Brené Brown, *The Gifts of Imperfection: Let Go of Who You Think You're Supposed to Be and Embrace Who You Are* (Center City, MN: Hazelden, 2010); Braco Pobric, *Habits and Happiness: How to Become Happier and Improve Your Wellbeing by Changing Your Habits* (Mercerville, NJ: High Impact Consulting, 2014); Tom Rath and Robert O. Clifton, *How Full Is Your Bucket: Positive Strategies for Work and Life* (New York: Gallup, 2004); Eckhart Tolle, *A New Earth: Awakening to Your Life's Purpose* (New York: Dutton, 2005); Paul Dolan, *Happiness By Design: Change What You Do, Not How You Think* (New York: Hudson Street Press, 2014).
79. Gretchen Rubin, *The Happiness Project: Or, Why I Spent a Year Trying to Sing in the Morning, Clean My Closets, Fight Right, Read Aristotle, and Generally Have More Fun* (New York: HarperCollins, 2009). For her web site, see http://gretchenrubin.com/about/. See also Gretchen Rubin, *Happier at Home: Kiss More, Jump More, Abandon a Project, Read Samuel Johnson, and My Other Experiments in Everyday Life* (New York: Crown, 2012) and Gretchen Rubin, *Better Than Before: Mastering the Habits of Our Everyday Lives* (New York: Crown, 2015).
80. Rubin, *Project*, xiii, 297–301; Sonja Lyubomirsky and promotional copy on book jacket.
81. Rubin, *Project*, 1, 2, 7.
82. Rubin, *Project*, 277.
83. Rubin, *Project*, 289.
84. Compared to the responses on Amazon.com to Rubin's books, those to books by the Mount Rushmore five attracted far fewer reviews, revealed a greater balance between responses from men and women, and elicited far less of a sense of dialogue and reciprocity between author and reviewer. On the other hand, Rubin's book and the ones by the Mount Rushmore five garnered a roughly similar balance between positive and negative responses and contained evidence that many readers read multiple books within the field.

CHAPTER 7

The Future Is Here

Positive Psychology Comes of Age

By the middle of the second decade of the twenty-first century, positive psychology had come of age. Scholarly practitioners had built key elements of a powerful, extensive infrastructure and, along with lay popularizers, had reached expansive audiences. A consensus vision of the field had developed, one that was capacious, bold, and integrated. Writers elaborated on long-familiar themes and suggested the dimensions of new ones. Relying on fresh research, scholars turned to four topics, discussed somewhat before 1998, that now came to the fore: character, religion and spirituality, science, and international comparisons.[1] Moreover, the field's often implicit political ideologies—neoliberalism especially, but not exclusively—became increasingly apparent.[2] Finally, as a sign of positive psychology's prominence, sustained criticisms now emerged, too recently to describe how they might change the field over time.

CHARACTER

Character, as a key to a meaningful life, was prominent among the issues present as a relatively minor note before and that now came to the fore among positive psychologists. Soon after Martin Seligman's 1998 presidential APA address, he collaborated with Christopher Peterson in providing the intellectual and strategic leadership that led to their massive 2004 *Character Strengths and Virtues: A Handbook and Classification*. If the *Diagnostic and Statistical Manual* (DSM) was the scientific guide to psychological disorders, their Values in Action (VIA) inventory was the counterpart for positive psychological strengths. Using the VIA Signature Strengths Questionnaire would enable people to figure out their strengths and then learn how to build on them. Peterson and Seligman listed six major strengths—wisdom and knowledge, courage, humanity, justice, temperance, and transcendence—each with several subcategories. If temperance meant self-control and prudence, the emphasis on justice required that citizens commit themselves to civic action that went beyond self-interest and could involve social protests or support of social causes. Transcendence, operating through spirituality or religiousness ("whether they be called universal, ideal, sacred, or divine"), involved a different dimension of moving beyond self-involvement.[3]

The emphasis on character strengths, historically linked with masculinity, developed as part of a larger vision of American society in historical perspective. Seligman and Peterson made clear their opposition to a "personless" or "radical environmentalism" that undermined self-determination by shifting responsibility for problems from the individual to external circumstances. Seligman's justification for the return to an emphasis on character as a counter to postmodernism and relativism was only part of the story. "After a detour through the hedonism of the 1960s, the narcissism of the 1970s, the materialism of the 1980s, and the apathy of the 1990s," Peterson and Seligman wrote, relying on oversimplified generalizations, "most everyone today seems to believe that character is important after all and that the United States is facing a character crisis on many fronts, from the playroom to the classroom to the sports arena to the Hollywood screen to business corporations to politics." The turn to character involved grappling with Aristotle's concept of eudaimonia "which holds," they underscored, that "well-being is not a consequence of virtuous action but rather an inherent aspect of such action."[4]

Moreover, central to the emphasis on character strengths was a recognition of the necessity to work through the consequences of the Easterlin Paradox. Since World War II the GDP of Western nations, including the United States, had increased considerably, but their citizens reported no greater happiness. Millions of people in developed nations struggled to move beyond materialism to meaning, to shift, as some positive psychologists had, from hedonic to eudaimonic. What made such a change difficult was how people were overwhelmed by excessive choices. They often found that what market economies delivered undermined happiness, cut people off from meaningful social relationships, increased inequalities in wealth and income, and bedeviled citizens with upward social comparisons. Rather than indulge in a culture of complaint in which grievances loomed large, people, advocates of character asserted, should see ways of transcending the self. As one observer put it in 2003, follow the findings of positive psychologists in realizing that being "forgiving, grateful, and optimistic . . . are actually essential to personal well-being."[5]

GRATITUDE AND ALTRUISM

Among the many character traits, several held a significant place in the practice of positive psychology, gratitude and altruism prominently among them. Emphasis on these values provides added evidence of how scholars in the field used language that in potentially powerful ways connected individualism and social obligations. Pre-1998 studies of the "Helper's High" and reciprocal altruism had established a connection between giving and happiness.[6] Now, however, this topic was the subject of more vigorous experiments and more prominent applications. "Gratitude," remarked Barbara Fredrickson, "opens your heart and carries the urge to give back— to do something good in return, either for the person who helped you or for someone else."[7] Several experimental exercises were especially notable. Researchers had long ago shown that there was a correlation between helping and happiness, but now positive psychologists claimed they relied on scientific experiments that moved beyond correlation to causation. For example, Sonja Lyubomirsky carried out an experiment in which, once a week, subjects recorded in a journal what they were grateful for. Compared with a control group, the journal keepers reported significantly greater satisfaction with their lives. Similarly, she noted, people could enhance their happiness by acts of kindness such as writing a letter to a loved one, doing a favor for a neighbor, or visiting a nursing home. "Doing five kind acts a week, especially all in a single day," a *Time* magazine reporter noted in 2005, "gave a measurable boost" to those she studied.[8]

Seligman carried out extensive gratitude experiments—in his classes, in controlled settings, and on the Internet. "The single most effective way to turbocharge your joy," a reporter for *Time* paraphrased him as saying in a 2005 article, "is to make a 'gratitude visit.' That means writing a testimonial thanking a teacher, pastor or grandparent—anyone to whom you owe a debt of gratitude—and then visiting that person to read him or her the letter of appreciation. 'The remarkable thing,' says Seligman, 'is that people who do this just once are measurably happier and less depressed a month later. But it's gone by three months.' Less powerful but more lasting, he says, is an exercise he calls three blessings—taking time each day to write down a trio of things that went well and why," in a way that underscored how psychological rituals tended to replace organized religion with highly personal spirituality. "'People are less depressed and happier three months later and six months later,'" Seligman remarked. "Gratitude exercises can do more than lift one's mood," the writer for *Time* reported in 2005, going on to mention the work of psychologist Robert Emmons, the most influential student of gratitude who "found they improve physical health, raise energy levels and, for patients with neuromuscular disease, relieve pain and fatigue."[9]

Other studies revealed the links between giving, happiness, and health. Especially important was the work of the medical ethicist Stephen Post, who with funds from the Templeton Foundation had founded the Institute for Research on Unlimited Love in 2001. In a series of books and articles written in the early twenty-first century, he combined reports on scientific studies (which he helped launch at more than a score of universities), inspirational stories, how-to instructions, and wisdom that mixed spirituality and religion. He showed how unselfish giving not only made people feel happier but also produced remarkable health benefits, including living longer and mitigation of chronic illnesses. Invoking a passage from Proverbs ("A generous man will prosper, he who refreshes others will himself be refreshed"), he insisted that while "genuine altruism is an action done without assuming reciprocal or reputational gains for the agent," nonetheless "by its very inward dynamic" it "enhances well-being and often contributes to health." Along similar lines, working at the HeartMath Institute, Rollin McCraty published "The Appreciative Heart: The Psychophysiology of Positive Emotions and Optimal Functioning," which claimed to rely on empirical scientific research to demonstrate the connection between positive emotions generated by giving to both improved performance and better health outcomes.[10]

The fullest exploration of the relationships between science, religion, and altruism—a key issue in the study of character—came together in an edited 2015 book, *Caring Economics: Conversations on Altruism and Compassion Between Scientists, Economists, and the Dalai Lama*, based on a 2010 conference planned in response to the 2008 Great Recession.[11] The economist Ernst Fehr carried out experiments that, going against the grain of colleagues who assumed people focused on their self-interest narrowly defined, revealed that people did take into account notions of fairness to others and that altruism undergirded the commitment to providing for the public good; indeed, altruistic people lived happier and healthier lives. The neuroscientist Tania Singer reported on studies of the brain that, relying on the research using fMRI imaging, revealed how the mapping of neural networks in the interoceptive cortex of the brain helped us understand socially positive behavior and human interconnectedness. In addition, experiments showed that training people in loving-kindness meditation helped novices express compassion that experts in mediation had long experienced. Similarly, giving people specific hormones or neuropeptides, such as oxytocin, decreased their fearfulness and enhanced their capacity to trust others. Using fMRI, the economist William Harbaugh examined the "warm-glow kind of altruism" that helped people make charitable gifts.[12]

Especially important in the conference discussions was the work of the psychologist Richard J. Davidson, who, relying on studies of children, long-time practitioners of compassionate meditation, and those who received training in compassion, presented evidence of a correlation between the amount of activation in the insula and amygdala and how predisposed people were to compassion. Subjects who in a laboratory setting redistributed money in a game reported "greater feelings of warmth and compassion and concern for the suffering of others" than did their experimental peers who did not redistribute funds. Moreover, evidence of the brain's plasticity was associated with altruism. More generally, contributors to the volume of essays worked to reconcile Western and Buddhist outlooks on caring. And no one was in a better position to do so than Matthieu Ricard, a Frenchman who, after earning his doctorate in molecular biology in 1972, devoted the rest of his life to the study and practice of Buddhism. It was possible, he insisted, to teach people to be compassionate, including toward their enemies.[13]

Elsewhere, learning to express gratitude took on some key characteristics of a social or cultural movement. The 2000 movie *Pay It Forward*, based on a novel of the same name, told the story of a seventh-grade student whose social studies teacher taught him to pay it forward by responding to a favor received by doing ones for three others, each of whom would do so for three more people, thus creating a rapidly multiplying network of gratitude. This in turn led to the Pay It Forward Movement and Foundation, established by the novel's author Catherine Ryan Hyde, which over time had circulated over a million Pay It Forward bracelets in over 100 nations. "The philosophy of Pay It Forward," its web site announced, "is that through acts of kindness among strangers, we all foster a more caring society." Then in 2007 came the Pay It Forward Day, which received global media coverage. Eventually its hope was to "inspire over 10 million acts of kindness around the world" such as buying a stranger a cup of coffee or helping out someone in need. "Imagine the difference that would make!" the web site announced. Four years later came the Newton Project, which by providing wristbands whose circulation could be followed, made it possible for a web site visitor to track acts of kindness. The project aimed "to empower individuals to make a difference one person at a time. Our goal," the web site announced, "is to create an ever-growing community of connected individuals who value and promote giving, compassion and love across the world."[14]

Resilience was another character strength that received considerable attention in the new century. Going back at least to writings of Viktor Frankl, psychologists have long been interested in how people responded positively when confronted with adversity. Now, however, researchers more explicitly explored the connections between character and what was known early on as posttraumatic growth. A key book on this topic is *The Resilience Factor: 7 Keys to Finding Your Inner Strength and Overcoming Life's Hurdles*, by Karen Reivich and Andrew Shatté, the former a co-author with Seligman on *The Optimistic Child* and co-director of the Penn Resiliency Project. Drawing on cognitive behavioral therapy, the authors' seven keys included challenging beliefs, putting thoughts into perspective, and understanding how patterns of response undermined positivity. Published in 2002, the book, like some by other positive psychologists, used responses to 9/11 to illustrate the benefits of positive psychology. That tragic day, they wrote, had threatened people's sense of safety and justice. Yet "just like we as a nation have done," they noted at the book's end, "in little ways, every day" the people whose lives they had described in the book "reconstructed their world by changing the way they think." Connecting the national and the personal, they insisted "they did it and so can you." In their final sentence they insisted "by changing the way you think, you can change your life for good." Interested before 9/11 in character strengths as a counter to victimology and unearned self-esteem, after that horrific event Seligman and his colleagues now redoubled their efforts to counter narcissistic happiness.[15]

Over the course of two decades, the Penn Resiliency Program supported its findings on character in experimental and real-world settings. Carrying out studies on over 3,000 children and adolescents, the experiments of Seligman, Reivich, and their colleagues revealed that it was possible to teach optimism, assertiveness, coping, and realistic problem solving. Relying on a $2.8 million grant from the United States Department of Education, they introduced positive psychology into a high school that, Seligman reported, "builds character strengths, relationships, and meaning, as well as raises positive emotion and reduces negative" ones—and in the process enhanced "the traditional goals of classroom learning."[16]

In 2008, Seligman began to collaborate with the Pentagon on the Comprehensive Soldier Fitness Program for returning vets stressed by years of rotating in and out of service in Afghanistan and Iraq (see Chapter 8), an effort subjected to sharp criticism for what many saw as compromises with professional standards in a misguided patriotic effort but that Seligman insisted was itself patriotic. Working together with Brigadier General Rhonda Cornum, Seligman and his colleagues developed a test to measure psychological fitness, courses that focused on self-improvement, and a pilot program for resilience training. The efforts were so successful that the Army eventually established twenty training centers that, according to the program's web site, taught soldiers and their families "things such as problem solving, how to think optimistically, and how to cope with adversity." The Army granted Seligman's center at Penn a $31 million no-bid contract to train American service members to be resilient and overcome tragic events.[17]

The Road to Character (2015), by *New York Times* columnist David Brooks, revealed the conservative implications of an emphasis on character that Seligman had alluded to briefly. "By successfully confronting sin and weakness," Brooks remarked as he both drew on positive psychology and made it even more accessible, "we have the chance to play our role in a great moral drama. We can shoot for something higher than happiness" by taking "advantage of every occasion to build virtue in ourselves and be of service to the world." Countering what he labeled the culture of the "Big Me," he called on people to develop character strengths that humbly recognized the importance of our connection to and caring for others. His advice on how to restore moral realism was capacious. Live for holiness, not happiness; purpose, not pleasure, he recommended. Understanding that we are "flawed creatures" will militate against "selfishness and overconfidence." Through acts of kindness, an embrace of humility, and a struggle against sinful pride, he wrote in ways that reflected his commitment to a Protestant tradition embodied in self-help literature, people would give up earthly success and instead choose inner, moral growth. His advice was to avoid short-term, banal, and material pleasures and commit oneself "to tasks that cannot be completed in a single lifetime." Whether from a loved one, a stranger, or God, one should work to achieve grace, a condition in which "gratitude fills the soul, and with it the desire to serve and give back." Whether working as a hedge fund manager or dedicating your life to helping the poor, mature people developed a sense of purpose that enabled them to move "from fragmentation to centeredness, . . . a state in which the restlessness is over, the confusion about meaning and purpose of life is calmed."[18]

Writing in the *New York Times* in 2015, literary critic and *New York Times* editor Parul Sehgal explored the immense popularity of resilience and critiqued its assumptions. She charted how resilience had "sprung into new life as a catchword in international development and Silicon Valley and among parenting pundits and TED-heads." Publishers had issued hundreds of books on the subject, telling eager audiences how to toughen their investment portfolios or their children. Organizations—from the United Nations to the Department of Homeland Security—added resilience to their mission statements. In response to terrorist attacks, to student protests on campuses, and even to Justin Bieber's fall and rise, people counseled resilience, something that was "so conveniently vacant that it manages to be profound and profoundly hollow." Yet, she noted, resilience was "indistinguishable from classic American bootstrap logic when it is applied to individuals, placing all the burden of success and failure on a person's character." As Alfie Kohn perceptively noted in a *Washington Post* op-ed, "the more we focus on levels of grit (or self-discipline more generally), the less likely we'll be to question larger policies and institutions."[19]

SPIRITUALITY AND RELIGION

In developing the Comprehensive Soldier Fitness Program, the Pentagon and Seligman recruited Ken Pargament to work on how to enhance resilience through spirituality. We have already met Pargament as the author of the 1997 *The Psychology of Religion and Coping: Theory, Research, and Practice*. His work marked a major turning point in the discussions of the connection between religion and happiness, a marker of the increasing acknowledgment of the importance of religion in American public life. Robert Emmons had reported in 1999 that despite their claims that they studied the whole person, psychologists failed to pay significant attention to the roles of religion and spirituality in people's lives, a trend Pargament's work now reversed, with support of the Templeton Foundation playing a key role.[20]

Indeed, Sir John Templeton wrote the foreword to the 2002 *Handbook of Positive Psychology*. He predicted that in the future those who contributed to this volume "will be recognized as visionary leaders, whose research helped to identify, elevate, and celebrate the creative potential of the human spirit." He looked forward to when "a group of scientists will publish findings that will advance humankind's understanding of a spiritual principle that had been at the core of my own life's purpose: *agape love*," since with unconditional love, unlike with money, the more "we give away, the more we have left."[21]

Often without being very specific about which faith traditions mattered, researchers increasingly showed that religion and spirituality improved the quality of life and extended longevity.[22] Of the Mount Rushmore five, Sonja Lyubomirsky offered the fullest and most nuanced discussions of the relationships between happiness and religion and/or spirituality. Although it was impossible to investigate God in the lab or quantify sacredness, she noted in a way that reflected what William James might have said, researchers could explore "the *consequences* of having religious beliefs." Studies demonstrated that religious people lived happier and healthier lives and were better able to recover from traumas. She considered but in the end rejected a commonly held assumption that the benefits of religion had "nothing to do with the substance of their religious and spiritual beliefs" but more with the social support that religious affiliations provided. She insisted on the importance of "the one 'ultimate' supportive relationship for many religious individuals, one that doesn't require any formal participation in religious services or programs, and that is their relationship to God"—one that provided comfort and enhanced self-esteem. In addition, "your sense that God has a purpose in everything helps you find meaning in ordinary life events as well as traumatic ones." Although she distinguished between religion and spirituality, she concluded that the benefits from the two approaches were basically the same. She raised the possibility that some religious traditions (such as those that envisioned a punishing God or fostered prejudice) were harmful but concluded that the results of specific studies were "not very generalizable to today's diversity of views, indicating that the vast majority of religious and spiritual individuals are more likely to be inclusive, compassionate, and open-minded than the reverse."[23]

The relationship between Buddhism and happiness deserves special note. After 1998, there was little new under the sun that earlier shone on Buddhism and meditation, except for two important changes. The scientific evidence for the positive health benefits of meditation, first reported in Herbert Benson's 1975 *Relaxation Response*, now accumulated dramatically. Second, and not unrelated, the relationships between Buddhism, mindfulness, and happiness garnered immense popular attention, at least equal to if not more so than any connection to Protestantism or Roman Catholicism.[24]

Ironically, given how prominent a role Jews have played in positive psychology, scholars in that field have written remarkably little on Jews and happiness. There are scores of books on happiness by Protestant ministers, some of whom doubled as psychologists, few if any by Roman Catholics priests, and few by rabbis. That may be changing. Recently, rabbis and other Jews have indeed focused on this topic, pointing out that although often problematic stereotypes allege that Jews are known for kvetching and anxiety, positive psychology shares and perhaps draws on much that is central to Judaism, including Tzedakah (the religious obligation to be righteously charitable), Tikkun Olam (to heal the world), the importance of social connections that a community provides, resilience in the face of adversity, or the joyful rituals such as Simchat Torah (the celebration of the conclusion of a cycle of Torah readings).[25] With further research, we may come to understand the conflict in visions of well-being between Judaism's communitarian commitments and Protestantism's individualistic ones.[26] Yet the connections between Jews, Judaism, and happiness has remained understudied.[27] At least two factors may be at work involving how Jews drew on religious traditions other than Judaism. A significant number of Jewish Buddhists (aka Jewbus or Jubus) have been major figures in both American Buddhism and happiness studies—Jon Kabat-Zinn, Jeffrey R. Rubin, Rodger Kamenetz, Jack Kornfield, Sylvia Boorstein, Herbert Benson, Richard J. Davidson, Alan Gettis, and Daniel Goleman come immediately to mind. However, Jewish writers learned to write and speak in Christian terms. For example, the words of David Brooks in *The Road to Character* of sin and redemption more likely echo the Protestantism of the Episcopal Grace Church School that he attended as a child and the findings of positive psychology he has explored than expressions of the Jewish faith of his ancestors.[28]

Overall, positive psychologists fudged or avoided all sorts of issues concerning religion and spirituality. Just as they and others watered down Buddhism to make it acceptable to mainstream Americans, so too and more generally they homogenized American religion. Terms like religiousness, religion, and spirituality seemed interchangeable. Most writers remained skeptical of any connection with a specific theology or view of God. They papered over or significantly avoided discussion of traditional struggles within American religious traditions, Protestantism especially—whether God was vengeful or kindly, whether or how humans could be damned or saved, whether or not a sinful life confined people to Hell. They did not vigorously follow up on suggestions of the differences between healthy and unhealthy religious experiences or connections. Notably, positive psychology came of age when a major restructuring of American religious traditions was well under way, when once central ones (for example, Presbyterianism, Irish Roman Catholicism, and Conservative Judaism) were challenged by once peripheral ones (Mormonism, Pentecostalism, Latino Roman Catholicism, Orthodox Judaism, and Buddhism). Yet reading what positive psychologists have written offers few insights into and little specificity about such changes.[29]

Several ironies marked the explorations of the connections between religion/spirituality and happiness after 1998, when experimenters and writers intensified their interest in the positive impact of religion on people's sense of well-being. First, such considerations began not with mainstream American faith traditions but with Buddhism.[30] Remember that in 1984 Diener concluded that the evidence of the impact of religion on subjective well-being was far from clear. Yet by then Herbert Benson had written *The Relaxation Response* and Jon Kabat-Zinn had already established the Stress Reduction Clinic at University of Massachusetts Medical School, both of which combined Buddhism and science. Thus focus on how Western religions enhanced happiness came late to the table. Second, despite the presence of so many Jews among positive psychologists—Martin Seligman, Tal

Ben-Shahar, Daniel Gilbert, Daniel Kahneman, Richard J. Davidson, Sonja Lyubomirsky, and Jonathan Haidt, to name a few—most of the research has focused on liberal American Protestantism; indeed, it may be that Jewish writers, often known for their angst, have marked their assimilation into American culture by embracing a certain Protestant vision of the world. Third, just as the incorporation of Buddhism into happiness studies involved a watering down of practice and beliefs, so too went the inclusion of Western religions. Positive psychologists talked of vague religious commitments or an even vaguer spirituality. Finally, it remained unclear whether religious practices and beliefs, as opposed to sociability and organizational life, were responsible for enhanced satisfaction with life. Thus a *Time* reporter noted in 2005 that "religious faith seems to genuinely lift the spirit, though it's tough to tell whether it's the God part or the community aspect that does the heavy lifting."[31]

SCIENCE AND HAPPINESS

Debates over whether traits and characteristics are biologically or socially constructed commanded considerable attention among scientists in the second half of the twentieth century. "If there has been a general trend in the human sciences over the past two or three decades," the historian Joel Isaac wrote in 2012, in a way that helps us understand changes in positive psychology, "it has centered on the increasing influence of biological forms of explanation—most notably the alliance of evolutionary accounts of human psychology with experimental work in the neurosciences."[32] As we have already seen in the work of Richard J. Davidson, Carol D. Ryff, and others from before 1998, that year was no magic marking point in the application of science to the study of happiness. Nonetheless, several things are notable for the very late twentieth century and the first decade and a half of the twenty-first. As scientific advances relevant to the study of subjective well-being intensified, writers more fully integrated scientific discoveries into their more general treatments. And popularizers offered research findings to a wide audience, even as researchers warned that their work had only begun and it was too early to draw certain conclusions or confidently make applications. At moments, researchers involved in positive psychology, nervous about scientific explanations of how the mind operates and sensitive to suspicion among other scientists that positive psychology was not scientific enough, had more serious reservations about how rigorous were the bases of conclusions. As one noted in 2009 in response to books by Matthieu Ricard and Eckhart Tolle, "they should not be treated with any credibility. They advocate an image of the human condition and well-being that is not based on a good and scientific under-standing of human nature."[33]

If by and large before 1998 summaries of the field had not fully integrated scientific findings, this changed considerably soon after.[34] An examination of writings by the Mount Rushmore five and other synthesizers reveals a consensus on the connections among science, health, and well-being. Fredrickson, like many researchers into emotions, relied on an emphasis on nature rather than nurture, as she invoked evolutionary biology to support her broaden-and-build theory. Over time our ancestors' "sparkle of good feelings" worked through natural selection to strengthen their positivity, making them "better prepared to survive future threats to life and limb."[35] If the Darwinian theory of natural selection was difficult to explore in a labo-ratory, the same was not true of other key elements of the scientific connec-tion between well-being and health. The use of EEG revealed that for happy people there was a connection between positive emotions and the brain's left prefrontal cortex.[36] The use of the fMRI provided evidence that was even more central to the neuroscience of happiness, despite how new and controversial it was.[37] Available by the mid-1990s, in the early twenty-first century this kind of neuroimaging became the gold standard for exploring the connections between positive well-being and the brain. Indeed, a grant of almost $6 million from the Templeton Foundation enabled Seligman to establish a Positive Neuroscience Project at Penn's Positive Psychology Center.

Initially researchers returned to the work that Robert Heath and James Olds had done in the 1950s using electrodes on the brain to enhance plea-sure, only to discover that the neuroscience of pleasure, though still promis-ing, was more elusive and complicated than earlier assumed.[38] Over time, if there was one focal point that commanded ample attention, it was the nexus between happiness and neuroscience, explored by positron emission tomography (PET) scans, EEG, and fMRI, and practiced by mindful medi-tation. In a 2007 booklet on fMRI, the American Psychological Association reported that Davidson's studies revealed that "meditation can help the brain learn to flex its happiness muscles." Studying Buddhist monks from Tibet and using a problematic analogy, what the APA called "the Olympic athletes of meditation," he and his colleagues revealed that meditation promoted "increased activity in a region of the brain associated with joy. But you don't have to spend decades in meditation to see effects. Even the control group—total beginners—saw changes in their brain activation. In short, you can improve your ability to be happy just like you can improve your tennis backhand or your golf swing."[39]

In the early twentieth-first century, Davidson, whose work on the rela-tionship between the brain and happiness had begun in the 1970s, emerged as the key figure in the neuroscience of happiness. In 2005, *Time* magazine exuberantly reported on his work under the title "Health: The Biology of Joy." "Known by his colleagues as the king of happiness research," the *Time* reporter remarked, in 2000 Davidson had noticed a Buddhist monk in his lab "sink deep into serene meditation" and, with electrodes attached to his skull, produce "electrical activity in the left prefrontal lobe" of his brain "shooting up at a tremendous rate." What Davidson witnessed made clear "that happiness isn't just a vague, ineffable feeling; it's a physical state of the brain—one that you can induce deliberately."[40]

Although much remained to be determined, such as what happiness meant scientifically and how the neuroscience of happiness operated, much was becoming more extensively explored. Studies using fMRI and EEGs helped locate the principal locus of happiness in the left prefrontal cortex. Researchers emphasized the importance of genetic predispositions to levels of happiness, the significance of a balance between negativity and positivity, and the likely role of neurotransmitters (especially dopamine and serotonin). "People with a sensitive version of the receptor that accepts dopamine," *Time* reported, "tend to have better moods, and researchers are actively studying the relationship of dopamine levels to feelings of euphoria and depression." Yet Davidson and others explored whether neuroplasticity meant that the happiness set point was not fixed, that mental activity could actually increase happiness long term.[41]

Davidson's career recapitulates the history of the relationships between happiness studies, science, and Eastern religions. He entered Harvard graduate school in psychology in 1972 when behaviorism was prominent; indeed, he had an awkward conversation with B. F. Skinner in, of all possibly significant places, an elevator in William James Hall. Determined to study the neurological basis of emotions, among what inspired him was the model David McClelland provided of "one foot very successfully planted in the world of academic psychology and one in the world of spiritual transcendence." In graduate school he carried out a key experiment that made clear that the left and right prefrontal cortices were connected to positive and negative emotions, respectively. In the same years, he encountered key figures who would serve as models of how to connect science and spirituality: not only Ram Das and Jon Kabat-Zinn, but also Daniel Goleman, with whom in graduate school Davidson began research on meditation. Learning how to meditate in 1974, during decades of professional achievement he nonetheless kept the academic and meditative aspects of his life separate because senior colleagues warned him that focusing his research on meditation would call his professionalism into question.[42]

That began to change when in 1992 he met the Dalai Lama, who facilitated introductions to long-term, expert meditators in Dharamsala,

Figure 7.1 Wearing a 128-channel geodesic sensor net, Buddhist monk Matthieu Ricard sits in a soundproof room and talks with Richard J. Davidson (right) before participating in an electroencephalography (EEG) test at the EEG facility in the Waisman Center at the University of Wisconsin–Madison on June 5, 2008. Ricard is a long-time participant in an ongoing research study led by Davidson that monitors a subject's brain waves during various forms of meditation including compassion meditation. Matthieu Ricard's arrival at the lab of Richard J. Davidson illustrates the joining of science and spirituality. Davidson is director of the Waisman Lab for Brain Imaging and Behavior (WLBIB) and the William James and Vilas Professor of Psychology and Psychiatry. (From Jeff Miller/University of Wisconsin-Madison, © UW-Madison University Communications.)

India, in order to see if such mental activity changed the brain. The Tibetan monks, skeptical of science and used to solitude, made carrying out the studies difficult, but Davidson and others persisted, aware that the Dalai Lama was open to science. Then in 2001 the French molecular geneticist turned master meditator Matthieu Ricard came to Davidson's lab. and with the Dalai Lama on hand, Davidson placed 256 sensors on Ricard's scalp to reveal "that engaging in specific forms of meditation," known as compassionate or loving-kindness meditation, "evokes dramatic changes in brain function that our tools could measure" (Figure 7.1).That was the moment, Davidson later wrote, when "the field of contemplative neuroscience had just been born." Over time Davidson proved that the Tibetan monks who had practiced meditation the longest and most intensely possessed the most favorable left-right ratio for the pre-frontal cortex, a ratio that increased the more they meditated. This made them, some claimed, among the happiest people on earth.[43]

In his 2012 *The Emotional Life of Your Brain: How Its Unique Patterns Affect the Way You Think, Feel, and Live—and How You Can Change Them*, written with science journalist Sharon Begley, Davidson melded the findings of hard science with key elements drawn from popular how-to books. His investigations led him to emphasize the concept of neuroplasticity, the ability of the brain "to change its structure and function in significant ways . . . in response to the experiences we have as well as the thoughts we think." Neuroplasticity was a tremendously important breakthrough in understanding the brain and its relationship to the mind. A science writer remarked that "the power of neuroplasticity to transform the emotional brain opens up new worlds of possibility," including how we have "the capacity to willfully direct which functions will flower . . . which moral capacities emerge . . . which emotions flourish." Davidson explored how mental training, achieved principally through meditation, could "alter patterns of activity in the brain to strengthen empathy, compassion, optimism, and a sense of well-being."[44]

Linking neuroscience and his long-standing experience with meditation, and providing questionnaires and exercises that would enable readers to benefit from practicing it, Davidson remarked that he hoped his book would help people transform their lives, as it had done his. "You can modify your Emotional Style," he told readers, "to improve your resilience, social intuition, sensitivity to your own internal emotional and psychological states, coping mechanisms, attention, and sense of well-being." The benefits of mindfulness were abundant. Not only did it help build compassion, focus, resilience, positivity, and social intuition, it also promoted healthful well-being, resulting in greater resistance to illnesses and longer lives. At the end of his book Davidson talked directly to his readers, telling them that he hoped what he wrote helped them see "that who you are today does not need to be who you are tomorrow, but that our Emotional Style is ours for the creating. Emotions," he insisted, "help us appreciate others and the world around us; they make life meaningful and fulfilling. May each and every one of you flourish in your well-being and help others to do the same."[45]

Davidson's book was part of an outpouring of work in the early twenty-first century on the relationships between neuroscience and well-being. The findings and recommendations appeared in varied genres—from cautious scholarly articles announcing new experimental findings, to books that summarized findings in sober and often technical terms, to books (like Davidson's) aimed at popular audiences, to how-to offerings that sometimes claimed more than evidence allowed.[46]

Davidson's work captured what had emerged by 2010 as a consensus among neuroscientists about the relationship between the brain and positive emotions, a consensus often shaped by the links between brain science and Buddhism. Writers worked to distinguish between hokum that could exaggerate the power of the mind over the body and scientific studies that offered a more careful assessment. New technologies, especially PET and fMRI, made possible what two scholars have called the "neuromolecular gaze"—the ability to visualize not only the brain but also how it functioned in ways that enhanced our understanding of emotions. There was no one part of the brain linked to pleasure, researchers discovered; rather, the connection involves a complicated set of regions and processes. Research made available a wide range of interventions; with training, it is possible for individuals to use their mind and emotions to change their brains. As Daniel Goleman remarked in the preface to a book by a leading science journalist, scientific investigations suggested that there may well be "a two-way street of causality, with systematic mental activity resulting in changes in the very structure of the brain." Research into how the brain works supposedly revealed that happiness goes along with social connections and a strengthened immune system. Every brain, scientists agreed, is different, in part because every person has a different genetic makeup. Still, all brains were capable of growth and change, making it possible to train the brain to make it, and ourselves, more open to positive thoughts and feelings. Neuroscience confirmed much of what positive psychologists had long emphasized: the importance getting off the status-driven hedonic treadmill and minimizing the power of social comparisons and of having commitments or interests larger than the self, especially through social connections, religion, or the experience of nature.[47]

For many writers, brain science revealed an inseparable connection between Eastern religions and meditation. Richard O'Connor, a therapist who acknowledged that he had suffered from clinical depression, insisted that "practicing mindfulness regularly is our best hope at resetting the happiness thermostat." Many positive psychologists preferred meditation to drugs, both because the evidence for meditation's beneficial effects was so strong and because drugs based on new findings by neuroscientists were not fully developed, were illegal, or had problematic side effects, including addiction.[48]

Researchers also explored the connection between positive psychology and favorable health outcomes. Sheldon Cohen and his colleagues carried out a key experiment (see Chapter 6). Based on this and other studies, the 2005 *Time* article reported that "people who rate in the upper reaches of happiness on psychological tests develop about 50% more antibodies than average in response to flu vaccines" and "that happiness or related mental states like hopefulness, optimism and contentment appear to reduce the risk or limit the severity of cardiovascular disease, pulmonary disease, diabetes, hypertension, colds and upper-respiratory infections as well." Similarly, a Dutch study whose certain conclusions seemed exaggerated revealed that "upbeat mental states reduced an individual's risk of death 50% over the study's nine-year duration," while other investigations revealed the people with greater subjective well-being became ill less frequently, recovered more quickly, and often had longer lives.⁴⁹

The dust jacket of a learned book aimed at a popular audience in 2007 summarized what neuroscientists had concluded. "Cutting-edge science and the ancient wisdom of Buddhism have come together to show how we all have the power to literally change our brains by changing our minds," remarked the publicist for Sharon Begley's *Train Your Mind, Change Your Brain: How a New Science Reveals Our Extraordinary Potential to Transform Ourselves*. Yet careful scientific researchers worried that, as the British behavioral scientist Daniel Nettle put it, the promise of increased happiness, by promoting "a plethora of therapies, alternative therapies, herbal products, alternative herbal products, spiritual systems, alternative systems," involved excessive "quackery and charlatanism." Too many self-help books and "self-administered therapies," he cautioned, seemed "to suggest that we can all become supermen and women, with no problems, perfect happiness, and limitless wealth and energy." In contrast, he had to admit that through therapy (especially cognitive behavioral therapy and pleasant activities training) or meditation, "happiness can be deliberately manipulated, with measurable if modest effects."⁵⁰

The serious, scientifically based study of the brain and happiness at times opened the gates to popular renditions that promised transformative changes. O'Connor wrote that "if you will seriously work on happiness for three months, you'll have a different brain, be a different person." John Medina, a developmental molecular biologist, insisted that "aerobic exercise just twice a week halves your risk of general dementia" and reduces "your risk of Alzheimer's by 60 percent." Two scientists offered a book that showed how to activate brain states, which would "give you the ability to gradually rewire your own brain—from the inside out—for greater well-being, fulfillment in your relationships, and inner peace." Others touted the social benefits of what brain science revealed. In *Social Intelligence* (2006), Daniel Goleman claimed that "neuroscience has discovered that our brain's very design makes it *sociable*, inexorably drawn into an intimate brain-to-brain linkup whenever we engage with another person. That neural bridge lets us affect the brain—and so the body—of everyone we interact with, just as they do us." In *Your Money and Your Brain: How the New Science of Neuroeconomics Can Help Make You Rich* (2007), *Money* magazine writer Jason Zweig reported on one implication of Davidson's work. Having more activity in the left prefrontal cortex, he remarked, meant "it's almost as if this area is a source of internal sunshine for the mind," which meant, among other things, that people who had such capacity were better investors. Understanding what neuroscience revealed about how we make investment decisions, he claimed, would provide investors with "financial peace of mind"—and greater wealth. This was one example—common among popularizers but not infrequent among scholars who wrote about neuroscience—of how conclusions and applications could outpace scientific findings.[51]

HAPPINESS INTERNATIONALLY

Positive psychologists responded to globalization of the economy and of intellectual life in several different and often conflicting ways. Where they faltered was in grappling with the ways cultural differences across national boundaries influenced the understanding of happiness. Part of the reason was their failure to incorporate insights and methods from anthropology. From early on positive psychologists had talked of integrating the social sciences with the behavioral ones. Economics had joined the fray, with consideration from public policy specialists coming along later. Yet by and large sociology and anthropology had remained on the sidelines.[52] The result, especially true with the absence of anthropology, was that on issues such as defining and measuring happiness, distinctive cultural perspectives often remained unexplored and by and large Western values—or, as someone inventively remarked, the perspectives of the WEIRD (Western, Educated, Industrialized, Rich, and Democratic)—reigned. There was at least one important issue on which cultural differences received significant attention. Researchers explored how the distinction between the individualism of Western societies and the collectivism of Eastern ones shaped notions of self-esteem, identity, motivation, and subjective well-being.[53]

After 1998 other international dimensions of positive psychology received markedly greater attention. New efforts built on earlier ones. In the United States surveys had appeared in the 1950s. Early on the scene was the World Data Base of Happiness, developed by Rutt Veenhoven decades before Seligman's 1998 presidential address. Then came the European Commission's Eurobarometer, launched in 1973; the European Values Study and the World Values Survey, both originating in 1981; and the Russian Longitudinal Monitoring Survey, which emerged shortly after the collapse of the Soviet Union. Beginning in the late 1990s, data collection spread, moving beyond developed nations to developing and even stagnant or deeply troubled ones. The Latinobarometro Survey appeared in 1996 and the Afrobarometer Survey in 1999. A handful of scholars collected data where one might normally expect to find little happiness, such as in war-torn Afghanistan, among the homeless in America, and on the streets of Calcutta. Initiated in 2005, the Gallup World Poll now covers 160 nations and 98 percent of the world's adults. These databases made possible the study of a host of issues, among which happiness was only one and even then sometimes indirectly.[54]

The connection between public policy and happiness across national borders was a related issue that received increasing attention in the early twenty-first century. Decades before, in 1972, the Kingdom of Bhutan had relied on a Buddhist outlook to replace the Gross Domestic Product with Gross National Happiness as a measure of a country's well-being. In the early twenty-first century international organizations, national governments in the developed and developing world, and even some cities proposed or developed happiness or well-being indices as a way of informing public policy.[55] The political and ideological implications of a shift from GDP to some measure of happiness or well-being varied, with no one perspective dominating. For many, the change emerged from consideration of the Easterlin Paradox—that after the achievement of a certain level of wealth, additional income or economic growth yielded few or diminishing increments of pleasure. Many who embraced well-being as a measure supported commitments to improve the environment; reduce inequalities of wealth, education, and income; and look at an economy less from on high than from a household level. As the authors of the United Nations report remarked, "rising incomes—beyond ensuring the fulfillment of essential needs—do not necessarily increase well-being much further." Rather, they commented, "surveys have indicated that an overall sense of security, including job security, strong family and friendship networks, as well as freedom of expression and other factors, strongly impact people's well-being."[56]

In some cases, social scientists from the left provided the key arguments, such as was true with the French report commissioned by President Nicolas Sarkozy and authored by Joseph E. Stiglitz, Amartya Sen, and Jean-Paul Fitoussi. Formed in 2008 and its report issued a year later, the Commission on the Measurement of Economic Performance and Social Progress remarked that standard economic data "did not alert us that the seemingly bright growth performance of the world economy between 2004 and 2007 may have been achieved at the expense of future growth." The report urged governments to focus on issues, many of which were irrelevant to a concentration on GDP but central to the anti-materialist strain among positive psychologists and others: environmental sustainability, inequalities of wealth and income, and well-being experienced at the household level.[57]

Yet it is hard to escape the conclusion that in some cases sponsors and consumers of government policy based on happiness had in mind more conservative purposes. For authoritarian leaders like the King of Bhutan, a focus on happiness took attention away from a lack of democracy and civil liberties. For nations struggling to develop economically in ways that reflected Western experiences, concentrating on well-being could undermine pleasures, such as traditional patterns of kinship or religion, that modernization might threaten. And for those on the right in developed nations, like Prime Minister David Cameron, an emphasis on happiness kept attention away from the failures of markets to provide economic justice and environmental protections. For example, Cameron used a concentration on happiness to argue against state control of the economy and for locally focused volunteerism, a Big Society rather than a Big Government. "A bigger, stronger more active society," Cameron remarked in 2011, "involves something of a revolt against the top-down, statist approach." Or as an op-ed writer in the *New York Times* commented in 2014, "if we may all be equally happy, irrespective of our circumstances, then that would equip" conservative politicians "with a convenient excuse to stop looking at structural issues like class, social and economic inequality or poverty."[58]

Correlating GNP with happiness or satisfaction with life leads to suggestive but not always indisputable conclusions.[59] A chart exploring levels of reported well-being with national wealth per person offers one telling perspective. Most of the nations where citizens report the highest degrees of satisfaction are in Northern Europe. The United States, with the highest GDP per capita, is not the happiest nation. Some relatively wealthy nations, such as France or Japan, do not report levels of personal satisfaction commensurate with their affluence. In contrast, others, such as the Philippines or Nigeria, display a sense of well-being one might not simplistically expect given their relatively lack of prosperity.[60]

The 2013 United Nations–sponsored World Happiness Report revealed similar dimensions of international comparisons, ones whose ironies and complications remind us not to put too much faith in the conclusions drawn from the data (Figure 7.2).[61] As usual, Denmark, Norway, Switzerland, and the Netherlands ranked highest, with sub-Saharan nations such as Benin and Togo at the bottom. Out of 156 nations surveyed, the United States ranked 17th, just behind Mexico. Overall, some indicators were more important than per capita GDP: the extensiveness of social connections, generosity, and perceptions of corruption. Researchers offered vitally important observations when they emphasized the strength of the safety net, social welfare policies, social trust, and relatively equal income distribution as factors, often more important than affluence—which help account for why some European nations outranked America.[62] Or as one science writer put it, "a civic sense, social equality, and control over our own lives constitute the magic triangle of well-being in society."[63] To many astute but perhaps unnecessarily optimistic observers, the policy implications of

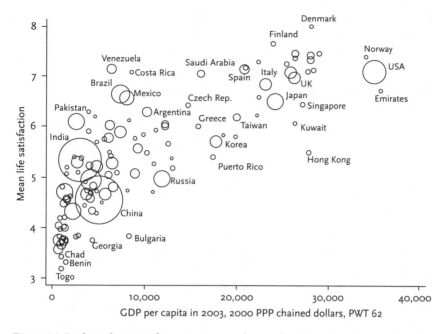

Figure 7.2 By the early twenty-first century, researchers explored the international relationship between Mean life satisfaction (vertical line) and GDP per capita (horizontal line). (From Angus Deaton, "Worldwide, Residents of Richer Nations More Satisfied," http://www.gallup.com/poll/104608/worldwide-residents-richer-nations-more-satisfied.aspx. Copyright © 2008, Gallup, Inc. All rights reserved. The content is used with permission; however, Gallup retains all rights of republication.)

international happiness comparisons were clear. Since constantly increasing growth in GDP does not produce significantly greater happiness in developed nations, the goal of public policy should shift to the promotion, as two writers advocated, of "the good things of life" such as friendship, health, respect, and leisure.[64]

POLITICAL IDEOLOGY AND OF POSITIVE PSYCHOLOGY

Positive psychologists hold varied, albeit patterned political positions. Although there are both exceptions and some signs of change, the most common stance, consonant with the personalism of psychology, emphasizes that change comes from individual transformations and that enhancing the individual's sense of well-being will help improve society.[65] Such promises have several major characteristics. When they offer examples, scholars most often focus on the impact that happiness has on a series of decreasingly important concentric circles, beginning with one's friends and family. They can be vague when it comes to the connection between the personal and broader social worlds. Thus in a widely used textbook in the field, the authors defined "collectivism" in a way no good socialist or communitarian might, as occurring "when the average person in a society is disposed to group interdependence."[66] Assuming as they do that social change comes from an individual or small group, there is among many positive psychologists remarkably little emphasis on collective action, social movements, or government interventions for social welfare.[67] Seligman spelled out one dimension of this when he remarked that changing external circumstances, such as poverty, "is usually impractical and expensive." If external circumstances such as affluence accounted for only 10 percent of subjective well-being, then happiness enhancement came not from social change but from individual transformation.[68]

This had come home to me when, at the beginning of the course I audited on "The Science of Happiness," I encountered a popular online questionnaire designed to indicate how satisfied I was with my life. Similar limitations emerged in an examination of the other major survey method—one developed by Martin Seligman and examined in Norbert Schwarz and Fritz Strack's 2003 "Reports of Subjective Well-Being: Judgmental Processes and Their Methodological Implications." Here the search was for what the survey called "Authentic Happiness." Once more, a respondent self-reports using an online survey, and the result is an assessment that comes from "The VIA Survey of Character Strengths." These strengths range widely and include hope, spiritualty, caution, perseverance, capacity to love and be loved, and open-mindedness. At least six of the twenty-four strengths might conceivably touch on a person's social and political commitments—"fairness, equity, and justice," "kindness and generosity," "curiosity and interest in the world," "social intelligence," "leadership" and "citizenship, teamwork, and loyalty." Yet when I looked at the questions and categories, I found an emphasis on small-scale interaction rather than political or social engagement with a wider world. Kindness and generosity covered one's ability to do good deeds for others, even if you do not know them well. Curiosity about the world captures how extensive your interest is, without giving any sense of what that "world" comprises. "Social intelligence," we learn, contains your awareness "of the motives and feelings of other people. You know what to do to fit in to different social situations, and you know what to do to put others at ease." "Fairness, equity, and justice" means "treating all people fairly," not letting "your personal feelings bias your decisions about other people," and giving "everyone a chance." The 240 questions reinforce this individualistic and small-group focus. For example, the questionnaire asks whether you ever deliberately hurt anyone or whether you have a "broad outlook on what is going on." Similarly, the survey asks whether "it is important to me that I live in a world of beauty," but not how important it is to live in a peaceful, more egalitarian, or more environmentally safe world.[69]

In the writings of leading positive psychologists, we can also see the vague promises of social change stemming from increases in individual happiness. From the outset, leading figures in the field promised to focus on institutions that fostered positivity, and over time a tremendous amount of research and consulting did indeed go into such efforts, at corporations and schools especially. Yet characteristically in their writings, major figures in the field were vague when it came to offering a capacious and specific social vision. For example, in a typical passage Fredrickson wrote of how positivity involved more than enhancing personal happiness. "Beyond feeling good," she insisted, people were "also *doing* good— adding value to the world" by being "highly engaged with their families, work, and communities." Positivity, she insisted, required "transcending self-interest enough to share and celebrate goodness in others and in the natural world." Yet her book offered no suggestions about the implications of such transcendence for political or social change. Moreover, like others who wrote in a way that discouraged working for comprehensive social transformations, she cautioned that flourishing "need not imply grand or grandiose actions." Similarly, Seligman talked of how "the Meaningful Life consists in belonging to and serving something that you believe is bigger than the self, and humanity creates all the positive institutions to allow this: religion, political party, being green, the Boy Scouts, or the family." Yet he offered readers little or no guidance of how to connect individual and social flourishing.[70]

Moreover, there is evidence that mainstream positive psychology resonates with cultural conservatism, especially among those who emphasize tough character traits more than emphatic or compassionate ones, adopting as they do the harsher aspects of the Protestant work ethic. Here there was some resemblance between people in the field and neoconservatives who, beginning in the late 1960s, decried what they saw as excessive self-expression and stood in an antagonistic relationship to emerging social movements of women and African Americans. Seligman's emphasis on how the choice of character over personality as a counter to relativism and postmodernism dovetails with cultural conservatism. In the section on character in *Flourish*, he remarked that while "I do not remotely advocate giving up on reform" that would undo "malignant circumstances," research in positive psychology made clear that interventions that involved "identifying and then shaping character" were centrally important. To him, self-control and grit were more important and effective than political engagement.[71]

Near the end of *Flourish* Seligman differentiated between the criticisms of life in the West in the early twenty-first century and what he called "New Prosperity." He wrote that "history, in the hands of postmodernists, is taught as 'one damn thing after another.'" In contrast, he underscored that North America, Western Europe, Japan, and Australia were "at a Florentine moment: rich, at peace, enough food, health, and harmony." For him, history was "the account of human progress," uneven to be sure but "nevertheless upward." The postwar world had seen the vanquishing of fascism and communism, the feeding of billions of people, the securing of "universal education and universal medical care," a five-fold increase in purchasing power, an extension of life expectancy, and "huge inroads into racial, sexual, and ethnic injustice. The age of the tyrant," he concluded, "is coming to an end, and the age of democracy has taken firm root." Of course, it is not hard to construct an opposing picture of recent developments, one that would emphasize the failure of the Arab Spring, growing hostility to outsider, the prevalence of homelessness or drug addiction, the rise of ISIS, the refugee crisis, the persistence of poverty in America, the anger of white working-class men, mass incarceration, and the growing gap between the very rich and the rest of us.[72]

Consequently, the historical vision of positive psychologists, one that was often implicit, was optimistic. For example, Seligman believes that positive psychology developed when it did because by the early twenty-first century suffering in the world had diminished significantly while affluence had increased. It is possible to counter or qualify such a perspective with several arguments. As Seligman himself predicted in his 1998 address, "the warfare the world faces in the next century will be ethnic in its roots and hatreds" with "the destruction of whole communities and the ongoing problems of refugees and human rights abuse" amplifying these problems. Although there are signs of hope, the failure of the Arab Spring, the continuing and violent turmoil in the Middle East, to say nothing of gun violence, personal depression, and the threat of a nuclear war or a supervirus, reminds us that suffering persists in much of the world. Moreover, the argument about the predominance of affluence correctly points to the hundreds of millions of people who have entered the middle class in recent years; yet in the West and especially in the United States, prosperity was prevalent during much of the postwar world, well before positive psychology emerged. Instead we might look elsewhere for a historical explanation of the emergence and spread of positive psychology. It is possible that positive psychology emerged when it did not because the world was getting better but because there was a disjuncture between people's optimistic expectations and more complicated, often depressing individual and social experiences.[73]

In important ways psychology reflected aspects of neoliberalism, which, like positive psychology's scholarship, came to increasing prominence in the 1980s and 1990s. We are familiar with the role neoliberalism has played in economics and public policy, but we can also see how many positive psychologists also reflect its importance. The emergence of positive psychology is a specific moment in a longer story of how Americans (and others) responded to affluence and consumer culture, often by realizing that there was something more to life than a seemingly unending pursuit of happiness through materialism. However, the more specific seedbed is the rise of neoliberalism amidst a period of economic transformations and turmoil. Unfortunately, we do not have systematic studies of the social location of proponents and consumers of positive psychology to make firm judgments, though my best guess is that both groups occupy positions of relative social privilege defined by race, income, and education.[74]

Neoliberalism involves self-government by the individual rather than the exercise of government power at the same time that it fosters government of the self by corporate capitalism's old and new cultural agencies. In the face of political deadlock and disenchantment with politics, it promises spheres of action where individuals operate effectively. Neoliberalism celebrates markets, competition, entrepreneurship, and freedom as opposed to centralized controls and forms of collective action; weakens the welfare state's social safety net; embraces the benefits of technological transformations and globalized free trade; and emphasizes voluntary organizations. Among many neoliberals, the business corporation, and not labor unions or the government, is the nation's central institution.[75] The sociologist Sam Binkley captured one consequence of these tendencies when he noted that "taking the market as a model for social conduct in all realms of life," neoliberalism "sets out to reinvent all social relations as market relations, and to remake individuals as market actors—profit-maximizing, calculating, self-interested individuals for whom every relation is conceived as an enterprise." Characteristically, there is remarkably little to no research on whether participating in a labor union or organized social movement affects a person's happiness.[76]

One link between positive psychology and neoliberalism came in the emphasis on psychological wealth as a way of measuring happiness, one example of the use of an economic term to describe something not usually seen as primarily economic. Lyubomirsky underscored another aspect of the connection between external conditions and the field's development when she speculated that happiness had emerged as a "hot topic . . . a symptom, perchance, of the Western twenty-first century individualistic zeitgeist."

Diener and Biswas-Diener, who spoke of "Psychological Wealth: The Balanced Portfolio," captured other implications of this relationship when they reported on studies that showed how in some circumstances money could buy happiness. "It might not seem fair," they wrote in 2008, "that some folks have not only big bucks but more happiness as well; but rather than begrudging folks for their good fortune," they continued in a way that went against what some others had identified as the risks of upward social comparison, "consider how money can boost happiness." Therefore, "the research linking money to happiness need not be an emotional death sentence for less affluent people," because, they noted, some homeless people "were actually faring well in terms of happiness." Similarly, Emmons had written of "emotional prosperity." Yet even among those closely involved with the development of positive psychology, there were those who critiqued key aspects of neoliberalism. From what I can gather, among prominent positive psychologists, Csikszentmihalyi is the one who has offered a critique of neoliberalism. In his *Good Business,* he remarked that "the most important functions of the society, which used to be relatively independent of the market, have now become servants of Wall Street," questioned the assumption that "happiness would be provided by the market," and called for a more direct confrontation with "the consequences of a purely market-driven view of the world." Another case in point is Barry Schwartz, who was present near the creation of the field and has worked closely with Seligman on a number of projects. He has criticized the excesses of free markets and consumer culture for undermining the pursuit of happiness—and hailed consumer education, government regulation, and religious commitments as ways of countering market excess.[77]

At a time when vast sectors of the broad middle range of Americans experienced tough times, the hope that they could avoid a consequential "death sentence" might serve as reassurance. The rise and growth of positive psychology occurred at a time when in the United States labor unions weakened, incomes for the vast majority of people stagnated, social welfare programs were cut, life-long marriages and jobs became rarer, and a very small percentage of wealthy people benefited disproportionately from increases in income and assets. For tens of millions of Americans, downsizing, outsourcing, the shift of retirement policies from defined benefit to defined contribution, and the spread of contingent labor arrangements powerfully undermined security. The focus on the question of whether money could buy happiness often meant that other economic issues, especially economic insecurities, got short shrift. In such contexts some observers could interpret the findings of positive psychologists in a reassuring manner. Since incomes in excess of $70,000 supposedly brought little or small increases in happiness, there was nothing to gain from being envious of the wealthy, albeit plenty to lament about the plight of the poor. An emphasis on accepting one's external lot in life (which after all accounted for only 10 percent of one's sense of well-being) and working to enhance one's individual happiness within the context of the givenness of externalities offered the best chance for a better, happier lot.

Yet it would be wrong to insist on a connection between positive psychology and any single set of political commitments. After all, empirical studies pointed in multiple directions. If the recognition that an income above a certain level suggested the futility of envy, it also pointed in the direction of increasing Gross Domestic Happiness by shifting economic policy from economic growth to taxation of the wealthy and to accepting more inflation in exchange for less unemployment.[78] Similarly, international comparisons could be construed as offering support to social democracy rather than neoliberal capitalism: after all, nations like Sweden and the Netherlands— with strong social programs, relatively equitable distribution of wealth and income, and heavy taxation—provided greater levels of happiness than obtained in the United States, with its relatively weak social safety net, lack of social trust, more inequitable distribution of wealth and income, and lower levels of taxation. Moreover, a relatively wealthy France and a relatively poor Mexico had roughly the same levels of happiness. As the subtitle of a 2010 book explained, there was a "Paradox of Happy Peasants and Miserable Millionaires." In the end, despite the dramatic growth of economists' interest in happiness, major issues—concerning definitions, research methods, and policy implications—remain unresolved.[79]

Critics point to evidence that liberals and leftists dominate the field of social psychology, but within positive psychology the situation is more complicated.[80] Indeed, it is possible to identify a spectrum of political positions within the field, something explored here but, as far as I know, nowhere else. At one end stands the British social democrat and economist Richard Layard, now a life peer who sits in the British House of Lords, but whose children cannot.[81] In his 2005 *Happiness: Lessons from a New Science*, which he dedicated to Kahneman, Layard followed authors of other summary books but broadened the scope of his social vision. Psychology, he noted, lacked "the comprehensive framework for policy analysis that economics" provided, especially economics not fundamentally indebted to the worship of free markets and rational citizen/consumers. Therefore incorporating economics into contemporary psychology would advance scholarship and reveal ways of enhancing happiness that reached beyond individualistic solutions. Like other positive psychologists, Layard stressed the importance of social connections, but he emphasized how in Britain and the United States they had eroded significantly, undermining people's sense of trust and security, with unemployment being "one of the worst things that can happen to anyone." Acknowledging the power of social comparisons and the hedonic treadmill, he cast serious doubt as to whether economic growth could increase levels of happiness in developed nations. Given that above a certain level added income produced relatively slight gains in happiness, there was considerable wastefulness in developed economies.[82]

Moreover, since people abhorred losses more than they valued gains and since well-to-do people garnered less happiness from more money than their poorer counterparts, egalitarian redistribution meant that "a country will have a higher level of average happiness the more equally its income is distributed." To bolster this assertion he pointed to Scandinavian nations that recorded high rates of happiness along with high taxes, a strong educational system, and "a culture of mutual respect." Layard also emphasized that research made clear that "it is more important to reduce suffering than to generate extreme happiness." The policy recommendations that followed from his analysis were clear: develop family-friendly social policies, "subsidize activities that promote community life," dramatically reduce unemployment, provide major funding to counter the emotional and economic costs of mental illness, use social policy "to fight the constant escalation of wants," and foster education that emphasized "the sense of an overall purpose wider than oneself."[83]

If Layard represents the social democratic left among happiness scholars, the cultural left appears most prominently in the work of University of California Berkeley psychology professor Dacher Keltner and the Greater Good Science Center of the University of California, of which he was the founding director. Keltner weaves together strands of the familiar tapestry comprised of Eastern religions, neuroscience, and Darwinism, though in his case it was the kindest and not the fittest who survived. The Center, like Keltner's research and writing, as well as Berkeley's Social Interaction Lab, relies heavily on an individualistic focus. Yet even here they differ from mainline positive psychology. Although both Seligman and Keltner emphasized altruism, when talking of character the former stressed grit and resilience; the latter, love and compassion. Moreover, if most positive psychologists were vague about how to move from the personalistic to the social and political, Keltner and his colleagues more fully explored such connections. Among the topics they focused on, but most positive psychologists avoided, were the dynamics of racism, social class, moral behavior on a large scale, environmental degradation, peaceful reconciliation, and the exercise of power.[84]

Another approach to policy, libertarian paternalism, has emerged in the work of behavioral economists and others interested in enhancing happiness. The key text is Richard H. Thaler and Cass R. Sunstein's *Nudge: Improving Decisions About Health, Wealth, and Happiness* (2008).

Using what they call choice architecture to move people to make wise decisions is its central recommendation. For example, when employers established procedures that automatically enrolled employees in pension plans but gave them the choice of opting out, they did not significantly interfere with their freedom but held the prospect of improving their long-term well-being. President Barak Obama invited Sunstein to direct the Office of Information and Regulatory Affairs, which made seemingly small but highly significant changes in government rules and procedures that in turn relied on the findings of behavioral economists and on how scholars such as Kahneman had carefully analyzed decision-making.[85]

In contrast to this libertarian paternalism, David G. Myers of Hope College has offered a centrist perspective on happiness that rested on an embrace of traditional values. In his 2000 *The American Paradox: Spiritual Hunger in an Age of Plenty*, he advocated policies that many on the left also called for, such as a progressive tax on consumption and the strengthening of the progressive income tax. Yet as the title of his book made clear, he placed his analysis within a religiously inspired emphasis on how Americans lived in a world that combined spiritual longing and material abundance. A tax on consumption, by curbing excessively wanton materialism, would help restore spiritual commitments. Moreover, family values were central to his policy recommendations that involved "government and corporate policies that actually value families." Opposed to rampant individualism and to the ways divorce adversely affected children, he called for countering the excesses of the sexual revolution, strengthening marriage and the family, linking reproduction with responsibility, and reducing Sunday work requirements to *"support the familial and religious roots of virtue."*[86]

A free market, conservative perspective appeared in Arthur C. Brooks's *Gross National Happiness: Why Happiness Matters for America—and How We Can Get More of It*. The book appeared in 2008, the same year that its author became president of the American Enterprise Institute and a few years before he joined the advisory board of Charles Koch's Well-Being Initiative. Brooks argued that the data revealed that in general conservatives were happier than liberals because of the quality of their marriages, the seriousness of their religious commitments, and the strength of their individualism. When he turned to the implications of such findings, he made clear he supported family-friendly social policies—not by government mandates but by using the law and the tax code to strengthen traditional marriages. The evidence also showed, he argued, that a combination of religious, political, and economic freedom enhanced people's happiness. When it came to moral freedoms, such as control over whom we could marry or the conditions that made obtaining an abortion easy or difficult, it was not the government but "individuals, families, and communities" that should establish "our own private standards of behavior" even if they were "very strict."[87]

The American tradition, he insisted, demanded a high ratio of freedom to security, with the government constantly attempting to lower the ratio, for example, by requiring us to wear seat belts, protecting us from second-hand smoke, or enforcing strict safety measures for airplane passengers. Brooks objected strenuously to how the "nanny state" eroded freedom and thus happiness, for instance, by having the government care for people who were capable of taking care of themselves. He asserted it undermined the ambition of poor people and depressed their spirits to tell them that because America was no longer a nation where equality of opportunity was possible, they should follow the Democratic Party in fighting for redistributive policies. Instead, it was charitable giving that improved individual and national happiness. Answering those who said nations could enhance their collective happiness by significantly taxing superfluous consumption, Brooks asserted that "although consumerism does not buy happiness, government spending does not, either," since "private prosperity brings us up, but government spending bring us back down." Above all, success under capitalism was the most important provider of happiness, he remarked in a way that reflected his unabashed and simplistic conservatism. It was not venal greed that motivated people but a natural desire "to succeed and create value."[88]

POSITIVE PSYCHOLOGY, THE SOCIAL SCIENCES, AND PUBLIC POLICY

From early on some social scientists had been central to the field of happiness studies, but positive psychologists had remained more insulated from fields that might have made their vision less individualistic and enabled them to engage more fully in public policy debates.[89] At first glance that seemed to change in the twenty-first century when social scientists, economists especially, entered the territory positive psychologists had traditionally occupied.

We have already seen the importance of early adopters such as Richard Easterlin, Tibor Scitovsky, Robert Frank, and Richard Layard. Until early in the twenty-first century they were rare among social scientists who focused on the relationships between policy and happiness. However, increasingly after that, national governments, international commissions, and scholars from a variety of disciplines turned their attention to the question of how to deploy public policy to increase individual and collective happiness. Given decades of research as to what made people happy, there was widespread agreement about what factors enhanced well-being—curbing the excesses of markets and individualism, reducing the damage unemployment or insecure employment causes, stemming the tide of environmental degradation, enhancing physical and mental health, and increasing people's sense of security and trust. Given how high are the stakes, recent the attention, and freighted the ideological issues, disagreements persist, especially about the nature of the connection between democracy and happiness and to what extent or whether there was a relationship between greater economic equality and happiness.[90]

Despite the interventions of economists into debates over public policy, to a considerable extent positive psychologists remained inattentive to many political issues. Indeed, over time Seligman actually moved away from a broad-scale public policy. In his 1998 APA presidential address he had announced major public policy initiatives. One involved the application of positive psychology to threats to human rights in ethno-political conflicts, in Northern Ireland and South Africa especially; another, support for social activism to alleviate inner city poverty. Similarly, if in his 1975 *Helplessness* he had talked of "effective protest" that would help residents of inner cities overcome helplessness and of how poverty could be solved by the "self-esteem-enhancing nature of social action," in the twenty-first century he turned away from a commitment to organized efforts to achieve social justice. The Comprehensive Soldier Fitness Program was a one major exception to the rule of public caution about focusing on policy issues in a major way, but it came at the initiative of the Army. Moreover, relying on an emphasis on character, it trained soldiers to overcome what they experienced in war rather than work for peaceful resolution of conflicts.[91]

CRITICISMS OF POSITIVE PSYCHOLOGY

Positive psychologists have acknowledged the validity of some of the criticisms of their field, although at some key moments they seem prone to avoid grappling with what critics say.[92] "What strikes me is how defensive people seem to be when anyone challenges the merits/values of positive psychology," remarked a New Zealand psychologist in early 2016. Nonetheless, at key moments insiders offered critiques of the field.[93]

One of the main issues involved the dangers of popularization. Thus, in 2013, Christopher Peterson insisted on distinguishing between what practitioners wrote in scholarly journals and in trade books. Popular books, he cautioned his peers, "should not be written as happiness cookbooks, replete with strong guarantees about the five easy steps toward lasting bliss." He had to admit that versions of the field that appeared in blogs and phone apps made it "difficult for the general public to sort through what is actually known versus what is simply hoped. Exaggerations do occur, and they tarnish all of positive psychology." Yet, he insisted, "criticizing all of positive psychology for occasional excesses in some quarters is akin to criticizing all of music based solely on what one hears in an elevator."[94] An even sharper critique from inside came in 2012 from positive psychologist Ilona Boniwell. The danger, she wrote, of jumping on a slogan-dominated ideological bandwagon included "a narrow mindset, resentment of any criticism, hero worship, self-perpetuating beliefs, arrogance and getting stuck in self-imposed positivity, leading to a lack of depth, lack of realism and simplifications."[95]

A June 2015 session at the International Positive Psychology Association meetings, titled "Critiques of Positive Psychology," covered many of the key points of criticism. Kim S. Cameron, co-founder of the University of Michigan's Center for Positive Organizational Scholarship, led off with a full and frank presentation of key elements of commonly offered criticisms. Some of what he mentioned could be true of many emerging fields claiming scientific validity to what they discovered, including that findings were often invalid, overstated, or misleading. Yet some of what he highlighted involved problems specific to those who studied subjective well-being. Positive psychology, he remarked, failed to live up to its promise to draw on and make alliances with other academic fields. Skeptics asserted that positive psychology relied on an ethnocentric vision that reinforced Western values (individualism especially, in ways that echoed criticism of the Me Generation) and institutions (capitalism, in particular). Closer to home, the field ran into trouble by reflecting the biases of the white middle class and in the process ignored the way poverty and repression adversely affected the plight of the poor and non-whites. When practitioners moved from the classroom and laboratory, their interventions, critics alleged, created conformity rather than freedom.[96]

One critic from outside the field has noted that, relying on recycled clichés of Norman Vincent Peale and allowing the pendulum to swing too far away from negativity, positive psychology underemphasized the negative and offered what someone else called nothing more "than naïve, crass happiology."[97] This last criticism, that positive psychologists underestimated the deleterious effects of excessive positivity and the importance of negative ones, has been prominently and extensively explored, leading some to develop Second Wave Positive Psychology, or PP2.0, and others to launch an even more fundamental challenge to the ways the field often embraces happiology.[98]

After Cameron's talk, several leading figures in the field responded. Especially notable was Seligman's reaction. Noting that he had spent his entire life as a critic, he went on to emphasize the difference between destructive and constructive varieties of criticism, the latter appearing especially on web blogs. This meant that most criticism was not peer reviewed, and he emphasized the need for what he called "malice detectors." Science, he insisted as he focused on the importance of academic standards, was the antidote to "junk skepticism."[99]

Yet as reassuring as were the comments by Cameron and his colleagues, it is hard to avoid the conclusion that many positive psychologists were unwilling to engage with the most trenchant critiques of this field. There is, for example, little in their reactions to reassure a skeptic that they had grappled with the kinds of issues Jackson Lears raised in a 2013 essay. The outpouring of courses and how-to books in positive psychology, he argued, was a small "part of a broad, obsessive and flourishing effort to pursue happiness more directly and systematically than ever before." For Lears, it did not "take a social scientist to see that a blizzard of how-to books on 'positivity' suggests its lack in everyday life," for "behind the facade of smiley-faced optimism, American culture seems awash in a pervasive sadness, or at least a restless longing for a sense of fulfillment that remains just out of reach." He castigated positive psychologists for offering clichéd, conventional bromides, ones based not on science but on scientism, especially "a strikingly vacuous worldview, one devoid of history, culture or political economy" that relied on hardly convincing "pop evolutionary psychology" and "pop neuroscience." Especially vexing to him was the individualism of happiness studies that avoided "being in the world, including the public world."[100]

Barbara Ehrenreich's 2009 *Bright-Sided: How Positive Thinking Is Undermining America* is among the most pointed, even angry critiques of positive psychology and certainly the best known. Several years later Peterson cited her book as evidence of "a recent backlash" that reprised "the centuries-old suspicion of optimism as indicative of stupidity or denial."[101]

Ehrenreich brought considerable strengths to the task of critiquing positive psychology—a doctorate in cell biology from Rockefeller University, a passionate feminist consciousness, and formidable talents as a writer whose previous books had commanded significant readership. [102] *Bright-Sided* was an intensely personal book, which Ehrenreich began with how she felt when people encouraged her to face a diagnosis of breast cancer by seeing the bright side but ended up as an impassioned attack on positive thinking, including that offered by psychologists. Calling "positive thinking" a "mass delusion" in general, she zeroed in on the "ultrafeminine theme of the breast cancer marketplace" characterized by "the cornucopia of pink-ribbon-themed breast cancer products" that evoked the advice of those who saw breast cancer as a gift, not a life-threatening or life-altering danger. As a trained scientist and skilled polemicist, she questioned those who offered scientific evidence that the right attitude would help you resist or recover.[103]

Within this larger context, Ehrenreich began her treatment of positive psychology with a discussion of Seligman as an academic entrepreneur who used a range of strategies—whether "scientific breakthrough or flamboyant bid for funding and attention"—to advance his career, his profession, and his ideas. She reported how in 2007 she went to see Seligman with some trepidation, having recently published an article in *Harper's* that was critical of positive psychology, including its pop incarnations. When he saw her, she remembered, he was "practically scowling" and he engaged in strategies to avoid talking with her by creating a series of what she called "barriers to a normal interview." The situation continued to deteriorate: when Ehrenreich raised questions about some of what Seligman had written, he reportedly responded testily, telling her to go home and Google what she apparently did not understand. When she did, she reported, she discovered that although in *Flourish* Seligman had used equations to make his "book look weightier and full of mathematical rigor," in fact it made him "look like the Wizard of Oz." Ehrenreich concluded her discussion of Seligman and positive psychology by reporting on what she saw as the problematic nature of the studies on which the field rested, especially those that established correlation but not causation, that engaged in media-driven positive spinning, and that defended the status quo by emphasizing that it was the individual's responsibility to change adverse situations.[104]

Two years later, writing in *Flourish*, Seligman responded to what Ehrenreich had written. Under the heading "Barbara ('I Hate Hope') Ehrenreich," he remarked that he found her book "uncongenial" and her analysis "wrongheaded and evidence-ignoring," going on to say that she did not see that "the evidence is robust, significance levels are high, and the findings replicate over and over." By confusing optimism with "'sugar coating,'" when she faced a cancer diagnosis, he remarked, she appeared "to be after a world in which human well-being follows only from externalities such as class, war, and money. Such a crumbling, Marxist worldview," he continued, "must ignore the enormous number of reflexive realities in which what a person thinks and feels goes on to influence the future," reflexive realities which were precisely what "the science of positive psychology" was about.[105]

Others on the left, whether Marxist, Foucauldian, or postmodern, offered critiques of positive psychology more profound and more fully articulated than Ehrenreich's. From what I can tell, people in the field know of Ehrenreich's criticism but few if any are aware of what those on the left—Marxists and Foucauldians—have written. Well into the twenty-first century came an analysis that emphasized how positive psychologists were involved in managing the consent of workers, citizens, and consumers—and in the process distracting attention from more urgent issues. "There are surely ample political and material problems to deal with right now," wrote the British sociologist William Davies in his *The Happiness Industry: How the Government and Big Business Sold Us Well-Being*, "before we divert quite so much attention towards the mental and neural conditions through which we individually experience them."[106] Although not focusing specifically on positive psychology, the cultural critic Lauren Berlant talked of late twentieth-century "cruel optimism," how in Western societies the promise of lives marked by security, social mobility, and equality persisted when neoliberalism made realization of such a dream increasingly unlikely. Others articulated how "happiness becomes a disciplinary technique," with positive psychologists promoting highly moral dimensions of subjective well-being that conventional bourgeois people pursued as part of emotionally laden performances infused with values shaped by the capitalist marketplace.[107]

Citing how the language of the marketplace (happiness as "a type of emotional currency that can be spent, like money, on outcomes in life you truly value" or as a liquid that operated in "the same way that monetary instruments such as stocks" did), the American sociologist Sam Binkley used a Foucauldian perspective to explore happiness as an instrument of government in a post-Keynesian world.[108] For him, "the new discourse on happiness" involved "a life resource whose potential resides at the disposal of a sovereign, enterprising, self-interested actor" who operated in a neoliberal world that promised "dynamic possibilities, risks and open horizons." In the process, the enterprising, responsible self, liberated from constraining negativity and dependence once fostered by the social welfare state, could pursue a world that seemed to be full of self-realized individualistic possibilities but was actually governed by imperatives and institutions beyond the individual's control.[109]

In her work on self-help and makeover cultures, Micki McGee explores how globalization and deindustrialization have undermined traditional values and institutions, replacing them with therapeutic makeover and self-help cultures. Old and new media, from bestselling books to life coaching and webinars, have emerged as "central to the compliance industries required for neoliberal governmentality" as they chase after the "liberal ideal of the pursuit of happiness." Crucial to these efforts are inspirational imperatives that in turn rely on religious and spiritual traditions, including the Protestantism in the Norman Vincent Peale tradition but also the Buddhism represented by the Dalai Lama and Jon Kabat-Zinn. For McGee and others, it was no coincidence that an abundance of calls on people to invest in, manage, and improve themselves occurred at the same time that economic insecurity affected tens of millions of Americans. Into the breach came self-help culture, including positive psychology, that promised to keep people afloat when faced with unprecedented challenges.[110]

McGee's particular contribution is to emphasize how the promise of a reborn self could lead people "into a new sort of enslavement: into a cycle where the self is not improved but endlessly belabored." For her the prominence of the belabored self, which she sees in American culture including the flourishing of positive psychology, is an essential component of how neoliberalism helps maintain the political and social status quo in part by emphasizing individualistic efforts rather than communitarian or political ones. Self-reinvention, and not political activism, promised to solve the problems of economic insecurity even though a new, fulfilled, and adequate self was impossible to achieve. Gender and religion play key roles in her analysis. She explores the gender dimensions of late twentieth- and early twenty-first-century self-help efforts, which in turn help us understand key impulses in positive psychology. Earlier, male-oriented traditions focused on gaining money, possessions, or status. Yet as women entered the paid workforce and became increasingly important in the marketplace for books, how-to literature increasingly focused on the intangible, highly subjective and elusive goals of self-fulfillment and happiness. One result was the increased importance of mindfulness, self-realization, and seeing one's life as a work of art—all of which required unending rounds of effort without necessarily guaranteeing arrival at the promised goal. Finally, she reminds us of how contemporary renderings of the successful, happy self rely on a reshaping of Protestant religious traditions. Applied to an understanding of positive psychology, her emphasis on the importance of a calling by work achievable through flow, along with the achievement of grace and rebirth by the self-actualized self, suggests a key component to realizing the promise of subjective well-being that is simultaneously religious and psychological.[111]

There is much merit in these critiques of positive psychology, although many critics missed that positivity as a world view encompassed a variety of political orientations. The dovetailing of the development of this field with a neoliberalism reinforced the individualism inherent in much of psychology and thus the difficulty many positive psychologists had in moving beyond vague promises of engaging social issues. As one observer perceptively noted of the emphasis on character, which could be applied more widely to the field's findings, maybe a better approach to character training would involve a greater willingness "to cast a critical eye on the peculiarly American cult of individual ascendency and instill grit while challenging social inequality, rather than inadvertently reproducing it."[112] Multiple social changes provided the seedbed of positive psychology, among them the opposing forces of neoliberalism's confidence in market forces in an age of economic travails and the way millions of people realized that affluence had limited potential to make lives happier. One important difference is that in the twenty-first century, scholars in happiness studies discussed income inequality and environmental degradation while those in positive psychology generally avoided these issues and focused instead on how terrorism enhanced character strengths. The future will reveal in what directions the fields of happiness studies and positive psychology will go, but if the past is any guide they will be multiple and often contradictory.

NOTES

1. It is impossible to cover the full range of new topics explored, but among others that deserve attention are the relationship between happiness and nature (Daniel M. Haybron, "Central Park: Nature, Context, and Human Wellbeing," *International Journal of Wellbeing* 1 [July, 2011]: 235–54) and the use the new social networks technologies (Lorenzo Coviello et al., "Detecting Emotional Contagion in Massive Social Networks," PLoSONE 9 [March 2014]). Another recent trend is the exploration of the eudaimonic turn, the connection between the humanities and positive psychology: for a summary, see James O. Pawelski, "Bringing Together the Humanities and the Science of Well-Being to Advance Human Flourishing," in *Well-Being and Higher Education: A Strategy for Change and the Realization of Education's Greater Purpose*, ed. Don Harward (Washington, DC: Bringing Theory into Practice, 2016).
2. Although some observers, including historians, see neoliberalism as a problematic description of late twentieth-century political economy, the evidence in positive psychology had led me to accept it as a useful analytical tool. For one take on this controversy, see Philip Mirowski, "The Political Movement That Dared Not Speak Its Own Name: The Neoliberal Thought Collective," https://ineteconomics.org/uploads/papers/WP23-Mirowski.pdf.
3. Christopher Peterson and Martin E. P. Seligman, *Character Strengths and Virtues: A Handbook and Classification* (New York: Oxford University Press, 2004), 370, 519. For a criticism of their work as relying too heavily on values of Western society, including individualism, see Konrad Banicki, "Positive Psychology on Character Strengths and Virtues: A Disquieting Suggestion," *New Ideas in Psychology* 33 (April 2014): 21–34. The Center for Positive Organization's faculty at the University of Michigan's Ross School of Business developed a similar approach, the Reflected Best Self™ Exercise: http://positiveorgs.bus.umich.edu/cpo-tools/reflected-best-self-exercise-2nd-edition. On the history of this concept, see Judy Hilkey, *Character Is Capital: Success Manuals and Manhood in Gilded Age America* (Chapel Hill: University of North Carolina Press, 1997).
4. Peterson and Seligman, *Character*, 5, 11, 18.
5. Gregg Easterbrook, *The Progress Paradox: How Life Gets Better While People Feel Worse* (New York: Random House, 2004), xix.
6. For some recent research, see Peggy N. Thoits and Lyndi N. Hewitt, "Volunteer Work and Well-Being," *Journal of Health and Social Behavior* 42 (June 2001): 115–31; Sara B. Algoe and Jonathan Haidt, "Witnessing Excellence in Action: The 'Other-Praising' Emotions of Elevation, Gratitude, and Admiration," *JPP* 4 (March 2009): 105–27; Elizabeth W. Dunn, Lara B. Aknin, and Michael I. Norton, "Spending Money on Others Promotes Happiness,"

Science 319 (March 21, 2008): 1687–88; Simone Schnall, Jean Roper, and Daniel M. T. Fessler, "Elevation Leads to Altruistic Behavior," *PS* 21 (March 2010): 315–20; Helen Y. Weng et. al., "Compassion Training Alters Altruism and Neural Responses to Suffering," *PS* 24 (July, 2013): 1171–80.

7. Barbara Fredrickson, *Positivity: Top-Notch Research Reveals the 3-to-1 Ratio That Will Change Your Life* (New York: MJF Books, 2009), 41. For other explorations of character strengths, see Todd Kashdan, *Curious? Discover the Missing Ingredient to a Fulfilling Life* (New York: William Morrow, 2009); Roy F. Baumeister and John Tierney, *Willpower: Rediscovering the Greatest Human Strength* (New York: Penguin, 2011); Lisa G. Aspinwall and Ursula M. Staudinger, *A Psychology of Human Strengths: Fundamental Questions and Future Directions for a Positive Psychology* (Washington, DC: American Psychological Association, 2003); Angela Duckworth, *Grit: The Power of Passion and Perseverance* (New York: Simon & Schuster, 2016).

8. Claudia Wallis, "The New Science of Happiness," *Time*, Jan. 9, 2005.

9. Wallis, "New Science of Happiness." Kathryn Lofton, *Oprah: the Gospel of an Icon* (Berkeley: University of California Press, 2011) explores the connections between keeping a journal and expressing happiness. See also Robert A. Emmons, *Thanks! How the New Science of Gratitude Can Make You Happier* (Boston: Houghton Mifflin, 2007); Robert A. Emmons. *Gratitude Works! A 21-Day Program for Creating Emotional Prosperity* (Hoboken, NJ: Wiley, 2013); Robert Emmons, "Spirituality: Recent Progress," in *A Life Worth Living: Contributions to Positive Psychology*, ed. Mihaly Csikszentmihalyi and Isabella Selega Csikszentmihalyi (New York: Oxford University Press, 2006), 62–81. For a critique of the emphasis on gratitude, see Barbara Ehrenreich, "The Selfish Side of Gratitude," *NYT*, Jan. 3, 2016.

10. Stephen G. Post, "General Introduction," in *Altruism and Health: Perspectives from Empirical Research*, ed. Stephen G. Post (New York: Oxford University Press, 2007), 6; http://store.heartmath.org/s.nl/it.A/id.615/.f. See also these works by Stephen G. Post: *Unlimited Love: Altruism, Compassion, and Service* (Philadelphia: Templeton Foundation Press, 2003); with Jill Neimark, *Why Good Things Happen to Good People The Exciting New Research That Proves the Link Between Doing Good, and Living a Longer, Healthier, Happier Life* (New York: Broadway, 2007); *The Hidden Gifts of Helping: How the Power of Giving, Compassion, and Hope Can Get Us Through Hard Times* (San Francisco: Jossey-Bass, 2011).

11. Tania Singer and Matthieu Ricard, eds., *Caring Economics: Conversations on Altruism and Compassion Between Scientists, Economists, and the Dalai Lama* (New York: Picador, 2015). For an exploration of the connections between religion, spirituality, neuroscience, and positivity, see George E. Vaillant, *Spiritual Evolution: A Scientific Defense of Faith* (New York: Broadway, 2008).

12. Ernst Fehr, "The Social Dilemma Experiment," in Singer and Ricard, *Caring*, 77–84; Ernst Fehr, "Altruistic Punishment and the Creation of Public Goods," in Singer and Ricard, *Caring*, 125–34; Tania Singer, "Empathy and the Interoceptive Cortex," in Singer and Ricard, *Caring*, 27–43; William Harbaugh, "Why People Give to Charity," in Singer and Ricard, *Caring*, 124. For the controversial and highly consequential debates over what investigations that rely on fMRI reveal about moral judgments, see Joshua D. Greene et al., "An fMRI Investigation of Emotional Engagement in Moral Judgment," *Science*, Sept. 14, 2001, 2105–8; Selim Berker, "The Normative Insignificance of Neuroscience," *Philosophy and Public Affairs* 37 (Fall 2009): 293–329.

13. Richard J. Davidson, "The Neural Basis of Compassion," in Singer and Ricard, *Caring*, 52; Matthieu Ricard, "A Buddhist Perspective on Altruism," in Singer and Ricard, *Caring*, 57–62.

14. See http://www.payitforwardfoundation.org/; http://payitforwardday.com/; TheNewton Project.com.

15. Karen Reivich and Andrew Shatté, *The Resilience Factor; 7 Keys to Finding Your Inner Strength and Overcoming Life's Hurdles* (New York: Crown, 2002), 321. On the importance of positivity and resilience in responding to 9/11, see also Fredrickson, *Positivity*, 99–103; Martin E. P. Seligman, *Authentic Happiness: Using the New Positive Psychology to Realize Your Potential for Lasting Fulfillment* (New York: Free Press, 2002), xiii–xiv. For another book on resilience, see Judith Rodin, *The Resilience Dividend: Being Strong in a World Where Things Go Wrong* (New York: Public Affairs, 2014).

16. Martin E. P. Seligman, *Flourish: A Visionary New Understanding of Happiness and Well-Being* (New York: Simon & Schuster, 2011), 83, 85.

17. See http://www.acsim.army.mil/readyarmy/ra_csf.htm. On this program, see Seligman, *Flourish*, 126–51. For criticisms of the program, see http://www.counterpunch.org/2011/03/24/the-dark-side-of-comprehensive-soldier-fitness/; https://www.washingtonpost.com/local/army-program-works-to-make-soldiers-fit-in-body-and-mind/2011/05/13/gHQAVsCqxH_story.html; the special issue of *American Psychologist* 66 on the program, Jan. 2011, as well as the ensuing discussion, along with Seligman's response, in *American Psychologist* 66 (Oct. 2011): 641–47. For a critique, see Jeffrey R. Rubin, "The Unhappy Truth About Positive Psychology," *Truthout*, July 18, 2012. On the crucial role wars more generally have played in the development of American psychology, see Ellen Herman, *The Romance of American Psychology: Political Culture in the Age of Experts* (Berkeley: University of California Press, 1995). Jennifer Mittelstadt, *The Rise of the Military Welfare State* (Cambridge, MA: Harvard University Press, 2015) tells the larger story of how the American military, beginning in the 1980s, worked to instill conservative values.

18. David Brooks, *The Road to Character* (New York: Random House, 2015), xiv–xv, 6, 261–67. On his religious view, see https://www.washingtonpost.com/news/acts-of-faith/wp/2015/05/01/interview-david-brooks-on-sin-augustine-and-the-state-of-his-soul/.

19. Parul Sehgal, "Brace Yourself" [online as "The Profound Emptiness of 'Resilience'"], *NYTM*, Dec. 6, 2015; Alfie Kohn, "The Downside of 'Grit,'" *Washington Post*, April 6, 2014.

20. Robert A. Emmons, "Religion in the Psychology of Personality: An Introduction," *Journal of Personality* 67 (Dec. 1999): 873–88. On spirituality, as distinguished from religion, as a source of happiness, see Sam Harris, *Waking Up: A Guide to Spirituality Without Religion* (New York: Simon & Schuster, 2014).

21. Sir John Templeton, "Foreword," in *Handbook of Positive Psychology*, ed. C. R. Snyder and Shane J. Lopez (New York: Oxford University Press, 2002), vii.

22. Tracy Balboni et al., "Religiousness and Spiritual Support Among Advanced Cancer Patients and Associations with End-of-Life Treatment Preferences and Quality of Life," *Journal of Clinical Oncology* 25 (Feb. 2007): 555–60; Kenneth Pargament, "Cultivating the Spiritual Dimension in Life: A Vital Aspect of Positive Psychology," talk at Fourth World Conference on Positive Psychology, June 25, 2015; Britt-Mari Sykes, *Questioning Psychological Health and Well-Being: Historical and Contemporary Dialogues Between Theologians and Psychologists* (Macon, GA: Mercer University Press, 2010). For the work of a sociologist who has extensively studied the positive impact of religion on American life, see Rodney Stark, *America's Blessings: How Religion Benefits Everyone, Including Atheists* (West Conshohocken, PA: Templeton Press, 2012).

23. Sonja Lyubomirsky, *The How of Happiness: A Scientific Approach to Getting the Life You Want* (New York: Penguin Press, 2008), 228, 230, 232, 235. For a more cautious view of the impact of religion on happiness, see Ed Diener and Robert Biswas-Diener, *Happiness: Unlocking the Mysteries of Psychological Wealth* (Malden, MA: Blackwell, 2008), 112–26.

24. The literature here is immense, and includes Dean Sluyter, *The Zen Commandments: Ten Suggestions for a Life of Inner Freedom* (New York: Penguin Putnam, 2001); Robert

A. F. Thurman, *Inner Revolution: Life, Liberty, and the Pursuit of Real Happiness* (New York: Riverhead, 1998); David Baird, *A Thousand Paths to Happiness* (Napierville, IL: Sourcebook, 2000); David P. Barash, *Buddhist Biology: Ancient Eastern Wisdom Meets Modern Western Science* (New York: Oxford University Press, 2014). On the growing popularity of meditation, see David Hochman, "Mindfulness: Getting Its Share of Attention," *NYT*, Nov. 1, 2013; Joel Stein, "Just Say Om," cover story of *Time*, Aug 4, 2003. For a critique of some scholars for overemphasizing the positive impact of mindfulness on mental health, see Anna Nowogrodzki, "Power of Positive Thinking Skews Mindfulness Studies," *Nature*, April 21, 2016.

25. To sample such discussions, see Rabbi Michael Knopf, "Where Positive Psychology and Judaism Overlap," *Haaretz*, June 3, 2013; R. Elchanan Poupko, "Born to Bentch: Judaism and Positive Psychology," *Torah Musings*, Feb. 20, 2014; Eliezer Schnall, Mark Schiffman, and Aaron Cherniak, "Virtues That Transcend: Positive Psychology in Jewish Texts and Tradition," in *Religion and Spirituality Across Cultures*, ed. Chu Kim-Prieto (Dordrecht, Netherlands: Springer, 2014), 21–45; Martha Mendelsohn, "The Jewish Happiness Project," *Jewish Week*, Oct. 3, 2011. Tal Ben-Shahar has been involved in teaching courses on Judaism and happiness: Rabbi Benjy Brackman, "Exciting Class on Jewish Positive Psychology in North Metro Denver," *Boulder Jewish News*, Oct. 20, 2014.

26. On the contrasting views, see Adam B. Cohen and Peter C. Hill, "Religion as Culture: Religious Individualism and Collectivism among American Catholics, Jews, and Protestants," *Journal of Personality* 75 (Aug. 2007): 709–42.

27. The only article from a database of scholarly articles using "Judaism" and "positive psychology" in searches is Katherine Darlsgaard, Christopher Peterson, and Martin E. P. Seligman, "Shared Virtue: The Convergence of Valued Human Strengths Across Culture and History," *Review of General Psychology* 9 (Sept. 2005): 203–13. As the title indicates, the authors, who included Judaism in their sample, were interested in common rather than distinctive outlooks of a wide range of religious traditions. For other articles on Jews and happiness, see Jeff Levin, "Religious Behavior, Health, and Well-Being Among Israeli Jews: Findings from the European Social Survey," *Psychology of Religion and Spirituality* 5 (Nov. 2013): 272–82; Adam B. Cohen, "The Importance of Spirituality for Well-Being for Jews and Christians," *JHS* 3 (Sept. 2002): 287–310. In *Authentic Happiness*, Seligman did report on the work by an undergraduate who revealed that fundamentalists, including Orthodox Jews, were significantly more optimistic than their counterparts, including Reform Jews: Seligman, *Authentic*, 60; elsewhere (*Authentic*, 258), as others have commonly done, he collapsed Judaism into part of "the Judeo-Christian tradition." On the role Jews played in American psychology, see Andrew R. Heinze, *Jews and the American Soul: Human Nature in the 20th Century* (Princeton, NJ: Princeton University Press, 2004).

28. Rodger Kamenetz, *The Jew in the Lotus: A Poet's Rediscovery of Jewish Identity in Buddhist India* (San Francisco: Harper, 1994) introduced the word Jubu to a broad audience.

29. Robert Wuthnow, *The Restructuring of American Religion: Society and Faith Since World War II* (Princeton, NJ: Princeton University Press, 1988).

30. After 1998, happiness books in genres available earlier continued to appear: among those that that combined the perspectives of Buddhism and psychology are Jack Kornfield, *After the Ecstasy, the Laundry: How the Heart Grows Wise on the Spiritual Path* (New York: Bantam Books, 2000); Alan Gettis, *The Happiness Solution: Finding Joy and Meaning in an Upside Down World* (Norwood, NJ: Goodman Beck, 2008); Alan Gettis, *Seven Times Down, Eight Times Up: Landing on Your Feet in an Upside Down World*, 2nd ed. (Norwood, NJ: Goodman, Beck, 2009); Matthieu Ricard, *Happiness: A Guide to Developing Life's Most Important Skill*, trans. Jesse Browner (2003; London: Atlantic Books, 2007). For inspirational homilies by a Protestant minister, see Tom Owen-Towle, *Being Happy in an Unhappy World* (San Diego: Barking Rocks Press, 2001).

31. Wallis, "New Science of Happiness."

32. Joel Isaac, *Working Knowledge: Making the Human Sciences from Parsons to Kuhn* (Cambridge, MA: Harvard University Press, 2012), 11. For a critique of neuroscience, with a focus on books that "show that brain science promises much and delivers little," see Adam Gopnik, "Mindless: The New Neuro-Skeptics," *New Yorker*, Sept. 9, 2013, 86. For another critique, in this instance for linking neuroscience and an emphasis on morality, see Tamsin Shaw, "The Psychologists Take Power," *NYRB*, Feb. 25, 2016. Nikolas Rose and Joelle M. Abi-Rached, *Neuro: The New Brain Sciences and the Management of the Mind* (Princeton, NJ: Princeton University Press, 2013) is a nuanced consideration of advances in neuroscience. See also the blog neurobabble.co.uk; William T. Uttal, *Mind and Brain: A Critical Appraisal of Cognitive Neuroscience* (Cambridge, MA: MIT Press, 2011); Suparna Choudhury and Jan Slaby, eds., *Critical Neuroscience: A Handbook of the Social and Cultural Contexts of Neuroscience* (Malden, MA: Wiley-Blackwell, 2012); Joseph Dumit, *Picturing Personhood: Brain Scans and Biomedical Identity* (Princeton, NJ: Princeton University Press, 2004); Natasha Dow Schüll and Caitlin Zaloom, "The Shortsighted Brain: Neuroeconomics and the Governance of Choice in Time," *Social Studies of Science* 41 (Aug. 2011): 515–38; Fernando Vidal, "Brainhood: Anthropological Figure of Modernity," *History of Human Sciences* 22 (Feb. 2009): 5–36.

33. M. Joseph Sirgy, "Can QOL of Life Researchers Learn Anything 'Scientifically' Meaningful from Popular Cultural Icons Who Speak on Happiness and Well-Being?" *JHS* 10 (Nov. 2009), 769–71. See also, for example, the caution expressed by Richard J. Davidson, "The Human Brain: Deconstructing Mindfulness," https://www.youtube.com/watch?v=0oynfJv7-NU, at the Davos World Economic Forum in early 2015. Critics also caution against inferring psychological states from physiological evidence: John T. Cacioppo and Louis G. Tassinary, "Inferring Psychological Significance from Physiological Signals," *AP* 45 (Jan. 1990): 16–28; Gregory A. Miller, "How We Think About Cognition, Emotion, and Biology in Psychopathology," *Psychophysiology* 33 (Nov. 1996): 615–28.

34. There were, however, limits to the incorporation of neuroscience into summary books: Seligman, *Flourish*, though it had a chapter titled "Positive Physical Health: The Biology of Optimism," contained no reference to Davidson, neuroscience, or fMRI in the index. Todd B. Kashdan and Michael F. Steger, "Challenges, Pitfalls, and Aspirations for Positive Psychology," in *Designing Positive Psychology: Taking Stock and Moving Forward*, ed. Kennon M. Sheldon, Todd B. Kashdan, and Michael F. Steger (New York: Oxford University Press, 2011), 16–17, note that positive psychologists often incorporate biological considerations in a perfunctory way.

35. Fredrickson, *Positivity*, 24. For a full statement of the role of evolution, see David M. Buss, "The Evolution of Happiness," *AP* 55 (Jan. 2000): 15–23. The impact of evolutionary theory on the field is hard to underestimate. For example, in 2011 two leading researchers spoke of "pleasure as an adaptive evolutionary feature" and suggested that "hedonic reactions have been too important to survival to be exclusively subjective": Kent C. Berridge and Morten L. Kringelbach, "Building a Neuroscience of Pleasure and Well-Being," *Psychological Well-Being: Theory, Research and Practice* 1 (Oct. 2011); 1–26.

36. Lyubomirsky, *How*, 60, relying on studies that Richard J. Davidson did well before 1998.

37. See, for example, Fredrickson, *Positivity*, 107–10. On the controversies surrounding the use of fMRI to explore emotions, see Edward Vul et al., "Puzzlingly High Correlations in fMRI Studies of Emotion, Personality, and Social Cognition," *Perspectives on Psychological Science* 4 (May, 2009): 274–90.

38. Morten Kringelbach and Kent C. Berridge, "The Joyful Mind," *Scientific American* 307 (Aug. 2012): 40–45. On scientific experiments with Deep Brain Stimulation as a way of increasing a sense of well-being, see Maartje Schermer, "Health, Happiness and Human

Enhancement—Dealing with Unexpected Effects of Deep Brain Stimulation," *Neuroethics* 6 (Dec. 2013): 435–45.

39. *Functional Magnetic Resonance Imaging: A New Research Tool* (Washington, DC: American Psychological Association, 2007), 1–5. For examples of the work of Davidson's lab, see Richard J. Davidson and Antoine Lutz, "Buddha's Brain: Neuroplasticity and Meditation," *IEEE Signal Processing Magazine* 25 (Sept. 2007): 172–76; Antoine Lutz et al., "Regulation of the Neural Circuitry of Emotion by Compassion Meditation: Effects of Meditative Expertise," *PLoS ONE*, March 26, 2008.

40. Michael D. Lemonick, "Health: The Biology of Joy," *Time*, Jan. 9, 2005. On the historical background for such studies, see John Tresch, "The Brain Multiple in the Laboratories of Post-Buddhism," paper at a conference, "Sorting Brains Out: Tasks, Tests, and Trials in the Neuro- and Mind Sciences, 1890–1915," University of Pennsylvania, Sept. 9, 2015.

41. Lemonick, "Health"; work of Richard J. Davidson, reported in Sharon Begley, *Train Your Mind, Change Your Brain. How a New Science Reveals Our Extraordinary Potential to Transform Ourselves* (New York: Ballantine, 2007), 228–33. For a cautious attempt to connect brain research with both hedonia and eudaimonia, see Berridge and Kringelbach, "Building," 1–26. On the role of genetics, see Ragnhild Bang Nes, "Happiness in Behaviour Genetics: Findings and Implications," *JHS* 11 (June 2010): 369–81. On the relationships between the genome and emotional states, see Aysu Okbay, "Genetic Variants Associated with Subjective Well-Being, Depressive Symptoms, and Neuroticism Identified Through Genome-Wide Analyses," *Nature Genetics*, 48 (April 18, 2016): 624–33.

42. Richard J. Davidson, with Sharon Begley, *The Emotional Life of Your Brain: How Its Unique Patterns Affect the Way You Think, Feel, and Live—and How You Can Change Them* (New York: Hudson Street Press, 2012), 179.

43. Davidson, *Emotional*, 194–96. For the study, see Antoine Lutz et al., "Long-Term Meditators Self-Induce High Amplitude Gamma Synchrony During Mental Practice," *Proceedings of the National Academy of Sciences* 101 (Nov. 16, 2004): 16369–73. On Benson, the Dalai Lama, and Davidson, see Anne Harrington, *The Cure Within: A History of Mind-Body Medicine* (New York: W.W. Norton, 2008), 230–42.

44. Davidson, *Emotional*, xix, 9; Norman Doidge, *The Brain's Way of Healing: Remarkable Discoveries and Recoveries from the Frontiers of Neuroplasticity* (New York: Viking, 2015), xv; Begley, *Train Your Mind*, 240–41. Davidson had chosen to name his position the William James Professorship; after all, James in 1890 talked of the brain's plasticity. For an example of how scholars in the field of positive psychology draw on James, see James O. Pawelski, *The Dynamic Individualism of William James* (Albany: State University of New York Press, 2007).

45. Davidson, *Emotional*, 10, 252.

46. The literature here is considerable. Jo Marchant, *Cure: A Journey into the Science of Mind Over Body* (New York Crown, 2016), by a science writer who earned a PhD in genetics and medical microbiology, is a good place to begin. Among other books aimed at wide audiences are Rick Hanson, with Richard Mendius, *Buddha's Brain: The Practical Neuroscience of Happiness, Love, and Wisdom* (Oakland, CA: New Harbinger, 2009); John Medina, *Brain Rules:12 Principles for Surviving and Thriving at Work, Home, and School* (Seattle: Pear Press, 2008); Jason Zweig, *Your Money and Your Brain: How the New Science of Neuroscience Can Help Make You Rich* (New York: Simon & Schuster, 2008); Lisa F. Barrett, *How Emotions Are Made: The New Science of the Mind and Brain* (Boston: Houghton Mifflin Harcourt, 2016); Jon Kabat-Zinn and Richard J. Davidson, eds., *The Mind's Own Physician: A Scientific Dialogue with the Dalai Lama on the Healing Power of Meditation* (Oakland, CA: New Harbinger, 2011). For an informed but somewhat skeptical assessment, see Miguel Farias and Catherine Wikholm, *The Buddha Pill: Can Meditation Actually Change You?* (London: Watkins, 2015). For an example of

magazine coverage aimed at a wide audience, see Sharon Begley, "The Brain: How the Brain Rewires Itself," *Time*, Jan. 19, 2007.

Among the many more scholarly books, some aimed at broad audiences are Davidson, with Sharon Begley, *Emotional*; Daniel Goleman, *Social Intelligence: The New Science of Human Relationships* (New York: Bantam Books, 2006); Daniel H. Pink, *A Whole New Mind: Moving from the Information Age to the Conceptual Age* (New York: Riverhead, 2005); Vaillant, *Spiritual Evolution*; Morten L. Kringelbach, *The Pleasure Center: Trust Your Animal Instincts* (New York: Oxford University Press, 2009); Norman Doidge, *The Brain That Changes Itself: Stories of Personal Triumph From the Frontiers of Brain Science* (New York: Viking, 2007).

47. Joelle M. Abi-Rached and Nikolas Rose, "The Birth of the Neuromolecular Gaze," *History of the Human Sciences* 23 (Feb. 2010): 11–36; Daniel Goleman, "Preface," in Begley, *Train Your Mind*, xii.

48. Richard O'Connor, *Happy at Last: a Thinking Person's Guide to Finding Joy* (New York: St. Martin's Press, 2008), 97–98. For recent developments in Third Wave therapies, which combine cognitive behavioral with other approaches, see http://www.3rdwavetherapy. com/what-is-third-wave-cognitive-behavioral-therapy/.

49. Lemonick, "Health." Diener and Biswas-Diener, *Happiness*, 29–46 summarizes the evidence. Among the key studies are Carol D. Ryff and Burton Singer, "From Social Structure to Biology: Integrative Science in Pursuit of Human Health and Well-Being," in Snyder and Lopez, *Handbook*, 541–55; Deborah D. Danner, David A. Snowdon, and Wallace V. Friesen, "Positive Emotions in Early Life and Longevity: Findings from the Nun Study," *JPSP* 80 (May 2001): 804–13; Corey L. M. Keyes, "Promoting and Protecting Mental Health as Flourishing: A Complementary Strategy for Improving National Mental Health," *AP* 62 (Feb.–March 2007): 95–108. For a summary of studies that demonstrated a connection between positivity, neuropsychology, and pro-social behavior, see Alice M. Isen, "A Role for Neuropsychology In Understanding the Facilitating Influence of Positive Affect on Social Behavior and Cognitive Professes," in Snyder and Lopez, *Handbook*, 528–40. For an important government study on the implications of scientific advances for happiness, see President's Council on Bioethics, *Beyond Therapy: Biotechnology and the Pursuit of Happiness* (Washington, DC: Government Printing Office, 2003).

50. Dust jacket for Begley, *Train Your Mind*; Daniel Nettle, *Happiness: The Science Behind Your Smile* (New York: Oxford University Press, 2005), 142–44.

51. O'Connor, *Happy*, 260; Medina, *Brain Rules*, 28; Hanson and Mendius, *Buddha's*, 2; Goleman, *Social Intelligence*, 4; Zweig, *Money*, 7, 240. Rose and Abi-Rachel, in *Neuro*, talk of exaggerated and premature promises in neuroscience.

52. Robb Willer is one exception in sociology; Gordon Matthews and Carolina Izquierdo in anthropology. The Winter 2015 issue of the *Journal of Ethnographic Theory* focused on happiness; in the introductory essay, "Values of Happiness," *Journal of Enthnographic Theory* 5 (Winter 2015): 1–23, Harry Walker and Iza Kavedžija make clear how late anthropologists were in coming to terms with the surge in happiness studies and how they could make distinctive contributions. Critical of how many economists and psychologists claim to measure subjective well-being, the contributors to the volume both accept and complicate the distinction between the hedonic and eudaimonic, make clear that not all cultures consider happiness a major goal, and offer varied and complex renderings of the relationships between social responsibility, values, and goals.

53. Ed Diener and Eunkook M. Suh, eds., *Culture and Subjective Well-Being* (Cambridge, MA: MIT Press, 2000) contains essays (especially by Eunkook Suh and Shigehiro Oishi) that grapple with cultural differences, but the volume, though focused on culture, contains no contribution by an anthropologist and many if not all by psychologists. Diener and Biswas-Diener, *Happiness*, 127–44 discuss how different cultures evaluate and experience

happiness. For an anthropologist's linking of his field and positive psychology, see Ted Fischer, "A Positive Anthropology," in "Anthropological Observations . . . On Economics, Politics, and Daily Life," July 16, 2010, at http://www.anthropologicalobservations. blogspot.com. On the distortions that result from how psychologists focus on WEIRD, see Joseph Henrich, Steven J. Heine, and Ara Norenzayan, "The Weirdest People in the World?" *Behavioral and Brain Sciences* 33 (June 2010): 61–136; James Coyne, "Positive Psychology Is Mainly For Rich White People," *PLOS Blogs*, Aug. 21, 2013.

54. A useful summary of the field is Carol Graham, *Happiness Around the World: The Paradox of Happy Peasants and Miserable Millionaires* (New York: Oxford University Press, 2009). Springer has a book series, "Cross-Cultural Advancements in Positive Psychology," which includes Alejandro Castro Solano, *Positive Psychology in Latin America* (Dordrecht, Netherlands: Springer, 2014) and Marié P. Wissing, *Well-Being Research in South Africa* (Dordrecht, Netherlands: Springer, 2013).

55. Among the early twentieth-century ones were the International Institute of Management's Gross National Happiness 2.0 or Gross National Well-Being; the Genuine Progress Indicator; Thailand's Green and Happiness Index; the Organization for Economic Co-operation and Development's Better Life Index; the UN World Happiness Report (following the General Assembly's resolution "Happiness: Towards a Holistic Approach to Development"); the Canadian Index of Wellbeing; Goa's Gross National Happiness; Seattle's index for measuring happiness; Prime Minister David Cameron's call for making happiness the new GDP; France's President Nicolas Sarkozy's advocacy of a Happiness Index; South Korea's Happiness Index; a report from the United States Office of Management and Budget and National Research Council of the National Academies titled "Subjective Well-Being"; Dubai Happiness Index; and EHERO, the Erasmus Happiness Economics Research Organization in the Netherlands.

56. United Nations, Happiness Resolution, "Happiness: Towards a Holistic Approach to Development," draft note, Nov. 6, 2012, 15.

57. Joseph E. Stiglitz, Amartya Sen, and Jean-Paul Fitoussi, *Report of the Commission on the Measurement of Economic Performance and Social Progress* (Paris: INSEE, 2015), 9.

58. David Cameron, quoted in "Prime Minister Defends Big Society Policy," *BBC News*, Feb. 13, 2011; Carl Cederstrom, "The Dangers of Happiness," *NYT*, July 18, 2015.

59. One example of conflicting conclusions: citizens of nations in Northern Europe with strong social welfare programs report very high levels of happiness, yet although Canada and Spain have more extensive programs than the United States and Mexico, their citizens are not notably happier.

60. For a summary of the field, see Paul Allin and David J. Hand, *The Wellbeing of Nations: Meaning, Motive and Measurement* (Chichester, UK: Wiley, 2014).

61. Caitlin Dewey, "A Fascinating Map of the World's Happiest and Least Happy Countries," *Washington Post*, Sept. 10, 2013. The 2016 World Happiness Report broke new ground when it paid significant attention to the impact of unequal distribution of well-being: Jena McGregor, "The U.S. Doesn't Crack the Top 10 Happiest Countries in the World," *Washington Post*, March 16, 2016.

62. For other works on this topic, see Ed Diener, Daniel Kahneman, and Norbert Schwarz, eds., *Well-Being: The Foundations of Hedonic Psychology* (New York: Russell Sage, 1999); Ed Diener, John F. Helliwell, and Daniel Kahneman, eds., *International Differences in Well-Being* (New York: Oxford University Press, 2010); Amartya Sen, "The Economics of Happiness and Capability," in *Capabilities and Happiness*, ed. Luigino Bruni, Flavio Comim, and Maurizio Pugno (New York: Oxford University Press, 2008): 16–27; Eric Weiner, *The Geography of Bliss: One Grump's Search for the Happiest Places in the World* (New York: Hachette, 2008); John Helliwell, "Well-Being, Social Capital, and Public Policy: What's New?" *Economic Journal* 116 (March, 2006): C 34–45.

63. Stefan Klein, *The Science of Happiness: How Our Brains Make Us Happy—and What We Can Do to Get Happier*, trans. Stephen Lehmann (New York: Marlowe, 2002), 252.

64. Robert Skidelsky and Edward Skidelsky, *How Much Is Enough: Money and the Good Life* (New York: Other Press, 2012), 123. For a summary of the work on the intersection between economics, public policy, and subjective well-being, see John F. Helliwell, "How Can Subjective Well-being Be Improved?" in *New Directions for Intelligent Government in Canada*, ed. Fred Gorbet, Andrew Sharpe, and Ian Stewart (Ottawa: Centre for Study of Living Standards, 2011), 283–308.

65. Some of the essays in Robert Biswas-Diener, ed., *Positive Psychology as Social Change* (New York: Springer, 2011) both critique the individualistic focus of discussions of social change among positive psychologists and begin the move toward alternatives. See, for example, Robert Biswas-Diener, "Editor's Foreword," v–xi; Robert Biswas-Diener and Lindsey Patterson, "Positive Psychology and Poverty," 137–38; Nicky Garcea and P. Alex Linley, "Creating Positive Social Change Through Building Positive Organizations: Four Levels of Intervention," 159, 173; Lara B. Aknin et al., "Investing in Others: Prosocial Spending for (Pro)Social Change," 231; Scott Sherman "Changing the World: The Science of Transformative Action," 336, 340; Barbara Frederickson, "Editor's Afterword," 349. However, the shift is only partial, focusing as the essays often do on a limited number of issues (especially poverty and environmentalism), avoiding discussions of power relationships, and concentrating more on analysis of problems than programs for change that involve social movements, other forms of mobilization, or government policies.

66. C. R. Snyder and Shane J. Lopez, *Positive Psychology: The Scientific and Practical Explorations of Human Strengths* (Thousand Oaks, CA: Sage, 2007), 462. Tim Lomas, Kate Hefferon, and Itai Itvzan, *Applied Positive Psychology: Integrated Positive Practice* (Los Angeles: Sage, 2014), by three psychologists at the University of East London, is a textbook that more fully integrates science, culture, and society than many of its counterparts.

67. Robert Biswas-Diener et al., "Positive Psychology as a Force for Social Change," in Sheldon, Kashdan, and Singer, *Designing*, 410–18, reveals both the strengths (a focus on the environment, educational and business organizations, and poverty) and limitations (an emphasis on a relatively narrow range of interventions, many of them personal) of the focus on the relationships between positive psychology and social change.

68. Seligman, *Authentic*, 50.

69. Norbert Schwarz and Fritz Strack, "Reports of Subjective Well-Being: Judgmental Processes and Their Methodological Implications," in Kahneman, Diener, and Schwarz, *Well Being*, 61–84; http://www.authentichappiness.sas.upenn.edu/testcenter.aspx.

70. Fredrickson, *Positivity*, 17; Seligman, *Flourish*, 12.

71. Seligman, *Flourish*, 105.

72. Seligman, *Flourish*, 237–38. For a criticism from an unnamed letter writer of Seligman for revealing that more money did not significantly enhance the happiness of those in poverty, see Seligman, *Authentic*, 280.

73. Martin E. P. Seligman, "The President's Address," 1998, *AP* 54 (Aug. 1999): 559–62. For his historical analysis, see Martin Seligman, conversation with author, May 19, 2016; in offering his assessment, Seligman may have been relying on, among other sources, Stephen Pinker, *The Better Angels of Our Nature: Why Violence Has Declined* (New York: Viking, 2011).

74. On neoliberalism, see Sam Binkley, *Happiness as Enterprise: An Essay on Neoliberal Life* (Albany: State University of New York Press, 2014); David Harvey, *A Brief History of Neoliberalism* (New York: Oxford University Press, 1990); Noam Chomsky, *Profit over People: Neoliberalism and Global Order* (New York: Seven Stories Press, 1999); Bethany Moreton, *To Serve God and Wal-Mart: The Making of Christian Free Enterprise* (Cambridge, MA: Harvard University Press, 2009); Wendy Brown, *Undoing the Demos: Neoliberalism's*

Stealth Revolution (New York: Zone Books, 2015); Anthony Giddens, *Modernity and Self-Identity: Self and Society in the Late Modern Age* (Stanford, CA: Stanford University Press, 1991); Nikolas Rose, *Governing the Soul: The Shaping of the Private Self* (London: Free Association Books, 1999). In *Saving the Modern Soul: Therapy, Emotions and the Culture of Self-Help* (Berkeley: University of California Press, 2008), Eva Illouz offers a critique of self-help culture and psychology for undermining communitarian engagement and instead embracing an atomistic individualism.

75. On the corporation's centrality, see Mihaly Csikszentmihalyi, *Good Business: Leadership, Flow, and the Making of Meaning* (New York: Viking, 2003), 12.

76. Binkley, *Enterprise*, 152.

77. Lyubomirsky, *How*, 2; Diener and Biswas-Diener, *Happiness*, 3, 110–11; Csikszentmihalyi, *Good Business*, 189, 190, 194; Barry Schwartz: *The Costs of Living: How Market Freedom Erodes the Best Things in Life* (New York: W.W. Norton, 1994) and *The Paradox of Choice: Why More Is Less* (New York: HarperCollins, 2004). For a summary of the implications of happiness studies for public policy, see Elizabeth Kolbert, "Everybody Have Fun: What Can Policymakers Learn from Happiness Research?" *New Yorker*, March 22, 2010.

78. On the 2009 proposal by Nicolas Sarkozy to shift the yardstick from Gross Domestic Product to measuring a nation's well-being by focusing on happiness, see Henry Samuel, "Nicolas Sarkozy Wants to Measure Economic Success in 'Happiness,'" *The Telegraph*, Sept. 14, 2009. In "Economic Growth and Subjective Well-Being: Reassessing the Easterlin Paradox," *Brookings Papers on Economic Activity* (Spring 2008), 1–102, Betsey Stevenson and Justin Wolfers conclude that the policy implication of the Easterlin Paradox lead in this direction.

79. Graham, *Happiness*, subtitle. Carol L. Graham, *The Pursuit of Happiness* (Washington, DC: Brookings Institution Press, 2011) explores the promises and challenges economists face when they turn their attention to the study of happiness.

80. Jonathan Haidt, "New Study Indicates Existence of Eight Conservative Social Psychologists," *Heterodox Academy*, Jan. 7, 2016. Haidt, a social psychologist active in positive psychology from early on, has explored political divisions in America: Jonathan Haidt, *The Righteous Mind: Why Good People Are Divided by Politics and Religion* (New York: Pantheon, 2012).

81. Richard Layard, *Happiness: Lessons from a New Science* (New York: Penguin, 2005). See also Richard Layard, "Happiness: Has Social Science a Clue?" Lionel Robbins Memorial Lectures, delivered at London School of Economics, March 3–5, 2003; Richard Layard, "The Economics of Happiness," in Singer and Ricard, *Caring Economics*, 97–114; Richard Layard and David M. Clark, *Thrive: How Better Mental Health Care Transforms Lives and Saves Money* (Princeton, NJ: Princeton University Press, 2014).

82. Layard, *Happiness*, 128, 155, 172.

83. Layard, *Happiness*, 52–53, 122, 233–34. Ferguson, "Happiness," discusses and critiques Layard's impact on British social policy, especially his advocacy of cognitive behavioral therapy as a treatment for depression.

84. This summary relies of Dacher Keltner, *Born to Be Good: The Science of a Meaningful Life* (New York: W.W. Norton, 2009); Jason Marsh, Rodolfo Mendoza-Denton, and Jeremy Adam Smith, eds., *Are We Born Racist? New Insights from Neuroscience and Positive Psychology* (Boston: Beason, 2010); Dacher Keltner, Jason Marsh, and Jeremy Adam Smith, eds., *The Compassionate Instinct: The Science of Human Goodness* (New York: W.W. Norton, 2010); Dacher Keltner, *The Power Paradox: How We Gain and Lose Influence* (New York: Penguin, 2016); and the web sites http://www.greatergood.berkeley.edu and http://www.socrates.berkeley.edu/~keltner/research.htm.

85. Richard H. Thaler and Cass R. Sunstein, *Nudge: Improving Decisions About Health, Wealth, and Happiness* (New Haven, CT: Yale University Press, 2008). See also Daniel Kahneman, *Thinking, Fast and Slow* (New York: Farrar, Straus and Giroux, 2011), 408–18.

86. David G. Myers, *The American Paradox: Spiritual Hunger in an Age of Plenty* (New Haven, CT: Yale University Press, 2000), 147, 156.

87. Arthur C. Brooks, *Gross National Happiness: Why Happiness Matters for America—and How We Can Get More of It* (New York: Basic Books, 2008), 100. On the Well-Being Initiative, see Chris Young, "Why Are the Kochs Investing in Happiness?" *Slate*, June 25, 2014.

88. Brooks, *Gross*, 128–29, 131.

89. To sample recent writings on the intersection of happiness and public policy, begin with Amitava K. Dutt and Benjamin Radcliff, eds., *Happiness, Economics, and Politics: Toward a Multi-Disciplinary Approach* (Northampton, MA: Edward Elgar, 2009); Bruno Frey, *Happiness: A Revolution in Economics* (Cambridge, MA: MIT Press, 2008); Derek Bok, *The Politics of Happiness: What Government Can Learn from the New Research on Well-Being* (Princeton, NJ: Princeton University Press, 2010). See also Amartya Sen, *The Idea of Justice* (Cambridge, MA: Harvard University Press, 2009); Robert E. Lane, *Loss of Happiness in Market Economies* (New Haven, CT: Yale University Press, 2000); Alexander Pacek and Benjamin Radcliff, "Assessing the Welfare State: The Politics of Happiness," *Perspectives on Politics* 6 (June 2008): 266–77; Robert D. Putnam, *Bowling Alone: The Collapse and Revival of American Community* (New York: Simon & Schuster, 2000); Bent Greve, *Happiness* (London: Routledge, 2012); and a series of articles by Rutt Veenhoven in the *Journal of Happiness Studies*, including "Greater Happiness for a Greater Number: Is That Possible or Desirable?" 11 (Oct. 2010): 605–29. For earlier writings, see Robert A. Easterlin, ed., *Happiness in Economics* (Northampton, MA: Edward Elgar, 2002).

90. On the key issue of equality and happiness, national differences may be important. That greater equality seems to enhance happiness in Western Europe but not in the United States, notes one scholar, "can be attributed to Americans' belief (probably an illusion) that there is a greater amount of upward social mobility in their society": Frey, *Happiness*, 2.

91. Martin E. P. Seligman, *Helplessness: On Depression, Development, and Death* (San Francisco: W.H. Freeman, 1975), 164.

92. For example, on Jan. 3, 2016, I received two notices about articles from the *New York Times* from Friends of Positive Psychology, but no mention of an essay by Barbara Ehrenreich that also appeared in the same newspaper that day, an essay critical of the field: Ehrenreich, "Selfish Side."

93. Kristen Hamling, posting on Friends of Positive Psychology list serve, Feb. 14, 2016.

94. Christopher Peterson, *Pursuing the Good Life: 100 Reflections on Positive Psychology* (New York: Oxford University Press, 2013), 33–34. For a warning that positive psychology needs to rethink its commitment to liberal individualism, see Barry Schwartz, "Pitfalls on the Road to a Positive Psychology of Happiness," in *The Science of Optimism and Hope: Research Essays in Honor of Martin E. P. Seligman*, ed. Jane Gillham (Radnor, PA: Templeton Foundation Press, 2000), 399–412.

95. Ilona Boniwell, *Positive Psychology in a Nutshell: The Science of Happiness*, 3rd ed. (Maidenhead, UK: Open University Press, 2012), 164.

96. Kim S. Cameron, opening comments on panel on "Critiques of Positive Psychology," Fourth World Conference on Positive Psychology, June 27, 2015; on the session and reactions to it, see http://positivepsychologyprogram.com/critiques-criticisms-positive-psychology. Sheldon, Kashdan, and Steger, *Designing* is a collection of essays that offer a balanced assessment of the field in the ten years since its inception. For critiques of the study or goal of happiness, see Richard S. Lazarus, "Does the Positive Psychology Movement Have Legs?" *Psychology Inquiry* 14 (April 2003): 93–109; Jennifer Hecht,

The Happiness Myth: Why What We Think Is Right Is Wrong (New York: HarperCollins, 2007); Daniel M. Haybron, *The Pursuit of Unhappiness: The Elusive Psychology of Well-Being* (Oxford: Oxford University Press, 2008); Kristján Kristjánsson, *Virtues and Vices in Positive Psychology: A Philosophical Critique* (New York: Cambridge University Press, 2013); Oliver Burkeman, *The Antidote: Happiness for People Who Can't Stand Positive Thinking* (New York: Faber and Faber, 2012); Simon Burnett, *The Happiness Agenda: A Modern Obsession* (New York: Palgrave Macmillan, 2012); Michael Bennett and Sarah Bennett, *F*uck Feelings: One Shrink's Practical Advice for Managing All Life's Impossible Problems* (New York: Simon & Schuster, 2015); John F. Schumaker, *In Search of Happiness: Understanding an Endangered State of Mind* (Westport, CT: Praeger, 2007). For a satire on self-help roads to happiness, see the novel by Will Ferguson, *Happiness™* (Edinburgh: Canongate, 2002). Although not dealing directly with positive psychology, several books critically explore the broader traditions of which it is a part: among them are Lauren G. Berlant, *Cruel Optimism* (Durham, NC: Duke University Press, 2011); Stephen Briers, *Psychobabble: Exploding the Myths of the Self-Help Generation* (Harlow, UK: Pearson Education, 2012); Mitch Horowitz, *One Simple Idea: How Positive Thinking Reshaped Modern Life* (New York: Crown, 2014); Dana Becker, *The Myth of Empowerment: Women and the Therapeutic Culture in America* (New York: New York University Press, 2005).

97. Kristjánsson, *Virtues*, 3. One essay that marked the shift to more complicated and balanced views of subjective well-being is Richard M. Ryan and Edward L. Deci, "On Happiness and Human Potentials: A Review of Research on Hedonic and Eudaimonic Well-Being," *Annual Review of Psychology* (Feb. 2001): 141–66. Emily Esfahani Smith, "There's More to Life Than Being Happy," *Atlantic*, Jan. 9, 2013, brought this discussion to public attention.

98. Among the works critical of positive psychology that criticize the excessive emphasis on positivity and emphasize the importance of negative feelings are Itai Ivtzan, Tim Lomas, Kate Hefferon, and Piers Worth, *Second Wave Positive Psychology: Embracing the Dark Side of Life* (New York: Routledge, 2016); Eric G. Wilson, *Against Happiness; In Praise of Melancholy* (New York: Farrar, Straus and Giroux, 2008); Julie K. Norem, *The Positive Power of Negative Thinking: Using Defensive Pessimism to Manage Anxiety and Perform at Your Peak* (New York: Basic Books, 2001); Barbara Held, *Stop Smiling, Start Kvetching: A 5-Step Guide to Creative Complaining* (Brunswick, ME: Audenreed, 1999); Barbara Held, "The Negative Side of Positive Psychology," *Journal of Humanistic Psychology* 44 (Jan. 2004): 9–46; Jane Gruber, "Four Ways Happiness Can Hurt You," *Greater Good: The Science of a Meaningful Life*, May 3, 2012; Ruth Whippman, *America the Anxious: How Our Pursuit of Happiness Is Creating a Nation of Nervous Wrecks* (New York: St. Martin's Press, 2016).

99. Martin E. P. Seligman, comments at "Critiques of Positive Psychology" panel. To sample some of the criticisms that have appeared in newspapers, blogs, and magazines, see Beth Azar, "Positive Psychology Advances, with Growing Pains," *Monitor on Psychology*, 42 (April 2011); Daniel M. Haybron, "Happiness and Its Discontents," *NYT*, April 13, 2014; Andrew Anthony, "The British Amateur Who Debunked The Mathematics of Happiness" *The Guardian*, Jan. 18, 2014; Cederstrom, "Dangers of Happiness"; Alistair Miller, "A Critique of Positive Psychology—or 'The New Science of Happiness,'" *Journal of Philosophy of Education* 42 (Aug./Nov. 2008): 591–608; essays in *Theory and Psychology* 18 (Oct. 2008), in *Psychological Inquiry*, 14 (2003), in *Review of General Psychology* 9 (June 2005), and in *Psychologist*, 16 (March 2003); Emory L. Cowen and Ryan P. Kilmer, "'Positive Psychology': Some Plusses and Some Open Issues," *Journal of Community Psychology* 30 (July 2002): 449–60; Gary Greenberg, "War on Unhappiness," *Harper's*, Sept. 2010, 27–35; Rubin, "Unhappy Truth." For a defense against criticisms, see [author unknown], "Positive Psychology Criticism: All That's Cracked Up To Be?" *Positive Psychology Articles*, Oct. 14, 2015.

100. Jackson Lears, "Get Happy!!: For Margaret Thatcher as for Today's Happiness Industry, There Is No Such Thing as Society," *Nation*, Nov. 6, 2013.
101. Barbara Ehrenreich, *Bright-Sided: How Positive Thinking Is Undermining America* (New York: Henry Holt, 2009); Peterson, *Pursuing*, 88.
102. For a critique of Ehrenreich's books, see David Van Nuys, "Popping the Happiness Bubble: The Backlash Against Positive Psychology," *Psychology Today*, Nov. 3 and 16, 2010.
103. Ehrenreich, *Bright-Sided*, 13, 22–23.
104. Ehrenreich, *Bright-Sided*, 149, 151–52, 158–72.
105. Seligman, *Flourish*, 201–2, 236.
106. William Davies, *The Happiness Industry: How the Government and Big Business Sold Us Well-Being* (London: Verso, 2015), 6; see also William Davies, *The Limits of Neoliberalism: Authority, Sovereignty and the Logic of Competition* (Thousand Oaks, CA: Sage, 2014). For Davies's critique of Layard, whom Prime Minister Tony Blair appointed as the nation's happiness tsar, for relying on cognitive behavioral therapy to enhance the efficiency of workers, see William Davies, "The Political Economy of Unhappiness," *New Left Review* 71 (Sept.–Oct. 2011): 65–80. For a sharp critique from the left of positive psychology, including its application by people like Layard to policy, see Iain Ferguson, "Neoliberalism, Happiness and Wellbeing," *International Socialism: A Quarterly Review of Socialist Theory* 117 (Dec. 2007).
107. Berlant, *Cruel Optimism*; Sara Ahmed, *The Promise of Happiness* (Durham, NC: Duke University Press, 2010), 8. Sara Ahmed, "The Happiness Turn," is the essay in a collection of essays on happiness: *New Formations*, 63 (Winter 2007/08): 7–14. Among other useful sources on neoliberalism are Bethany Moreton, "S'More Inequality: The Neoliberal Marshmallow and the Corporate Reform of Education," *Social Text*, 32 (Fall 2014): 29–48; Andrew Lakoff, "Adaptive Will: The Evolution of Attention Deficit Disorder," *Journal of the History of the Behavioral Sciences* 36 (Spring 2000): 149–69.
108. Robert Biswas-Diener, *Practicing Positive Psychology Coaching: Assessment, Activities, and Strategies for Success* (Hoboken, NJ: Wiley, 2010), 40. Rose, *Governing the Soul* is a classic study of how psychology seeks exercise political power by governing people.
109. Binkley, *Enterprise*, 1. In important ways Binkley's observations echo what Daniel T. Rodgers wrote in *Age of Fracture* (Cambridge, MA: Harvard University Press, 2011).
110. Micki McGee, "From Makeover Media to Remaking Culture: Four Directions for the Critical Study of Self-Help Culture," *Sociology Compass* 6 (Sept. 2012): 686.
111. Micki McGee, *Self-Help, Inc.: Makeover Culture in American Life* (New York: Oxford University Press, 2005), 12, 19, 42–43, 49–110.
112. Judith Shulevitz, review of Angela Duckworth, *Grit: The Power of Passion and Perseverance*, *NYTBR*, May 8 2016, 14.

CHAPTER 8

The Business of Happiness

Around the world, but especially in America, happiness is big business. Tens of millions of people and organizations spend billions of dollars in efforts to increase subjective well-being. Some of this occurs in forms that antedate the arrival of positive psychology—sales of bestselling how-to books; attendance at workshops or churches; payments to therapists; and purchase of drugs. However, some phenomena are of more recent vintage—funding from government agencies or private foundations; watching a TED talk; visiting a web site; purchasing an app; talking to a coach trained in positive psychology; and working with consultants in schools or corporations. With happiness already so fully imbedded in the culture of late twentieth- and early twenty-first-century culture, absent these innovations positive psychology would have emerged in the late twentieth century and then flourished even more in the twenty-first. New media nonetheless enhanced the prominence and power of positive psychology—reinforcing and at times exaggerating the field's individualistic emphasis and the hold of neoliberalism. Whether old media or new, time-tested interventions or innovative ones, happiness enterprises have amplified the power of the pursuit of enhanced subjective well-being.[1]

The organized pursuit of happiness has swept into virtually every corner of American life, and done so at a time when tens of millions of Americans experienced economic stagnation and uncertainty. By early in the twenty-first century these efforts had pumped billions of dollars into the economy. Money flows into efforts to understand how the brain works in order to enhance people's sense of well-being. The National Institute of Health had poured funds into neuroscience research, the main aim of which is countering mental illness and increasing mental health. Pharmaceutical and medical device corporations rush to translate findings of basic research into practical applications. More popular but similar in spirit are efforts by entrepreneurs to sell products that promise to make you feel happier. Authors of popular books, like Martin Seligman and Shawn Achor, set their speaker's fees at $25,000 and up. Market researchers now examine people's brains in the laboratory as they interact with various items; facial expressions and eye movements are studied in customers roaming the store aisles, all in an effort to capture the subtle—and even subconscious—emotions that products elicit. Positive psychologists and behavioral economists might assert that greater income does not significantly increase happiness, but as one observer notes, "the vast assemblage of consumer psychologists, consumer neuroscientists and market researchers" are "dedicated to ensuring that we do achieve some degree of emotional satisfaction by spending money." In 2000 there were fifty new and popular non-fiction titles that focused on happiness, a number that increased annually.[2] Sprawling organizations and writers-turned-entrepreneurs that investigate and promote happiness have emerged—one thinks of a corporate organization like Gallup and an entrepreneurial psychologist like Rick Hanson.[3]

Wait, there is more. Not only can you buy over-the-counter drugs at CVS but even grocery stores offer nootropics—smart drugs, supplements, or specialized foods that promise improved cognition, memory, or functioning and, ultimately a sense of greater well-being. Available from www.Amazon.com is the Kindle edition of *Nootropics: Boost Your Brainpower, Increase Your Memory, IQ, Happiness Level, Cure Anxiety and More*, by the appropriately named William James (an Australian author living in the early twenty-first century, not the American philosopher from a hundred years earlier). Americans annually spend billions of dollars on health-related mindfulness practices.[4] Web sites proliferate that offer happiness for consumption, in the form of products, ideas, and yardsticks. www.Successories.com offers a full range of products—including posters, pens, mugs—that seek to motivate people to be positive. www.extrahappiness.com boasts the "Best B vitamins to boost mood, brain power and happiness." www.abundance-and-happiness.com promises that "Mind Power" will help you explore and discover "The Infinite and Creative Power of the Human Mind." You can join www.HappinessClub.com and then "Be Happy right now and for every moment to come for the rest of your life." Over 1½ million people have logged on to a web site Martin Seligman developed, www.authentichappiness.sas.upenn.edu, and taken tests to "measure character strengths and different aspects of happiness and well-being."[5] Experts offer ways of monetizing the happiness value of social media platforms such as Twitter and Facebook.[6] Reflecting this zeitgeist, in 2014 Pharrell Williams's ebullient popular tune "Happy" ("Clap along if you feel like happiness is the truth") topped Billboard's chart. "There are happiness institutes, camps, clubs, classes, cruises, workshops, and retreats," a skeptical British observer noted in 2006. "Universities are adding courses in Happiness Studies," he continued. "Fast-growing professions include happiness counselling, happiness coaching, 'life-lift' coaching, 'joyology' and happiness science. Personal happiness is big business and everyone is selling it. Being positive is mandatory, even with the planet in meltdown."[7] Many academic positive psychologists may have recoiled at some of the excesses of promotional happiology, seen vividly in Oprah enterprises and in the prosperity gospel of televangelists, even though as was true with how-to books, prominent figures in the field did not shy away from promotional efforts that some might question as excessive.

TED TALKS

With their powerful visuals, compelling stories, and immense reach, TED talks are the first of a series of happiness enterprises that deserve focused attention. They occupy a key, innovative position in public life that augments the flourishing of positive psychology and happiness studies. They sprang initially from the imagination of Richard Saul Wurman, who trained as an architect and whose work I first encountered when I used his graphically innovative ACCESS city guidebooks, which revealed how imaginatively he understood the relationships between **T**echnology, **E**ducation, and **D**esign. He launched what would become TED talks in 1984 with an initial conference in Monterey, California, that was sufficiently unsuccessful in financial terms that the second one did not take place until 1990. In 2000 the new media entrepreneur Chris Anderson purchased the franchise from Wurman. A year later Anderson turned the enterprise into a non-profit foundation, with attendance remaining by invitation or application. Over time these conferences, and the talks they feature, took hold and entered the problematic formulaic zone. The TED project really took off beginning in 2006 when TED talks, held at a conference center to which entrance required a substantial fee, were first streamed free online. That year the talks attracted 2 million views, a number that grew to 200 million in 2009 to more than a billion by 2012. Over time TED became an empire—in addition to the original conference came a variety of venues, including e-books, TED Global and more independent, satellite TEDx conferences in well over 100 nations.[8]

A place where new technologies made initial or early appearances, a TED conference, remarked a *New Yorker* writer, has "become in recent years a showroom for the intellectual style of the digital age . . . . it is today home to one of the fastest-growing, best-educated, and wealthiest creative communities in America." Like the World Economic Forum at Davos, Sundance Film Festival, or the meetings convened by the Clinton Global Initiative, TED conferences are among a handful of new elite public spaces created since the early 1970s. Giving a talk at TED, the technology journalist Steven Levy has written, is "a rite of passage for an Internet-age intellectual." Yet if TED conferences are public spaces where members of new elites meet as they weave together economic, cultural, and social capital, TED talks are something else. They are the modern-day equivalent of speeches at nineteenth-century lyceums and town commons—democratic areas, open to anyone who has access to broadband and a computer, where a knowledgeable and/or aspiring public can gain access to ideas that are at once familiar and transformative.[9]

TED talks follow a well-honed pattern. Presenters audition and, once approved, they refine their talks through rehearsals and responses from friends and strangers on social media. They follow well-tested dramatic forms: as a knowledgeable observer stated, "an opening of direct address, a narrative of personal stake, a research summary, a précis of potential applications, a revelation to drive it home, and an ending that says, Go forth and help humanity" form their basic arcs. Though some are longer and some shorter, the goal is an eighteen-minute presentation, carefully but often lightly edited. Multiple cameras film them, heightening the sense of dramatic theater they offer. The most successful among them rely on a well-framed story filled with anecdotes and a compelling message. Delivery is as important as content. A talk may be memorized but is most effective if it appears to be delivered extemporaneously, passionately, and authentically. Stage presence matters: establishing eye contact with a handful of people in the audience; using smiles and hand gestures to sustain connections; and presenting PowerPoints that avoid words the speaker will offer and rely solely on visuals.[10]

Google turns up almost three score TED talks on happiness, but the most popular one is "The Surprising Science of Happiness" by Harvard psychologist Dan Gilbert, filmed in February 2004 and viewed over 12 million times since. Dressed informally—plain black T-shirt, crumpled light grey cotton pants, and casual shoes—Gilbert strode back and forth across the stage, speaking in colloquial language, energetically conveying his findings, and unobtrusively using a small hand-held clicker to shift from one visual image to another. He began with an attention-grabbing statement: "When you have 21 minutes to speak, 2 million years seems like a really long time." He then went on to discuss the importance of evolution and the development of the brain, "the almost three-pound meatloaf that everybody here has between their ears." He quickly turned to the neuroscience behind his talk, discussing how brains were "experience simulators" that allowed humans, unlike any other species, to "have experiences in their heads before they try them out in real life." This enabled them, he remarked, using a dramatic and easily understood example, to know that they would not enjoy Ben and Jerry's liver-and-onion ice cream. Having experience simulators, he insisted, was "up there with opposable thumbs and standing upright and language as one of the things that got our species out of the trees and into the shopping mall."

Next came examples—backed up by the study of lottery winners and paraplegics, of "impact bias"—of how poor we are at judging the emotional influence of future events. To drive home his point that dramatic, often traumatic events usually and over the long term have little impact on us, he emphasized that happiness is not something we find but that people can synthesize by relying on a "psychological immune system," governed by "largely non-conscious cognitive processes, that help them change their views of the world, so that they can feel better about the worlds in which they find themselves." Using stories that surprised and evoked laughter, he insisted that we incorrectly think natural happiness, getting what we desire, is better than synthetic happiness, "what we make when we don't get what we wanted." Americans, he noted, believed natural happiness was superior, because "what kind of economic engine would keep churning if we believed that not getting what we want could make us just as happy as getting it?" After all, he noted as he drove home his point, "a shopping mall full of Zen monks is not going to be particularly profitable, because they don't want stuff enough."

Gilbert then shifted to a series of experiments that illustrated how people synthesized happiness when they expressed satisfaction with the choices they made. These studies showed that freedom, "the ability to make up your mind and change your mind," was "the friend of natural happiness." Maximizing choices from "among all those delicious futures" was "the enemy of synthetic happiness."

At the end of his talk, Gilbert brought together his consideration of neuroscience and experiments to underscore that we can best achieve happiness if we understand how complicated the relationships actually are between desire, expectations, and actual experience. It is risky, he noted, if "preferences drive us too hard and too fast" and we overrate one future over another. Unbounded ambition "leads us to lie, to cheat, to steal, to hurt others, to sacrifice things of real value." In contrast, "when our ambition is bounded, it leads us to work joyfully." He ended his talk with this lesson: "our longings and our worries are both to some degree overblown, because we have within us the capacity to manufacture the very commodity we are constantly chasing when we choose experience." What the science of happiness thus revealed is that although we can manufacture happiness, the limits on our predicting how we will feel when reality takes over should make us cautious about what we plan for and what we desire. Perhaps our experiences in shopping centers, to which he referred twice in the talk, did not usually measure up to our expectations. Put another way, as he made clear in the advertisements he did for widely viewed television advertisements for Prudential Financial, perhaps saving prudentially was more important than spending recklessly. Gilbert's TED talk was just one example of how new media has helped enhance the connection between business and happiness.[11]

HAPPY CORPORATE LIFE

Shawn Achor, an influential happiness consultant to corporations, appears in one of the twenty most popular TED talks, "The Happy Secret to Better Work," first shown in May 2011 and which since has since garnered over 12 million views.[12] Then in 2012, PBS aired "The Happiness Advantage with Shawn Achor." He also offered his inspiring applications of positive psychology to the world of work in two books—*The Happiness Advantage: The Seven Principles that Fuel Success and Performance at Work* (2010) and *Before Happiness: 5 Actionable Strategies to Create a Positive Path to Success* (2013).[13] He came to these tasks with proper bona fides: a BA from Harvard, followed by an MA in Christian and Buddhist Ethics from Harvard Divinity School, a teaching assistant in Tal Ben-Shahar's popular happiness course, founder of consulting companies Aspirant and GoodThinkInc that helped organizations apply happiness scholarship. GoodThinkInc.com provides, the web site promises, "research services to companies in order to raise employee engagement and success by offering Metrics for evaluating engagement and employee performance" and "identifying return on investment for different interventions and training programs." With his wife, Michelle Gielan, Achor also founded the Institute for Applied Positive Research, whose mission is to "bridge the gap between cutting-edge research in the field of positive psychology and best practices within corporate and community cultures around the world." Traveling to more than fifty countries, Achor has served as a consultant for many Fortune 500 corporations. Although many of the companies he and his wife have worked with were high-tech ones, they also consulted for Walmart. At a time when a higher minimum wage and better benefits might have helped, they embarked, Shawn Achor wrote, "on an ambitious initiative aimed at raising the happiness levels of their 1.5 million associates who are struggling to make ends meet in face of complicated family and educational issues."[14]

Arguing that happiness led to success, rather than the other way around, Achor advised readers and clients on how positivity would enhance competitiveness and achievement. Backed by research in positive psychology and neuroscience, he asserted that the Happiness Advantage, aka the "competitive edge . . . makes us more motivated, efficient, resilient, creative, and productive, which drives performance upward." In the aftermath of the Great Recession, when "employees at all levels had found their legs yanked out by forces beyond their control," he deployed a range of positive psychology approaches, packaged in the vernacular, that promised a better day: relying on posttraumatic growth by using a crisis as a catalyst for productive change, overcoming learned helplessness, and employing cognitive behavioral therapy to change one's explanatory style. His "5 Actionable Strategies to Create a Positive Path to Success" promised uplift, engagement, and achievement. Choosing *the most valuable reality* would lead "to positive growth." Mapping *your meaning markers* set you on "the best route to accomplishing your goals." Canceling *the noise* meant boosting "the signal that points to greater opportunities, possibilities, and resources." Creating *positive inception* made it possible "to amplify the effects of a positive mindset by transferring your positive reality to others." In other words, consonant with both positive psychology and neoliberalism, in face of stagnant incomes and job losses due to downsizing, take advantage of adversity by developing positive goals, increasing engagement, and achieving greater success. As the copy on the back on Achor's book *Before Happiness* stated, "The ability to create a reality in which all things are possible is one of the greatest precursors of success, performance and even happiness," to say nothing of the presumptive privilege of being able to assume this.[15]

Achor's work only begins to encompass the extensive interventions of happiness studies and positive psychology into the corporate world, part of the explosion of applications generated beginning in the 1990s that was an essential part of the process of commodifying and packaging happiness. Consultants advise executives to empower employees by fostering confidence and creativity, promoting a variety of tasks, building on strengths, making flow more possible, and emphasizing team building. Marketing experts use neuroimaging and neuro-marketing, along with big data, to better understand and influence consumers' behavior. In 2010 Tony Hsieh, who sold his Internet company to Microsoft for $256 million and then joined Zappos, where he became CEO, offered *Delivering Happiness: A Path to Profits, Passion, and Purpose* (2010). In 2007 he had developed an interest in positive psychology, and one day it hit him, delivering shoes was "*about delivering happiness to the world.*" So in 2009 Zappos changed its mission to "Delivering Happiness" and offered a Science of Happiness class to employees.[16]

Many corporations have embraced the strategies of positive psychology. Motivational speakers cheer on executives, managers, and workers, in the workplace or at retreats, while coffee mugs and posters remind them to keep their minds on positivity. Similarly, corporations employ Chief Fun Officers, Chief Happiness Officers, Jolly Good Fellows, or Happiness Engineers to enhance their employees' sense of well-being. Major corporations include in their mission statements a commitment to make the world a better place, a commitment that dovetails with the boom in the business of happiness. They hire consultants to develop a Gross Happiness Index for a workplace. At the World Economic Forum in Davos in 2014, meditation was prominently promoted for economic elites, thanks in part to appearances by Matthieu Ricard and Richard J. Davidson. Attendees were given a gadget that attached to their bodies and sent messages to their smartphones to assess their well-being. Happiness, wrote one critic, "as a measurable, visible, improvable entity," had "penetrated the citadel of global economic management," and if Davos was a guide, capitalism now depended "on our ability to combat stress, misery and illness, and put relaxation, happiness and wellness in their place."[17]

If consulting firms are one vehicle by which positive psychology enters the corporate world, business schools are another—and here the Center for Positive Organizations at the University of Michigan's Ross School of Business is pre-eminent. Given how disengaged many employees are, the Center offers "a valuable opportunity for organizations to increase purpose, passion, performance—and profit—through positive business practices that energize and engage workers." The Center promises to apply "Positive Organizational Scholarship" in order to energize and transform organizations and their leaders. "The study and perspective of Positive Organizational Scholarship," leaders of the Center insist, "is committed to revealing and nurturing the highest level of human potential."

Organizational leaders could do this by "bringing empathy, compassion, and energy into the workplace," in the process creating "a generative business setting" and acting "as a catalyst in the discovery of human potential," reminiscent of what Abraham Maslow had also done in his work with corporations. In "Restoring Hope During Trying Times," Ross School of Business professor Gretchen M. Spreitzer suggested what this might mean in practice, especially "in the context of survivor responses to organizational downsizing." She encouraged "survivors" to overcome fear and respond proactively and constructively as they countered the "Walking Wounded" and the "Carping Critics." Along similar lines, in "The Michigan Model of Leadership," four scholars in 2013 wrote on "Developing Adaptive Leaders for Turbulent Times," which made it possible for leaders "who utilize the process of Mindful Engagement" to have a positive impact on the world by relying on "empathy, drive, integrity, and courage—across society and throughout organizational hierarchies—whose core purpose is to make a positive difference in the lives of others."[18]

Positive interventions into American corporate life drew heavily on positive psychology during "turbulent" and "trying times," when downsizing—to say nothing of income stagnation, family disruption, weakened labor unions, and increasing disparities in wealth and income—became common. These efforts relied on the language of human potential, empathy, courage, compassion, and energy as markers of positivity. Given their penchant for accenting the positive, it should come as no surprise that positive psychologists focused remarkably little in their scholarship on the consequences for happiness of the 2008 worldwide economic crisis. The *Journal of Positive Psychology* paid almost no attention to the 2008 economic crisis and its consequences for well-being; characteristically given its greater interest in public policy, the *Journal of Happiness Studies* devoted most of an issue to this topic.[19]

The University of Michigan Center's vision expressed in *Positive Organizational Scholarship* (2003) both critiqued the neoliberal economy and suggested how to counter its harshest aspects—without overturning its most sacred principles of free markets and pursuit of profits.[20] Its leading figures remarked that positive psychology revealed how it was possible to overcome "difficult, threatening, ambiguous, and turbulent conditions," such as downsizing, by drawing on forces such as "resilience, transcendence, meaningfulness, cascading vitality, virtuousness, callings, courageous principles action," and "social networks."[21]

OPRAH

Oprah Winfrey "is a woman on a mission," remarked an observer writing in *Christian Century*, and at the center of that mission was "the message: Make yourself happy." Especially after she mirrored a similar turn in positive psychology by transforming the focus of her TV shows from talking about people's problems to emphasizing their opportunities for achieving happiness, Oprah has been America's most influential promoter of positivity and happiness. Her power and prominence are legendary. Indeed, her own awakening through and to personal development from a life marked early on by poverty and sexual molestation has both led and mirrored the broader American turn toward positivity.[22]

The Oprah Winfrey Show, which aired from 1986 to 2011, initially to almost 50 million viewers in America and eventually to audiences in over 100 nations, had an enormous following. Oprah has her own cable network and on Sirius her own radio show. *O, The Oprah Magazine,* commands the attention of more than 2.5 million readers. Her book club wielded immense power, transforming the lives of authors and readers alike. Her web site, www.oprah.com, complete with message boards, support groups, and chat rooms, receives 20,000 emails daily and attracts more than 6 million users a month. Worth more than $3 billion and able to reach those with considerable wealth and modest resources alike, she promotes social change and liberal causes by her philanthropy and inspiration.

Oprah's connections to happiness generally and mainstream positive psychology specifically are extensive. She has promoted meditation. Psychologists used a moment from the Oprah Winfrey Show in experiments that revealed that watching an inspirational clip causes subjects to extend help to others. She hosted in 2009 "Oprah on Location: The Happiest People on Earth," a series of interviews she did in Denmark that provided evidence of what scientists had discovered—that environmentalism, alternatives to traditional marriages, and an ample social safety net really did enhance subjective well-being.

Oprah's enterprises draw on the work of a broad array of public figures—from the spiritual to the scientific—who offer guidance on positivity.[23] She promoted Rhonda Byrne's 2006 self-help book *The Secret,* whose pseudoscientific claims academic positive psychologists would reject even as they were aware of yet another example of the spread of key elements of their field into popular culture. Oprah's media empire features the work of social worker Brenée Brown and spiritualist Eckhart Tolle, whose books have incorporated some of the findings of positive psychologists. Soon after the publication of Ed Diener and Robert Biswas-Diener's *Happiness: Unlocking the Mysteries of Psychological Wealth* in 2008, www.Oprah.com featured an interview with the father/son duo by Liz Brody, titled "Which Way to Happy? Two Authors Weigh In." Here they responded to her questions in careful, sober terms, countering readers' expectations, remarking that rather than achieving happiness by following one set of beliefs or practices, it was best to think of doing so by means of a long-term journey toward achieving goals. And then in January 2010 the web site featured an essay by Biswas-Diener, "The 11th Hour: How Working Under Pressure Can Be a Strength." Distinguishing between procrastinators and incubators and preferring the less pejorative term, he praised "bright, creative people with an amazing gift to work hard under pressure" who could be "very dependable in work situations that require last-minute changes or tight deadlines."[24]

Oprah's enterprises have featured other members of the Mount Rushmore five. *O, The Oprah Magazine* offered an interview with Barbara Fredrickson soon after she published *Love 2.0* in 2013. Drawing on recent findings in neuroscience, Fredrickson talked about how love—not romance

but the common everyday social contacts even with strangers who provided what she termed "micromoments" of connections—improved a
person's health. In "How to Be an Optimist," a writer for Oprah's magazine presented Seligman's take on optimism, as what Seligman called "the
skeleton of hope," even as he cautioned against versions that were blind
to reality. The magazine's 2014 "The Ohm of Happiness" reported Sonja
Lyubomirsky's finding that happier people responded to the world "in
relatively more positive and more adaptive ways." An earlier issue of the
magazine, drawing on the work of Mihaly Csikszentmihalyi, reported that
men found it easier to find pleasure in flow because women tended to juggle
multiple tasks simultaneously.[25]

Oprah's career and appeal reverberated with issues of gender, race,
American self-help and therapeutic traditions, and neoliberalism. In the
mid-1990s, several years before Seligman's announcement of his turn from
negative to positive, Oprah reconfigured her show to shift its focus from
problems like child abuse and drug addiction to hopeful opportunities
built on positive thinking. As she remarked in the opening of the season
that began in September 1998, coincidentally but importantly around the
same time as Seligman's APA presidential address, "I am more dedicated
than ever to try to do television that inspires us to make positive changes in
our lives."[26] Her messages were especially important, as one observer put it,
to "women in the middle: middle-class, middle-American and, like Oprah,
middle-aged. They are people caught in the middle of families, interpersonal conflicts, too many good intentions, and an overlong to-do list. These
are women trying to manage busy lives and households, address personal
and social concerns, and maybe also lose some weight." Oprah offered a
brand of feminism focused not on transforming institutions but on depo-
liticized empowerment that would transform the self. An African American
woman deeply committed to the uplift of her people, Oprah promised her
broader audience the transcendence of race through an emphasis not on
institutional racism but on personal responsibility. Contradicting what
she had discovered in Denmark, her typical offerings dovetailed with
neoliberalism—with an emphasis on self-help, individual empowerment
and responsibility, and the enterprising self. Her very being reaffirmed the
power of the American dream in troubled economic times.[27]

Nothing summed up Oprah's advocacy of happiness and positivity better
than Louisa Jewell's 2011 essay about the last episode of *The Oprah Winfrey
Show*. A graduate of Penn's Master of Applied Positive Psychology program,
Jewell announced herself as "president of Positive Matters and a consultant,
facilitator and speaker who works with organizations around the world
to develop positive leaders and nurture productive teams." For twenty
years, she reported, watching the television show had become "a positive

intervention," though ever since she read about Barbara Fredrickson's positivity ratio, in order to avoid "unnecessary negative emotions," she stopped viewing shows that emphasized tragedies. "When Oprah wanted to fill you with positive emotions she was the master," so "day after day I sat in awe as she filled my bucket" bringing to life "many lessons taught by positive psychologists around the world."

Jewell reported that on this, her final show, Oprah offered her most important lessons. Every individual had the power to change her life and learn that she was not alone, something exemplified by Oprah's own life and the lives of people she featured on her show. Referring to the work of scholars such as Jane Dutton and Barbara Fredrickson, Jewell underscored Oprah's message that happiness was contagious. Oprah called on everyone to develop a calling, with Jewell pointing to the work of Yale psychologist Amy Wrzesniewski on how members of custodial staffs derived satisfaction from their work in a hospital.

Seligman's research on helplessness reverberated with Oprah's remark that "There is a difference between thinking you deserve to be happy and knowing you are worthy of happiness." "Realistic optimism and a strong belief in ourselves," Jewell remarked, underscoring the match between what Oprah said and what positive psychologists found, "can have a profound impact on our lives." Finally, Oprah ended her show by emphasizing gratitude. Drawing on the work of Jonathan Haidt, Jewell mentioned that Oprah stressed that giving was more important than receiving—as she pointed to Oprah's giving everyone in the audience a trip to Australia and remembered a show when everyone in the audience brought a pair of pajamas to donate to children in homeless shelters. "Robert Emmons demonstrated the power of gratitude through his research," Jewell noted as she unintentionally reminded us that what positive psychologists often did was confirm well-worn and obvious precepts, "and Oprah brought it to the masses by encouraging people to keep a daily gratitude journal. She didn't need a PhD to know the power of appreciation." Finally, Jewell applauded how Oprah ended the show. After embracing several staff members as she passed them in a long narrow hallway, with "her high heels in her hand, she picks up her dog Sadie, gives her a big hug, and walks off into the distance. Her show ends with this final act of love."[28]

HAPPY TELEVISION EVANGELISTS

The timing of the *The Oprah Winfrey Show*, at least in the Chicago area, an observer remarked, "has a whiff of morning service. It is an hour-long ritual each weekday at 9 A.M., adding up to a lot more pulpit time per week than the average pastor enjoys, and in front of a lot bigger congregation." Competing with Oprah for the public's attention in promoting positivity were Protestant ministers who use television shows to highlight a prosperity gospel. In important ways these religious leaders were successors of earlier New Thought movements, which emphasized that true human selfhood is Divine, that sickness is in the mind, and that healing can be found in positive thinking. These preachers wrote bestselling books, appeared on television and in mega-churches, in the process offering a vision of God-given health and wealth. Bishop T. D. Jakes and Joel Osteen are among the most prominent, the former African American and the latter white. Their ministries reflect the even more widespread turn among American Christians away from sin and suffering and toward an optimistic faith that emphasizes the possibilities of success and well-being.[29]

On the *Steve Harvey Show* in April 2015 Jakes offered "5 Simple Steps to Be Happy." Reflecting positive psychology's insistence that personal responsibility was more important than possessions, he began telling audience members that rather than believing a big house would make you happy, you had to "own your own happiness." Then, reflecting the advice of cognitive behavioral therapists, he called on people to "challenge your own story" rather than beating "yourself to death" with a narrative that worked imperfectly. Just as positive psychologists insisted on focusing on the present, Jakes recommended enjoying "the journey and not the destination." Although he said that "nature teaches us there is no fruit without relationships," he might as well have remarked that positive psychologists offered the same advice, in their case based on scientific findings. Finally, much as scholarship had done, he insisted on the balance between work and play. In his sermonic preaching he typically talked of God's power and biblical wisdom, but on this particular program, before an audience with more whites than blacks, his language was mostly secular even though his rhetorical style drew on African American spiritual traditions.[30]

Whereas Jakes's voice was booming and his manner exuberant, Rev. Joel Osteen conveyed a sense of well-being by his ever-present smile, self-deprecating humor, and mild, reassuring manner. In his January 2015 sermon "Happiness in Your Life" delivered in a cavernous auditorium to a mostly white audience, Osteen emphasized the importance of laughter. "Happiness is always a choice," he notably remarked elsewhere. "You can't wait for circumstances to get better. . . . So look for ways to be happy every day." In the first and more extensive part of his sermon, he spoke in mostly secular terms. As if summarizing the findings of positive psychologists and neuroscientists, he discussed how experts emphasized the benefits of laughter: it lowered blood pressure, stimulated the immune system, released endorphins, and increased brain functioning. All of this helped people solve problems, enhanced social interaction by bringing down the barriers between people, and made people more creative. Then he shifted the basis of authority for happiness from science to God and the Bible. Quoting John 8:21, he intoned "He will fill your mouth with laughter and your lips with shouts of joy." When we laugh, he insisted, we release the healing power God has placed in us.[31]

In his number one bestseller *Your Best Life Now: 7 Steps to Living at Your Full Potential* (2004), Osteen offered his gospel of happiness and prosperity, one much more exuberantly positive than what most academic psychologists articulated. He told a story that illustrated an issue surrounding the relation between the spiritual and material. Following in a long line of ministers who preached the power of positive thinking, he advised his readers to develop a positive self-image, generate a prosperous outlook, raise their expectations, and dream big dreams to summon victory, greatness, and prosperity. Most of his examples combined success at work, the ability to garner a higher standard of living, and the receipt of God's gift of preferential treatment. He also made clear that he was directing his advice at an audience struggling to achieve and gladly accept the fruits of social mobility, something that reverberated in the narrative of his own life. Even his emphasis on the importance of giving was linked to a promise of prosperity. "If you want Him to pour out his blessings and favor in your life, then you're going to have to get your mind off yourself." Indeed, though he backed his sermon-like chapters with biblical references, Heaven seemed virtually non-existent in his soothing and prosperous world. Many evangelicals would find his positions beyond the pale. He seems too worldly, optimistic—paying insufficient attention to God's power and the temporary, sinful nature of people's life on earth.[32]

POSITIVE PSYCHOLOGY, NEW MEDIA, AND THE ENHANCEMENT OF HAPPINESS

Among the forces that amplified the power and spread of positive psychology (and simplified or exaggerated its findings) were new media—blogs, apps, and web sites among them. Inherent in both phenomena, with one reinforcing the other, was the prevalence of cheerful expressions of positivity. The coincidental timing could not have been more perfect. The term "World Wide Web" was first coined in early 1990s, and the first blogs appeared in 1994. The first iPhone came out in 2007, with apps appearing very soon afterward. By 2015, more than 1.5 million apps and blogs were available. As the media and communications scholar Henry Jenkins has written, content flows "across multiple media platforms," "multiple media industries" cooperate, and active media consumers migrate as they "go almost anywhere in search of" desired experiences that are easy to exchange and collaborate around. What new technologies like Fitbit and apps such as Unstuck did for self-improvement more generally, other innovations did to help transform the ways of achieving happiness. Positive psychology and happiness studies would have existed in any case, but new technologies changed the tone and dynamics of these fields and catalyzed the process of amplification by exploding the niches scholars formerly operated in. This made the ideas of positive psychology researchers more accessible and easier to circulate; their consumption more interactive and participatory. These technologies made it possible for conversations to take place and for ideas to spread, through networks of people who had a good deal in common but might not have interacted otherwise. Old media is top-down, often driven by powerful elites; new media to a considerable extent is bottom-up, capable of enabling a wider range of people to enter the fray and lead.[33]

Among the most popular happiness blogs are Gretchen Rubin's "Happiness Project" and Sonja Lyubomirsky's "How of Happiness," but Evelyn Lim's "Abundance Tapestry" topped the list that Google turned up. Lim offers two kinds of consulting—one on self-love and another on money and wealth, references to resources, and an online store selling books and downloadable programs. A wife and mother from Singapore who left a highly compensated job in the corporate world to embark on a more independent and entrepreneurial path, Lim promotes herself as "an Abundance Alchemy Coach" whose vision is "to turn dreams into reality through self-awareness, inspiring others to do the same," through her training as a Certified Emotional Freedom Technique Practitioner, an Intuitive Consultant, and a Vision Board Counselor—newly minted, ingenious, and slippery terms.[34]

Apps also proliferate. In 2015, Cat Johnson used a web site to offer a list of her favorite happiness ones. "Since smartphones quicken the pace of life and work," she remarked, "it only seems fair that they should also help us recover from all that quickening—give us a way to wind down and brighten our moods, right? While no app can compare to time with loved ones, nature, meditation, and exercise," she insisted, "there are plenty that promise to boost our happiness, calm us, and make us more grateful." Topping her list of apps promoting mindfulness, calm, better sleep, and improved relationships was the "Gratitude Journal," available for $1.99. Writing down five things you are grateful every day, its web site promised, would "change your life forever." Seligman and others had touted the benefits of expressing gratitude and but this journalist went farther. A "sweet way to stay focused on the good things in life," the app amplified the journal's power by letting "you look back on all the other things that have sparked feelings of gratitude," as well as making it possible for you to "add photos, tag Facebook friends, geotag your entries, and share what you're grateful for with loved ones."[35]

Web sites offered a comprehensive range of happy possibilities, reinforcing the power of positivity as a cultural movement. The web site www.actionforhappiness.org bills itself as a movement dedicated to "build a happier and more caring world," in which "people care less about what they can get just for themselves and more about the happiness of others." You can subscribe to www.positivepsychologynews.org to locate a coach, a book, or an article. Through www.gretchenrubin.com, the author of *The Happiness Project* extends the range of her bestselling book by offering access to podcasts, newsletters, tips, daily quotes, and quizzes, as well as information on her book tours, how to launch a habits group, or how to engage in a 21-day project. The site www.happify.com™ presents "Cutting-edge science-based activities and games to overcome negative thoughts, anxiety, and everyday stress." Logging on to "Start My Journey" takes you to a statement that asserts that "Happiness is a complex state of mind" and offers skills that take only minutes a day to learn, yet "can quietly but profoundly change the way you see the world." *Live Happy Magazine*, launched in October 2013, promises "90 Days to a Happier You" and "How to Find Your Happiness Trigger." Developed at Penn by Martin Seligman and his colleagues, www.authentichappiness.sas.upenn.edu offers one of the most serious and comprehensive sites, providing visible evidence of how scholars took advantage of the opportunities the new media offered. In six languages, it provides access to over twenty questionnaires, profiles of leading figures in the field of positive psychology, news of upcoming conferences, and access to information on materials in multiple media. In a mission statement honed over the years, it describes positive psychology as being "founded on the belief that people want to lead meaningful and fulfilling lives, to cultivate what is best within themselves, and to enhance their experiences of work and play," and as "the scientific study of the strengths and virtues that enable individuals and communities to thrive."

Launched in 2013 with venture capitalist support, and touted by major news outlets, www.happier.com relies on software to build a social network dedicated to promoting happiness. "We created Happier with one mission in mind," the site announces, "To help you find more moments of joy, kindness, and meaning in your everyday life." "Inspired by scientific research," its products reveal how "gratitude, mindfulness, and staying connected to people you care about create the foundation for a happier and healthier life." Hundreds of thousands have used its offerings—including Nutrition for Your Soul™, coaching programs, smartphone apps, and short-term courses—all designed to "inspire you to make your own well-being a priority and offer simple and enjoyable ways to help you improve it."

An attractively designed web site, www.happpier.com has many windows and doors. The banner of "Celebrate the Good Around You" leads to "Supportive Community and Awesome Courses"; "15 affordable luxuries when you need a pick me up"; "3 things you should do to avoid dreading Sunday evening"; "5 interior design tips to make you feel more awesome at home"; "9 photos that will make you ridiculously happy right now"; and "10 positive quotes you'll want to share with your bestie." Clicking on "Science" leads you to the usual suspects, with references to the studies from which the happiness recommendations spring: express gratitude; "surround yourself with happier people"; rather than spending money on material goods, do so on experiences; perform acts of kindness for others; and increase the level of your social interaction. Under "Work and Money," you can learn whether you have a terrible boss, how to write a letter you will never send, and not take rude comments personally. You can learn how to allocate money more wisely by spending free time with a friend or asking a salesperson for a discount. All these suggestions, and others that appear so commonly in both scholarly investigations and popular advice literature, seem so obvious as to suggest that they serve the cultural function of reassuring advice in a world many experienced as out of control.

NEW MEDIA AND CULTURAL CHANGE

We are familiar with the role of new media in social movements such as the Arab Spring, but less explored are their impact on cultural movements.[36] A phenomenon like positive psychology extends its reach well beyond the academy by multiple means that connect people who rarely encounter each other in person, let alone at street protests or at an organizing meeting. To the extent that new media promote connectivity, participation, social relationships, denser social networks, helpfulness, sharing, and gratitude, then they have contributed considerably both to the power and spread of positive psychology as a cultural movement and to people's sense of well-being.[37] Moreover, new media individualizes experiences, promotes ideas of personal self-help, fosters superficial and opportunistic relationships, and doubtlessly enhances the power of neoliberalism.[38]

My own preliminary exploration of a prominent listserv and Facebook reveals the power and the limitations of new media.[39] Reading of two years of postings on Friends of Positive Psychology, one of the most important listservs in the field, provides one way of assessing the nature of the impact of new media. People relatively new to the field write in asking for leads that might answer questions that interest them. Many of the entries come from a handful of correspondents, people who act unofficially as moderators or informants. Many of the postings reaffirm widely agreed-upon findings—for example, that character strengths matter; that there is a correlation if not causation between subjective well-being and health; or that there are limits to how more money can enhance happiness. Postings pay special attention to acknowledging the field's importance in the media. Rarely, if ever, is notice taken, let alone engagement offered, of critics of positive psychology who work outside the boundaries of the field—such as Barbara Ehrenreich, William Davies, or Sam Binkley. With relative infrequency, disagreements do erupt. For example, in February 2016, Dr. Lynn Johnson, who founded the Brief Therapy Center in 1984 and later developed the site and program "Real Thriving," sparked a heated discussion about whether progressive taxation, redistribution of wealth, and the pursuit of social justice more generally inevitably involved acts of violence or totalitarianism. Were Liberty and Equality compatible, discussants asked. A month later, a spirited debate emerged over the relationship between positive psychology and religion/spirituality, especially fundamentalism and meditation, both secular and Buddhist.

On Facebook, the relationship between positive psychology and new media is more complicated, although cause and effect between the two forces is far from clear. What is clear is that Facebook promotes both social connections and individualism, prominent features of millions of exchanges on this and other social media. Some sites link positivity and activism—for example, www.facebook.com/brenebrown, developed by an author of books on happiness, has raised millions of dollars for refugees in Syria and the homeless in America. However, much more prevalent is the way the use of Facebook makes possible exchanges consistent with the findings and recommendations of positive psychologists. As is true with other self-improvement arenas, frequently visited web sites offer books for sale, techniques for practice, and personal advice for the lovelorn that spread the gospel of positive psychology. Social networks that by their nature often rely on some combination of ephemeral, superficial, and virtual relationships provide opportunities for expressions of gratitude, the development of social connections and positive feelings, perhaps best exemplified by range of happy emojis. Anyone who peruses Facebook entries finds evidence of how people offer each other—be it close friends or people they probably do not know—expressions of affirmation, gratitude, congratulations, encouragement, and inspiration that reflect, even if only implicitly so, key findings of positive psychology. Moreover, Facebook itself experiments with ways of enhancing the well-being of its users through algorithms.[40]

Therapeutic interventions and coaching, another way of spreading the gospel of positive psychology, come in a variety of forms. In several instances they draw on earlier therapeutic traditions, including cognitive behavioral therapy, which, with its insistence on helping people change distorted beliefs, was one of the formative influences in shaping the new field. Carl Rogers emphasized patient-centered therapy and people's inherent tendency toward personal growth decades before Seligman's 1998 talk. In the twenty-first century, when interest grew in developing positive therapeutic approaches, attention to the application of Rogers's theories intensified. There were other variants that involved the application of positive psychology to interventions that were more fully and explicitly indebted to positive psychology, among them positive therapy or emotional fitness coaching.[41] What these approaches have in common is an emphasis on promoting personal growth and an antipathy to focusing on mental disorders—not reducing symptoms but making more positive functioning possible.[42]

Distinctions between positive therapy and positive coaching are often hard to discern or maintain. In general, positive therapy requires a greater level of training and certification, while coaching draws more on experience than formal credentials. Coaching is more future and results oriented than its counterpart; more concerned with action than how understanding leads to action; and more involved in mentoring than probing for insight. Coaches are more inclined to relate to their clients as partners than as experts. A coach helps a client not to overcome past traumas but to take advantage of present and future opportunities.[43]

Robert Biswas-Diener's 2010 *Practicing Positive Psychology Coaching: Assessment, Activities, and Strategies for Success* provides an introduction to the field and reflects both the unresolved nature of professionalization and the more resolved sense of what it means to apply positive psychology to coaching. Acknowledging that positive psychology coaching was "fairly poorly defined," he was especially dismayed by "the number of people who hang up shingles and market themselves as 'positive psychology coaches' with limited knowledge of both standard coaching techniques and the science of positive psychology." He also separated himself from happiologists, a frequently used and derogatory term that describes those popularizers who naively and excessively promote happiness. He noted that "while I would stop well short of calling these people charlatans, I do find an advertised promise of happiness to be problematic."[44] To remedy this situation, he supported efforts to standardize nomenclature, formal training, and certification.

Biswas-Diener accurately described the uneven state of training and credentialing. At the high end are graduate programs that do not focus specifically or exclusively on positive psychology coaching, such as a Master of Applied Positive Psychology at Penn, a masters in coaching at Harvard Medical School, or a masters program at the University of East London, which was the first in the world to offer a degree program that combines positive psychology and coaching. Then come a host of certificate programs and short-term seminars. A single course can cost several hundred dollars, and entire programs, which might take a year to complete, up to $5,000 or more. Most of them rely on new media, as does the practice of coaching itself—a virtual classroom, tele-classes, tele-conferences, prerecorded classrooms, DVDs, webinars, telephone or Skype conversations, and online discussions and materials. Full certification also requires various levels of supervised practice. All of them insist that their coaching relies on up-to-date, scientifically based research in the burgeoning field of positive psychology.[45]

These programs offer students a range of skills and approaches. One example will suffice. Those at Whole Being Institute, offered in several locations and online, rely on these techniques: "appreciative inquiry" that will help "clients to focus on what works in order to inspire ideas, confidence, and motivation for change"; "asking powerful questions" that will assist clients in achieving "greater understanding" and how "to make progress toward their goals"; stories that will "generate insights, narrative coherence, and goal clarity"; "empathetic listening"; and "solutions focus," which will help clients "develop paths to solutions that work." The outcome, claimed another program, was empowering "individuals to break through to new levels of performance, productivity and optimal living." Such programs, one observer noted, aim to train people to help clients gain "fast personality changes through the setting and acquisition of goals . . . explicitly concerned with the promotion of well-being and performance." By focusing on strengths, they concentrate on the positive in an attempt to improve what is right rather than fix what is wrong.[46]

If professional standards often remained unclear, the basis on which the field of positive psychology coaching rested was strong and clear. The relationship between coaches and clients relied on authentic cooperation to "look for solutions rather than explore obstacles" with the trained expert working to "show people what is possible and then wake them up to the idea that they have the personal resources to enact this change in their own lives." Ideally, what differentiated the practice from self-help schemes and from other types of coaching was its grounding in science, especially research on character strengths and on the relationship between positivity and performance. Thus what positive coaching claimed to offer was a scientifically grounded and testable focus on strengths as a way "to promote energy, effectiveness, productivity, and a sense of meaning" and on positivity as "a powerful resource for facilitating change and achieving success." Given the changes in the world of work, including the erosion of loyalty, the shift of responsibility for security from employer to employee, and the trade-off between certainty and freedom, Biswas-Diener argued, coaching based on positive psychology helped clients "craft the perfect job." Coaching, rather than focusing on the problematic past, emphasizes the possible future, relying on what one observer called "the agency and autonomy of the enterprising individual."[47]

Critics have questioned positive coaching on several grounds. One insisted that positive psychology coaching involved "manufacturing half-baked professionals" who had only brief training and then engaged in superficial, short-term practice, both of which were unregulated. In 2004 a British critic, noting that "life coaches will certainly outnumber dentists," suggested that "a disillusioned dentist might be advised to take up life-coaching, given that people seem readier to pay up to £100 an hour to talk to unqualified strangers about how to transform their lives, relationships and careers than they are to pay a trained dentist."[48]

SCHOOLS

Positive psychology has also had a tremendous impact on education, something that with its emphasis on well-being goes against the grain of the focus on standardized testing and preparation for worldly success. Developed by Seligman at Penn and by others elsewhere, with a focus on the importance of strengthening personal character, the use of positive psychology in schools has spread in the United States and abroad, at all levels but especially the pre-collegiate one. An online offering, www.strengthsquest.com, takes students through a series of exercises that enables them to identify their strengths such as competitiveness or empathy. Offered by Gallup and based on the work of Donald O. Clifton, cited by the American Psychological Association as the "grandfather of positive psychology," the program promises to help "Students, Staff, and Faculty Achieve Academic, Career, and Personal Success." Having done that, they can craft an educational present and professional future that enables them to take full advantage of the opportunities their strengths make possible. In a variety of schools, stand-alone courses or units within other courses draw on findings of positive psychology that emphasize the beneficial effect of social relations, resilience, flow, and positivity.[49]

The most intriguing examples involve infusing positive psychology into entire schools. The Penn Resiliency Program sets out to enhance students' well-being by promoting optimism, realistic thinking, assertiveness, and relaxation. With a $2.8 million grant from the Department of Education, researchers from Penn tested the application of the discipline in a rigorous experiment at Strath Haven High School by focusing on meaning, character strengths, and social relations. In Australia, the Geelong Grammar School offers its Model of Positive Education, by providing "a road map of what people want for themselves, the students and their children. Good health, frequent positive emotions, supportive relationships, a sense of purpose and meaning, and moments of complete immersion and absorption—a life where a person uses their character strengths in ways that support the self and others, and that has flourishing at the heart." Teachers use Shakespeare plays to examine character strengths and geographical comparisons to explore the relationships between well-being and culture, while coaches talk to athletes about the deployment of resilience. Turning away from asking students to repair their deficiencies, all these programs teach their students to identify and build character strengths.[50]

Ian Morris directs one of the best known education programs, the Well-Being program at Wellington College in Berkshire, England. Launched in 2006, supported by headmaster Anthony Seldon, and taught to 4th and 5th form students, the program has had remarkable success in improving students' performance on standard exams. Such results, however, are a byproduct of much broader and transformative goals. Learning how to ride the elephant, the subtitle of Morris's 2009 book that relied on an analogy Jonathan Haidt had offered, is how Morris described the goal of education: creating a harmonious relationship between the student/rider, "the conscious thinking self," and the elephant, "the vast, powerful set of forces" that the rider tries to control, "all of the myriad unnoticed processes of the brain and all of the extraordinary panoply of events which take place in the body."[51]

To do so, what worked in the school classroom were techniques such as game playing, journal writing, and sharing. The key concepts drew heavily on positive psychology: avoiding the traps of affluent society such as social comparison and running on the hedonic treadmill, pursuing true happiness, enhancing personal attachments and social relationships, fostering the emotions, identifying and building on character strengths especially resilience, relying on mindful meditation, teaching alternative explanatory styles, and experiencing flow. "Well-being should be the *primary* function of all education," Morris wrote as he advocated "finding, drawing out and building upon the strengths of individuals, and enabling them to excel." In the foreword to the book by Morris, Richard Layard, whose work as an economist has had tremendous influence on British social policy, made clear how ambitious was the agenda of those advocating the centrality of positive psychology in the education system. Young people want to be happy, Layard wrote, not selfishly but in a way that promotes flourishing. The British government had begun to acknowledge this and had "made the teaching of well-being an integral part of the national curriculum."[52]

FOUNDATIONS

Private philanthropy was crucial in launching positive psychology and giving the field the prominence and shape it came to have, though the field would have existed without such support or with it at a less generous level. Nonetheless, present at the creation of positive psychology, several private foundations were especially influential—including Atlantic Philanthropies, the Annenberg Sunnylands Trust, Mayerson (which established VIA Institute on Character and more generally played a key role in the work of Martin Seligman and Christopher Peterson on character and virtues), the Robert Wood Johnson Foundation, and one private corporation, Gallup. One organization in particular, the John Templeton Foundation, stands out; it is hard to think of another example of a private foundation that in the late twentieth and early twenty-first centuries played such a commanding, transformative role in the development of a field of inquiry.

American-born Sir John Templeton made his money in international mutual funds and then dispensed it through conservative, values-oriented philanthropies centrally interested in the relationship between science and religion. A Yale graduate and Rhodes Scholar, Templeton began as an international investor on Wall Street in 1938 and launched his first Templeton Fund in 1954. Knighted by Queen Elizabeth in 1987, he created his foundation that same year. A friend of Norman Vincent Peale in the postwar period, Templeton wanted to ground many of the minister's ideas in scientific evidence. A Presbyterian by upbringing and affiliation, Templeton was a devoted and at times idiosyncratic inquirer into the nature of a broad range of spiritual values and traditions. In 1987 he offered his philosophy of life in *The Templeton Plan: 21 Steps to Personal Success and Real Happiness*, a book whose outlook resembled what positive psychologists would later emphasize: genuine happiness, positivity, altruism and gratitude, personal character strengths and virtues, the triumph of productive thoughts over unproductive ones, the importance of social relations, and the power of faith and spirituality.[53]

Shaped by its founder's vision, the Templeton Foundation focuses much of its effort on Big Questions, especially the relationship between religion or spirituality and science. "Declaring that relatively little is known about the divine through scripture and present-day theology," the foundation's web site states that its founder "predicted that 'scientific revelations may be a gold mine for revitalizing religion in the 21st century.' To his mind, 'All of nature reveals something of the creator. And god is revealing himself more and more to human inquiry, not always through prophetic visions or scriptures but through the astonishingly productive research of modern scientists.'" If, as the site claims, Templeton was an "unorthodox" and "relentless questioner and contrarian," on one subject his mind was made up and his views orthodox. One of its core funding priorities is "Individual Freedom and Free Markets": Templeton believed prosperity was only possible when societies "recognized and established broad principles of freedom, competition, and personal responsibility . . . without economic freedom, individual freedom was fragile and vulnerable." Consequently, the foundation supports "a range of programs intended to liberate the initiative of individuals and nations and to establish the necessary conditions for the success of profit-making enterprise."[54]

The Templeton Foundation's support of positive psychology has been extensive. It has generously funded studies of character development, positive emotions, the importance of social relationships in fostering subjective well-being, and the relationships between meditation, the brain, and emotions. The list of connections between patron and recipients in the field is long. With a grant of $2.7 million, from 1996 to 2005 the foundation supported Herbert Benson's work on whether prayer helped patients undergoing coronary bypass surgery. In 2000 Barbara Fredrickson won the first Templeton Positive Psychology Prize; in *Love 2.0* she remarked that what launched her on the "path toward getting these new ideas on love from my mind into yours began when Brian McCorkle invited me to serve as Templeton Research Fellow for a series on religious and psychological well-being at the Danielson Institute at Boston University." In 2001 the foundation funded the Institute for Research on Unlimited Love at SUNY–Stony Brook. Sonja Lyubomirsky received the Templeton Positive Psychology Prize in 2002 and was later the recipient of two grants from the foundation, totaling $715,000. Templeton himself wrote the Forward to the 2002 *Handbook of Positive Psychology*. The foundation supported Mihaly Csikszentmihalyi's work on *Good Business: Leadership, Flow, and the Making of Meaning* (2003). There he remarked that the "soul is manifested in the vision of leaders . . . *by doing something of benefit to others.* Sir John Templeton expressed this value in its pithiest form: 'Those who give, get; those who try to get, don't.'" A grant of $5.6 million for Expanding the Science and Practice of Gratitude underwrote the work of Robert Emmons at University of California–Davis and the Greater Good Science Center at the University of California at Berkeley.[55]

The most extensive and formative examples of the Templeton Foundation's support of positive psychology involved the work of Seligman and his colleagues at Penn. The relationship began in 1996. The foundation had an endowment that would grow to $3.3 billion in 2013 and was located a dozen or so miles from the Penn campus. Members of the staff (at the time only five people) were asking themselves how they would fulfill their founder's mission. The key member was Arthur Schwartz, Vice President in charge of Character Development Programs beginning in 1995, who had earned his doctorate at Harvard's Graduate School of Education that year, with a dissertation titled "A Philosophical Inquiry into the Structure and Function of the Moral Ideals Concept: Implications for Character Education Strategies During Adolescence." Schwartz contacted Seligman, who had recently published two books on optimism, and together they developed a conference on the relationship between science and hope. Seligman's outlook on positive psychology, remarked the author of the preface to the book that published the symposium's papers, "is consonant with Sir John Templeton's vision of a science that explores the virtues that enhance life."[56] Among the 100 people in attendance on February 10, 1998, were members of the foundation's board of trustees and advisory board. Templeton came to dinner and listened to Seligman give the keynote address. After the talk Templeton raised his hand and Seligman called on him. This is a wonderful set of issues, he remarked before asking how the foundation could help place hope on a scientific footing.[57]

The rest is history. When he delivered the APA presidential address, Seligman announced the creation of the Templeton Positive Psychology Prize. The foundation, as well as the Atlantic Philanthropies, provided substantial funding for the meetings at Akumal and the networks of scholars, senior and junior, that Seligman and his colleagues built. In 2000 the Templeton Foundation Press published the results of the symposium: *The Science of Optimism and Hope: Research Essays in Honor of Martin E. P. Seligman*. From 2001 to 2007, the foundation provided $2.2 million to help establish the Positive Psychology Center at Penn. As principal investigator, Seligman arranged for the involvement of a who's who in the field, broadly conceived and notable for its inclusion of social scientists such as Richard Easterlin, Robert Frank, and Robert Putman. From 2005 to 2010, the foundation granted the Penn Center $350,000 for research on grit. Then beginning in 2009, Seligman headed a foundation-funded, $5.8 million grant for research into the connections between positive psychology and neuroscience.

The relationships between foundations and scholars is complicated, symbiotic but not fully reciprocal, having for scholars a strong but less than binding sense of expectations.[58] For several reasons, this mutually beneficial situation was unusual. It is very rare in the social and behavioral sciences for private philanthropy to play such a prominent role and for foundations to have such a significant role in the development and communication of an academic field. Csikszentminhalyi caught the dynamics in the acknowledgments to *Good Business*. He remarked that the Templeton Foundation's "generosity matched their discretion—no strings were attached to the grant," but went on to "hope that our results will not disappoint them."[59]

In 2002, Seligman described the dynamics of a time when he encountered Templeton. Templeton had invited him, his family, and some colleagues to the Lyford Cay Club in the Bahamas, the country where his host lived. "I haven't felt so out of place," Seligman whispered to his father-in-law, "since I had dinner at the Ivy Club my freshman year at Princeton." Moreover, he remarked, "the only Yacht Club I'd been in before was at Disneyland." But here he was with "liveried servants speaking in hushed Caribbean-British accents, and stunning palatial homes owned by movie stars, European royalty, and billionaires from all over the world." His host, who had given up his American citizenship, joined other residents who were "enjoying the lenient Bahamian tax structure. It is to this incongruous setting that I have come to put forward my ideas about finding meaning in life." Seligman went on to note that even with Templeton's "history of benevolence and tolerance," there was "palpable unease—even fear" in the room "that his geniality does not quite dispel. Seasoned academics," he continued, "are overly dependent on the generosity of private foundations," though he might have noted that scholars awarded a Guggenheim, ACLS, or NEH fellowship had no such relationship with a funding source. "When in the august presence of the donors themselves," he went on, "academics worry that they will slip and say something that displeases their host," thereby jeopardizing "years of careful scholarship and assiduously cultivating foundation executives." Like others scholars in the room, Seligman was "hoping for more" of "Sir John's largesse."[60]

Seligman and his colleagues benefited from the generosity of the Templeton Foundation, something that could have conflicted with their emphasis on self-reliance but not on their commitment to the importance of social networks. The foundation in turn needed scholars like Seligman and many of his colleagues who shared an interest in providing a scientific basis for positive psychology. The foundation controlled the purse strings, and it did not take a genius to figure out what they would and would not fund. Would mainstream positive psychology have focused so abundantly on values and character, often with a conservative emphasis, had no money been forthcoming from Templeton? Hard to say for sure, but in moving in the direction he did, Seligman, committed to a conservative view of the world early on, did not compromise his principles or skew his ideology, despite how sensitive he was to the types of research endeavors funding agencies supported. Positive psychology and Seligman's career would have developed under different circumstances, but Templeton's support gave the field one of its most important figures some direction and greater focus than it might otherwise have had.

Still, it is possible that under different conditions the story of how positive psychology developed would not have been quite the same—or had quite the same emphases or asked quite the same questions. We can approach these issues using a counterfactual approach. Atlantic Philanthropies, with its origins in the fortune built by the Irish-American Charles Feeney's creation of Duty Free Shoppers Group, its web site remarks, is "focused on promoting education, health, peace, reconciliation and human rights." It was Feeney's interest in ethno-political conflicts and reconciliation that enabled Seligman to announce in his presidential address initiatives to resolve conflicts on the Emerald Isle (to which Feeney had given hundreds of millions, of which the grant to Seligman was a very small part) and in South Africa.[61] It is not clear what happened in the relationship between Seligman and the Atlantic Philanthropies after the initial burst of cooperation. Had that relationship flourished, or had one with the Ford Foundation begun and developed, perhaps Seligman and his colleagues would have focused their research on public issues, and perhaps from a more left-liberal orientation than they did.

GOVERNMENT

Federal funding of positive psychology has been formative. The list of sources is extensive: the Departments of Defense and Education; the National Science Foundation; the National Institutes of Mental Health, Health, Aging, and Nursing Research; the National Cancer Institute; the National Center for Complementary and Integrative Health; and the Public Health Service. Federal funding for the field dwarfs that from private foundations. Hundreds of millions of dollars have flowed from Washington to universities around the nation for work in the field of positive psychology.

As with funding decisions of private foundations, those of government agencies involve choices among alternatives that are always significant and sometimes controversial. Federal funding for positive psychology is no exception. Choosing whether to allocate research dollars toward positive psychology, psychotropic drugs, cognitive behavioral therapy, behaviorism, or Freudianism not only rests on considerations pertaining to the best use of government funds but also brings in issues that are sometimes ideologically inflected. Ditto for how to balance funding for homeopathic versus allopathic medicine; for treating cancer with prescription drugs as opposed to positive thinking. The generous funding of positive psychology and studies of happiness meant implicitly reinforcing the fields' various ideological proclivities: their focus on personalism, their assumption that it was preferable to enhance subjective well-being by positivity rather than by changes in social structures, or their emphasis on an often conservative version of character formation. Sometimes, as was true with positive psychology's interventions into education, controversy erupted over why an emphasis on character was more important than focusing on basic skills or on traditional subjects or raising the salaries of teachers or reducing the poverty of their students. A different issue is that the insistence of federal agencies on exploring the biological foundations of behavior largely shaped programs of research and experimental designs.

Among the most controversial of positive psychology's government-funded endeavors was the Comprehensive Soldier Fitness (CSF) Program, in 2012 renamed the Comprehensive Soldier and Family Fitness Program and eventually an Army-wide effort with twenty training centers in the United States and abroad.[62] In 2008 the army's chief of staff, concerned about the psychological and financial costs of PTSD among soldiers returning from Iraq and Afghanistan, contacted Seligman in an effort to explore how his work on how character strengths might help military personnel overcome helplessness, anxiety, and depression. Right away, agreement emerged on an ambitious program of research and application. The *American Psychologist*, the flagship publication of the American Psychological Association, devoted its entire January 2011 issue to a presentation of the program, which supporters saw as professionally relevant, but detractors saw as tantamount to an infomercial. The issue opened with Chief of Staff General George W. Casey Jr.'s "A Vision for Psychological Resilience in the U.S. Army" and ended with Martin Seligman and Raymond D. Fowler's "Comprehensive Soldier Fitness and the Future of Psychology." In between were eleven essays by scholars sympathetically explaining aspects of the program. Written at a time when there were more than 100,000 American troops in Iraq and Afghanistan, many of them deployed for long and multiple tours of duty, the program raised significant issues about what the government's support for psychologists' involvement meant in terms of citizenship, professionalism, and patriotism.[63]

General Casey made clear how "nearly a decade of protracted war" during "an era of persistent conflict" called for "leveraging the science of psychology in order to improve our force's resilience." Faced with "unprecedented levels of posttraumatic stress disorder, depression, suicide, and anxiety along with a need for a resilient Army capable of meeting the persistent warfare of the foreseeable future," Seligman and Fowler had expansive goals for the program. They hoped it might "transform the practice of psychology and psychology's relation to medicine and education" by dramatically shifting focus from treatment of the negative to the promotion of the positive. They acknowledged that some, including psychologists, would "look askance on working with the military in any way," but went on to argue that withholding "professional and scientific support" for those defending the nation as a result of democratically arrived-at governmental decisions was "simply wrong." They envisioned several objections to the program, including that "aiding the military will make people who kill for a living feel better about killing and help them do a better job of it" and that the profession should not lend its support to the nation's foreign policy. They responded by saying that scientists should not withhold their expertise when it might improve the lives of others and that enhancing the fitness of troops would produce, on balance, more good than harm. Above all, they asserted that just as powerful military action, which psychology had "materially aided" and "in doing so carved out its identity," had successfully fought back against attempts by fascists and communists to "overthrow democracy," so too in the battle against "jihadist Islam" psychologists should support the use of the military in "self-defense." They ended the issue by remarking that "we are proud to aid our military in defending and protecting our nation right now, and we will be proud to help our soldiers and their families into the peace that will follow."[64]

Nine months later, the journal featured half a dozen letters critical of the program. Writers opposed the methods the Comprehensive Soldier Fitness Program used. Worried about professional responsibility, they questioned the way the scholarly association and journal involved itself in what appeared to be uncritical one-sided advocacy, especially when members of the profession had recently come under attack for their support of torture. "The APA and the American Psychologist need to stay grounded in science, not sell infomercials. The line between the two can be fuzzy," remarked one observer caustically. They cast skeptical eyes on whether America's past and present military interventions were as noble, innocent, and responsible as the program's advocates asserted. Having supported terrible dictators in the past, now "we invaded and occupied a foreign nation that had not attacked us, and in so doing we killed thousands of Iraqi civilians. When we finally leave, we will leave a devastated and divided society."[65]

Dismayed, angered, and shamed by "the current state of my profession," psychologist Sean Phipps offered the most impassioned and capacious critique. He had considered himself a positive psychologist but was now disinclined to describe himself that way. He lamented that the contributors to the original issue were "all blindly accepting the military's premise that this interminable warfare is unavoidable." Why not, he asked, apply "positive psychology principles to the reduction of conflict between nations, to the prevention of war, or to the promotion of peace" or use spirituality for promoting peace rather than for inspiring soldiers, as psychologist Kenneth Pargament seemed to have done? What the special issue of the *American Psychologist* and the government grant to Penn's Positive Psychology Center revealed was that some professional psychologists were eager to gain a share of Department of Defense dollars. There was nothing positive in a psychology, he continued, that trained "our soldiers to experience more death, destruction, and depredation with less distress." This placed the profession on "a slippery slope, a short step to creating psyches that can engage in waterboarding or other forms of human degradation without the experience of distress, guilt, or remorse." He concluded by asserting that "a true positive psychology should be primarily addressed to eradicating the disease of war, not to supporting those who fight it."[66]

Seligman responded to his critics. Long interested in the costs of ethno-political conflict, he defended the program and his involvement (which he noted he had done pro bono) against the criticisms that it was proceeding on grounds that violated ethical standards, those protected both by international law and by his profession's commitments. He insisted that he did not blindly accept the military's assertion that it was impossible to avoid unending wars. He admitted that he could not evaluate whether this was likely, but since it was possible, he wrote, "the Army must be prepared for it, and CSF is an evidence-based way of preparing our soldiers to meet such a possibility." He went on to argue that those who objected to American foreign policy "would have us withhold psychological knowledge on those grounds. Would they, on those grounds," he continued, "also withhold their professional skills from individual American soldiers who came to them for treatment?"

Seligman was proud that he and his co-authors "provide our knowledge and our skills to American soldiers" from which he hoped they would benefit. Without mentioning his presidential initiatives more than a dozen years earlier along these lines, he asserted that he was "strongly for peace and for conflict resolution, and that is what advocacy directed to Congress and to the White House is for. The Army, however," he continued, "carries out the orders of our politicians, and in doing so, deserves the very best that psychology can offer by way of prevention and treatment." Seligman ended his defense of the program and his involvement by asserting that his patriotism, far from being blind, was grounded in familial experience. America, he noted, was "the country that gave my grandparents, persecuted unto death in Europe, a safe haven where their children and grandchildren would flourish. I view the U.S. Army as the force that stood between me and the Nazi gas chambers, and thus I count my days with the sergeants and the generals as the most fulfilling of my life."[67]

This controversy came at a critical moment in national and professional history. For many Americans, support for intervention in Iraq and Afghanistan was waning, even as the cost of those efforts to American troops and their families was intensifying. Supporters and opponents of CSF had divergent visions of American history, citizenship, democracy, and professional responsibility. Seligman believed that previous American interventions were carried out with the best of intentions, while opponents focused on evidence of self-serving national motives and brutal results. In some ways, the two groups interpreted the legacies of the 1960s differentially—Seligman as a warning against how liberals let conservatives capture patriotism and how the left turned against the military, even against the returning vets. In contrast, critics of the program drew from the war in Vietnam very different lessons, ones that led them to be careful about how decisions were made and how costly and deadly wars could be. Seligman envisioned foreign policy decisions made by democratic political processes; others understood that the military actively shaped decisions about whether and how to go to war. Seligman linked citizenship, science, and professionalism, while others were acutely aware of how science was sometimes used to advance questionable goals made in the name of science or how presidents and other political leaders manipulated information. The controversy over the CSF program came at a time when members of professional organizations—of psychologists, anthropologists, and medical doctors—clashed over the meaning of professional obligation. If Seligman and his colleagues took conservative positions on such matters, they were hardly alone.

ACADEMIC ENTREPRENEURSHIP

"Some commentators say Seligman and his colleagues are already the greatest entrepreneurs in the history of psychology," remarked one observer in 2013, "and that positive psychology is the largest growth industry in psychology."[68] Academic entrepreneurship, a subject to which scholars have paid considerable attention when it comes to biotechnology and medicine, comes in many forms. Federal and state funds, income from endowments, money from private foundations, corporations, and wealthy donors come together in often complex mixtures to support the work of programs, centers, institutes, and laboratories. Especially at leading private and public universities such enterprises abound. They vary in the sources of their funding, the role of faculty in their development, and their relationship to the outside world.[69]

If Yale has its Center for Emotional Intelligence, Wisconsin its Center for Healthy Minds, and Harvard its Lee Kum Sheung Center for Health and Happiness, the University of California at Berkeley's Greater Good Science Center provides an example that is exemplary in its commitments and reach. Founded in 2001 by Dacher Keltner, who remains its director, and with Jason Marsh as its director of programs and the editor-in-chief of its award-winning online magazine *Greater Good*, the GGSC combines a commitment to science and its application, promising to study "the psychology, sociology, and neuroscience of well-being" and teaching "skills that foster a thriving, resilient, and compassionate society." Its web site, www.greatergood.berkeley.edu, attracts half a million unique visitors a month. Its MOOC, "The Science of Happiness," taught by Keltner and Emiliana Simon-Thomas, has registered 400,000 students in the five times it has been offered, with 20,000 completing it. EdX has listed it in the top 10 percent in enrollment of those offered on its platform, where it is competing with many more purely practical offerings such as statistics and computer science. Its six-day Summer Institute for Educators spreads the wisdom of positive psychology to teachers, most of them K–12.

In a field where many practitioners are leery of political engagement, "woven into its DNA" Marsh reports, is a commitment to "commit the self to causes and communities bigger than the self," seen, for example, in its efforts to foster reconciliation, cooperative behavior, and the understanding of racism and sexism. The web site for Greater Good in Action, www.ggia.berkeley.edu, which has 30,000 unique visitors monthly, fosters the application of traits such as compassion and empathy. In the wake of Donald Trump's election, at a time when the scarce emails from Friends of Positive Psychology insisted on not being political, GGSC took a different approach. Although not a political platform or party, it expressed its distress at "the message of hate, violence, and divisiveness that propelled its candidate to victory." It went on to redouble its commitment to "the values of kindness, compassion, humility, and empathy" that that transcend any single candidate and "to help people forge connections and see commonalities with others who might seem different from themselves."[70]

The development of centers is especially common and extensive in professional schools. At business schools, professors enhance their income and reach by consulting, lecturing, and offering short-term, non-degree programs. At medical schools, researchers build labs that disappear when they retire, though sometimes what they build survives. We have already seen this in the work and contributions of Herbert Benson and Jon Kabat-Zinn.

Moreover, in biomedicine, biotechnology, computer science, and related fields, professors in the arts and sciences and in professional schools make discoveries that lead to commercially viable products. Universities and their researchers struggle over the issue of who owns the resulting intellectual properties. Sometimes professors choose to remain within the academic community; sometimes they leave and play key roles in corporate enterprises, patenting their findings and starting spin-off companies; some use a revolving door to exit and re-enter. The commercialization of science is a major locus of entrepreneurship and growth: one need only look at two of those most thoroughly studied—the Langer Lab at MIT in biomedicine or the Whitesides Lab in Chemistry, which in 1982 moved from MIT to Harvard.[71] Some universities, especially Stanford with Silicon Valley and MIT with Route 128 and the area near Kendall Square, have spawned transformative commercial projects.[72]

Building an extensive operation is most common in the hard sciences but occurs in positive psychology as well. The University of Wisconsin neuroscientist Richard J. Davidson, for example, reported that in 2011 he had "eleven graduate students, ten postdoctoral fellows, four computer programmers, twenty-one additional research and administrative staff members, and some twenty million dollars in research grants from the National Institutes of Health and other sources."[73] Such an enterprise is rare in the humanities or soft social sciences—where financial support for scholarship is not as essential as it is in positive psychology. There are exceptions. One thinks of the empire that Henry Louis Gates Jr. built at Harvard, now the Hutchins Center for African and African American Research, which houses seven institutes, initiatives, studios, or projects. In my own field, history, academic entrepreneurs come in at least two varieties. Some enhance their incomes and advance their careers by writing textbooks and/or serving as public historians, especially by working as consultants and talking heads on television. Rarer is the development of institutes, such as the Charles Warren Center for Studies in American History at Harvard or the Shelby Cullom Davis Center in the Princeton History Department. Neither of these, however, has committed itself to or relied on leadership by a scholar/ entrepreneur dedicated to the development and transformation of a field. Nor are they organized to turn a profit. Such ambitious ventures are common in the social and behavioral sciences, as we have seen with the University of Michigan's Institute for Social Research, which dates to 1949. With five research centers, it touts itself as "the world's largest academic social science survey and research organization."

Within positive psychology, and even beyond, Seligman is the academic entrepreneur par excellence. His contributions cover almost every possible area related to the applications of the field. He has written, co-authored, and edited a score of books (some translated into as many as 34 languages) and more than 250 articles. He has played major roles in founding, editing, advising, and writing for a wide range of publications—from specialized scholarly ones to *Parents Magazine* and *Reader's Digest*. He has held leadership positions at Penn and in professional organizations. All of this, though impressive, falls within the range of what many scholars and professors do, though not usually so extensively. Even more impressive are his involvements in a range of activities that place him and his work fully in the public sphere. He has delivered a TED talk and had his work featured in *O, The Oprah Magazine*. He has worked with corporations, for example, helping MetLife improve its hiring practices and chairing the scientific board of Foresight, Inc.[74]

Seligman has masterfully used new media, web sites especially, to promote positive psychology. In 2002 he partnered with Ben Dean to create the Authentic Happiness Coaching Program, which used teleconferencing to train more than 1,000 coaches in 19 nations. Through Penn's Positive Psychology Program for Educators, his work has impacted pre-collegiate education at home and abroad. He has garnered support from private foundations. The National Institute of Mental Health, the National Institute of Aging, the National Science Foundation, and the Department of Education have funded his work, but his greatest source of federal support has been for the Army's CSF program. Seligman lacks a pulpit like that used by Osteen or Jakes, although the meetings of the International Positive Psychology Association and other organizations help him spread the word. Moreover, Penn's positive psychology web site, www.positivepsychology.org, with its promotion of labs, institutes, degree programs, projects, research initiatives, and therapeutic strategies, is the among field's most robust and comprehensive bully pulpits, with bestselling books by Seligman and others not far behind. In addition to support from his university, Seligman musters an extraordinary and sustained combination of ambition, chutzpah, ability to work with others, intelligence, inventiveness, energy, and organizational skills. Other fields have their leading entrepreneurs and scholars, but what is significant in positive psychology is that one if its leading scholars is also its most prominent entrepreneur.

In the field of psychology more broadly, it is possible to hear calls for translating science from bench to practice. If some of his peers are critical of Seligman's robust entrepreneurship, he nonetheless well understood how to accomplish this. He knew that the way to carry out this translation was to proceed on many fronts—garnering support from public and private sources; through Penn's Master of Applied Positive Psychology training cadres of practitioners; communicating to broad publics through multiple media; and skillfully marrying his efforts with cultural and political predispositions that already existed. If all this meant getting his hands dirty and encountering skepticism from peers, his efforts nonetheless helped spread the findings of positive psychology.

CONCLUSION

An examination of the business of happiness underscores the many dimensions of the relationship between scientifically grounded positive psychology and various degrees of the proliferating, popularized happiology. With serious practitioners giving TED talks, appearing on *Oprah*, and deploying new media, it was sometimes possible to distinguish between the two and, other times, not. As was true of books promoting and summarizing the field, academics both policed and crossed the border between the scientific and the possibly improper popular. The emphasis on a balance between negativity and positivity, and on the distinction between corrupting and meaningful pleasure, helped maintain the claims positive psychologists had that they occupied higher ground. Yet the insistence on such distinctions also underscored the danger they faced and could not always successfully avoid.

Following the money trail highlights some important dimensions of happiness studies and positive psychology. Old media and new contributed to spreading the force of their approaches. These fields would have gained significant traction under different conditions, but TV evangelism, Oprah's enterprises, TED talks, blogs, web sites, and apps greatly accelerated and amplified their reach. Support from private foundations and government agencies also helped launch, build, and define their presence, inside and more notably outside university walls. So, too, did opportunities to spread positive coaching and positive institution building. All these factors helped reinforce the race, class, and gender dynamics of positive psychology, topics whose importance they generally avoided given that the primary scholarly focus and popular audiences were white, middle-class subjects. The separate tracks of black and white TV evangelism, as well as Oprah's attempt at racial transcendence and the discipline's minimal focus on race, all mattered. Class and gender were ever-present but understudied and not extensively acknowledged or explained. The manly virtues of character strength sat uneasily with the omnipresence of women as consumers of positive coaching, mindful meditation, and bestselling self-help books.

Spencer Johnson's *Who Moved My Cheese? An Amazing Way to Deal with Change in Your Work and in Your Life*, published in the same year as Seligman's APA presidential address, offered a parable that drove home the possibility of uplift in a downsizing world. On the bestseller list for almost 5 years and translated into 37 seven languages, it sold over 25 million copies.[75] If events surrounding World War II helped give birth to key elements of happiness studies, Johnson's book underscores the importance of a different set of challenging circumstances that helped shape positive psychology. Among them were globalization and the spread of affluence. Yet it was hardly coincidental that positive psychology appeared and flourished at the same time the social and economic conditions of vast stretches of working-class and middle-class Americans and people in other highly developed nations were deteriorating. Downsizing, globalization, technological unemployment, migration patterns, the Great Recession, familial dysfunction, and drug addiction came together to create a perfect storm of insecurity and even misery. Although the relationships between these forces and the appeal of positivity is hardly simple, depressing and disorienting realities provided fertile ground for positivity.[76] In these contexts, what positive psychology offered was a largely private, reassuringly optimistic world. As we have seen, advocates of the field occupied a range of political positions, from right-center to left-center; yet many, without necessarily being aware they were doing so, wed positivity and neoliberalism. Opportunity, enterprise, uplift, entrepreneurship, determination, and resilience comprised key elements in the familiar project of how experts in a capitalist world set out to engineer emotions. Positive psychologists had ambitious plans for transforming America by shaping emotional responses and transforming people's internal conditions despite their social situation.[77]

The pursuit of happiness involved an attempt to use science to optimize positivity by managing both feelings and consent. Despite all the research carried out in the field, what remains too often neglected are the who, why, how, and with what results ordinary consumers gain from all the money and time they spend on pursuing positive psychology by reading books, attending workshops, and carrying out recommended exercises. My own guess is that this is a world of serial searchers, people who move from one approach to another as they incorporate specific elements of what the field offers but rarely embrace in an integrated manner all that is on offer. Nonetheless, it is likely that millions of people derived genuine satisfaction, in ways that enhanced their subjective well-being, despite—or because of—what powerful forces and institutions set out to accomplish.

NOTES

1. For summaries of the business of happiness, see Barbara Ehrenreich, *Bright-Sided: How Positive Thinking Is Undermining America* (New York: Henry Holt, 2009), 97–122; William Davies, *The Happiness Industry: How the Government and Big Business Sold Us Well-Being* (London: Verso, 2015); Sam Binkley, *Happiness as Enterprise: An Essay on Neoliberal Life* (Albany: State University of New York Press, 2014); Ruth Whippman,

America the Anxious: How Our Pursuit of Happiness Is Creating a Nation of Nervous Wrecks (New York: St. Martin's Press, 2017); Ilona Boniwell, *Positive Psychology in a Nutshell: The Science of Happiness*, 3rd ed. (Maidenhead, UK: Open University Press, 2012), 154–58; Jeff Wilson, *Mindful America: The Mutual Transformation of Buddhist Meditation and American Culture* (New York: Oxford University Press, 2014); C. R. Snyder and Shane J. Lopez, *Positive Psychology: The Scientific and Practical Explorations of Human Strengths* (Thousand Oaks, CA: Sage, 2007), 379–472; Roger Dooley, *Brainfluence: 100 Ways to Persuade and Convince Consumers with Neuromarketing* (Hoboken, NJ: Wiley, 2012); Elizabeth Weil, "Happiness Inc.," *NYT*, April 19, 2013; Oliver Burkeman, "Who Goes to Work to Have Fun?" *NYT*, Dec. 11 2013; Raffi Khatchadourian, "We Know How You Feel," *New Yorker*, Jan. 19, 2015; http://isj.org.uk/neoliberalism-happiness-and-wellbeing/; Barbara Gunnell, "The Happiness Industry," *New Statesman*, Sept. 6, 2004. Mitch Horowitz, *One Simple Idea: How Positive Thinking Reshaped Modern Life* (New York: Crown, 2014), a cultural history of positive thinking, not positive psychology, pays attention to happiness ministers and Oprah but hardly to all the elements under discussion here.

2. Davies, *Happiness Industry*, 74. For another critique of the business of happiness, see Laura Freeman, "Our Sinister, Soup-Sapping Happiness Industry," *Spectator*, June 25, 2016. On products and services that promise to enhance happiness by activating the brain, see Jonna Brenninkmeijer, "Taking Care of One's Brain: How Manipulating the Brain Changes People's Selves," *History of the Human Sciences* 23 (Feb. 2010): 107–26. On the proliferation of books, see Carlin Flora, "The Pursuit of Happiness," *Psychology Today*, Jan. 1, 2009; Micki McGee, *Self-Help, Inc.: Makeover Culture in American Life* (New York: Oxford University Press, 2005), 11 reports on the tremendous growth in the number of self-help books in the 1990s.

3. The Gallup organization is a major player in the business of happiness. Donald O. Clifton's organization Scientific Research Inc. acquired the Gallup Organization in 1988 and maintained the better-known name. As it continued to broaden its reach beyond political polling, the Gallup Organization expanded its activity in measuring and promoting well-being. Along the most important results were the Gallup-Healthways Well-Being Index, as well as the work of Shane Lopez, *Making Hope Happen: Create the Future You Want for Yourself and Others* (New York: Atria, 2013) and Tom Rath, *Wellbeing: The Five Essential Elements* (New York: Gallup, 2010). Rick Hanson, a Senior Fellow at the Center, has a widespread set of outlets of his own, not only bestselling books on parenting, happiness, and neuroplasticity, but also newsletters and online programs: http://www.rickhanson.net.

4. Wilson, *Mindful America*, 2; for his discussion of the commercial marketing of mindfulness, see 133–58. On the corporate commercialization of meditation, see David Gelles, "The Hidden Price of Mindfulness Inc.," *NYT*, March 20, 2016.

5. Gary Greenberg, "The War on Unhappiness: Goodbye Freud, Hello Positive Thinking," *Harper's*, Sept. 2010, 32; with the quote from https://www.authentichappiness.sas.upenn.edu/.

6. David Kravitz, *How to Monetize Twitter, Facebook, Snapchat, LinkedIn and Other Social Media Sites* (n.p: Create Space Publishing, 2016).

7. John F. Schumaker, "The Happiness Conspiracy," *New Internationalist*, July 2006.

8. See https://en.wikipedia.org/wiki/TED; https://www.ted.com/about/programs-initiatives/ted-talks; Chris Anderson, *TED Talks: The Official TED Guide to Public Speaking* (Boston: Houghton Mifflin Harcourt, 2016).

9. Nathan Heller, "Listen and Learn: TED Talks Reach Millions Around the World. How Has a Conference Turned into an Industry?" *New Yorker*, July 9, 2012; Steven Levy, quoted in Benjamin Wallace, "Those Fabulous Confabs," *New York*, Feb. 26, 2012.

10. Heller, "Listen and Learn." On successful TED talks, see Chris Anderson, "How to Give a Killer Presentation," *Harvard Business Review* 91 (June 2013): 121–25 and http://www.scienceofpeople.com/2015/03/secrets-of-a-successful-ted-talk/.

11. See https://www.ted.com/talks/dan_gilbert_asks_why_are_we_happy?language=en; for Mihaly Czikszentmihalyi's TED talk, see "Flow, The Secret to Happiness," Feb. 2004.

12. "Oprah and Shawn Achor: The Secrets of Happy People," Oprah.com, May 25, 2014. On the more general issue of the application of the discipline, see Stephen Joseph, ed., *Positive Psychology in Practice: Promoting Human Flourishing in Work, Health, Education, and Every Day Life*, 2nd ed. (Hoboken, NJ: Wiley, 2015).

13. Shawn Achor, *The Happiness Advantage: The Seven Principles that Fuel Success and Performance at Work* (New York: Random House, 2010); Shawn Achor, *Before Happiness: 5 Actionable Strategies to Create a Positive Path to Success* (New York: Crown Business, 2013).

14. See http://goodthinkinc.com/research/; Achor, *Before Happiness*, xiv–xv. In *To Serve God and Wal-Mart: The Making of Christian Free Enterprise* (Cambridge, MA: Harvard University Press, 2009), Bethany Moreton explores the factors that shape this corporation.

15. Achor, *Advantage*, 4, 107; Achor, *Before Happiness*, xvii; back cover of paperback of *Before Happiness*.

16. Tony Hsieh, *Delivering Happiness: A Path to Profits, Passion, and Purpose* (New York: Hachette, 2010), 230. On the corporation, see Aimee Groth, *The Kingdom of Happiness: Inside Tony Hsieh's Zapponian Utopia* (New York: Touchstone, 2017).

17. Davies, *Happiness*, 3; this section also draws on 1–11 and 104–13. On the spread of mindful meditation among business elites and others, see Lizzie Widdicombe, "The Higher Life," *New Yorker*, July 6 and 13, 2015, 40–47. For a French high-tech entrepreneur's statement at the World Economic Forum in Davos that meditation was an example of how "we created our own problem that we are now trying to solve," see Loic Le Meur, quoted in Matthew Campbell and Jacqueline Simmons, "At Davos, Rising Stress Spurs Goldie Hawn Meditation Talk," *Bloomberg News*, Jan. 21, 2014.

18. This draws on http://positiveorgs.bus.umich.edu, including Gretchen M. Spreitzer, "Restoring Hope During Trying Times" and Scott DeRue et. al., "Developing Adaptive Leaders for Turbulent Times: The Michigan Model of Leadership."

19. Antonella Delle Fave, "Well-Being in Times of Crisis: Interdisciplinary Evidence and Policy Implications," *JHS* 15 (Feb. 2014), 119–23; see also Francis Green et al., "Job-Related Well-Being Through the Great Recession," *JHS* 17 (Feb. 2016): 389–411.

20. Kim S. Cameron, Jane E. Dutton, and Robert E. Quinn, "Foundations of Positive Organizational Scholarship," in *Positive Organizational Scholarship*, ed. Kim S. Cameron, Jane E. Dutton, and Robert E. Quinn (San Francisco: Berrett-Koehler, 2003), 3 began the introductory essay by contrasting worlds organized around "greed, selfishness, manipulation" and "appreciation, collaboration, virtuousness."

21. Kim S. Cameron et al., "Developing a Discipline of Positive Organizational Scholarship," in Cameron, Dutton, and Quinn, *Positive Organizational Scholarship*, 262, 370. For the discussion of downsizing, see Kim S. Cameron, "Organizational Virtuousness and Performance," in Cameron, Dutton, and Quinn, *Positive Organizational Scholarship*, 48–65.

22. Marcia Z. Nelson, "Oprah on a Mission: Dispending a Gospel of Health and Happiness," *Christian Century*, Sept. 25, 2002, 21–25. Kathryn Lofton, *Oprah: The Gospel of an Icon* (Berkeley: University of California Press, 2011) is especially perceptive in helping us understand Oprah as involved in a cultural movement that fuses religion, celebrity, and consumer cultures with new dynamics of capitalism. See also Kathleen Rooney, *Reading with Oprah: The Book Club That Changed America* (Fayetteville: University of Arkansas Press, 2005).

23. See http://www.oprah.com also featured a July 8, 2012, "Be Happy: An 8-Day Happiness Course" by the positive psychologist Robert Holden: http://www.oprah.com/own-super-soul-sunday/Be-Happy-An-8-Day-Happiness-Course.

24. See http://www.oprah.com/spirit/Which-Way-to-Happy-Two-Experts-Weigh-In; http://www.oprah.com/spirit/Working-Under-Pressure-Can-Be-a-Strength-Robert-Biswas-Diener; see also Ed Diener and Robert Biswas-Diener, "5 Ways You Can Buy Happiness (Really!)" http://www.oprah.com, Sept. 9, 2009.

25. Nicole Frehsée, "Spread the Love: the Health Benefits of Bonding," *O, The Oprah Magazine*, Feb. 2013; Lise Funderburg, "How to Be an Optimist," *O, The Oprah Magazine*, Feb. 2002 and Seligman quoted in same; Sonja Lyubomirsky, quoted in "The Ohm of Happiness," *O, The Oprah Magazine*, Aug. 2014; Cynthia King, "The One Way to Discover Your Truest Self," *O, The Oprah Magazine*, May 2001.

26. Oprah Winfrey, *Oprah Winfrey Show*, Sept. 8, 1998, quoted in Janice Peck, *The Age of Oprah: Cultural Icon for the Neoliberal Era* (Boulder, CO: Paradigm, 2008), 6.

27. Nelson, "Oprah," 20. This paragraph draws heavily on Peck, *Oprah*, especially 1–13. On how Oprah draws on African American religious traditions, see Eva Illouz, *Oprah Winfrey and the Glamour of Misery: An Essay on Popular Culture* (New York: Columbia University Press, 2003). On uplift in African American life, see Kevin K. Gaines, *Uplifting the Race: Black Leadership, Politics, and Culture in the Twentieth Century* (Chapel Hill: University of North Carolina Press, 1996).

28. See http://positivepsychologynews.com/news/louisa-jewell/2011052717921.

29. Nelson, "Oprah," 21. For a critique of this movement, see David W. Jones and Russell S. Woodbridge, *Health, Wealth and Happiness: Has the Prosperity Gospel Overshadowed the Gospel of Christ?* (Grand Rapids, MI: Kregel, 2011). For its history, see Kate Bowler, *Blessed: A History of the American Prosperity Gospel* (New York: Oxford University Press, 2013). For the turn away from sin, see Andrew Delbanco, *The Death of Satan: How Americans Have Lost the Sense of Evil* (New York: Farrar, Straus and Giroux, 1995); Paula M. Kane, *Sister Thorn and Catholic Mysticism in Modern America* (Chapel Hill: University of North Carolina Press, 2013); R. Marie Griffith, *Born Again Bodies: Flesh and Spirit in American Christianity* (Berkeley: University of California Press, 2004); Robert A. Orsi, *Thank You, St. Jude: Women's Devotion to the Patron Saint of Hopeless Causes* (New Haven, CT: Yale University Press, 1996); John Piper, *Desiring God* (Sisters, OR: Multnomah 2003).

30. See http://www.empoweringeverydaywomen.com/td-jakes-shares-5-steps-to-happiness-steve-harvey-eew-magazine.html; on Jakes, see Jonathan L. Walton, *Watch This! The Ethics and Aesthetics of Black Televangelism* (New York: New York University Press, 2009), 103–23.

31. See https://www.youtube.com/watch?v=gQXyTgztEPI.

32. Joel Osteen, *Your Best Life Now: 7 Steps to Living at Your Full Potential* (New York: Warner Faith, 2004), 221. On his importance, see Phillip L. Sinitiere, *Salvation with a Smile: Joel Osteen, Lakewood Church, and American Christianity* (New York: New York University Press, 2015).

33. The scholarship on new media is considerable, but among the places to begin are the optimistic Henry Jenkins, *Convergence Culture: Where Old and New Media Collide* (New York: New York University Press, 2006), 2; see also Henry Jenkins, Sam Ford, and Joshua Green, *Spreadable Media: Creating Value and Meaning in a Networked Culture* (New York: New York University Press, 2013). More skeptical is Laurie Ouellette and James Hay, *Better Living Through Reality TV: Television and Post-Welfare Citizenship* (Malden, MA: Blackwell, 2008). Micki McGee, "From Makeover Media to Remaking Culture: Four Directions for the Critical Study of Self-Help Culture," *Sociology Compass* 6 (Sept. 2012): 688–90 explores the debate over convergence.

34. See http://www.abundancetapestry.com/about-me/.

35. Cat Johnson, "15 Apps To Boost Your Happiness," http://www.shareable.net/blog/15-apps-to-boost-your-happiness.
36. See, for example, Mohamed Zayani, *Networked Publics and Digital Contention: The Politics of Everyday Life in Tunisia* (New York: Oxford University Press, 2015).
37. Among the sources on the transformative cultural power of new media are Nicholas Negroponte, *Being Digital* (New York: Knopf, 1995); Lev Manovich, *The Language of New Media* (Cambridge, MA: MIT Press, 2002); Yochai Benkler, *The Wealth of Networks: How Social Production Transforms Markets and Freedom* (New Haven, CT: Yale University Press, 2006); Axel Bruns, *Blogs, Wikipedia, Second Life, and Beyond: From Production to Produsage* (New York: Peter Lang, 2008); José Van Dijck, *The Culture of Connectivity: A Critical History of Social Media* (New York: Oxford University Press, 2013); José Van Dijck, "Flickr and the Culture of Connectivity: Sharing Views, Experiences, Memories," *Memory Studies* 4 (Oct. 18, 2010): 401–15.
38. Dan Schiller, *Digital Capitalism: Networking the Global Market System* (Cambridge, MA: MIT Press, 2000); Trebor Scholz, ed., *Digital Labor: The Internet as Playground and Factory* (New York: Routledge, 2013).
39. There is an emerging literature on what sophisticated tools using Big Data reveal about happiness, a literature far more rigorous than my preliminary explorations. I am grateful to Sarah A. Murray for identifying these studies. See, for example, Peter Sheridan Dodds et al., "Temporal Patterns of Happiness and Information in a Global Social Network: Hedonometrics and Twitter," *PLoSOne*, 6 (Dec. 7, 2011); Yu-Hsiang Lin, Cheng-Hsi Fang, and Chia-Lin Hsu, "Determining Uses and Gratifications for Mobile Phone Apps," *Future Information Technology* 309 (Jan. 1, 2014): 661–68; Logan Longbourne, "Happiness Apps: Reinforcing Happiness-Promoting Behaviour Through Software," Ph.D. diss., Auckland University of Technology, 2015; Jill Belli, "Unhappy? There's an App for That: Tracking Well-Being Through the Quantified Self," *Digital Culture and Society* 2 (March 2016): 89–104.
40. I am grateful to Luma Muhtadie for helping me research and think through this topic. http://www.facebook.com/pages/Positive-psychology/112107518806508 is the official Positive Psychology Facebook page. Other important web pages include http://www.facebook.com/Happinessinyourlife; http://www.facebook.com/TheMindUnleashed; http://www.facebook.com/mysimplereminders; http://www.facebook.com/theofficial-robinsharmapage/. See also Whippman, *America the Anxious*, 166–86, on how the social norms of Facebook rely on the pretenses of happiness exchanges but actually erode a sense of subjective well-being.
41. Robert Biswas-Diener, *Practicing Positive Psychology Coaching: Assessment, Activities, and Strategies for Success* (Hoboken, NJ: John Wiley, 2010); Stephen Joseph, *Positive Therapy: Building Bridges Between Positive Psychology and Person-centred Therapy*, 2nd ed. (New York: Routledge, 2015). See also Warren Redman, *Emotional Fitness Coaching: How to Develop a Positive and Productive Workplace for Leaders, Managers and Coaches* (London: Kogan Page, 2012), whose author is president of Emotional Fitness Institute; Elaine Cox, Tatiana Bachkirova, and David Clutterbuck, eds., *The Complete Handbook of Coaching* (Los Angeles: Sage, 2010). I am also grateful to Melissa Schnapp for a Feb. 16, 2016, telephone conversation about coaching.
42. For a discussion of the impact of positive psychology on coaching, see Margaret Moore, "How Coaching Works: Positive Psychology," *Psychology Today*, Jan. 22, 2010.
43. For a good discussion of the difference between therapy and coaching, one that links the latter to neoliberalism's emphasis on helping someone to take advantage of opportunity, see Binkley, *Happiness*, 168–71.
44. Biswas-Diener, *Practicing*, 6, 147.

45. Biswas-Diener founded positiveacorn.com, which leads to a certificate as a Positive Psychology Coach, a program approved, as are many others, by the International Coach Federation; others include the CaPP Institute's one in coaching and positive psychology; the Wholebeing Institute's in positive psychology coaching; the School of Coaching Master's training for a position as a Certified Positive Psychology Coach; Caroline Adams Miller's Positive Psychology Masterclass for Coaches and Professionals. For a guide to programs in positive psychology, see https://positivepsychologyprogram.com/positive-psychology-courses-programs-workshops-trainings/.

46. See http://www.wholebeinginstitute.com; http://www.cappinstitute.com. Boniwell, *Nutshell*, 143–44.

47. Biswas-Diener, *Practicing*, 4, 10, 38, 146. Robert Biswas-Diener and Ben Dean, *Positive Psychology Coaching: Putting the Science of Happiness to Work for Your Clients* (Hoboken, NJ: John Wiley, 2997), 189–91; Sam Binkley, "Psychological Life as Enterprise: Social Practice and the Government of Neo-Liberal Interiority," *History of Human Sciences* 24 (July 2011): 95.

48. Boniwell, *Nutshell*, 144; Gunnell, "Happiness Industry." The key moment that left opened coaching unregulated came with a 2004 court decision in Colorado that exempted the field from government regulation because of its orientation to the present and future.

49. For a review of programs, see Boniwell, *Nutshell*, 149–53; Snyder and Lopez, *Positive Psychology*, 379–406; Seligman, *Flourish*, 78–97. For a critique of these efforts, see Kristján Kristjánsson, *Virtues and Vices in Positive Psychology: A Philosophical Critique* (New York: Cambridge University Press, 2013); Alistair Miller, "A Critique of Positive Psychology—or, 'The New Science of Happiness,'" *Journal of Philosophy of Education* 42 (Aug.–Nov. 2008): 591–608.

50. See https://www.ggs.vic.edu.au/School/Positive-Education/What-is-Positive-Education-/Our-Positive-Education-Model.

51. Ian Morris, *Teaching Happiness and Well-Being in Schools: Learning to Ride Elephants* (London: Continuum International, 2009), 2; Anna Tyzack, "Happiness at School: 'Since Wellbeing Lessons Started, Grades Have Gone Up,'" *Telegraph*, Feb. 18, 2012.

52. Morris, *Teaching*, 14; Richard Layard, "Foreword" to Morris, *Teaching*, [vi].

53. *The Templeton Plan: 21 Steps to Personal Success and Real Happiness*, as described by John M. Templeton to James Ellison (New York: Harper & Row, 1987). Two of Peale's books (*The Power of Positive Thinking* and *A Guide to Confident Thinking*) were among the eighteen listed at the book's end.

54. See http://www.templeton.org. When Sir John died in 2008, his son John Templeton Jr. (less interested in a broad range of religious traditions and more committed to conservative causes than his father) took over until he died in 2015, when Heather Templeton Dill, the founder's granddaughter, assumed the foundation's presidency.

55. Barbara Fredrickson, *Love 2.0: How Our Supreme Emotion Affects Everything We Feel, Think, Do, and Become* (New York: Penguin, 2013), 200; Mihaly Csikszentmihalyi, *Good Business: Leadership, Flow, and the Making of Meaning* (New York: Viking, 2003), 148.

56. [Jane E. Gillham?], "Preface," in *The Science of Optimism and Hope: Research Essays in Honor of Martin E.P. Seligman*, ed. Jane E. Gillham (Philadelphia: Templeton Foundation Press, 2000), x; this volume contains the essays from the symposium, including one on the neurobiology of optimism and one on the neurochemistry of resilience.

57. Arthur Schwartz, telephone conversation with author, Jan. 21, 2016.

58. Mark Solovey, *Shaky Foundations: The Politics-Patronage-Social Science Nexus in Cold War America* (New Brunswick, NJ: Rutgers University Press, 2013) explores the complex, often reciprocal nature of patron/client relationships in funding research. Full disclosure: in 2004 I received an honorarium of $10,000 from the Templeton Foundation to

write a paper on thrift and attend a conference on the same topic. For recent work on patronage of science, see articles on the topic in *ISIS* 103 (June 2012): 310–55.

59. Csikszentmihalyi, *Good Business*, v.

60. Martin E. P. Seligman, *Authentic Happiness: Using the New Positive Psychology to Realize Your Potential for Lasting Fulfillment* (New York: Free Press, 2002), 250–52. Seligman remarked that when he first worked with the foundation, he made clear that neither he nor positive psychology were "for rent, unable to avoid what sounded to me like a touch of ungrateful self-righteousness": Seligman, *Authentic Happiness*, 252. However, a long conversation with Arthur Schwartz, the foundation executive, reassured him.

61. See http://www.atlanticphilanthropies.org. Early in the twenty-first century, according to Seligman, after the Atlantic Philanthropies had turned down his request for funds to continue his work on public conflicts, he called to CEO to say "we don't need any further funding because positive psychology is now self-supporting": Martin E. P. Seligman, *Flourish: A Visionary New Understanding of Happiness and Well-Being* (New York: Simon & Schuster, 2011), 8–9. For information on Feeney's support of Irish universities and of the peace process between north and south, see Conor O'Clery, *The Billionaire Who Wasn't: How Chuck Feeney Secretly Made and Gave Away a Fortune* (New York: Public Affairs, 2007), 267–85. In late January 1997, Feeney stepped out from his anonymity and made public his philanthropic activities.

62. In *Head Strong: How Psychology is Revolutionizing War* (New York: Oxford University Press, 2014), Michael D. Matthews, the key figure in connecting Seligman and his work with the military, discusses the roles psychology has played in the military, including (79–89) on the development of the Comprehensive Soldier Fitness Program.

63. See the following essays in *American Psychologist* 66 (Jan. 2011): George W. Casey Jr., "Comprehensive Soldier Fitness: A Vision for Psychological Resilience in the U.S. Army," 1–3; Martin E. P. Seligman and Raymond D. Fowler, "Comprehensive Soldier Fitness and the Future of Psychology," 82–86. For responses, see *American Psychologist*, 66 (Oct. 2011): Sean Phipps, "Positive Psychology and War: An Oxymoron," 641–42; Joachim I. Krueger, "Shock Without Awe," 642–43; Roy Eidelson, Marc Pilisuk, and Stephen Soldz, "The Dark Side of Comprehensive Soldier Fitness," 643–44; John Dyckman, "Exposing the Glosses in Seligman and Fowler's (2011) Straw-Man Arguments," 644–45; James C. Quick, "Missing: Critical and Skeptical Perspectives on Comprehensive Soldier Fitness," 645. For Seligman's response to critiques in the Oct. issue, see "Helping American Soldiers in Time of War: Reply to Comments on the Comprehensive Soldier Fitness Special Issue," 646–47. Extensive criticism of CSF has focused on its methods and morality, as well as the favoritism in the Army's funding. For the background history on the relationship between scholars and the state, see Sarah Bridger, *Scientists at War: The Ethics of Cold War Weapons Research* (Cambridge, MA: Harvard University Press, 2015; Joy Rohde, *Armed with Expertise: The Militarization of American Social Research during the Cold War* (Ithaca, NY: Cornell University Press, 2013).

64. Casey, "Comprehensive," 1; Seligman and Fowler, "Comprehensive," 82, 85, 86.

65. Quick, "Missing," 645; Dyckman, "Glosses," 644.

66. Phipps, "Oxymoron," 641–42.

67. Seligman, "Helping American Soldiers," 646–47. For a full description of the program, and Seligman's role in its development, see Seligman, *Flourish*, 126–51.

68. Kristjánsson, *Virtues and Vices*, 2. On the accolades and controversy Seligman has engendered, see Stacey Burling, "The Power of a Positive Thinker," http://www.philly.com, May 30, 2010.

69. The issue of academic entrepreneurship has received some attention from scholars: see, as examples, Toby E. Stuart and Waverly W. Ding, "When Do Scientists Become Entrepreneurs? The Social Structural Antecedents of Commercial Activity in the

Academic Life Sciences," *American Journal of Sociology* 122 (July 2006): 97–144; Steve Shapin, *The Scientific Revolution* (Chicago: University of Chicago Press, 1996); and two books by Sheldon Krimsky, *Biotechnics and Society: The Rise of Industrial Genetics* (New York: Praeger, 1991) and *Science in the Private Interest: Has the Lure of Profits Corrupted Biomedical Research?* (Lanham, MD: Rowman and Littlefield, 2003). Joel Isaac, *Working Knowledge: Making the Human Sciences from Parsons to Kuhn* (Cambridge, MA: Harvard University Press, 2012) offers case studies of program building but does not pay much attention to funding or, explicitly, to entrepreneurship.

70. Jason March, conversations with author Feb. 24, 2016, (in person) and Nov. 10, 2016 (telephone); http://www.greatergood.berkeley.edu; https://mail.google.com/mail/u/0/?tab=cm#inbox/15853f82ba218e01. For evaluations of the impact of the Center's work, see "Highlights from the 2015 GGSC Audience Survey"; Emiliana Simon-Thomas, "Science of Happiness Impact Summary"; SIE 2016 Evaluations, copies of author's possession. In the days immediately after the 2016 election, I received only one relevant email from Friends of Positive Psychology, "This is NOT a political post," wrote Dr. Karen of www.brainand-health.com, "It IS a post about what I would have hoped this group [i.e., Friends of Positive Psychology] could have come up with instead of the push me–pull you that erupted," as she offered as link to a video that showed "one couple who's managing to do what we could not."

71. H. Kent Bowen et al., "Langer Lab: The Commercializing Science," Harvard Business School Case 605-017, Oct. 2004; H. Kent Bowen and Francesca Gino, "The Whitesides Lab," Harvard Business School Case 606-064, March 2006.

72. To sample the extensive literature on academic entrepreneurship and its funding, see Susan Rosegrant and David R. Lampe, *Route 128: Lessons from Boston's High-Tech Community* (New York: Basic, 1992); Alan R. Earls, *Route 128 and the Birth of the Age of High Tech* (Charleston, SC: Arcadia Publishing, 2002); AnnaLee Saxenian, *Regional Advantage: Culture and Competition in Silicon Valley and Route 128* (Cambridge, MA: Harvard University Press, 1994); Margaret P. O'Mara, *Cities of Knowledge: Cold War Science and the Search for the Next Silicon Valley* (Princeton, NJ: Princeton University Press, 2005); Rebecca S. Lowen, *Creating the Cold War University: The Transformation of Stanford* (Berkeley: University of California Press, 1997); Mark Solovey, *Shaky Foundations*; Jennifer Washburn, *University, Inc.: The Corporate Corruption of American Higher Education* (New York: Basic, 2005).

73. Richard J. Davidson, with Sharon Begley, *The Emotional Life of Your Brain: How Its Unique Patterns Affect the Way You think, Feel, and Live—and How You Can Change Them* (New York: Hudson Street Press, 2012), xii.

74. This draws on his 2010 c.v.: http://truth-out.org/archive/files/seligmanvita.pdf.

75. Spencer Johnson, *Who Moved My Cheese? An Amazing Way to Deal with Change in Your Work and in Your Life* (New York: Putnam, 1998).

76. Each in distinctive ways—Ehrenreich, *Bright-Sided*, 112–21, Binkley, *Happiness*, 1–13, Davies, *Happiness*, 104–08, and Peter Kramer, *Listening to Prozac* (New York: Viking Penguin, 1993), 271–72—make similar connections.

77. Tamsin Shaw, "The Psychologists Take Power," *NYRB*, Feb. 25, 2016, connects the two efforts.

The Happiest Place on Earth

In late June 2015, my wife, the historian Helen L. Horowitz, and I attended the Fourth World Congress on Positive Psychology at Disney World in Lake Buena Vista, Florida. Disney World struck me as an appropriate place for those interested in promoting happiness to gather. After all, Roy Disney, Walt's younger brother, remarked in 1971 at the opening of the Florida Magic Kingdom that he hoped it would "bring Joy and Inspiration and New Knowledge to all who come to this happy place." Moreover, visitors were more likely to come if they had incomes over $70,000 a year, arrived with people with whom they had social relationships, and had some taste for liberty, adventure, enchantment—and joyful, programmed play.

Sponsored by the International Positive Psychology Association (IPPA), it attracted 1,200 participants from 48 nations and every continent in the world. Half of those there were from the United States, with Australia accounting for 7.6 percent; Canada, 6.3; China, 4.3; the United Kingdom, 3.9; Japan, 2.9; Mexico, 2.6; Brazil, 2.2; Germany, 1.7; Denmark, 1.6; Netherlands, 1.3; and Israel, 1.1. Most of those attending were professors, students, practitioners, and researchers.[1] IPPA has in excess of 3,000 members in more than 70 countries. About 45 percent of its members are either practicing psychologists or academic researchers; another 20 percent are practitioners (coaches, consultants) applying findings to business and educational organizations, as well as individuals; 25 percent are students; and 10 percent are people from varied backgrounds interested in the field.[2]

As someone accustomed to attending conferences for historians, I was in for many surprises, even as I now recognize that meetings of academics have a dramatically different tone, orientation, and agenda than do those that attract businesspeople and others more interested in inspiration and practical applications than in the most current, perhaps esoteric research.

Registration for a meeting of the Organization of American Historians cost less than $200; for the IPPA it was $800. Exhibits at historians' meetings feature extensive displays of books, but little more. The IPPA meeting had a few booths displaying books but many offering information on other commercial goods such as glossy magazines, popular web sites, or card games. Also among the sponsors, advertisers and exhibitors were university-based and free-standing educational programs and research centers. And then there were offerings of commercial products and services, some of them useful and compelling and others seemingly vacuous. Borrowing a page from popular books on happiness, I list them here with bullet points.

- Happify, a company "pioneering online emotional fitness by integrating the science of happiness into daily activities and games that help people build skills for a happier, more fulfilling life."[3]
- HeartMath, claiming its "two decades of scientific research has proven that thoughts and action have an impact on heart rate variability and health outcomes" with its emWave® and Inner Balance™ technologies providing "education and training on the body's response to stress."[4]
- Live Happy and its magazine, "dedicated to promoting and sharing authentic happiness through education, integrity, gratitude, and community awareness . . . by bringing the happiness movement to a personal level and inspiring people to engage in living purpose-driven, healthy, meaningful lives."[5]
- The Resilience Doughnut, "Combining Strengths to Thrive," a "practical, strengths-based model for developing resilience in children, young people and adults," graphically illustrated by "Nine strengths around the periphery and in the middle, 'I Have, I Am, I Can.'"[6]
- Positive IQ, "founded on the philosophy that nurturing and strengthening twelve key character traits, such as commitment and kindness, will more fully enable the development of worthwhile goals that, through attention, discipline and passion, will lead to personal growth and positive living."[7]
- QoL-X, "dedicated to helping people around the world learn how to personally experiment with quality of life improvements for themselves and those they care about."[8]
- BIGUAcademy, "the world's #1 direct sales and marketing organization, providing virtual training courses on the science of happiness, neuroscience, positive psychology and personal development to individuals and organizations around the globe."
- MassPensamientoPositivo, "Positive technology solutions for Latin America, introducing the world's happiest characters—Los Felicios."

- Life Energy, "The Guide to Enhanced Well-Being—One Decision at a Time."
- Positive Acorn, "Training Professionals in the Science of Positive Psychology."

With 14 pre-Congress talks (entry to which required additional fees); 7 plenary sessions; 10 invited speakers; almost 100 sessions on a range of topics, such as virtues, health, mindfulness, and education; and over 300 poster sessions, the offerings were extensive. Then there were special events. One evening featured the 2013 movie *Saving Mr. Banks*. The program announced that it was "the perfect positive psychology movie for IPPA in Orlando!" one that brought together P. L. Travers, the author of *Mary Poppins*, and Walt Disney. "Look," the program announced, "for themes of creativity, playfulness, positive relationships, character strengths overuse/underuse, perseverance, nostalgia, personal transformation, hope/optimism, re-imagination of one's past, and transcending problems." Following this came "IPPA Rocks the World: Saturday Night Celebration with Soaringwords + Zumba.®" Soaringwords, I learned, is "a nonprofit organization that lessens the negative impact of serious illness by embracing hospitalized children and families to encourage positive health and healing." Participants would also "Rock the World with a Zumba Master Class." The evening, the program promised, allowed people to "have a blast and meet new friends in a fun and energizing experience" with "action-packed social activity" that enabled you to "harness your unique character strengths to create a paper-bag puppet to donate to a hospitalized child."[9]

Talks at history conventions, even presidential addresses, tend to be sober and understated, delivered in ways not unlike how a professor might address a large lecture class at a university. At this conference, some speakers talked in such a manner, but many others relied on a more dynamic, TED-style approach—wearing a small portable microphone, moving around the platform, and gesturing dramatically. Some talks were scholarly; others added a full measure of inspiration as if we were at a religious revival, which in some ways we were. In his message, the IPPA's president, the Spanish psychologist Carmelo Vazquez, set the tone for much of what went on, appropriately for a meeting that focused on happiness. Since "this is a Congress of positive people," he remarked, "I am certain that this will be a space not only for learning and knowledge, but also for joy and enthusiasm."[10]

Not surprisingly but equally striking was how some sessions offered entertainment. For example, one meeting, titled "Idea Bounce," was a "case competition like event" in which participants were "to form teams and compete for the 'best' solution to their positive psychology 'problem.'"[11] At other sessions, I encountered an approach that, in my scholarly insularity, I had experienced quite rarely: turning to someone sitting next to me, introducing myself, and then engaging in conversation with that person. More dramatic and unexpected was the way some plenary sessions began. The person introducing the meeting would start by saying "Welcome." When the audience did not respond or did so tepidly, the host would work to elicit a loud and enthusiastic call back.

Reinforcing the gender dynamics of positive psychology, what Helen heard impacted her personally more than it did me, although as a scholar writing the field's history I learned much that was informative. Having discovered relaxation techniques in college, Helen now found out about the science behind them. Working to come to terms with the death of her mother six months earlier, what she listened to in some sessions about balancing negativity and positivity struck home. In facing grief, one presenter asked, what are the steps that lead to acceptance of the inevitable? More generally, in dealing with rejection or conflict, she found meaningful ways that relied on positive solutions to turn a "no" into a "yes."

The conference opened my eyes to things that as a researcher I had only half-known or not fully understood—New Knowledge, Roy Disney called it. The global reach of positive psychology was very much in evidence, albeit mostly from developed nations—especially through the presence of so many who had come from Western Europe, Australia, and Japan. Even more striking were the numbers and enthusiasm of attendees from Australia, many of whom had flown back and forth between Sydney or Melbourne and Orlando just to be at the IPPA meeting. I was well aware of how many scholars were active in the field, but only once there did I realize how many coaches, educators, and other practitioners were actively applying positive psychology in the realms of education, sports, business, and therapy. Before I arrived I had done a good deal of research into what those in the field had written, but only once there did I realize the extensiveness and importance of the scholarship that connected positive psychology, on the one hand, with either neuroscience or religion, on the other.

I found several talks especially useful in suggesting where my own research into the history of positive psychology should go. I listened with rapt attention to Richard J. Davidson deliver his talk on "Well-Being: Perspectives from Affective and Contemplative Neuroscience," in which he told the audience how his life changed in 1992 when his meeting with the Dalai Lama persuaded him to shift the focus of his research from depression to compassion. He then focused on four findings of neuroscience: neuroplasticity, epigenetics, bi-directional communication between brain and body, and, most controversially, innate human goodness. With "Past, Present and Future Perspectives on Eudaimonic Well-Being," Carol Ryff showed me more complicated ways of understanding philosophical and scientific aspects of subjective well-being, especially the importance of resilience and a balance between positivity and negativity. Another eye-opener came from Kenneth Pargament's "Cultivating the Spiritual Dimension in Life: A Vital Aspect of Positive Psychology." I was familiar with how many social scientists did not want to take religion seriously and that early happiness studies had revealed how minimal was the impact of spirituality on life satisfaction. In contrast, Pargament alerted me to the scholarship on how engagement with religion and spirituality enhanced the quality of life and even extended its length.[12]

Almost all of the sessions made sense to me, more as a scholar than as a potential practitioner. However, one in particular made clear to me that some in the field could easily move from hard science to New Age mysticism, which to me seemed in conflict with both science and my own this-worldliness. With "Heart-Brain Dynamic: The Role of Self-Regulation and Psychophysiological Coherence in Optimal Functioning," Rollin McCraty, Director of Research of the HeartMath Research Center at the Institute of HeartMath, began his talk with an impressive and convincing discussion of mind–body connections worthy of his talk's and his own title. Toward the end of his presentation, the notes I took at the time indicate my skepticism when he spoke of the "invisible magnetic" solar signals that affect "human activity levels" with "bursts of human creativity correlating with solar activity." As a consequence "solar energy promoted positive feelings."[13]

Above all, what intrigued me were contrasting statements of the political implications of positive psychology. In the Harvard undergraduate seminar that I audited on "The Science of Happiness," we worked our way through Jonathan Haidt's *The Happiness Hypothesis: Finding Modern Truth in Ancient Wisdom* (2006), a book that juxtaposed canonical works by philosophers, novelists, poets, and playwrights with contemporary scientific findings. In a speech on "Capitalism, Values, and Large Scale Flourishing," Haidt hailed the dramatic improvement in people's lives achieved by capitalism's impact since 1800, which accelerated even further after 1950, despite the fact that people who understood the power of the hedonic treadmill might be skeptical. Although he acknowledged the downside of these transformations, Haidt offered the limited choice of going forward with a capitalism bolstered by an ethical dimension or going back to the horrors of a precapitalist world. "Get capitalism right," my notes indicate him saying, "and this will enhance happiness." Haidt used a PowerPoint presentation showing which nations were happiest—those that combined relative equality, a high GDP, and social trust. With those as the metrics, the Scandinavian nations stood at the top, with the United States clearly below. What surprised me at the time was that Haidt evidenced no awareness of what I took to be the implications of such an international survey—that the goal was not simply more ethical corporations but more equitable distribution of wealth and a social welfare net that fostered a sense of greater trust. In other words, to me, although individual and corporate actions mattered, national policies mattered as well.[14]

During his talk, Haidt did an informal survey of the politics of the audience. Out of about 800 present, I estimated that 20 identified as conservatives; the rest, with the center or left of the political spectrum. The reaction to a talk by Mihaly Csikszentmihalyi proved that the results of Haidt's survey were correct. Few of the presentations at the IPPA meetings received a standing ovation; Csikszentmihalyi's on "Positive Psychology and the Importance of Culture" did. Positive psychologists, Csikszentmihalyi argued, had paid "too much attention to proximal institutions such as family, schools, and the workplace." Instead, he called on those in the field to broaden the range of their interventions and focus on issues such as inequality, social justice, social trust, and the environment. "It is easy to focus on individual hedonic well-being," he noted, but positive psychologists "should use our professional skills for the common good and the future."[15] That members of the audience responded more enthusiastically to Csikszentmihalyi's talk than to Haidt's exposed both differences of political opinion among positive psychology's leaders and great unanimity among its followers. Positive psychology had some widely held assumptions but never an enforced political orthodoxy. From the outset a tension has existed between the individual pursuit of happiness and the collective commitment to a more robustly just social good. Clearly the field is at a fork in the road, uncertain what combination of conservative commitments grounded in character strengths and liberal activism will provide the way forward.

NOTES

1. Most of the information on the conference comes from *Fourth World Congress on Positive Psychology Program*, from relevant web sites, and from the Esther Hill, the IPPA administrator.
2. Martin E. P. Seligman, *Flourish: A Visionary New Understanding of Happiness and Well-Being* (New York: Simon & Schuster, 2011), 271.
3. *Program*, 70. Where not cited, information on vendors comes from their web sites.
4. *Program*, 70.
5. *Program*, 72.
6. See http://www.theresiliencedoughnut.com.au/about/resilience/.
7. *Program*, 72.
8. *Program*, 73.
9. *Program*, 43.

10. Carmelo Vazquez, "Message from the President of IPPA," *Program*, 8.
11. *Program*, 34.
12. Richard J. Davidson, "Well-Being: Perspectives from Affective and Contemplative Neuroscience," June 26, 2015; Carol Ryff, "Past, Present and Future Perspectives on Eudaimonic Well-Being," June 26, 2015; Kenneth Pargament, "Cultivating the Spiritual Dimension in Life: A Vital Aspect of Positive Psychology," June 25, 2015.
13. Rollin McCraty, "Heart-Brain Dynamic: The Role of Self-Regulation and Psychophysiological Coherence in Optimal Functioning," June 27, 2015.
14. Jonathan Haidt, "Capitalism, Values, and Large Scale Flourishing," June 26, 2015.
15. Mihaly Csikszentmihalyi, "Positive Psychology and the Importance of Culture," June 28, 2015.

INDEX

References to figures are denoted by an italic *f*.

posttraumatic growth (PTG), 115
poverty, 19, 138, 143, 186n.54, 208, 210,
    212, 219–20, 247, 266
Powell, John, 136, 137
The Power of Positive Thinking (Peale), 4,
    11n.7, 32–34, 131, 140
Practicing Positive Psychology Coaching
    (Biswas-Diener), 257
Prager, Dennis, 136
Princeton University, 18, 154, 264, 271
professional infrastructure,
    building, 153–55
prospect theory, 71–72
Protestantism, 2, 197, 198
Prozac, 80, 101–4, 121n.18
Psychiatric Times (journal), 102
psychobiology, 79
The Psychology of Religion and Coping
    (Pargament), 117, 196
psychopharmacology, 53
psychotropic medicines, 57n.30
Public Health Service, 265
The Pursuit of Happiness (Myers), 143, 146
Putnam, Robert, 7, 263

QoL-X, 284
Quarterly Journal of Economics (journal), 111

Razell, Peter, 88n.18
Reader's Digest (magazine), 272
Reagan, Ronald, 5, 21, 94, 101, 143
reciprocal altruism, evolutionary biology
    and, 64–66
Reivich, Karen, 194
relaxation, better living through, 75–78
Relaxation Response (Benson), 75–78, 104,
    197, 198
religion, 117
    American life, 227n.22
    spirituality and, 196–99
resilience, character of, 194–96, 260–61
Resilience Doughnut, 284
Ricard, Matthieu, 164, 199, 202, 202f, 246
Ridley, Matt, 116
Riesmann, Frank, 52
The Road to Character (Brooks), 195, 198
Robertson, James, 38
Robert Wood Johnson Foundation, 261
Rockefeller, Laurence, 78
Rockefeller University, 221

Rogers, Carl, 23, 70, 96, 174, 257
Roman Catholicism, 197, 198
Roosevelt, Eleanor, 43
Roosevelt, Theodore, 155
Rosenblatt, Seymour, 81
Rubin, Gretchen, 177–81, 253–54
Rubin, Jeffrey R., 198
Rubin, Robert, 180
Russian Longitudinal Monitoring
    Survey, 206
Ryan, M. J., 176–77
Ryff, Carol, 99, 119, 145, 174–75,
    199, 286

Sanity, Insanity and Common Sense (Suarez
    and Mills), 136
Sarkozy, Nicolas, 207, 232n.55, 234n.78
satisfaction surveys, 72–75
    see also international surveys
Saving Mr. Banks (movie), 285
scholarly consensus, happiness, 141–44
schools, business of happiness, 259–61
Schuller, Robert, 134, 139
Schwartz, Arthur, 263
Schwartz, Barry, 174, 214
Schwarz, Norbert, 111, 210
Schweitzer, Albert, 43
science
    brain, 98–101
    Csikszentmihalyi and Seligman
        works, 129–35
    happiness and, 199–206
    popularization and, 155–65
    scholarly consensus, 141–44
    see also neuroscience; popularization
Scientific American (journal), 45
Scitovsky, Tibor, 82, 218
season's greetings, 66–67
Second Wave Positive Psychology
    (PP2.0), 220
The Secret (Byrne), 248
Secure Base (Bowlby), 38
Sehgal, Parul, 195
Seldon, Anthony, 260
selective serotonin reuptake inhibitor
    (SSRI), 101
self-actualization, Maslow and,
    40–44, 91n.47
self-destructive behavior, 91n.47
self-esteem, 87n.12